THE MEDIEVAL WORLD

300–1300

THE
MEDIEVAL
WORLD

300-1300

SECOND EDITION

EDITED BY

NORMAN F. CANTOR

Brandeis University

The Macmillan Company
Collier-Macmillan Limited, London

PRINTING 67891011 YEAR 3456789

Earlier edition © copyright 1963 by The Macmillan Company.

Library of Congress catalog card number: 68-10120

THE MACMILLAN COMPANY
866 THIRD AVENUE, NEW YORK, NEW YORK 10022
COLLIER-MACMILLAN CANADA, LTD., TORONTO, ONTARIO

PRINTED IN THE UNITED STATES OF AMERICA

PREFACE

To repeat what I said in the first edition, this volume presents the main ideas and institutions of medieval civilization in roughly chronological order of emergence. Approximately equal attention is devoted to the early Middle Ages (300–1050) and the high Middle Ages (1050–1300). I believe that all aspects of medieval civilization are presented in one way or another. The introductions to the readings and documents, it will be noted, lead into one another and can be read consecutively as a short sketch of medieval history. The Moslem world and Byzantium after the sixth century have been excluded on the grounds that they are not part of the history of western civilization. I have kept the extracts from Augustine's *Confessions* and *The City of God* and Thomas Aquinas' writings to a minimum because these are the medieval works most readily available to students in cheap editions. At the end I have included works by Dante and William of Occam, although they were products of the early fourteenth century, because they seem to me to round off and finish the pattern of medieval history.

Mrs. Elaine G. Robison did several of the translations from Latin with great skill. Dr. John Benton of the California Institute of Technology kindly directed my attention to document number 51-A and contributed a felicitous translation.

In the second edition, I have added several selections to illustrate aspects of medieval civilization that were excluded or inadequately dealt with in the first edition: the Moslem and Jewish attitudes (the Koran in No. 24 and Judah Halevi in No. 41); the new sensibility and ideal of romantic love in the twelfth century (Chrétien de Troyes in No. 42B, Wolfram von Eschenbach in No. 42C, and Andreas Capellanus in No. 42D); additional illustration of bourgeois life and outlook (Milan in 1288 as described by Bonvesin della Riva, in No. 43B); additional examples of political ideals and practice in the high Middle Ages (the Anglo-Saxon Chronicle on William the Conqueror in No. 44A and Roger of Wendover on King John and the Barons in No. 52B); and the social criticism found in Jean de Meun's part of the *Romance of the Rose* (No. 53). I wish to thank the many teachers of western civilization and medieval history courses who have offered valuable suggestions. I regret that I could not include several other documents of great importance, because of limitations of space.

N. F. C.

CONTENTS

I / THE EARLY MIDDLE AGES

Historians tend to divide the period between 300 and 1300 A.D. into two distinct eras. The first of these is generally called the early Middle Ages; it is a very long era extending from the beginning of the fourth to the middle of the eleventh century. During the early Middle Ages a distinctive Western civilization emerged out of the background—one might almost say the clash—of Christian, Graeco-Roman, and Germanic institutions and ideas. Depending on one's choice of metaphor, the early Middle Ages is the infancy and youth, or the springtime, of the European world. It is a period marked by a great deal of chaos and turbulence as Western Europe was racked by internal disunity and invasion from without by alien peoples frequently exhibiting a low level of culture. Largely under the guidance of the Church, Western Europe struggled first of all to develop its distinctive ideals; then it faced the task, even more difficult, of developing the institutions which would embody and activate these ideals in everyday life.

1 / A. D. NOCK: WHY CHRISTIANITY TRIUMPHED IN THE ROMAN WORLD

Medieval history begins with the advance of Christianity to its paramount position in the religious life of the Roman world and its triumph over other popular religions such as Isis and Mithra. The authority on ancient religion, A. D. Nock, here suggests the causes for the triumph of Christianity.[1]

[1] A. D. Nock, *Conversion* (Oxford: The Clarendon Press, 1933), pp. 267–79. Reprinted by permission of The Clarendon Press.

1

. . . The advance of Christianity stands out as a phenomenon which does not stand alone but has parallels which make its success not wholly incomprehensible. There were other forms of belief at the time which won adherents among men who were not called to them by anything in their antecedents. And yet these very analogies enable us to see the differences more clearly. The other Oriental religions in Roman paganism . . . were neither Oriental nor religious in the same degree. They had not brought a compact body of doctrine or of accessible sacred literature from the Nearer East with them; in so far as they appealed to men who did not come from the lands of their origin it was in forms which were fully hellenized, at least fully hellenized in matters of fundamental thought and above all in their expectations of the hereafter. This is true in spite of the exotic appearance which they had and sometimes artificially adopted for purposes of effect. Christianity avoided the exotic in externals and retained it in doctrine, in its doctrine of the last things and of the hereafter, in its sacred literature, available to all and sundry but not accommodated to classical style and classical thought, in its peculiar and unbending view of history. The Oriental mystery religions were not Oriental in the same sense as Christianity. Neither were they religions in the same sense. Theology might be and was applied to them: beliefs and hopes and interpretations clustered around them, but they were fluid and the interpretations came from outside, from Greek speculation and from the earlier habits of the Greek mind in religious things. And . . . there was no body of faithful throughout the world, no holy Isiac or Mithraic church—no Isiacs even, except as the members of a local association, with a devotion and belief which an Isiac from elsewhere could recognize.

Greek philosophy was applied to Christianity as to its unequal competitors. But, as applied to Christianity, it was applied to what was already much more of an entity. In Christianity it was used for the interpretation of a body of doctrine widely held by men speaking Greek and Latin. In its rivals it was used to give substance and meaning to what was essentially a cult and a mythology. This may sound a little less than just to Mithraism, which had in its origins a dualism and a cosmic expectation. Yet it must be borne in mind that Mithraism reached the Mediterranean world in a casual and sporadic way, as the worship of groups of Persians left without a country, and not starting with anything like the original urge of Zoroastrianism, which lay centuries and centuries behind. As we know it, the early theological element is very much obscured, and the core of the matter has become individual deliverance: certainly the cosmic expectation and the doctrine of the resurrection have faded. Christianity represents just such a movement as might have resulted from Zoroastrianism had it come into being at the beginning of our era and been promptly forced to leave Persian soil while still in its first vigour. So Christianity was different. And yet it was capable of being made intelligible and it was removed from Judaea early enough to become part of the larger world.

2 / CONSTANTINE, THE CHRISTIAN EMPEROR

Constantine the Great (312–337), the first Christian emperor, greatly influenced the development of the Roman Empire and the Christian Church in the fourth century, and in many ways the effect of his policies endured for centuries. The emperor's character, motives, and aims have been the subject of much controversy among modern writers. Our knowledge of Constantine is derived for the most part from the writings of his friend, adviser, and biographer, Bishop Eusebius of Caesarea in Palestine, and from Constantine's own decrees and letters. In the following selections, Eusebius describes important aspects of the emperor's life in a work which served as a model for biographies of medieval kings at least until the thirteenth century (A); Eusebius states his view of the ideology of imperial rule, the first clear expression of the doctrine of Caesaropapism and sacred Christian monarchy (B); Constantine intends to help the Church by imperial decree (C); [2] *finally we have the Nicene Creed, which Constantine imposed on the Church at the Council of Nicea in 325 in an attempt to end the Arian controversy over the nature of the Trinity (D).* [3]

A. EUSEBIUS: THE LIFE OF CONSTANTINE

Purpose of the Work

It is my intention . . . to pass over the greater part of the royal deeds of this thrice-blessed prince; as, for example, his conflicts and

[2] A, B, and C from *The Library of the Nicene and Post-Nicene Fathers*, P. Schaff and H. Wace, eds., Vol. I, *Church History, Life of Constantine*, and *Oration in Praise of Constantine*, pp. 484–5, 489–91, 494–5, 584, 591, 595, 381, 382–3 (New York: The Christian Literature Company, 1890).

[3] *Library of the Nicene and Post-Nicene Fathers*, Vol. XIV (New York: Charles Scribner, 1905), p. 3. Translation by A. C. McGiffert, E. C. Richardson, and H. R. Percival.

engagements in the field, his personal valor, his victories and successes against the enemy, and the many triumphs he obtained: likewise his provisions for the interests of individuals, his legislative enactments for the social advantage of his subjects, and a multitude of other imperial labors which are fresh in the memory of all; the design of my present undertaking being to speak and write of those circumstances only which have reference to his religious character.

And since these are themselves of almost infinite variety, I shall select from the facts which have come to my knowledge such as are most suitable, and worthy of lasting record, . . .

The Conversion of Constantine

Being convinced, however, that he needed some more powerful aid than his military forces could afford him,[4] on account of the wicked and magical enchantments which were so diligently practiced by the tyrant [Maxentius], he sought Divine assistance, deeming the possession of arms and a numerous soldiery of secondary importance, but believing the cooperating power of Deity invincible and not to be shaken. He considered, therefore, on what God he might rely for protection and assistance. While engaged in this enquiry, the thought occurred to him, that, of the many emperors who had preceded him, those who had rested their hopes in a multitude of gods, and served them with sacrifices and offerings, had in the first place been deceived by flattering predictions, and oracles which promised them all prosperity, and at last had met with an unhappy end, while not one of their gods had stood by to warn them of the impending wrath of heaven; while one alone who had pursued an entirely opposite course, who had condemned their error, and honored the Supreme God during his whole life, had found him to be the Saviour and Protector of his empire, and the Giver of every good thing. Reflecting on this, and well weighing the fact that they who had trusted in many gods had also fallen by manifold forms of death, without leaving behind them either family or offspring, stock, name, or memorial among men: while the God of his father had given to him, on the other hand, manifestations of his power and very many tokens: and considering farther that those who had already taken arms against the tyrant, and had marched to the battle-field under the protection of a multitude of gods, had met with a dishonorable end (for one of them had shamefully retreated from the contest without a blow, and the other, being slain in

[4] In 312 A.D., Constantine, who ruled Gaul and Britain, was about to invade Italy and try to gain the throne of the western empire by defeating Maxentius, who ruled Rome.

the midst of his own troops, became, as it were, the mere sport of death); reviewing, I say, all these considerations, he judged it to be folly indeed to join in the idle worship of those who were no gods, and after such convincing evidence, to err from the truth; and therefore felt it incumbent on him to honor his father's God alone.

Accordingly he called on Him with earnest prayer and supplications that he would reveal to him who He was, and stretch forth His right hand to help him in his present difficulties. And while he was thus praying with fervent entreaty, a most marvelous sign appeared to him from heaven, the account of which it might have been hard to believe had it been related by any other person. But since the victorious emperor himself long afterwards declared it to the writer of this history, when he was honored with his acquaintance and society, and confirmed his statement by an oath, who could hesitate to accredit the relation, especially since the testimony of after-time has established its truth? He said that about noon, when the day was already beginning to decline, he saw with his own eyes the trophy of a cross of light in the heavens, above the sun, and bearing the inscription, CONQUER BY THIS. At this sight he himself was struck with amazement, and his whole army also, which followed him on this expedition, and witnessed the miracle.

He said, moreover, that he doubted within himself what the import of this apparition could be. And while he continued to ponder and reason on its meaning, night suddenly came on; then in his sleep the Christ of God appeared to him with the same sign which he had seen in the heavens, and commanded him to make a likeness of that sign which he had seen in the heavens, and to use it as a safeguard in all engagements with his enemies.

At the dawn of day he arose, and communicated the marvel to his friends: and then, calling together the workers in gold and precious stones, he sat in the midst of them, and described to them the figure of the sign he had seen, bidding them represent it in gold and precious stones. And this representation I myself have had an opportunity of seeing.

Now it was made in the following manner. A long spear, overlaid with gold, formed the figure of the cross by means of a transverse bar laid over it. On the top of the whole was fixed a wreath of gold and precious stones; and within this, the symbol of the Saviour's name, two letters indicating the name of Christ by means of its initial characters, the letter P being intersected by X in its centre [5]; and these letters the emperor was in the habit of wearing on his helmet at a later period. From the cross-bar of the spear was suspended a cloth, a royal

[5] Chi Rho: ☧.

piece, covered with a profuse embroidery of most brilliant precious stones; and which, being also richly interlaced with gold, presented an indescribable degree of beauty to the beholder. This banner was of a square form, and the upright staff, whose lower section was of great length, bore a golden half-length portrait of the pious emperor and his children on its upper part, beneath the trophy of the cross, and immediately above the embroidered banner.

The emperor constantly made use of this sign of salvation as a safe-guard against every adverse and hostile power, and commanded that others similar to it should be carried at the head of all his armies.

These things were done shortly afterwards. But at the time above specified, being struck with amazement at the extraordinary vision, and resolving to worship no other God save Him who had appeared to him, he sent for those who were acquainted with the mysteries of His doctrines, and enquired who that God was, and what was intended by the sign of the vision he had seen.

They affirmed that He was God, the only begotten Son of the one and only God: that the sign which had appeared was the symbol of immortality, and the trophy of that victory over death which He had gained in time past when sojourning on earth. They taught him also the causes of His advent, and explained to him the true account of His incarnation. Thus he was instructed in these matters, and was impressed with wonder at the divine manifestation which had been presented to his sight. Comparing, therefore, the heavenly vision with the interpretation given, he found his judgment confirmed; and, in the persuasion that the knowledge of these things had been imparted to him by Divine teaching, he determined thenceforth to devote himself to the reading of the inspired writings.

Constantine and the Bishops

He [Constantine] exercised a peculiar care over the church of God: and whereas, in the several provinces there were some who differed from each other in judgment, he, like some general bishop consti-tuted by God, convened synods of his ministers. Nor did he disdain to be present and sit with them in their assembly, but bore a share in their deliberations, ministering to all that pertained to the peace of God. He took his seat, too, in the midst of them, as an individual amongst many, dismissing his guards and soldiers, and all whose duty it was to defend his person; but protected by the fear of God, and surrounded by the guardianship of his faithful friends. Those whom he saw inclined to a sound judgment, and exhibiting a calm and conciliatory temper, received his high approbation, for he evidently delighted in a general harmony of sentiment; while he regarded the unyielding with aversion.

B. EUSEBIUS: CONSTANTINE AS VICE-REGENT OF GOD

This is He who holds a supreme dominion over this whole world, Who is over and in all things, and pervades all things visible and invisible: the Word of God. From Whom and by Whom our divinely favored emperor, receiving, as it were, a transcript of the Divine sovereignty, directs, in imitation of God himself, the administration of this world's affairs. . . . Invested as he [the Emperor Constantine] is with a semblance of heavenly sovereignty, he directs his gaze above, and frames his earthly government according to the pattern of that Divine original, feeling strength in its conformity to the monarchy of God. And this conformity is granted by the universal Sovereign to man alone of the creatures of this earth: for He only is the author of sovereign power, who decrees that all should be subject to the rule of one. And surely monarchy far transcends every other constitution and form of government. . . . Hence there is one God, and not two, or three or more. . . .

. . . Such were the dealings of the Supreme Sovereign, who ordained an invincible champion to be the minister of his heaven-sent vengeance (for our emperor's surpassing piety delights in the title of Servant of God) and him He has proved victorious over all that opposed him. . . . Our emperor is one, appointed by, and representative of, the one Almighty Sovereign. . . . As truly worthy of the name of VICTOR, he has subdued the twofold race of barbarians: soothing the savage tribes of men by prudent embassies, compelling them to know and acknowledge their superiors, and reclaiming them from a lawless and brutal life to the governance of reason and humanity; at the same time that he proved by the facts themselves that the fierce and ruthless race of unseen spirits had long ago been vanquished by a higher power. . . .

. . . Our emperor as the one ruler on earth, . . . as a skillful pilot, sits on high at the helm of state, and directs the vessel with unerring course. . . . Meanwhile God himself, the great Sovereign, extends the right hand of his power from above for his protection, giving him victory over every foe, and establishing his empire by a lengthened period of years: and He will bestow on him yet higher blessings. . . .

C. CONSTANTINE'S PRONOUNCEMENTS ON THE CHURCH

Necessity of Maintaining the Unity of the Church

1. It seems to me a very serious thing that in those provinces which Divine Providence has freely entrusted to my devotedness, and in which there is a great population, the multitude are found following the baser course, and dividing, as it were, into two parties, and the bishops are at variance, . . . I have such reverence for the legitimate Catholic Church that I do not wish you to leave schism or division in any place. . . .

It has happened that those very ones who ought to hold brotherly and harmonious relations toward each other, are shamefully, or rather abominably, divided among themselves, and give occasion for ridicule to those men whose souls are aliens to this most holy religion. Wherefore it has seemed necessary to me to provide that this dissension, which ought to have ceased after the judgment had been already given by their own voluntary agreement, should now, if possible, be brought to an end by the presence of many.

2. Constantine Augustus to Caecilianus, bishop of Carthage. . . .

Since I have learned that some men of unsettled mind wish to turn the people from the most holy and catholic Church by a certain method of shameful corruption, do thou know that I gave command to Anulinus, the proconsul, and also to Patricius, vicar of the prefects, when they were present, that they should give proper attention not only to other matters but also above all to this, and that they should not overlook such a thing when it happened. Wherefore if thou shouldst see any such men continuing in this madness, do thou without delay go to the abovementioned judges and report the matter to them; that they may correct them as I commanded them when they were present.

Exemption of the Clergy from Secular Duties

Since it appears from many circumstances that when that religion is despised, in which is preserved the chief reverence for the most holy celestial Power, great dangers are brought upon public affairs; but that when legally adopted and observed it affords the most signal prosperity to the Roman name and remarkable felicity to all the affairs of men, through the divine beneficence. . . . Wherefore it is my will that those . . . in the catholic Church, who give their services to this holy religion, and who are commonly called clergymen, be entirely exempted from all public duties, that they may not by any error or sacrilegious negligence be drawn away from the service due to the Deity, but may devote themselves without any hindrance to their own law. For it seems that when they show greatest reverence to the Deity the greatest benefits accrue to the state.

D. THE NICENE CREED

We believe in one God, the Father Almighty, maker of all things visible and invisible; and in one Lord Jesus Christ, the Son of God, the only-begotten of his Father, of the substance of the Father, God of God, Light of Light, very God of very God, begotten not made, being of one substance with the Father. By whom all things were made, both which be in heaven and in earth. Who for us men and for our salvation came down [from heaven] and was incarnate and was made man. He suffered and the third day he rose again, and ascended into heaven. And he shall come again to judge both the quick and the dead. And [we believe] in the Holy Ghost. And whosoever shall say that there was time when the Son of God was not, or that before he was begotten he was not, or that he was made of things that were not, or that he is of a different substance or essence [from the Father] or that he is a creature, or subject to change or conversion—all that so say, the Catholic and Apostolic Church anathematizes them.

3 / DECLINE AND FALL

The great efforts by Constantine and his immediate prede-cessor, Diocletian, to reorganize the empire and prevent its col-lapse had only limited and short-term success. By the end of the fourth century the western, Latin-speaking part of the empire was disintegrating in the face of the Germanic invasions. What was wrong with the Roman world? Why was it unable to with-stand the invaders whose numbers were relatively small? What general factors are responsible for the vast changes in culture, society, and economy that constitute the beginning of medieval civilization and the end of the ancient world? In the following selections are presented seven of the most important and at-tractive answers to "the greatest problem in history." Two con-

temporary churchmen, Salvian (A)[6] *and St. Jerome (B),*[7] *give remarkably different interpretations of the causes of the disasters of their era; this is followed by the classic analysis by the eighteenth-century historian Edward Gibbon, whose* Decline and Fall of the Roman Empire *inaugurated the modern study of medieval civilization (C).*[8] *Four interpretations by twentieth-century scholars are then juxtaposed: Ferdinand Lot, the enormously erudite French medievalist (D);*[9] *J. B. Bury, the outstanding historian of Byzantium (E);*[10] *Michael Rostovtzeff, the great Russian authority on ancient history who found refuge in the United States after the Bolshevik revolution (F);*[11] *Arnold J. Toynbee, the English philosopher of history (G);*[12] *and finally André Piganiol, the French historian of the fourth century (H).*[13]

A. SALVIAN: THE CONSEQUENCES OF SIN

What hope, I ask you, can there be for the Roman state when barbarians are more chaste and pure than the Romans? What I say is all too little: what hope of life or pardon, I ask, can we have in the sight of God when we see chastity in the barbarians and even so are not willing to be chaste ourselves? Should we not feel shame and confusion at this? . . .

If my human frailty permitted, I should wish to shout beyond my strength, to make my voice ring through the whole world: Be ashamed, ye Roman people everywhere, be ashamed of the lives you lead. No

[6] Salvian, *On the Government of God*, transl. E. M. Sanford, in *Records of Civilization*, Vol. 12 (New York: Columbia University Press, 1930), p. 223. Reprinted by permission of Columbia University Press.

[7] *Library of Nicene and Post-Nicene Fathers*, Vol. VI, transl. W. H. Fremantle (New York: 1893), p. 237.

[8] E. Gibbon, *The Decline and Fall of the Roman Empire* (Philadelphia: Birch and Small, 1805), Chapter 38.

[9] F. Lot, *The End of the Ancient World*, transl. P. and M. Leon (London: Routledge & Kegan Paul, Ltd., 1931), pp. 185–86. Reprinted by permission of Routledge & Kegan Paul.

[10] J. B. Bury, *Selected Essays*, introduced by H. Temperley (Cambridge: Cambridge University Press, 1930), pp. xxiv, xxv–xxvii. Reprinted by permission of H. A. Dickie and J. B. Bury Will Trust.

[11] M. Rostovtzeff, *The Social and Economic History of the Roman Empire*, Vol. I, 2nd ed. (Oxford: The Clarendon Press, 1957), pp. 534, 541. Reprinted by permission of The Clarendon Press.

[12] A. J. Toynbee, *Civilization on Trial* (New York: Oxford University Press, 1948), pp. 13, 60. Reprinted by permission of Oxford University Press.

[13] A. Piganiol, *L'Empire Chrétien* (Paris: Presses Universitaires de France, 1947), pp. 421–2. By permission of Presses Universitaires de France.

cities are free of evil haunts, no cities anywhere are free from inde-
cency, except those in which barbarians have begun to live. Do we
then wonder that we are wretched who are so impure, that we are
conquered by the enemy who are outdone by them in honor, that
they possess our properties who abjure our wickedness? It is neither
the natural strength of their bodies that makes them conquer nor the
weakness of our nature that makes us subject to defeat. Let no one
think or persuade himself otherwise—it is our vicious lives alone that
have conquered us.

B. ST. JEROME: THE BARBARIAN TRAITOR

Who will hereafter credit the fact or what histories will seriously
discuss it, that Rome has to fight within her own borders not for
glory but for bare life; and that she does not even fight but buys the
right to exist by giving gold and sacrificing all her substance? This
humiliation has been brought upon her not by the fault of her emperors [Arcadius and Honorius] who are both most religious men,
but by the crime of a half-barbarian traitor [Stilicho] who with our
money has armed our foes against us. . . . But now, even if complete
success attends our arms, we can wrest nothing from our vanquished
foes but what we have already lost to them. The poet Lucan describing
the power of the city in a glowing passage says:

If Rome be weak, where shall we look for strength?

We may vary his words and say:

If Rome be lost, where shall we look for help?

C. EDWARD GIBBON: GENERAL CAUSES AND EFFECT OF CHRISTIANITY

. . . The decline of Rome was the natural and inevitable effect of
immoderate greatness. Prosperity ripened the principle of decay; the
causes of destruction multiplied with the extent of conquest; and as
soon as time or accident had removed the artificial supports, the stu-
pendous fabric yielded to the pressure of its own weight. The story of
its ruin is simple and obvious; and instead of inquiring *why* the Roman
Empire was destroyed, we should rather be surprised that it had sub-
sisted so long. The victorious legions, who, in distant wars, acquired
the vices of strangers and mercenaries, first oppressed the freedom
of the republic, and afterwards violated the majesty of the purple. The
emperors, anxious for their personal safety and the public peace, were

reduced to the base expedient of corrupting the discipline which rendered them alike formidable to their sovereign and to the enemy; the vigour of the military government was relaxed and finally dissolved by the partial institutions of Constantine; and the Roman world was overwhelmed by the deluge of barbarians. . . .

As the happiness of a *future* life is the great object of religion, we may hear without surprise or scandal that the introduction, or at least the abuse of Christianity, had some influence on the decline and fall of the Roman Empire. The clergy successfully preached the doctrines of patience and pusillanimity; the active virtues of society were discouraged; and the last remains of military spirit were buried in the cloister: a large portion of public and private wealth was consecrated to the specious demands of charity and devotion; and the soldiers' pay was lavished on the useless multitudes of both sexes who could only plead the merits of abstinence and chastity. Faith, zeal, curiosity, and more earthly passions of malice and ambition, kindled the flame of theological discord; the church, and even the state, were distracted by religious factions . . . and the persecuted sects became the secret enemies of their country. Yet party-spirit, however pernicious or absurd, is a principle of union as well as of dissension . . . [and] the pure and genuine influence of Christianity may be traced in its beneficial, though imperfect, effects on the barbarian proselytes of the North. If the decline of the Roman Empire was hastened by the conversion of Constantine, his victorious religion broke the violence of the fall, and mollified the ferocious temper of the conquerors.

D. FERDINAND LOT: THE FUNDAMENTAL CAUSE

The fundamental cause of the decay and later of the breaking up of the Roman Empire appears to us to have been the following:

The Empire had become too vast, too cunning and too complicated a mechanism; the Mediterranean world, economically retrograde since the third century, could no longer support its weight. It split in two, the *pars Orientis* and the *pars Occidentis*, from the end of this century. Even for the exercise of its authority, the State was under the necessity of narrowing its field of action. The same necessity was soon to force the West to break up into half-Roman, half-barbarian States. The latter in their turn would become subdivided, and the territorial splitting up was to go on increasingly without a stop for long centuries, until the twelfth century. This narrowing of political action was accompanied by a narrowing of public spirit, which was destined to go as far as the annihilation of the conception of public interest, and the disappearance of the notion of a State in the period of the barbarians.

Thus, under a still majestic appearance, the Roman Empire, at the end of the fourth century, was no longer anything but a hollow husk. It was powerless to withstand a violent shaking and soon it was to suffer a new and terrible shaking from the barbarians. The East was destined to emerge from it as best it could, but the West was to be shivered in pieces.

There is something deeper and more stable than political forms, which are always ephemeral, and that is what is called civilization. In its highest reaches, literature, the arts, philosophy and religion, the changes are no less striking than in the political sphere. . . . Science and philosophy succumbed under the competition of Oriental mysticism which brought about a real transformation of values.

This transformation is as phenomenal as if a sleeper on waking should see other stars shining above his head.

E. J. B. BURY: A SERIES OF CONTINGENCIES

[Bury's interpretation as summarized by Harold Temperley]

Bury laid down that history was a science to be studied by scientific methods but he did not believe that it proceeded wholly along fixed lines and according to mathematical laws. As history never repeated itself the past history of man could not be exactly deduced, nor the future precisely predicted. The accidents of history were such as to disturb any calculations. . . . [The] theory of "contingency" . . . bulks . . . large in Bury's later studies. He came finally to assert that general causes did not usually explain the great events of history. And he thus reached, by another road, a conclusion or lack of conclusion which is often held by great practical men. Few of these will admit that the causes of great events are simple or ascertainable, and some . . . ascribe everything to chance. . . .

The best application of Bury's idea is to be found in his view of the causes of the fall of the Roman Empire. In his earliest study he adopted conventional explanations. In his latest (1923) he adopted the "contingency" throughout. If there was any cause of the fall of the Roman Empire, it was that the German barbarians "peacefully penetrated" it, and finally took so many posts in the army that they rendered discipline impossible. "This was, of course, a consequence of the decline in military spirit, and of depopulation, in the old civilized Mediterranean countries." But he asserts that "this policy need not have led to the dismemberment of the Empire" and that the barbarian infiltration is explained not by "any general considerations," but by "the actual events."

It was the conflux of coincidences which proved decisive. The first contingent cause was the invasion of the Huns from Asia, a "historical surprise" and resulting from "events in Central Asia strictly independent of events in Europe." It was an "Asian mystery" how these Huns arose and poured into Europe. And to this first contingency was added a second, for the valiant Goths fled before them and poured into the Roman Empire. In their flight they met and defeated a Roman army and slew a Roman Emperor. This great defeat was mainly due to the contingent accident that the Roman Emperor was incompetent and rash. Theodosius, who succeeded Valens, sets "the unfortunate precedent" of settling the Visigoths—a new barbarian people—as a unit inside his borders. The fact that he died at the age of fifty was "a third contingency," for had he lived longer his great ability might have averted the evils of his blunder. But a fourth great event, dependent on causes which had nothing to do with the condition of the Empire, was the mediocrity of his two sons who divided his Empire. The Eastern Arcadius was incompetent, and the Western Honorius was "feeble-minded." The final or fifth event was the fact that in the West poor Honorius was controlled by a German, Stilicho. His character is "a puzzle," and he admitted barbarians wholesale into the Roman Empire till he brought disaster on himself and it. When he died the mischief was done, Italy, Gaul and Spain were overrun by barbarians and "his Roman successors could not undo the results of events which need never have happened." It is thus that the true historian delicately poises his conclusion.

F. MICHAEL ROSTOVTZEFF: THE REVOLT OF THE MASSES

. . . There is one prominent feature in the development of the ancient world during the imperial age, alike in the political, social, and economic and in the intellectual field. It is a gradual absorption of the higher classes by the lower, accompanied by a gradual levelling down of standards. This levelling was accomplished in many ways. There was a slow penetration of the lower classes into the higher, which were unable to assimilate the new elements. There were violent outbreaks of civil strife: the lead was taken by the Greek cities, and there followed the civil war of the first century B.C. which involved the whole civilized world. In these struggles the upper classes and the city-civilization remained victorious on the whole. Two centuries later, a new outbreak of civil war ended in the victory of the lower classes and dealt a mortal blow to the Graeco-Roman civilization of the cities. Finally, that civilization was completely engulfed by the inflow of barbarous elements from outside partly by penetration, partly by conquest, and in its dying condition it was unable to assimilate even a small part of them. . . .

[Thus] the main phenomenon which underlies the process of decline [of ancient civilization] is the gradual absorption of the educated classes by the masses and the consequent simplification of all the functions of political, economic, and intellectual life, which we call the barbarization of the ancient world.

The evolution of the ancient world has a lesson and a warning for us. Our civilization will not last unless it be a civilization not of one class, but of the masses. The Oriental civilizations were more stable and lasting than the Graeco-Roman, because, being chiefly based on religion, they were nearer to the masses. Another lesson is that violent attempts at levelling have never helped to uplift the masses. They have destroyed the upper classes, and resulted in accelerating the process of barbarization. But the ultimate problem remains like a ghost, ever present and unlaid: Is it possible to extend a higher civilization to the lower classes without debasing its standard and diluting its quality to the vanishing point? Is not every civilization bound to decay as soon as it begins to penetrate the masses?

G. ARNOLD J. TOYNBEE: THE PATTERN OF SOCIAL DISINTEGRATION

. . . The regular pattern of social disintegration is a schism of the disintegrating society into a recalcitrant proletariat and a less and less effectively dominant minority. The process of disintegration does not proceed evenly; it jolts along in alternating spasms of rout, rally, and rout. In the last rally but one, the dominant minority succeeds in temporarily arresting the society's lethal self-laceration by imposing on it the peace of a universal state. Within the framework of the dominant minority's universal state the proletariat creates a universal church, and after the next rout, in which the disintegrating civilization finally dissolves, the universal church may live on to become the chrysalis from which a new civilization eventually emerges. To modern Western students of history, these phenomena are most familiar in the Graeco-Roman examples of the *Pax Romana* and the Christian Church. The establishment of the *Pax Romana* by Augustus seemed, at the time, to have put the Graeco-Roman world back upon firm foundations after it had been battered for several centuries by perpetual war, misgovernment, and revolution. But the Augustan rally proved, after all, to be no more than a respite. After two hundred and fifty years of comparative tranquillity, the Empire suffered in the third century of the Christian era a collapse from which it never fully recovered, and at the next crisis, in the fifth and sixth centuries, it went to pieces irretrievably. The true beneficiary of the temporary Roman Peace was the Christian Church. . . .

The destruction of the Graeco-Roman civilization through the failure to replace an international anarchy by some kind of international law and order occupies the history of the four hundred years from 431 to 31 B.C. . . . The epitaph of the Roman Empire is "too late." The Graeco-Roman society did not repent until it had inflicted mortal wounds on itself with its own hands. The *Pax Romana* was a peace of exhaustion, a peace which was not creative and therefore not permaent. It was a peace and an order which came four centuries after its due time.

H. ANDRÉ PIGANIOL: BARBARIAN ASSASSINATION

It is a mistake to say that [in the fourth century] Rome was decadent. Pillaged, disfigured by the barbarian invaders of the third century, she rose again from her ruins. At the price of a grave crisis, a work of internal metamorphosis was accomplished at the same time: There was formed a new conception of imperial power, which is Byzantium's, a new conception of truth and beauty, which is medieval, and a new conception of collective and interdependent work in the service of social welfare. And all the ills from which the Empire suffered—the crushing taxation, the ruin of fortunes and social classes—originate not in this fruitful work of metamorphosis, but in the perpetual war conducted by the unorganized bands of those Germans who had succeeded in living for centuries at the frontiers of the Empire without being civilized.

It is too easy to claim that at the coming of the barbarians into the empire "all was dead" . . . or that the Roman empire in the West was not destroyed by a brutal blow, but rather that she "fell asleep."

Roman civilization did not die this beautiful death.

It was assassinated.

4 / AUSONIUS: ATTITUDES AND INTERESTS OF A FOURTH-CENTURY RHETORICIAN AND COURTIER

The autobiographical writings of a late fourth-century rhetorician and courtier provide us with a valuable insight into the ideals and mores of the imperial ruling class while imperial power was slowly crumbling.[14]

I

My father was Ausonius and I bear the same name. Who I am, and what is my rank, my family, my home, and my native land, I have written here, that you might know me, good Sir, whoever you may have been, and when you know me, might honour me with a place in your memory. . . . I myself was born at Bordeaux: four ancient cities contribute to the origin of my family. Thus my connexions are widely spread: many, if so they please, may adopt names which are derived from my house. . . . My father practised medicine—the only one of all the arts which produced a god; I gave myself up to Grammar, and then to Rhetoric, wherein I gained sufficient skill. I frequented the Courts as well, but preferred to follow the business of teaching, and won some repute as a grammarian. . . . My renown . . . was high enough to let me look upon the teachers of my day, men famous in Aquitaine, as their equal rather than their inferior.

Afterwards, when three decades with all their festivals were passed, I left my toils as a provincial teacher, receiving the command to enter the Emperor's golden palace. There I taught the young prince Grammar, and in due time Rhetoric; for, indeed, I have good reason for satisfaction and my boasting rests upon firm ground. . . . My pupil reigns over the whole world, which is his own. He created me Companion and Quaestor, and crowned my honours with the prefectship

[14] Ausonius, *Works,* transl. H. G. Evelyn White (New York: G. P. Putnam, 1919), Vol. I, pp. 3–7, 15, 23, 25, 27–29, 269, 271, 273; Vol. II, pp. 19, 27. Reprinted by permission of the publishers from The Loeb Classical Library, *Ausonius,* translated by Hugh G. Evelyn White, Cambridge, Mass.: Harvard University Press.

of the provinces of Gaul, Libya, and Italy. I became consul, too, and was given the precedence on assuming the insignia and the curule chair, so that my colleague's name stood after mine.

Such, then, is Ausonius: and you, on your part, do not despise me because I ask your favour for these songs of mine, without your seeking.

II

Hi, boy! Get up! Bring me my slippers and my tunic of lawn: bring all the clothes that you have ready now for my going out. Fetch me spring water to wash my hands and mouth and eyes. Get me the chapel opened, but with no outward display: holy words and guilt-less prayers are furniture enough for worship. I do not call for incense to be burnt nor for any slice of honey-cake: hearths of green turf I leave for the altars of vain gods. I pray to God and to the Son of God most high, that co-equal Majesty united in one fellowship with the Holy Spirit. And lo, now I begin my prayers: my heart feels Heaven is near and trembles. Have faith and hope, then, anything to fear? . . .

Now I have prayed enough to God, albeit we sinful men can never entreat Heaven enough. Boy! Bring me my morning coat. I must exchange my "Hail" and "Farewell" with my friends. . . .

And now the time for inviting my friends draws on. So, that no fault of mine may make them late for lunch, hurry at your best pace, boy, to the neighbours' houses—you know without my telling who they are—and back with you before these words are done. I have invited five to lunch; for six persons, counting the host, make the right number for a meal: if there be more, it is no meal but a mêlée. . . .

Hi, boy! My secretary, skilled in dashing shorthand, make haste and come! Open your folding tablets wherein a world of words is compassed in a few signs and finished off as if it were a single phrase. I ponder works of generous scope; and thick and fast like hail the words tumble off my tongue. . . .

Strange monsters disturb my calm slumbers. . . . Now the courts pass before my eyes with suits at law, and now the spacious theatre with its shows. Here I endure the sight of troops of cavalry cutting down brigands: or in the bloody arena some wild beast tears my face, or I am butchered with the sword. I go afoot across the wrecking sea, bound at a stride across the straits, and flit above the air on new-found wings. Then, too, in dreams we undergo amours unspeakable, and night's foul shames, and unions which are the themes of tragedy. Yet there is escape from these whenever shame bursts through the bonds of sleep, scattering the horrors of our dreams, and the mind free from filthy fancying keeps watch. Then the hands untainted feel about the bed nor find cause for remorse: the sinful guilt of luxury departs, and as the dream fades from us, so its stain. Now, I see myself applauding, one of a triumphant throng: again I am dragged through the street a disarmed Alan prison of war. And now I gaze upon the temples of the gods, their sacred portals and golden palaces; or seem to recline at a feast upon a couch of Sarran (Tyrian) purple, and presently sit feasting at the table of some steamy eating-house. . . .

III

First among cities, the home of gods, is golden Rome. Carthage yields precedence in rank to Constantinople, but will not stand a full step lower; for she scorns to be counted third, yet dares not hope for the second place, which both have held. One has the advantage in her ancient wealth, the other in her new-born prosperity. The one has seen her day, the other is now rising and by the loftiness of new achievements eclipses old-time renown, forcing Elissa to give place to Constantine. Carthage reproaches Heaven, now fully shamed if this time also she must give place who scarcely brooked the pre-eminence of Rome. . . .

Third would be Antioch, . . . if Alexander's settlement were willing to be placed fourth: both hold the same rank. These also doth frenzied ambition drive into rivalry of vices: each is disordered with her mob, and half-crazed with the riots of her frantic populace. This, fertile and secure, vaunts herself because she has the Nile for bulwark and is deep-embayed in her sheltered site; that, because her rival power confronts the faithless Persians. . . .

Long has Gaul, mighty in arms, yearned to be praised, and that royal city of the Treveri (Trèves), which, though full near the Rhine, reposes unalarmed as if in the bosom of deep profound peace, because she clothes and arms the forces of the Empire. Widely her wall stretches forward over a spreading hill; besides her bounteous Moselle glides past with peaceful stream, carrying the far-brought merchandise of all races of the earth.

At Milan also are all things wonderful, abundant wealth, countless stately houses, men able, eloquent, and cheerfully disposed; besides, there is the grandeur of the site enlarged by a double wall, the Circus, her people's joy, the massy enclosed Theatre with wedge-like blocks of seats, the temples, the imperial citadels, the wealthy Mint, and the quarter renowned under the title of the Baths of Herculeus; her colonnades all adorned with marble statuary, her walls piled like an earthen rampart round the city's edge:—all these, as it were rivals in the vast masses of their workmanship, are passing grand; nor does the near neighbourhood of Rome abase them.

IV

In the first days after holy Easter I long to visit my estate. For I am weary at the sight of throngs of people, the vulgar brawls at the cross-roads, the narrow lanes a-swarm, and the broadways belying their name for the rabble herded there. Confused Echo resounds with a babel of cries: "Hold!"—"Strike!"—"Lead!"—"Give!"—"Look out!" Here is a mucky sow in flight, there a mad dog in fell career, there oxen too weak for the waggon. No use to steal into the inner chamber and the recesses of your home: the cries penetrate through the house. These, and what else can shock the orderly, force me to leave the walled city and seek again the sweet peace of the retired country and the delights of trifling seriously; . . .

Enough experience have I had of toil ere now, friend Paulus, both as a pleader in the courts and in the thankless professorial chair at Schools of Rhetoric, and got therefrom no profit. But now has all that youthful energy oozed from these limbs, trembling old age is nigh, and my strong-box grown light furnishes means for outlay less readily. For the helpless draws no salary from the Exchequer, and the bed-ridden dotard earns no golden fees. Yet if only thou wilt be of un-ruffled mind and rather see good in everything, thy toil and poverty will find oblivion. But this is the very best of all, from all the Muses everywhere—not without bowl and wine, comrade of the true Muses—to seek soothing consolation for a troubled heart. Here shalt thou find the fruit of Demeter, rich in crops, here fat swine, here capacious goblets if thou wouldst mix the nectar of good wine. So shall we twain cheer the blank hours of our life, so long as means and age allow and the Three Sisters spin their purple thread.

5 / ATHANASIUS:
ST. ANTONY,
THE IDEAL MONK

The imperial political failure does not preclude the fact that the fourth century was, in the fields of religion and thought, one of the most creative periods in the history of Western civil-

ization. The greater part of the ideas which dominated Western thought during the early middle ages are derived from fourth-century writers and religious leaders. Among these ideas was the monastic withdrawal from the world in order to prepare for the kingdom of heaven. The leaders of the monastic movement were the "Fathers of the Desert," who fled from the sophisticated and tempting urban life of their day to the Egyptian desert and lived as hermits. The most famous of these anchorites was St. Antony, whose biography by Bishop Athanasius of Alexandria inspired many medieval monks and served as a model for the vast hagiographical literature of the early middle ages.[15]

And so for nearly twenty years he continued training himself in solitude, never going forth, and but seldom seen by any. After this, when many were eager and wishful to imitate his discipline, and his acquaintances came and began to cast down and wrench off the door by force, Antony, as from a shrine, came forth initiated in the mysteries and filled with the Spirit of God. Then for the first time he was seen outside the fort by those who came to see him. And they, when they saw him, wondered at the sight, for he had the same habit of body as before, and was neither fat, like a man without exercise, nor lean from fasting and striving with the demons, but he was just the same as they had known him before his retirement. And again his soul was free from blemish, for it was neither contracted as if by grief, nor relaxed by pleasure, nor possessed by laughter or dejection, for he was not troubled when he beheld the crowd, nor overjoyed at being saluted by so many. But he was altogether even as being guided by reason, and abiding in a natural state. Through him the Lord healed the bodily ailments of many present, and cleansed others from evil spirits. And He gave grace to Antony in speaking, so that he consoled many that were sorrowful, and set those .at variance as one, exhorting all to prefer the love of Christ before all that is in the world. And while he exhorted and advised them to remember the good things to come, and the loving-kindness of God towards us, "Who spared not His own Son, but delivered Him up for us all," he persuaded many to embrace the solitary life. And thus it happened in the end that cells arose even in the mountains, and the desert was colonised by monks, who came forth from their own people, and enrolled themselves for the citizenship in the heavens. . . .

[15] *Library of the Nicene and Post-Nicene Fathers,* Vol. IV, Athanasius' *Life of St. Antony,* transl. A. Robertson (New York: Christian Literature Co., 1892), pp. 200, 219, 221.

Thus, therefore, he warned the cruel. But the rest who came to him he so instructed that they straightway forgot their lawsuits, and felicitated those who were in retirement from the world. And he championed those who were wronged in such a way that you would imagine that he, and not the others, was the sufferer. Further, he was able to be of such use to all, that many soldiers and men who had great possessions laid aside the burdens of life, and became monks for the rest of their days. And it was as if a physician had been given by God to Egypt. For who in grief met Antony and did not return rejoicing? Who came mourning for his dead and did not forthwith put off his sorrow? Who came in anger and was not converted to friendship? What poor and low-spirited man met him who, hearing him and looking upon him, did not despise wealth and console himself in his poverty? What monk, having been neglectful, came to him and became not all the stronger? What young man having come to the mountain and seen Antony, did not forthwith deny himself pleasure and love temperance? Who when tempted by a demon, came to him and did not find rest? And who came troubled with doubts and did not get quietness of mind? . . . Cheering those who were troubled with doubts, he taught them how to defeat their plans, telling them of the weakness and craft of those who possessed them. Thus each one, as though prepared by him for battle, came down from the mountain, braving the designs of the devil and demons. How many maidens who had suitors, having but seen Antony from afar, remained maidens for Christ's sake? And people came also from foreign parts to him, and like all others, having got some benefit, returned, as though set forward by a father. And certainly when he did, all as having been bereft of a father, consoled themselves solely by their remembrances of him, preserving at the same time his counsel and advice. . . .

Even if this account is small compared with his merit, still from this reflect how great Antony, the man of God, was. Who from his youth to so great an age preserved a uniform zeal for the discipline, and neither through old age was subdued by the desire of costly food, nor through the infirmity of his body changed the fashion of his clothing, nor washed even his feet with water, and yet remained entirely free from harm. For his eyes were undimmed and quite sound and he saw clearly; of his teeth he had not lost one, but they had become worn to the gums through the great age of the old man. He remained strong both in hands and feet; and while all men were using various foods, and washings and divers garments, he appeared more cheerful and of greater strength. And the fact that his fame has been blazoned everywhere; that all regard him with wonder, and that those who have never seen him long for him, is clear proof of his virtue and God's love of his soul. For not from writings, nor from worldly wisdom, nor through any art, was Antony renowned, but solely from his piety towards God. That this was the Gift of God no one will deny. For from whence into Spain and into Gaul, how into Rome and Africa, was the man heard of who abode hidden in a mountain, unless it was God who maketh His own known everywhere, who also promised this to Antony at the beginning?

6 / THE PROBLEM OF FREEDOM OF RELIGION IN A CHRISTIAN STATE

If Christianity is the true religion, can any other religions be tolerated in a Christian state? This question was debated in the fourth century, and the outcome of the debate had enormous consequences for medieval civilization. In 313 Constantine, the western emperor, and Licinius, the eastern emperor, who was not a Christian, in the so-called Edict of Milan (A) [16] *agreed to allow freedom of worship in the empire. But by the second half of the century, when the great majority of the population and all the emperors were members of the Church, the leaders of the Church demanded proscription of paganism. In the eighth decade of the century the emperor removed the Altar of Victory, the symbol of Rome's association with the ancient gods, from the senate house. A fundamental debate on the question of freedom of religion followed (B)* [17] *between Symmachus, the leader of the pagan Roman aristocracy, and St. Ambrose, the bishop of Milan, the most vigorous and skilled spokesman of the Church in Italy. In the following decade Ambrose won a complete victory when the orthodox emperor Theodosius I prohibited the worship of*

[16] "The Edict of Milan," according to Lacantius, *The Death of the Persecutors,* from the text in C. Mirbt, ed., *Quellen zur Geschichte des Papsttums* (Tubingen: J. C. B. Mohr (Paul Siebeck), 1924), pp. 39–40. By permission of J. C. B. Mohr (Paul Siebeck).

[17] *The Library of the Nicene and Post-Nicene Fathers,* Vol. X, transl. E. de Romestin and H. I. F. Duckworth (New York: Christian Literature Co., 1896), pp. 414–15, 417–18, 420.

the ancient Roman gods and made Christianity the sole legal religion.

A. THE EDICT OF MILAN

When, happily, I, Constantine Augustus, and I, Licinius Augustus, had met at Milan, we dealt with all matters which pertained to public advantage and security. We believed that these things among others, in which reverence of divinity was contained, and which we saw would profit the majority of men, should be ordained first. We desired to give Christians and all other men the free right of following the religion which they wished, so that whatever Divinity is on the celestial throne might be placated and propitious to us and to all those who are placed beneath our power. And so, with beneficial and correct reasoning, we believed that this plan should be adopted: no man at all should be denied this faculty, whether he had given preference to the rite of the Christians, or to that religion which he felt was most suitable for him, so that the highest God Whose worship we observe with free minds, might vouchsafe His accustomed benevolence to us in every way. Wherefore it is necessary that your Reverence know that it is our pleasure that all those conditions which were contained in earlier letters sent to your office concerning the subject of Christians, and which seemed to be utterly improper and foreign to our clemency, be removed. Now each and every man who has the desire to observe the Christian religion may do so freely and openly, without any disturbance or molestation. We desired that these things be very fully brought to your attention, so that you might know that we have given the Christians the free and unconditional right to practice their religion. When you perceive that we have granted this indulgence to these people, your Reverence will also understand that similarly, in accordance with the serenity of our reign, we have granted the open and free right of belief and observance to others, so that each man shall have the opportunity of worshipping as he pleases. We have done this so that it will not seem that we detract anything from any man's dignity or religion. Moreover, we decided in the case of the Christians that if any places at which they were formerly accustomed to assemble, about which a plan had been included in the letters sent to your office, seem to have been purchased either by our treasury or by any private person whatsoever, these same places should be restored to the Christians without money or any other consideration of price, and without any deception or ambiguity. Those who received such places as gifts shall likewise restore them to the Christians as quickly as possible. If those who bought these places or received them as gifts should seek any satisfaction from our benevolence, let them ask it of our deputy, who will take care of their interests through our clemency. It is necessary that all these things be handed over to the body of Christians through your intercession and without delay. And since the Christians are known to have possessed not only those places at which they were accustomed to assemble, but also others, which belonged to them as a body, that is, to their churches and not to individual men, we have included all these places in the law mentioned above. You will order them to be restored to the Christians, that is, to their community or conventicles, without any further ambiguity or controversy. The preceding regulation will apply here, namely that those who restore these places without price, as we have commanded, may hope for an indemnity for our benevolence. In all these matters, you ought to exhibit your most effective intercession in behalf of the aforementioned community of Christians, so that our injunction may be obeyed as quickly as possible, and so, also, that the public tranquillity may be aided through our clemency. In this way it will come about that divine favor, which we have experienced in our greatest undertakings, shall continue through our entire reign for our own success as well as for the public weal. Moreover, so that the form of this ordinance and of our benevolence may come to the attention of all men, it will be convenient for you to promulgate these letters everywhere and bring them to the knowledge of all, so that the ordinance of our benevolence may not be hidden.

B. THE DEBATE BETWEEN SYMMACHUS AND ST. AMBROSE ON FREEDOM OF RELIGION

The Memorial of Symmachus on the Occasion of the Removal of the Altar of Victory from the Senate House

The most honourable Senate, always devoted to you, . . . bade me be once again the delegate to utter its complaints. But through wicked men audience was refused me by the divine Emperor, otherwise justice would not have been wanting, my lords and emperors, of great renown, Valentinian, Theodosius, and Arcadius, victorious and triumphant, ever august.

In the exercise, therefore, of a twofold office, as your Prefect I attend to public business, and as delegate I recommend to your notice the charge laid on me by the citizens. . . . It is our task to watch on behalf of your Graces. For to what is it more suitable that we defend the institutions of our ancestors, and the rights and destiny of our country, than to the glory of these times, which is all the greater when you understand that you may not do anything contrary to the custom of your ancestors? We demand then the restoration of that condition of religious affairs which was so long advantageous to the state. . . .

Who is so friendly with the barbarians as not to require an Altar of Victory? We will be careful henceforth, and avoid a show of such things. But at least let that honour be paid to the name which is refused to the goddess—your fame, which will last for ever, owes much and will owe still more to victory. Let those be averse to this power, whom it has never benefited. Do you refuse to desert a patronage which is friendly to your triumphs? That power is wished for by all, let no one deny that what he acknowledges is to be desired should also be venerated.

But even if the avoidance of such an omen were not sufficient, it would at least have been seemly to abstain from injuring the ornaments of the Senate House. Allow us, we beseech you, as old men to leave posterity what we received as boys. The love of custom is great. . . . We are anxious for the permanence of your glory and your name, that the time to come may find nothing which needs correction.

Where shall we swear to obey your laws and commands? By what religious sanction shall the false mind be terrified, so as not to lie in bearing witness? All things are indeed filled with God, and no place is safe for the perjured, but to be urged in the very presence of religious forms has great power in producing a fear of sinning. That altar preserves the concord of all, that altar appeals to the good faith of each. . . .

Everyone has his own customs, everyone his own rites. The divine Mind has distributed different guardians and different cults to different cities. As souls are separately given to infants as they are born, so to peoples the genius of their destiny. Here comes in the proof from the advantage, which most of all vouches to man for the gods. For, since our reason is wholly clouded, whence does the knowledge of the gods more rightly come to us, than from the memory and evidence of prosperity? Now if a long period gives authority to religious customs, we ought to keep faith with so many centuries, and to follow our ancestors, as they happily followed theirs.

Let us now suppose that Rome is present and addresses you in these words: "Excellent princes, fathers of your country, respect my years to which pious rites have brought me. Let me use the ancestral ceremonies, for I do not repent of them. Let me live after my own fashion, for I am free. This worship subdued the world to my laws, these sacred rites repelled Hannibal from the walls, and the Senones from the capitol. Have I been reserved for this, that in my old age I should be blamed? I would consider what it is thought should be set in order, but tardy and discreditable is the reformation of old age."

We ask, then, for peace for the gods of our fathers and of our country. It is just that all worship should be considered as one. We look on the same stars, the sky is common, the same world surrounds us. What difference does it make by what pains each seeks the truth? We cannot attain to so great a secret by one road. . . .

St. Ambrose's Reply

Ambrose, Bishop, to the most blessed prince and most gracious Emperor Valentinian, the august. . . .

Let . . . that invidious complaint of the Roman people come to an end. Rome has given no such charge. She speaks with other words. "Why do you daily stain me with the useless blood of the harmless herd? Trophies of victory depend not on the entrails of the flocks, but on the strength of those who fight. I subdued the world by a different discipline. . . . There is no shame in passing to better things. This alone was common to me with the barbarians, that of old I knew not God. Your sacrifice is a rite of being sprinkled with the blood of beasts. Why do you seek the voice of God in dead animals. Come and learn on earth the heavenly warfare; we live here, but our warfare is there. Let God Himself, Who made me, teach me the mystery of heaven, not man, who knew not himself. Whom rather than God should I believe concerning God? How can I believe you, who confess that you know not what you worship?"

By one road, says he, one cannot attain to so great a secret. What you know not, that we know by the voice of God. And what you seek by fancies, we have found out from the very Wisdom and Truth of God. Your ways, therefore, do not agree with ours. You implore peace for your gods from the Emperors, we ask for peace for the Emperors themselves from Christ. You worship the works of your own hands, we think it an offence that anything which can be made should be esteemed God. God wills not that He should be worshipped in stones. And, in fine, your philosophers themselves have ridiculed these things.

But if you deny Christ to be God, because you believe not that He died (for you are ignorant that that death was of the body not of the Godhead, which has brought it to pass that now no one of those who believes dies), what is more thoughtless than you who honour with insult, and disparage with honour, for you consider a piece of wood to be your god . . . ?

But, says he, let the altars be restored to the images, and their ornaments to the shrines. Let this demand be made of one who shares in their superstitions; a Christian Emperor has learnt to honour the altar of Christ alone. Why do they exact of pious hands and faithful lips the ministry to their sacrilege? Let the voice of our Emperor utter the Name of Christ alone, and speak of Him only, Whom he is conscious of, for, "the King's heart is in the hands of the Lord." Has any heathen Emperor raised an altar to Christ? While they demand the restoration of things which have been, by their own example they show us how great reverence Christian Emperors ought to pay to the religion which they follow, since heathen ones offered all to their superstitions. . . .

But, he says, the rites of our ancestors ought to be retained. But what, seeing that all things have made progress towards what is better? . . . The lands freed from the misty darkness wondered at the new sun. The day does not shine in the beginning, but as time proceeds, it is bright with increase of light, and grows warm with increase of heat.

7 / ST. JEROME: CHRISTIANITY AND CLASSICAL CULTURE

The three great Latin Church fathers, St. Jerome, St. Ambrose, and St. Augustine, writing at the end of the fourth and the beginning of the fifth century, gave to the church well-informed and judicious opinions on every aspect of Christian life and civilization. Their opinions were authoritative for the early Middle Ages, and profoundly affected the ideals and attitudes of Christians throughout the medieval period and, in fact, even to the present day. St. Jerome (d. 420), the translator of the Bible into the authoritative Catholic form of the Vulgate, was particularly concerned about the proper relationship between Christianity and classical culture. His views were always cited by those medieval writers who took a favorable attitude toward the value of the classical legacy.[18]

JEROME'S DREAM

Many years ago, when for the kingdom of heaven's sake I had cut myself off from home, parents, sister, relations, and—harder still— from the dainty food to which I had been accustomed: and when I was

[18] *Library of the Nicene and Post-Nicene Fathers*, Vol. VI, transl. W. H. Fremantle (New York: Christian Literature Co., 1893), pp. 35–36, 149, 130.

on my way to Jerusalem to wage my warfare, I still could not bring myself to forego the library which I had formed for myself at Rome with great care and toil. And so, miserable man that I was, I would fast only that I might afterwards read Cicero. After many nights spent in vigil, after floods of tears called from my inmost heart, after the recollection of my past sins, I would once more take up Plautus. And when at times I returned to my right mind, and began to read the prophets, their style seemed rude and repellent. I failed to see the light with my blinded eyes; but I attributed the fault not to them, but to the sun. While the old serpent was thus making me his plaything, about the middle of Lent a deep-seated fever fell upon my weakened body, and while it destroyed my rest completely—the story seems hardly credible—it so wasted my unhappy frame that scarcely anything was left of me but skin and bone. Meantime preparations for my funeral went on; my body grew gradually colder, and the warmth of life lingered only in my throbbing breast. Suddenly I was caught up in the spirit and dragged before the judgment seat of the Judge; and here the light was so bright, and those who stood around were so radiant, that I cast myself upon the ground and did not dare to look up. Asked who and what I was I replied: "I am a Christian." But He who presided said: "Thou liest, thou art a follower of Cicero and not of Christ. For 'where thy treasure is, there will thy heart be also.'" Instantly I became dumb, and amid the strokes of the lash—for He had ordered me to be scourged—I was tortured more severely still by the fire of conscience, considering with myself that verse, "In the grave who shall give thee thanks?" Yet for all that I began to cry and to bewail myself, saying: "Have mercy upon me, O Lord: have mercy upon me." Amid the sound of the scourges this cry still made itself heard. At last the bystanders, falling down before the knees of Him who presided, prayed that He would have pity on my youth, and that He would give me space to repent of my error. He might still, they urged, inflict torture on me, should I ever again read the works of the Gentiles. Under the stress of that awful moment I should have been ready to make even still larger promises than these. Accordingly I made an oath and called upon His name, saying: "Lord, if ever again I possess worldly books, or if ever again I read such, I have denied Thee." Dismissed, then, on taking this oath, I returned to the upper world, and, to the surprise of all, I opened upon them eyes so drenched with tears that my distress served to convince even the incredulous. And that this was no sleep nor idle dream, such as those by which we are often mocked, I call to witness the tribunal before which I lay, and the terrible judgment which I feared. May it never, hereafter, be my lot to fall under such an inquisition! I profess that my shoulders were black and blue, that I felt the bruises long after I awoke from my sleep, and that thenceforth I read the books of God with a zeal greater than I had previously given to the books of men.

THE VALUE OF SECULAR LITERATURE

You ask me at the close of your letter why it is that sometimes in my writings I quote examples from secular literature and thus defile the whiteness of the church with the foulness of heathenism. I will now briefly answer your question. . . . Who is there who does not know that both in Moses and in the prophets there are passages cited from Gentile books and that Solomon proposed questions to the philosophers of Tyre and answered others put to him by them. . . . That leader of the Christian army, that unvanquished pleader for the cause of Christ skillfully turns a chance inscription into a proof of the faith. For he had learned from the true David to wrench the sword of the enemy out of his hand and with his own blade to cut off the head of the arrogant Goliath. He had read in Deuteronomy the command given by the voice of the Lord that when a captive woman had had her head shaved, her eyebrows and all her hair cut off, and her nails pared, she might then be taken to wife. Is it surprising that I too, admiring the fairness of her form and the grace of her eloquence, desire to make that secular wisdom which is my captive and my handmaid, a matron of the true Israel? Or that shaving off and cutting away all in her that is dead whether this be idolatry, pleasure, error, or lust, I take her to myself clean and pure and beget by her servants for the Lord of Sabaoth? My efforts promote the advantage of Christ's family, my so-called defilement with an alien increases the number of my fellow-servants.

"THE ROMAN WORLD IS FALLING"

I shudder when I think of the catastrophes of our time. For twenty years and more the blood of Romans has been shed daily between Constantinople and the Julian Alps. Scythia, Thrace, Macedonia, Dardania, Dacia, Thessaly, Achaia, Epirus, Dalmatia, the Pannonias—each and all of these have been sacked and pillaged and plundered by Goths and Samatians, Quades and Alans, Huns and Vandals and Marchmen. How many of God's matrons and virgins, virtuous and noble ladies, have been made the sport of these brutes! Bishops have been made captive, priests and those in minor orders have been put to death. Churches have been overthrown, horses have been stalled by the altars of Christ, the relics of martyrs have been dug up.

> Mourning and fear abound on every side
> And death appears in countless shapes and forms.

The Roman world is falling: yet we hold up our heads instead of bowing them. What courage, think you, have the Corinthians now, or the Athenians, or the Lacedaemonians or the Arcadians, or any of the Greeks over whom the barbarians bear sway? I have mentioned only a few cities, but these were once the capitals of no mean states. The East, it is true, seemed to be safe from all such evils: and if men were panic-stricken here, it was only because of bad news from other parts. But lo! in the year just gone by the wolves (no longer of Arabia but of the whole North) were let loose upon us from the remotest fastnesses of Caucasus and in a short time overran these great provinces. What a number of monasteries they captured! What many rivers they caused to run red with blood! They laid siege to Antioch and invested other cities on the Halys, the Cydnus, the Orontes, and the Euphrates. They carried off troops of captives. Arabia, Phoenicia, Palestine and Egypt, in their terror fancied themselves already enslaved.

8 / ST. AMBROSE:
CHRISTIAN DUTY

St. Ambrose (d. 397) was the leader of the Latin Church in the last two decades of the fourth century. Before his election as archbishop of Milan he had held high positions in the Roman government, and his pronouncements on the Christian life show the moral, social, and political concerns of a lawyer and states-man. He sees the Church as a state in itself, and emphasizes the duties and obligations of the members of the Christian community. He had the courage not to shrink from the conclusion that in the areas of faith and morals the Church was an autonomous institution and that the bishops, not the emperors, were the governors in these realms. Ambrose's views on church and state mark the beginning of the development of a hierocratic political doctrine which contradicts Caesaropapism.[19]

THE DUTIES OF THE CLERGY

I do not therefore claim for myself the glory of the apostles (for who can do this save those whom the Son of God Himself has chosen?); nor the grace of the prophets, nor the virtue of the evangelists, nor the

[19] *Library of the Nicene and Post-Nicene Fathers*, Vol. X, transl. H. de Romestin (New York: Christian Literature Co., 1896), pp. 1, 16, 32, 53–54, 61, 62, 365, 367–8, 8, 11, 436, 427, 440–1.

cautious care of the pastors. I only desire to attain to that care and diligence in the sacred writings, which the Apostle has placed last among the duties of the saints; and this very thing I desire, so that, in the endeavour to teach, I may be able to learn. For one is the true Master, Who alone has not learnt, what He taught all; but men learn before they teach, and receive from Him what they may hand on to others.

But not even this was the case with me. For I was carried off from the judgment seat, and the garb of office, to enter on the priesthood, and began to teach you, what I myself had not yet learnt. So it happened that I began to teach before I began to learn. Therefore I must learn and teach at the same time, since I had no leisure to learn before. . . .

Why dost thou not spend the time which thou hast free from thy duties in the church in reading? Why dost thou not go back again to see Christ? Why dost thou not address Him, and hear His voice? We address Him when we pray, we hear Him when we read the sacred oracles of God. What have we to do with strange houses? There is one house which holds all. They who need us can come to us. What have we to do with tales and fables? An office to minister at the altar of Christ is what we have received; no duty to make ourselves agreeable to men has been laid upon us. . . .

But again, no one must retire through cowardice, or give up his faith from fear of danger. With what grace must the soul be equipped, and the mind trained and taught to stand firm, so as never to be disturbed by any fears, to be broken by any troubles, or to yield to any torments! With what difficulty indeed are they borne! But as all pains seem less in the fear of greater pains, so also, if thou dost build up thy soul by quiet counsel, and dost determine not to go from thy course, and layest before thee the fear of divine judgment and the torment of eternal punishment, canst thou gain endurance of mind.

If a man thus prepares himself, he gives signs of great diligence. On the other hand it is a sign of natural ability, if a man by the power of his mind can foresee the future, and put as it were before his eyes what may happen, and decide what he ought to do if it should take place. It may happen, too, that he will think over two or three things at once, which he supposes may come either singly or together.

Therefore it is the duty of a brave man not to shut his eyes when anything threatens, but to put it before him and to search it out as it were in the mirror of his mind, and to meet the future with foreseeing thought, for fear he might afterwards have to say: This has come to me because I thought it could not come about. If misfortunes are not looked for beforehand, they quickly get a hold over us. In war an unexpected enemy is with difficulty resisted, and if he finds the others unprepared, he easily overcomes them; so evils unthought of readily break down the soul.

In these two points, then, consist the excellency of the soul: so that the soul, trained in good thoughts, and with a pure heart, first, may see what is true and virtuous (for "blessed are the pure in heart, for they shall see God"), and may decide that only to be good which is virtuous; and, next, may never be disturbed by business of any kind, nor get tossed about by any desires. Not that this is an easy thing for any one. . . .

The rule of economy and the authority of self-restraint befits all, and most of all him who stands highest in honour; so that no love for his treasures may seize upon such a man, and that he who rules over free men may never become a slave to money. It is more seemly that in soul he should be superior to treasures, and in willing service be subject to his friends. For humility increases the regard in which one is held. It is praiseworthy and right for the chief of men to have no desire for filthy lucre in common with Syrian traders and Gilead merchants, nor to place all their hope of good in money, or to count up their daily gains and to calculate their savings like a hireling. . . .

I think, then, that one should strive to win preferment, especially in the Church, only by good actions and with a right aim; so that there may be no proud conceit, no idle carelessness, no shameful disposition of mind, no unseemly ambition. A plain simplicity of mind is enough for everything, and commends itself quite sufficiently.

When in office, again, it is not right to be harsh and severe, nor may one be too easy; lest on the one hand we should seem to be exercising a despotic power, and the other to be by no means filling the office we had taken up. . . .

Never protect a wicked man, nor allow the sacred things to be given over to an unworthy one; on the other hand, do not harass and press hard on a man whose fault is not clearly proved. Injustice quickly gives offence in every case, but especially in the Church, where equity ought to exist, where like treatment should be given to all, so that a powerful person may not claim the more, nor a rich man appropriate the more. For whether we be poor or rich, we are one in Christ. Let him that lives a holier life claim nothing more thereby for himself; for he ought rather to be the more humble for it.

In giving judgment let us have no respect of persons. Favour must be put out of sight, and the case be decided on its merits. Nothing is so great a strain on another's good opinion or confidence, as the fact of our giving away the cause of the weaker to the more powerful in any case that comes before us. The same happens if we are hard on the poor, whilst we make excuses for the rich man when guilty. Men are ready enough to flatter those in high positions, so as not to let them think themselves injured, or to feel vexed as though overthrown. But if thou fearest to give offence then do not undertake to give judgment.

IN PRAISE OF VIRGINITY

Virginity is not praiseworthy because it is found in martyrs, but because it itself makes martyrs.

But who can comprehend that by human understanding which not even nature has included in her laws? Or who can explain in ordinary language that which is above the course of nature? Virginity has brought from heaven that which it may imitate on earth. And not unfittingly has she sought her manner of life from heaven, who has found for herself a Spouse in heaven. She, passing beyond the clouds, air, angels, and stars, has found the Word of God in the very bosom of the Father, and has drawn Him into herself with her whole heart. For who having found so great a Good would forsake it? For "Thy Name is as ointment poured out, therefore have the maidens loved Thee, and drawn Thee." And indeed what I have said is not my own, since they who marry not nor are given in marriage are as the angels in heaven. Let us not, then, be surprised if they are compared to the angels who are joined to the Lord of angels. Who, then, can deny that this mode of life has its source in heaven, which we don't easily find on earth, except since God came down into the members of an earthly body? Then a Virgin conceived, and the Word became flesh that flesh might become God. . . .

I am not indeed discouraging marriage, but am enlarging upon the benefits of virginity. . . . Let us compare, if it pleases you, the advantages of married women with that which awaits virgins. Though the noble woman boasts of her abundant offspring, yet the more she bears the more she endures. Let her count up the comforts of her children, but let her likewise count up the troubles. She marries and weeps. How many vows does she make with tears! She conceives, and her fruitfulness brings her trouble before offspring. She brings forth and is ill. How sweet a pledge which begins with danger and ends in danger, which will cause pain before pleasure! It is purchased by perils, and is not possessed at her own will.

Why speak of the troubles of nursing, training, and marrying? These are the miseries of those who are fortunate. A mother has heirs, but it increases her sorrows. . . . Why should I further speak of the painful ministrations and services due to their husbands from wives, to whom before slaves God gave the command to serve? . . . And in this position spring up those incentives to vice, in that they paint their faces with various colours, fearing not to please their husbands; and from staining their faces, come to think of staining their chastity. What madness is here, to change the fashion of nature and seek a painting, and while fearing a husband's judgment to give up their own. . . .

And next, what expense is necessary that even a beautiful wife may not fail to please? Costly necklaces on the one hand hang on her neck, on the other a robe woven with gold is dragged along the ground. Is this display purchased, or is it a real possession? And what varied enticements of perfumes are made use of! The ears are weighed down with gems, a different colour from nature is dropped into the eyes. What is there left which is her own, when so much is changed? The married woman loves her own perceptions, and does she think that this is to live?

But you, O happy virgins, who know not such torments, rather than ornaments, whose holy modesty, beaming in your bashful cheeks, and sweet chastity are a beauty, ye do not, intent upon the eyes of men, consider as merits what is gained by the errors of others. You, too, have indeed your own beauty, furnished by the comeliness of virtue, not of the body, to which age puts not to an end, which death cannot take away, nor any sickness injure. Let God alone be sought as the judge of loveliness, Who loves even in less beautiful bodies the more beautiful souls. You know nothing of the burden and pain of childbearing, but more are the offspring of a pious soul, which esteems all as its children, which is rich in successors, barren of all bereavements, which knows no deaths, but has many heirs.

So the holy Church, ignorant of wedlock, but fertile in bearing, is in chastity a virgin, yet a mother in offspring. She, a virgin, bears us her children, not by a human father, but by the Spirit. She bears us not with pain, but with the rejoicings of the angels. She, a virgin, feeds us, not with the milk of the body, but with that of the Apostle, wherewith he fed the tender age of the people who were still children. For what bride has more children than the holy Church, who is a virgin in her sacraments and a mother to her people, whose fertility even holy Scripture attests, saying, "For many more are the children of the desolate than of her that hath an husband"? She has not an husband, but she has a Bridegroom, inasmuch as she, whether as the Church amongst nations, or as the soul in individuals, without any loss of modesty, she weds the Word of God as her eternal Spouse, free from all injury, full of reason.

POVERTY AND WEALTH

The blessedness of individuals must not be estimated at the value of their known wealth, but according to the voice of their conscience within them. For this, as a true and uncorrupted judge of punishments and rewards, decides between the deserts of the innocent and the guilty. The innocent man dies in the strength of his own simplicity, in the full possession of his own will; having a soul filled as it were with marrow. But the sinner, though he has abundance in life, and lives in the midst of luxury, and is redolent with sweet scents, ends his life in the bitterness of his soul, and brings his last day to a close, taking with him none of those good things which he once enjoyed—carrying away nothing with him but the price of his own wickedness. . . .

Is not he unjust who gives the reward before the end of the contest? Therefore the Lord says in the Gospel: "Blessed are the poor in spirit, for theirs is the kingdom of heaven." He said not: "Blessed are the rich," but "the poor." By the divine judgment blessedness begins there whence human misery is supposed to spring. . . . A reward future and not present,—in heaven not on earth,—has He promised shall be given. What further dost thou expect? What further is due? Why dost thou demand the crown with so much haste, before thou dost conquer? Why dost thou desire to shake off the dust and to rest? Why dost thou long to sit at the feast before the course is finished? As yet the people are looking on, the athletes are in the arena, and thou—dost thou already look for ease?

Perhaps thou sayest: Why are the wicked joyous? Why do they live in luxury? Why do they not toil with me? It is because they who have not put down their names to strive for the crown are not bound to undergo the labours of the contest. They who have not gone down into the race-course do not anoint themselves with oil nor get covered with dust. For those whom glory awaits trouble is at hand. The perfumed spectators are wont to look on, not to join in the struggle, nor to endure the sun, the heat, the dust, and the showers. Let the athletes say to them: Come, strive with us. The spectators will but answer: We sit here not to decide about you, but you, if you conquer, will gain the glory of the crown and we shall not.

They, then, who have devoted themselves to pleasures, luxury, robbery, gain, or honours are spectators rather than combatants. They have the profit of labour, but not the fruits of virtue. They love their ease; by cunning and wickedness they heap up riches; but they will pay the penalty of their iniquity, though it be late. Their rest will be in hell, thine in heaven; their home in the grave, thine in paradise. . . .

Do not, therefore, understand, or speak, or think as a child; nor as a child claim those things now which belong to a future time. The crown belongs to the perfect. Wait till that which is perfect is come, when thou mayest know—not through a glass as in a riddle, but face to face—the very form of truth made clear. Then will be made known why that person was rich who was wicked and a robber of other men's goods, why another was powerful, why a third had many children, and yet a fourth was loaded with honours.

THE AUTONOMY OF THE CHURCH

The church belongs to God, therefore it ought not to be assigned to Caesar. For the Temple of God cannot be Caesar's by right. . . . The emperor is within the church, not above it.

Who is there can deny that in a matter of faith—in a matter I say of faith—bishops are wont to judge Christian emperors, while emperors are not the judges of bishops.

There is nothing in a priest so full of peril as regards God or so base in the opinion of men as not freely to declare what he thinks. . . . In the cause of God whom will you listen to if not the priest, at whose greater peril sin is committed? [20] Who will dare to tell you [O, emperor] the truth if the priest dare not?

9 / THE AUGUSTINIAN WORLD-VIEW

The writings of St. Augustine (354–430), bishop of Hippo in North Africa, do not comprise an organized and finished intellectual and religious system. Augustine never had the leisure to organize his ideas in this way. But his doctrines, propounded over a long career in answer to problems that bothered his flock, are among the most seminal in Western civilization. Augustine is the greatest thinker of the early Middle Ages, and his writings, at all times in the Middle Ages and in many eras of the modern world, exercised a great influence on other leading theologians and philosophers. Augustine may best be viewed as the most profound and fertile of Christian thinkers, the sower of ideas which have been debated from his day until ours. He has exercised a particularly strong influence on periods of disintegration and apparent political failure—the early and late Middle Ages and the twentieth century.[21]

---

[20] I.e., the priest, who is responsible to God as the minister of God and the shepherd of His flock, will be called to account if he neglects his duty to reprove sin.

[21] I. *On Christian Doctrine,* transl. J. F. Shaw, 3rd ed. (Edinburgh: T. & T. Clark, 1892), 75–6.

II. *Confessions,* transl. F. J. Sheed (New York: Sheed & Ward, 1943), pp. 141,

I. UTILITY OF THE CLASSICAL HERITAGE

. . . If those who are called philosophers, and especially the Platonists, have said aught that is true and in harmony with our faith, we are not only not to shrink from it, but to claim it for our own use from those who have unlawful possession of it. For, as the Egyptians had not only the idols and heavy burdens which the people of Israel hated and fled from, but also vessels and ornaments of gold and silver, and garments, which the same people when going out of Egypt appropriated to themselves, designing them for a better use, not doing this on their own authority, but by the command of God, the Egyptians themselves, in their ignorance, providing them with things which they themselves were not making a good use of; in the same way all branches of heathen learning have not only false and superstitious fancies and heavy burdens of unnecessary toil, which every one of us, when going out under the leadership of Christ from the fellowship of the heathen, ought to abhor and avoid; but they contain also liberal instruction which is better adapted to the use of the truth, and some most excellent precepts of morality; and some truths in regard even to the worship of the One God are found among them. Now these are, so to speak, their gold and silver, which they did not create themselves, but dug out of the mines of God's providence which are everywhere scattered abroad, and are perversely and unlawfully prostituting to the worship of devils. These, therefore, the Christian, when he separates himself in spirit from the miserable fellowship of these men, ought to take away from them, and to devote to their proper use in preaching the gospel. Their garments, also,—that is, human institutions such as are adapted to that intercourse with men which is indispensable in this life—we must take and turn to a Christian use.

II. THE NATURE OF EVIL

Thus, O God my aid, from those chains You have freed me. But I was still seeking what might be the source of evil and I could see no answer. Yet with all the ebb and flow of my thought You did not let me be carried away from the faith by which I believed that You were, and

---

146–7. From the *Confessions of St. Augustine* in the translation of F. J. Sheed. Copyright 1943 Sheed & Ward, Inc., New York.

III. *The City of God*, transl. M. Dods (Edinburgh: T. & T. Clark, 1872), Vol. II, pp. 49–51, 326–8.

IV–VI. *The Works of Aurelius Augustine*, Marcus Dods, ed. (Edinburgh: T. & T. Clark, 1875–1892), Vol. IX, pp. 318–19, Vol. VI, pp. 300, 302, 303, 191–3, 195, Vol. XIII, pp. 347, 352–3.

that Your substance was unchangeable, and that You cared for men and would judge them; and that in Christ Your Son Our Lord, and in the Holy Scriptures which the authority of Your Catholic Church acknowledges, You had established the way of man's salvation unto that life which is to be after death. But with these truths held safe and inviolably rooted in my mind, I was still on fire with the question whence comes evil. What were the agonies, what the anguish of my heart in labour, O my God!

. . . Whatsoever things are, are good; and that evil whose origin I sought is not a substance, because if it were a substance it would be good. For either it would be an incorruptible substance, that is to say, the highest goodness; or it would be a corruptible substance, which would not be corruptible unless it were good. Thus I saw and clearly realized that You have made all things good, and that there are no substances not made by You.

. . . To You, then, evil utterly is not—and not only to You, but to Your whole creation likewise, evil is not: because there is nothing over and above Your creation that could break in or derange the order that You imposed upon it. But in certain of its parts there are some things which we call evil because they do not harmonize with other things; yet these same things do harmonize with still others and thus are good; and in themselves they are good. All these things which do not harmonize with one another, do suit well with that lower part of creation which we call the earth, which has its cloudy and windy sky in some way apt to it.

III. THE TWO CITIES

. . . Of the bliss of Paradise, of Paradise itself, and of the life of our first parents there, and of their sin and punishment, many have thought much, spoken much, written much. We ourselves, too, have spoken of these things in the foregoing books, and have written either what we read in the Holy Scriptures, or what we could reasonably deduce from them. . . . Yet I trust we have already done justice to these great and difficult questions regarding the beginning of the world, or of the soul, or of the human race itself. This race we have distributed into two parts, the one consisting of those who live according to man, the other of those who live according to God. And these we also mystically call the two cities, or the two communities of men, of which the one is predestined to reign eternally with God, and the other to suffer eternal punishment with the devil. This, however, is their end, and of it we are to speak afterwards. At present, as we have said enough about their origin, whether among the angels, whose numbers we know not, or in the two first human beings, it seems suitable to attempt an account of their career, from the time when our two first parents began to propagate the race until all human generation shall cease. For this whole time or world-age, in which the dying give place and those who are born succeed, is the career of these two cities concerning which we treat.

Of these two first parents of the human race, then, Cain was the first-born, and he belonged to the city of men; after him was born Abel, who belonged to the city of God. For as in the individual the truth of the apostle's statement is discerned, "that is not first which is spiritual, but that which is natural, and afterward that which is spiritual," whence it comes to pass that each man, being derived from a condemned stock, is first of all born of Adam evil and carnal, and becomes good and spiritual only afterwards, when he is grafted into Christ by regeneration: so was it in the human race as a whole. When these two cities began to run their course by a series of deaths and births, the citizen of this world was the first-born, and after him the stranger in this world, the citizen of the city of God, predestinated by grace, elected by grace, by grace a stranger below, and by grace a citizen above. By grace,—for so far as regards himself he is sprung from the same mass, all of which is condemned in its origin; but God, like a potter (for this comparison is introduced by the apostle judiciously, and not without thought), of the same lump made one vessel to honour, another to dishonour. But first the vessel to dishonour was made, and after it another to honour. For in each individual, as I have already said, there is first of all that which is reprobate, that from which we must begin, but in which we need not necessarily remain; afterwards is that which is well-approved, to which we may by advancing attain, and in which, when we have reached it, we may abide. Not, indeed, that every wicked man shall be good, but that no one will be good who was not first of all wicked; but the sooner any one becomes a good man, the more speedily does he receive this title, and abolish the old name in the new. Accordingly, it is recorded of Cain that he built a city, but Abel, being a sojourner, built none. For the city of the saints is above, although here below it begets citizens, in whom it sojourns till the time of its reign arrives, when it shall gather together all in the day of the resurrection; and then shall the promised kingdom be given to them, in which they shall reign with their Prince, the King of the ages, time without end.

. . . But the families which do not live by faith seek their peace in the earthly advantages of this life; while the families which live by faith look for those eternal blessings which are promised, and use as pilgrims such advantages of time and of earth as do not fascinate and divert them from God, but rather aid them to endure with greater ease, and to keep down the number of those burdens of the corruptible body which weigh upon the soul. Thus the things necessary for this mortal life are used by both kinds of men and families alike, but each has its own peculiar and widely different aim in using them. The earthly city, which does not live by faith, seeks an earthly peace, and the end it proposes, in the well-ordered concord of civic obedience and rule, is the combination of men's will to attain the things which are helpful to his life. The heavenly city, or rather the part of it which sojourns on earth and lives by faith, makes use of this peace only because it must, until this mortal condition which necessitates it shall pass away. Consequently, so long as it lives like a captive and a stranger in the earthly city, though it has already received the promise of redemption, and the gift of the Spirit as the earnest of it, it makes no scruple to obey the laws of the earthly city, whereby the things necessary for the maintenance of this mortal life are administered; . . . This heavenly city, then, while it sojourns on earth, calls citizens out of all nations, and gathers together a society of pilgrims of all languages, not scrupling about diversities in the manners, laws, and institutions whereby earthly peace is secured and maintained, but recognising that, however various these are, they all tend to one and the same end of earthly peace. It therefore is so far from rescinding and abolishing these diversities, that it even preserves and adopts them so long only as no hindrance to the worship of the one supreme and true God is thus introduced. Even the heavenly city, therefore, while in its state of pilgrimage, avails itself of the peace of earth, and, so far as it can without injuring faith and godliness, desires and maintains a common agreement among men regarding the acquisition of the necessaries of life, and make this earthly peace bear upon the peace of heaven; for this alone can be truly called and esteemed the peace of the reasonable creatures, consisting as it does in the perfectly ordered and harmonious enjoyment of God and of one another in God. When we shall have reached that peace, this mortal life shall give place to one that is eternal, and our body shall be no more this animal body which by its corruption weighs down the soul, but a spiritual body feeling no want, and in all its members subjected to the will. In its pilgrim state the heavenly city possesses this peace by faith; and by this faith it lives righteously when it refers to the attainment of that peace every good action towards God and man; for the life of this city is a social life.

IV. THE SIX AGES OF THE WORLD

Five ages of the world, accordingly, having been now completed (there has entered the sixth). Of these ages the first is from the beginning of the human race, that is, from Adam, who was the first man that was made, down to Noah, who constructed the ark at the time of the flood. Then the second extends from that period on to Abraham, who was called the father indeed of all nations which should follow the example of his faith, but who at the same time in the way of natural descent from his own flesh was the father of the destined people of the Jews; which people, previous to the entrance of the Gentiles into the Christian faith, was the one people among all the nations of all lands that worshipped the one true God: from which people also Christ the Saviour was decreed to come according to the flesh. For these turning-points of those two ages occupy an eminent place in the ancient books. On the other hand, those of the other three ages are also declared in the Gospel, where the descent of the Lord Jesus Christ according to the flesh is likewise mentioned. For the third age extends from Abraham on to David the king; the fourth from David on to that captivity whereby the people of God passed into Babylonia; and the fifth from that transmigration down to the advent of our Lord Jesus Christ. With His coming the sixth age has entered on its process; so that now the spiritual grace, which in previous times was known to a few patriarchs and prophets, may be made manifest to all nations; to the intent that no man should worship God but freely, fondly desiring of Him not the visible rewards of His services and the happiness of this present life, but that eternal life alone in which he is to enjoy God Himself: in order that in this sixth age the mind of man may be renewed after the image of God, even as on the sixth day man was made after the image of God. For then, too, is the law fulfilled, when all that it has commanded is done, not in the strong desire for things temporal, but in the love of Him who has given the commandment.

V. AGAINST THE DONATISTS: THE NATURE OF THE CHURCH AND THE OFFICE OF THE PRIESTHOOD

1. Hear, O Donatists,[22] what the Catholic Church says to you: "O ye sons of men, how long will ye be slow of heart? Why will ye love vanity and follow after lies?" Why have you severed yourselves, by the heinous impiety of schism, from the unity of the whole world? . . . Your imagination that you are separating yourselves, before the time of

---

[22] The Donatist heretics claimed that the ministration of the sacraments by an unworthy priest was invalid. They advocated a select church of the morally pure. Against them Augustine formulated the doctrine of the Church and the priesthood which has been the Catholic view to the present day. While limited to North Africa in Augustine's time the Donatist heresy was widespread in France and Italy, and later England and Germany, in the high and late Middle Ages, and is one of the intellectual roots of Protestantism. Augustine's dispute with the Donatists is therefore of fundamental importance for Western civilization.

the harvest, from the tares which are mixed in with the wheat, proves that you are only tares. For if you were wheat, you would bear with the tares, and not separate yourselves from that which is growing in Christ's field. Of the tares, indeed, it has been said, "Because iniquity shall abound, the love of many shall wax cold"; but of the wheat it is said, "He that shall endure unto the end, the same shall be saved." What grounds have you for believing that the tares have increased and filled the world, and that the wheat has decreased, and is found now in Africa alone? You claim to be Christians, and you disclaim the authority of Christ. He said, "Let both grow together till the harvest"; He said not, "Let the wheat decrease, and let the tares multiply." He said, "The field is the world"; He said not, "The field is Africa." He said, "The harvest is the end of the world"; . . . But you, by charging the good wheat with being tares, have proved yourselves to be tares; and what is worse, you have prematurely separated yourselves from the wheat. . . .

He is the associate of wicked men who consents to the deeds of wicked men; not he who suffers the tares to grow in the Lord's field unto the harvest, or the chaff to remain until the final winnowing time. If you hate those who do evil, shake yourselves free from the crime of schism. . . . Finally, wherein has the Christian world offended you, from which you have insanely and wickedly cut yourselves off? . . . Wherein has the peace of Christ offended you, that you resist it by separating yourselves from those whom you calumniate?

2. Since you were pleased to acquaint us with the letter sent to you by a Donatist presbyter, although, with the spirit of a true Catholic, you regarded it with contempt, nevertheless, to aid you in seeking his welfare if his folly be not incurable, we beg you to forward to him the following reply. He wrote that an angel had enjoined him to declare to you the episcopal succession of the Christianity of your town; to you, forsooth, who hold the Christianity not of your own town only, nor of Africa only, but of the whole world, the Christianity which has been published, and is now published to all nations. This proves that they think it a small matter that they themselves are not ashamed of being cut off, and are taking no measures, while they may, to be engrafted anew; they are not content unless they do their utmost to cut others off, and bring them to share their own fate, as withered branches fit for the flames. . . . For to you it was proclaimed by the voice of the Lord Jesus Christ Himself, that His "gospel shall be preached unto all nations, and then shall the end come." To you it has moreover been proclaimed by the writings of the prophets and of the apostles, that the promises were given to Abraham and to his Seed, which is Christ, when God said unto him: "In thy seed shall all nations of the earth be

blessed." Having then such promises, if an angel from heaven were to say to thee, "Let go the Christanity of the whole earth, and cling to the faction of Donatus, the episcopal succession of which is set forth in a letter of their bishop in your town," he ought to be accursed in your estimation; because he would be endeavouring to cut you off from the whole Church, and thrust you into a small party, and make you forfeit your interest in the promises of God.

For if the lineal succession of bishops is to be taken into account, with how much more certainty and benefit to the Church do we reckon back till we reach Peter himself, to whom, as bearing in a figure the whole Church, the Lord said: "Upon this rock I will build my Church, and the gates of hell shall not prevail against it!" The successor of Peter was Linus and his successor in unbroken continuity were these:— Clement, . . . and Siricius, whose successor is the present Bishop Anastasius. In this order of succession no Donatist bishop is found. . . . Now, even although some traitor had in the course of these centuries, through inadvertence, obtained a place in that order of bishops, reaching from Peter himself to Anastasius, who now occupies that see, —this fact would do no harm to the Church and to Christians having no share in the guilt of another; for the Lord, providing against such a case, says, concerning officers in the Church who are wicked: "All whatsoever they bid you observe, that observe and do; but do not ye after their works: for they say, and do not." Thus the stability of the hope of the faithful is secured, inasmuch as being fixed, not in the man, but in the Lord, it never can be swept away by the raging of impious schism. . . .

We rely . . . on the Holy Scriptures, wherein a dominion extending to the ends of the earth among all nations is promised as the heritage of Christ, separated from which by their sinful schism they reproach us with the crimes which belong to the chaff in the Lord's threshing-floor, which must be permitted to remain mixed with the good grain until the end come, until the whole be winnowed in the final judgment. From which it is manifest that, whether these charges be true or false, they do not belong to the Lord's wheat, which must grow until the end of the world throughout the field, i.e., the whole earth; as we know, not by the testimony of a false angel such as confirmed your correspondent in his error, but from words of the Lord in the Gospel.

VI. JUSTIFICATION OF THE USE OF FORCE ON BEHALF OF THE CHURCH

The aim towards which a good will compassionately devotes its efforts is to secure that a bad will be rightly directed. For who does not know that a man is not condemned on any other ground than because his bad will deserved it, and that no man is saved who has not a good will? Nevertheless, it does not follow from this that those who are loved should be cruelly left to yield themselves with impunity to their bad will; but in so far as power is given, they ought to be prevented from evil and compelled to good.

For if a bad will ought to be always left to its own freedom, why were the disobedient and murmuring Israelites restrained from evil by such severe chastisements, and compelled to come into the land of promise? If a bad will ought always to be left to its own freedom, why was Paul not left to the free use of that most perverted will with which he persecuted the Church? Why was he thrown to the ground that he might be blinded, and struck blind that he might be changed, and changed that he might be sent as an apostle, and sent that he might suffer for the truth's sake such wrongs as he had inflicted on others when he was in error? If a bad will ought always to be left to its own freedom, why is a father instructed in Holy Scripture not only to correct an obstinate son by words of rebuke, but also to beat his sides, in order that, being compelled and subdued, he may be guided to good conduct. . . .

I hear that you have remarked and often quote the fact recorded in the gospels, that the seventy disciples went back from the Lord, and that they had been left to their own choice in this wicked and impious desertion, and that to the twelve who alone remained the Lord said, "Will ye also go away?" But you have neglected to remark, that at that time the Church was only beginning to burst into life from the recently planted seed, and that there was not yet fulfilled in her the prophecy: "All kings shall fall down before Him; yea, all nations shall serve Him"; and it is in proportion to the more enlarged accomplishment of this prophecy that the Church wields greater power, so that she may not only invite, but even compel men to embrace what is good. This our Lord intended then to illustrate, for although He had great power, He chose rather to manifest His humility. This also He taught, with sufficient plainness, in the parable of the Feast, in which the master of the house, after he had sent a message to the invited guests, and they had refused to come, said to his servants: "Go out quickly into the streets and lanes of the city, and bring in hither the poor, and the maimed, and the halt, and the blind. And the servant said, Lord, it is done as thou hast commanded, and yet there is room. And the Lord said unto the servant, Go out into the highways and hedges, and compel them to come in, that my house may be filled." Mark, now, how it was said in regard to those who came first, "bring them in"; it was not said, "compel them to come in,"—by which was signified the incipient condition of the Church, when it was only growing towards the position in which it would have strength to compel men to come in. Accordingly, because it was right that when the Church had been strengthened, both in power and in extent, men should be compelled to come in to the feast of everlasting salvation, it was afterwards added in the parable, "The servant said, Lord, it is done as thou hast commanded, and yet there is room. And the Lord said unto the servants, Go out into the highways and hedges, and compel them to come in."

10 / OROSIUS: A PROVIDENTIAL VIEW OF HISTORY

Augustine had begun to write The City of God *to refute the claim of pagan critics that Rome was falling in Christian days as a consequence of the desertion of the traditional deities. His initial idea was to show that there were many even greater distasters before the coming of Christ. Eventually Augustine went on to more sophisticated historical thinking, but he handed over to a disciple, a Spanish priest named Orosius, the task of writing a world history showing that Providence had treated the world worse before the empire had accepted Christianity. Orosius'* Seven Books Against the Pagans *was very popular in the Middle Ages and strongly encouraged subsequent historians in the medieval period to write accounts of the events of their eras from a providential point of view. His treatise represents the most widely held theory of history in medieval society.*[23]

I have obeyed your instructions, blessed Augustine, and may my achievement match my good intentions. . . . You bade me reply to the empty chatter and perversity of those who, aliens to the City of God, are called "pagans" because they come from the countryside and the crossroads of the rural districts, or "heathen" because of their wisdom in earthly matters. Although these people do not seek out the future and moreover either forget or know nothing of the past, nevertheless they charge that the present times are unusually beset with

---

[23] Orosius, *Seven Books Against the Pagans,* transl. I. W. Raymond, *Records of Civilization,* Vol. 26 (New York: Columbia University Press, 1936), pp. 29, 30–31, 397–8. Reprinted by permission of Columbia University Press.

calamities for the sole reason that men believe in Christ and worship God while idols are increasingly neglected. You bade me, therefore, discover from all the available data of histories and annals whatever instances past ages have afforded of the burdens of war, the ravages of disease, the horrors of famine, of terrible earthquakes, extraordinary floods, dreadful eruptions of fire, thunderbolts and hailstorms, and also instances of the cruel miseries caused by parricides and disgusting crimes. I was to set these forth systematically and briefly in the course of my book. It certainly is not right for your reverence to be bothered with so trifling a treatise as this while you are intent on completing the eleventh book of your work against these same pagans. When your ten previous books appeared, they, like a beacon from the watchtower of your high position in the Church, at once flashed their shining rays over all the world. Also your holy son, Julian of Carthage, a servant of God, strongly urged me to carry out his request in this matter in such a way that I might justify his confidence in asking me.

I started to work and at first went astray, for as I repeatedly turned over these matters in my mind the disasters of my own times seemed to have boiled over and exceeded all usual limits. But now I have discovered that the days of the past were not only as oppressive as those of the present but that they were the more terribly wretched the further they were removed from the consolation of true religion. My investigation has shown, as was proper it should, that death and a thirst for bloodshed prevailed during the time in which the religion that forbids bloodshed was unknown; that as the new faith dawned, the old grew faint; that while the old neared its end, the new was already victorious; that the old beliefs will be dead and gone when the new religion shall reign alone. We must, of course, make an exception of those last, remote days at the end of the world when Antichrist shall appear and when judgment shall be pronounced, for in these days there shall be distress such as there never was before, as the Lord Christ by His own testimony predicted in the Holy Scriptures. At that time, according to that very standard which now is and ever shall be—yes, by a clearer and more searching discrimination—the saints shall be rewarded for the unbearable sufferings of those days and the wicked shall be destroyed. . . .

I have set forth with the help of Christ and according to your bidding, most blessed father Augustine, the passions and the punishments of sinful men, the tribulations of the world, and the judgments of God, from the Creation to the present day, a period of five thousand six hundred and eighteen years, as briefly and as simply as I could, but separating Christian times from the former confusion of unbelief because of the more present grace of Christ. Thus I now enjoy the sure reward of my obedience, the only one that I have a right to enjoy; for the quality of my little books, you who asked for this record will be responsible. If you publish them, they must be regarded favorably by you; if you destroy them, they must be regarded unfavorably.

11 / TACITUS: GERMANIC INSTITUTIONS

Tacitus' Germania, published in 98 A.D., is the only detailed account we have of Germanic life before the great invasions of the fourth and fifth centuries. It is easy to question the reliability of this account by the Roman aristocratic historian on the grounds that he never visited the German Rhine-Danube frontier and that he allowed his work to be influenced by the preconceived notion that the more primitive Germans were more vigorous and moral than the supposedly decadent and corrupt citizens of the civilized Roman world. But Tacitus, as one of the prominent political leaders of his day, had access to the reports of eyewitnesses, and his work is so circumstantial, and so many of the institutions he describes are confirmed by accounts of the life of the invaders three centuries later, that his work must be accepted as substantially a true and reliable description.[24]

THE INHABITANTS; ORIGIN OF THE NAME "GERMANY"

Chapter 2

The Germans themselves I should regard as aboriginal, and not mixed at all with other races through immigration or intercourse. For, in former times, it was not by land but on shipboard that those who sought to emigrate would arrive; and the boundless and, so to speak, hostile ocean beyond us, is seldom entered by a sail from our world. And, beside the perils of rough and unknown seas, who would leave Asia, or Africa, or Italy for Germany, with its wild country, its inclement skies, its sullen manners and aspect, unless indeed it were his home? In their ancient songs, their only way of remembering or recording the past, they celebrate an earth-born god, Tuisco, and his son Mannus, as

[24] *The Agricola and Germany of Tacitus,* transl. A. J. Church and W. J. Brodribb (London: Macmillan, 1885), pp. 87–107.

the origin of their race, as their founders. To Mannus they assign three sons, from whose names, they say, the coast tribes are called Ingaevones; those of the interior, Herminones; all the rest, Istaevones. Some, with the freedom of conjecture permitted by antiquity, assert that the god had several descendants, and the nation several appellations, as Marsi, Gambrivii, Suevi, Vandilii, and that these are genuine old names. The name Germany, on the other hand, they say, is modern and newly introduced, from the fact that the tribes which first crossed the Rhine and drove out the Gauls, and are now called Tungrians, were then called Germans. Thus what was the name of a tribe, and not of a race, gradually prevailed, till all called themselves by this self-invented name of Germans, which the conquerors had first employed to inspire terror.

THE NATIONAL WAR-SONGS; LEGEND OF ULYSSES

Chapter 3

They say that Hercules, too, once visited them; and when going into battle, they sing of him first of all heroes. They have also those songs of theirs, by the recital of which ("baritus," they call it), they rouse their courage, while from the note they augur the result of the approaching conflict. For, as their line shouts, they inspire or feel alarm. It is not so much an articulate sound, as a general cry of valour. They aim chiefly at a harsh note and a confused roar, putting their shields to their mouth, so that, by reverberation, it may swell into a fuller and deeper sound. Ulysses, too, is believed by some, in his long legendary wanderings, to have found his way into this ocean, and, having visited German soil, to have founded and named the town of Asciburgium, which stands on the bank of the Rhine, and is to this day inhabited. They even say that an altar dedicated to Ulysses, with the addition of the name of his father, Laertes, was formerly discovered on this same spot, and that certain monuments and tombs, with Greek inscriptions, still exist on the borders of Germany and Rhaetia. These statements I have no intention of sustaining by proofs, or of refuting; every one may believe or disbelieve them as he feels inclined.

PHYSICAL CHARACTERISTICS

Chapter 4

For my own part, I agree with those who think that the tribes of Germany are free from all taint of intermarriages with foreign nations, and that they appear as a distinct, unmixed race, like none but themselves. Hence, too, the same physical peculiarities throughout so vast a population. All have fierce blue eyes, red hair, huge frames, fit only for a sudden exertion. They are less able to bear laborious work. Heat and thirst they cannot in the least endure; to cold and hunger their climate and their soil inure them.

CLIMATE AND SOIL; PRECIOUS METALS

Chapter 5

Their country, though somewhat various in appearance, yet generally either bristles with forests or reeks with swamps; it is more rainy on the side of Gaul, bleaker on that of Noricum and Pannonia. It is productive of grain, but unfavourable to fruit-bearing trees; it is rich in flocks and herds, but these are for the most part undersized, and even the cattle have not their usual beauty or noble head. It is number that is chiefly valued; they are in fact the most highly prized, indeed the only riches of the people. Silver and gold the gods have refused to them, whether in kindness or in anger I cannot say. I would not, however, affirm that no vein of German soil produces gold or silver, for who has ever made a search? They care but little to possess or use them. You may see among them vessels of silver, which have been presented to their envoys and chieftains, held as cheap as those of clay. The border population, however, value gold and silver for their commercial utility, and are familiar with, and show preference for, some of our coins. The tribes of the interior use the simpler and more ancient practice of the barter of commodities. They like the old and well-known money, coins milled, or showing a two-horse chariot. They likewise prefer silver to gold, not from any special liking, but because a large number of silver pieces is more convenient for use among dealers in cheap and common articles.

ARMS, MILITARY MANOEUVRES, AND DISCIPLINE

Chapter 6

Even iron is not plentiful with them, as we infer from the character of their weapons. But few use swords or long lances. They carry a spear (*framea* is their name for it), with a narrow and short head, but so sharp and easy to wield that the same weapon serves, according to circumstances, for close or distant conflict. As for the horse-soldier, he is satisfied with a shield and spear; the foot-soldiers also scatter showers of missiles, each man having several and hurling them to an immense distance, and being naked or lightly clad with a little cloak. There is no display about their equipment: their shields alone are marked with very choice colours. A few only have corselets, and just one or two here and there a metal or leathern helmet. Their horses are remarkable neither for beauty nor for fleetness. Nor are they taught various evolutions after our fashion, but are driven straight forward, or so as to make one wheel to the right in such a compact body that none is left behind another. On the whole, one would say that their chief strength is in their infantry, which fights along with the cavalry; admirably adapted to the action of the latter is the swiftness of certain foot-soldiers, who are picked from the entire youth of their country, and stationed in front of the line. Their number is fixed,—a hundred from each canton; and from this they take their name among their countrymen, so that what was originally a mere number has now become a title of distinction. Their line of battle is drawn up in a wedge-like formation. To give ground, provided you return to the attack, is considered prudence rather than cowardice. The bodies of their slain they carry off even in indecisive engagements. To abandon your shield is the basest of crimes; nor may a man thus disgraced be present at the sacred rites, or enter their council; many, indeed, after escaping from battle, have ended their infamy with the halter.

GOVERNMENT

Chapter 7

They choose their kings by birth, their generals for merit. These kings have not unlimited or arbitrary power, and the generals do more by example than by authority. If they are energetic, if they are conspicuous, if they fight in the front, they lead because they are admired. But to reprimand, to imprison, even to flog, is permitted to the priests alone, and that not as a punishment, or at the general's bidding, but, as it were, by the mandate of the god whom they believe to inspire the warrior. They also carry with them into battle certain figures and images taken from their sacred groves. And what most stimulates their courage is that their squadrons or battalions, instead of being formed by chance or by a fortuitous gathering, are composed of families and clans. Close by them, too, are those dearest to them, so that they hear the shrieks of women, the cries of infants. *They* are to every man the most sacred witnesses of his bravery—*they* are his most generous applauders. The soldier brings his wounds to mother and wife, who shrink not from counting or even demanding them and who administer both food and encouragement to the combatants.

INFLUENCE OF WOMEN

Chapter 8

Tradition says that armies already wavering and giving way have been rallied by women who, with earnest entreaties and bosoms laid bare, have vividly represented the horrors of captivity, which the Germans fear with such extreme dread on behalf of their women, that the strongest tie by which a state can be bound is the being required to give, among the number of hostages, maidens of noble birth. They even believe that the sex has a certain sanctity and prescience, and they do not despise their counsels, or make light of their answers. In Vespasian's days we saw Veleda, long regarded by many as a divinity. In former times, too, they venerated Aurinia, and many other women, but not with servile flatteries, or with sham deification.

DEITIES

Chapter 9

Mercury is the deity whom they chiefly worship, and on certain days they deem it right to sacrifice to him even with human victims. Hercules and Mars they appease with more lawful offerings. Some of the Suevi also sacrifice to Isis. Of the occasion and origin of this foreign rite I have discovered nothing, but that the image, which is fashioned like a light galley, indicates an imported worship. The Germans, however, do not consider it consistent with the grandeur of celestial beings to confine the gods within walls, or to liken them to the form of any human countenance. They consecrate woods and groves, and they apply the names of deities to the abstraction which they see only in spiritual worship.

AUGURIES AND METHOD OF DIVINATION

Chapter 10

Augury and divination by lot no people practice more diligently. The use of the lots is simple. A little bough is lopped off a fruit-bearing tree, and cut into small pieces; these are distinguished by certain marks, and thrown carelessly and at random over a white garment. In public questions the priest of the particular state, in private the father of the family, invokes the gods, and, with his eyes towards heaven, takes up each piece three times, and finds in them a meaning according to the mark previously impressed on them. If they prove unfavourable, there is no further consultation that day about the matter; if they sanction it, the confirmation of the augury is still required. For they are also familiar with the practice of consulting the notes and the flights of birds. It is peculiar to this people to seek omens and monitions from horses. Kept at the public expense, in these same woods and groves, are white horses, pure from the taint of earthly labour; these are yoked to a sacred car, and accompanied by the priest

and the king, or chief of the tribe, who note their neighings and snort-
ings. No species of augury is more trusted, not only by the people and
by the nobility, but also by the priests, who regard themselves as the
ministers of the gods, and the horses as acquainted with their will.
They have also another method of observing auspices, by which they
seek to learn the results of an important war. Having taken, by whatever means, a prisoner from the tribe with whom they are at war,
they pit him against a picked man of their own tribe, each combatant
using the weapon of their country. The victory of the one or the other
is accepted as an indication of the issue.

COUNCILS

Chapter 11

About minor matters the chiefs deliberate, about the more important
the whole tribe. Yet even when the final decision rests with the people,
the affair is always thoroughly discussed by the chiefs. They assemble,
except in the case of a sudden emergency, on certain fixed days, either
at new or at full moon; for this they consider the most auspicious
season for the transaction of business. Instead of reckoning by days
as we do, they reckon by nights, and in this manner fix both their ordinary and their legal appointments. Night they regard as bringing on
day. Their freedom has this disadvantage, that they do not meet simultaneously or as they are bidden, but two or three days are wasted in
the delays of assembling. When the multitude think proper, they sit
down armed. Silence is proclaimed by the priests, who have on these
occasions the right of keeping order. Then the king or the chief,
according to age, birth, distinction in war, or eloquence, is heard, more
because he has influence to persuade than because he has power to
command. If his sentiments displease them, they reject them with
murmurs; if they are satisfied, they brandish their spears. The most
complimentary form of assent is to express approbation with their
weapons.

PUNISHMENTS; ADMINISTRATION OF JUSTICE

Chapter 12

In their councils an accusation may be preferred or a capital crime
prosecuted. Penalties are distinguished according to the offence. Traitors and deserters are hanged on trees; the coward, the unwarlike, the
man stained with abominable vices, is plunged into the mire of the
morass, with a hurdle put over him. This distinction in punishments
means that crime, they think, ought, in being punished, to be exposed,

while infamy ought to be buried out of sight. Lighter offences, too, have penalties proportioned to them; he who is convicted, is fined a certain number of horses or of cattle. Half of the fine is paid to the king or to the state, half to the person whose wrongs are avenged and to his relatives. In these same councils they also elect the chief magistrates, who administer law in the cantons and the towns. Each of these has a hundred associates chosen from the people, who support him with their advice and influence.

TRAINING OF THE YOUTH

Chapter 13

They transact no public or private business without being armed. It is not, however, usual for anyone to wear arms till the state has recognized his power to use them. Then in the presence of the council one of the chiefs, or the young man's father, or some kinsman, equips him with a shield and a spear. These arms are what the "toga" is with us, the first honour with which youth is invested. Up to this time he is regarded as a member of a household, afterwards as a member of the commonwealth. Very noble birth or great services rendered by the father secure for lads the rank of a chief; such lads attach themselves to men of mature strength and of long approved valour. It is not shame to be seen among a chief's followers. Even in his escort there are gradations of rank, dependent on the choice of the man to whom they are attached. These followers vie keenly with each other as to who shall rank first with his chief, the chiefs as to who shall have the most numerous and the bravest followers. It is an honour as well as a source of strength to be thus always surrounded by a large body of picked youths; it is an ornament in peace and a defense in war. And not only in his own tribe but also in the neighbouring states it is the renown and glory of a chief to be distinguished for the number and valour of his followers, for such a man is courted by embassies, is honoured with presents, and the very prestige of his name often settles a war.

WARLIKE ARDOUR OF THE PEOPLE

Chapter 14

When they go into battle, it is a disgrace for the chief to be surpassed in valour, a disgrace for his followers not to equal the valour of the chief. And it is an infamy and a reproach for life to have survived the chief, and returned from the field. To defend, to protect him, to ascribe one's own brave deeds to his renown, is the height of loyalty. The chief fights for victory; his vassals fight for their chief.

If their native state sinks into the sloth of prolonged peace and repose, many of its noble youths voluntarily seek those tribes which are waging some war, both because inaction is odious to their race, and because they win renown more readily in the midst of peril, and cannot maintain a numerous following except by violence and war. Indeed, men look to the liberality of their chief for their warhorse and their blood-stained victorious lance. Feasts and entertainments, which, though inelegant, are plentifully furnished, are their only pay. The means of this bounty comes from war and rapine. Nor are they as easily persuaded to plough the earth and to wait for the year's produce as to challenge an enemy and earn the honour of wounds. Nay, they actually think it tame and stupid to acquire by the sweat of toil what they might win by their blood.

HABITS IN TIME OF PEACE

Chapter 15

Whenever they are not fighting, they pass much of their time in the chase, and still more in idleness, giving themselves up to sleep and to feasting, the bravest and most warlike doing nothing, and surrendering the management of the household, of the home, and of the land, to the women, the old men, and all the weakest members of the family. They themselves lie buried in sloth, a strange combination in their nature that the same men should be so fond of idleness, so averse to peace. It is the custom of the states to bestow by voluntary and individual contribution on the chiefs a present of cattle or of grain, which, while accepted as a compliment, supplies their wants. They are particularly delighted by gifts from neigbouring tribes, which are sent not only by individuals but also by the state, such as choice steeds, heavy armour, trappings, and neckchains. We have now taught them to accept money also.

ARRANGEMENT OF THEIR TOWNS; SUBTERRANEAN DWELLINGS

Chapter 16

It is well known that the nations of Germany have no cities, and that they do not even tolerate closely contiguous dwellings. They live scattered and apart, just as a spring, a meadow, or a wood has attracted them. Their villages they do not arrange in our fashion, with the buildings connected and joined together, but every person surrounds his dwelling with an open space, either as a precaution against the disasters of fire, or because they do not know how to build. No use is made by them of stone or tile; they employ timber for all purposes, rude masses without ornament or attractiveness. Some parts of their buildings they stain more carefully with clay so clear and bright that it resembles painting, or a coloured design. They are wont also to dig out subterranean caves, and pile on them great heaps of dung, as a shelter from winter and as a receptacle for the year's produce, for by such places they mitigate the rigour of the cold. And should an enemy approach, he lays waste the open country, while what is hidden and buried is either not known to exist, or else escapes him from the very fact that it has to be searched for.

DRESS

Chapter 17

They all wrap themselves in a cloak which is fastened with a clasp, or, if this is not forthcoming, with a thorn, leaving the rest of their persons bare. They pass whole days on the hearth by the fire. The wealthiest are distinguished by a dress which is not flowing, like that of the Sarmatae and Parthi, but is tight, and exhibits each limb. They also wear the skins of wild beasts; the tribes on the Rhine and Danube in a careless fashion, those of the interior with more elegance, as not obtaining other clothing by commerce. These select certain animals, the hides of which they strip off and vary them with the spotted skins of beasts, and the produce of the outer oceans, and of seas unknown to us. The women have the same dress as the men, except that they generally wrap themselves in linen garments, which they embroider with purple, and do not lengthen out the upper part of their clothing into sleeves. The upper and lower arm is thus bare, and the nearest part of the bosom is also exposed.

MARRIAGE LAWS

Chapter 18

Their marriage code, however, is strict, and indeed no part of their manners is more praiseworthy. Almost alone among barbarians they are content with one wife, except a very few among them, and these not from sensuality, but because their noble birth procures for them many offers of alliance. The wife does not bring a dower to the husband, but the husband to the wife. The parents and relatives are present, and pass judgment on the marriage-gifts, gifts not meant to suit a woman's taste, nor such as a bride would deck herself with, but oxen, a caparisoned steel, a shield, a lance, and a sword. With these presents the wife is espoused, and she herself in her turn brings her husband a gift of arms. This they count their strongest bond of union, these their sacred mysteries, these their gods of marriage. Lest the woman should think herself to stand apart from aspirations after noble deeds and from the perils of war, she is reminded by the ceremony which inaugurates marriage that she is her husband's partner in toil and danger, destined to suffer and to dare with him alike both in peace and in war. The yoked oxen, the harnessed steed, the gift of arms, proclaim this fact. She must live and die with the feeling that she is receiving what she must hand down to her children neither tarnished nor depreciated, what future daughters-in-law may receive, and may be so passed on to her grand-children.

GERMANIC VIRTUE

Chapter 19

Thus with their virtue protected they live uncorrupted by the allurements of public shows or the stimulant of feastings. Clandestine correspondence is equally unknown to men and women. Very rare for so numerous a population is adultery, the punishment for which is prompt, and in the husband's power. Having cut off the hair of the adulteress and stripped her naked, he expels her from the house in the presence of her kinsfolk, and then flogs her through the whole village. The loss of chastity meets with no indulgence; neither beauty, youth, nor wealth will procure the culprit a husband. No one in Germany laughs at vice, nor do they call it the fashion to corrupt and to be corrupted. Still better is the condition of those states in which only maidens are given in marriage, and where the hopes and expectations of a bride are then finally terminated. They receive one husband, as having one body and one life, that they may have no thoughts beyond, no further-reaching desires, that they may love not so much the husband as the married state. To limit the number of their children or to destroy any of their subsequent offspring is accounted infamous, and good habits are here more effectual than good laws elsewhere.

THEIR CHILDREN; LAWS OF SUCCESSION

Chapter 20

In every household the childen, naked and filthy, grow up with those stout frames and limbs which we so much admire. Every mother suckles her own offspring, and never entrusts it to servants and nurses. The master is not distinguished from the slave by being brought up with greater delicacy. Both live amid the same flocks and lie on the same ground till the freeborn are distinguished by age and recognised by merit. The young men marry late, and their vigour is thus unimpaired. Nor are the maidens hurried into marriage; the same age and a similar stature is required; well-matched and vigorous they wed, and the offspring reproduce the strength of the parents. Sisters' sons are held in as much esteem by their uncles as by their fathers; indeed, some regard the relation as even more sacred and binding, and prefer it in receiving hostages, thinking thus to secure a stronger hold on the affections and a wider bond for the family. But every man's own children are his heirs and successors, and there are no wills. Should there be no issue, the next in succession to the property are his brothers and his uncles on either side. The more relatives he has, the more numerous his connections, the more honoured is his old age; nor are there any advantages in childlessness.

HEREDITARY FEUDS; FINES FOR HOMICIDES; HOSPITALITY

Chapter 21

It is a duty among them to adopt the feuds as well as the friendships of a father or a kinsman. These feuds are not implacable; even homicide is expiated by the payment of a certain number of cattle and of sheep, and the satisfaction is accepted by the entire family, greatly to the advantage of the state, since feuds are dangerous in proportion to a people's freedom.

No nation indulges more profusely in entertainments and hospitality. To exclude an human being from their roof is thought impious; every German, according to his means, receives his guest with a well-furnished table. When his supplies are exhausted, he who was but now the host becomes the guide and companion to further hospitality, and without invitation they go to the next house. It matters not; they are entertained with like cordiality. No one distinguishes between an acquaintance and a stranger, as regards the rights of hospitality. It is usual to give the departing guest whatever he may ask for, and a present in return is asked with as little hesitation. They are greatly charmed with gifts, but they expect no return for what they give, nor feel any obligation for what they receive.

HABITS OF LIFE

Chapter 22

On waking from sleep, which they generally prolong to a late hour of the day, they take a bath, oftenest of warm water, which suits a country where winter is the longest of the seasons. After their bath they take their meal, each having a separate seat and table of his own. Then they go armed to business, or no less often to their festal meetings. To pass an entire day and night in drinking disgraces no one. Their quarrels, as might be expected with intoxicated people, are seldom fought out with mere abuse, but commonly with wounds and bloodshed. Yet it is at their feasts that they generally consult on the reconciliation of enemies, on the forming of matrimonial alliances, on the choice of chiefs, finally even on peace and war, for they think that at no time is the mind more open to simplicity of purpose or more warmed to noble aspirations. A race without either natural or acquired cunning, they disclose their hidden thoughts in the freedom of the festivity. Thus the sentiments of all having been discovered and laid bare, the discussion is renewed on the following day, and from each occasion its own peculiar advantage is derived. They deliberate when they have no power to dissemble; they resolve when error is impossible.

FOOD

Chapter 23

A liquor for drinking is made out of barley or other grain, and fermented into a certain resemblance to wine. The dwellers on the river-bank also buy wine. Their food is of a simple kind, consisting of wild-fruit, fresh game, and curdled milk. They satisfy their hunger without elaborate preparation and without delicacies. In quenching their thirst they are not equally moderate. If you indulge their love of drinking by supplying them with as much as they desire, they will be overcome by their own vices as easily as by the arms of an enemy.

SPORTS; PASSION FOR GAMBLING

Chapter 24

One and the same kind of spectacle is always exhibited at every gathering. Naked youths who practise the sport bound in the dance amid the swords and lances that threaten their lives. Experience gives them skill, and skill again gives grace; profit or pay are out of the question; however reckless their pastime, its reward is the pleasure of the spectators. Strangely enough they make games of hazard a serious occupation even when sober, and so venturesome are they about gaining or losing, that, when every other resource has failed, on the last and final throw they stake the freedom of their own persons. The loser goes into voluntary slavery; though the younger and stronger, he suffers himself to be bound and sold. Such is their stubborn persistency in a bad practice; they themselves call it honour. Slaves of this kind the owners part with in the way of commerce, and also to relieve themselves from the scandal of such a victory.

SLAVERY

Chapter 25

The other slaves are not employed after our manner with distinct domestic duties assigned to them, but each one has the management of a house and home of his own. The master requires from the slave a certain quantity of grain, of cattle, and of clothing, as he would from a tenant, and this is the limit of subjection. All other household functions are discharged by the wife and children. To strike a slave is a rare occurrence. They often kill them, not in enforcing strict discipline, but on the impulse of passion, as they would an enemy, only it is done with impunity. The freedmen do not rank much above slaves, and are seldom of any weight in the family, never in the state, with the exception of those tribes which are ruled by kings. There indeed they rise above the freeborn and the noble; elsewhere the inferiority of the freedman marks the freedom of the state.

OCCUPATION OF LAND; TILLAGE

Chapter 26

Of lending money on interest and increasing it by compound interest they know nothing—a more effectual safeguard than if it were prohibited.

Land proportioned to the number of inhabitants is occupied by the whole community in turn, and afterwards divided among them according to rank. A wide expanse of plains makes the partition easy. They till fresh fields every year, and they have still more land than enough; with the richness and extent of their soil, they do not laboriously exert themselves in planting orchards, inclosing meadows, and watering gardens. Grain is the only produce required from the earth; hence even the year itself is not divided by them into as many seasons as with us. Winter, spring, and summer have both a meaning and a name; the name and blessings of autumn are alike unknown.

FUNERAL RITES

Chapter 27

In their funerals there is no pomp; they simply observe the custom of burning the bodies of illustrious men with certain kinds of wood.

They do not heap garments or spices on the funeral pile. The arms of the dead man and in some cases his horse are consigned to the fire. A turf mound forms the tomb. Monuments with their lofty and elaborate splendour they reject as oppressive to the dead. Tears and lamentations they soon dismiss; grief and sorrow but slowly. It is thought becoming for women to bewail, for men to remember, the dead.

Such on the whole is the account which I have received of the origin and manners of the entire German people.

12 / BEOWULF: THE DEATH OF A GREAT LORD

Tacitus' account of Germanic life may be compared with, and is substantially confirmed by, the great Anglo-Saxon epic Beowulf, *which comes to us in a form written down by an Anglo-Saxon Christian writer of the eighth century, but which circulated orally for many decades and probably centuries before. Two or three of the characters and events in this myth are confirmed by mention in historical sources of the fifth century, and we are probably justified in taking* Beowulf *as a source for Germanic institutions at the time of the invasions, when lordship and the war-band had become even more central to Germanic life than at the end of the first century. This selection is from the third and concluding part of the poem and describes the death of the great hero and lord* Beowulf.[25]

Beowulf spoke; for the last time he uttered boastful words: "In the days of my youth I ventured on many battles; and even now will I, the aged guardian of my people, go into the fight and do memorable deeds, if the great destroyer come forth to me out of his cavern." Then for the last time he greeted each of the men, bold helmet-wearers, his own dear companions. "I would not bear a sword or any weapon against the Serpent, if I knew how else I could maintain my boast against the monster, as I did of old against Grendel. But I look for hot

[25] *Beowulf,* transl. C. B. Tinker (New York: Newsom & Co., 1902), pp. 120–37.

battle-fire there, for the venomous blast of his nostrils; therefore I have upon me shield and byrnie. I will not fleet one foot's breadth from the keeper of that mound, but it shall be with us twain at the wall as Wyrd, lord of every man, allotteth. I am eager in spirit, so that I forbear boasting against the wingèd warrior. But do ye men tarry upon the mound with your armor upon you, clad in your byrnies, to see which of us twain after the strife shall survive the deadly woundings. It is no exploit for you, nor for the might of any man, save mine alone to measure strength with the monster and do heroic deeds. I will boldly win the gold, or else battle, yea an evil death, shall take away your lord."

Then the mighty warrior rose up with his shield, stern under his helmet; he bore his battle-mail beneath the stony cliffs; he trusted in his single strength. That is no coward's way! And he beheld hard by the wall,—he of noble worth, who had passed through many wars and clashing battles when armed hosts close in fight,—where stood an arch of stone and a stream breaking out thence from the mound; the surge of the stream was hot with battle-fire. The hero could not abide near the hoard anywhile unburned, because of the dragon's flame.

Then the lord of the Geats, for he was wroth, sent forth a word from his breast. The stout-hearted warrior stormed; his voice battle-clear, entered in and rang under the hoary rock. The keeper of the hoard knew the speech of men, and his hatred was stirred. There was no more time to seek for peace. First came fourth out of the rock the breath of the evil beast, the hot reek of battle. The earth resounded. The hero 'neath the mound, lord of the Geats, swung up his shield against the awful foe, and the heart of the coiled monster grew eager to go out to the strife. Already the good warrior-king had drawn his sword, that olden heirloom, undulled of edge. Each of those destroyers was struck with terror by the other. Stouthearted stood that prince of friends against his tall shield, while the dragon coiled himself quickly together; Beowulf awaited him in his armor.

Then the flaming dragon, curving like a bow, advanced upon him, hastening to his fate. A shorter time did the shield protect well the life and body of the mighty king than his hopes had looked for, if haply he were to get victory in the combat at that time, early in the day; but Wyrd did not thus appoint for him. The lord of the Geats lifted his hand and smote the hideous-gleaming foe with his weighty sword, in such wise that the brown blade weakened as it fell upon the bone, and bit less deeply than its lord had need of, when sore beset. Then, at the sword-stroke, the keeper of the mound was furious in spirit. He cast forth devouring fire. Far and wide shot the deadly flame. The lord of the Geats nowise boasted of victory, for his naked war-sword, his excellent blade, weakened in the fight, as was not meet. It was no easy course for the son of Ecgtheow to forsake this earth for ever; yet he was doomed against his will to take up his abode in a dwelling otherwhere. So every man must quit these fleeting days.

It was not long ere the fighters closed again. The keeper of the hoard plucked up his courage; his breast heaved anew with his venomous breathing. He who erewhile ruled the people was hard put to it, being encompassed by fire. In nowise did his own, companions, sons of heroes, surround him in a band with warlike valor, but they took refuge in the wood to save their lives. There was but one among them whose heart surged with sorrows. Naught can ever put aside the bond of friendship in him who thinketh aright.

He was called Wiglaf, son of Weohstan, a beloved warrior, lord of the Scylfings, kinsman of Aelfhere. He saw his lord suffering the heat under his helmet; and he remembered all the benefits which Beowulf had given him in time past, the rich dwelling-place of the Waegmundings, and every folk-right which his father possessed. And he could not forbear, but seized the shield, the yellow lined, with his hand, and drew forth his old sword. This was known among men as an heirloom of Eanmund, son of Ohthere, whom, when a friendless exile, Weohstan slew in fight with the edge of the sword; he bore to his kinsman the brown-hued helmet, the ringèd byrnie, the old giant-sword that Onela had given him; they were his comrade's war-harness, his ready armor. He spoke not of the feud, though he had killed his brother's son. He held the spoils, the sword and byrnie, for many years until his son could do a hero's deeds, like his father before him. Then he gave to him, among the Geats, war-harness of all kinds without number, when, full of years, he passed forth out of life along his last way.

This was the first time that the young warrior was to engage in the storm of war with his high lord. But his heart melted not within him, nor did his kinsman's heirloom weaken in the fight. That the dragon learned after they had come together.

Wiglaf spoke many fitting words, saying to his companions,—for his soul was sad within him: "I can remember the time when, as we drank the mead in the beer-hall, we promised our lord, him who gave us these rings, that we would repay him for the war-harness, for helmets and hard swords, if need like this befell him. Of his own will he choose us from his host for this adventure, urged us to do gloriously, and gave me these treasures, since he deemed us good spearmen, keen helm-bearers, albeit our lord, defender of his people, had thought to do this mighty work alone, for that he of all men hath performed most of famed exploits and daring deeds. Now the day is come when our lord needs the might of good warriors. Let us on to his help, whilst the heat is upon him, and the grim terror of the fire.

"God knows of me that I would much rather that the flame should enwrap my body with my king's. Methinks it unseemly that we should bear our shields back to our home, unless we can first strike down the foe and defend the life of the Weders' king. Full well I know that it is not according to his old deserts that he alone of all the Geatish force should endure the pain and sink in the fight. There shall be one sword and one helmet, one shield and one byrnie in common to us."

Then he sped through the noisome smoke, bearing his war-helmet to the aid of his lord; he spoke a few words: "Belovèd Beowulf, now do thou all things well, as thou of old sworest in the days of thy youth that thou wouldst not let thy glory fade while thou didst live. Now, O resolute hero, famed for the deeds, thou must defend thy life with all thy might. Lo, I will help thee."

After these words, the dragon, awful monster, flashing with blazing flames, came on all wroth a second time to meet his hated foe-men. Wiglaf's shield was burned away to the boss in the waves of fire; the byrnie could give no help to the young spear-warrior. But the youth went quickly under his kinsman's shield, since his own had been burned to ashes in the fire. Then again the war-king took thought for his glory; mightily he smote with his battle-sword so that it stood in the dragon's head, driven by force. Naegling was shivered in pieces; Beowulf's sword, old and gray-marked, weakened in the fight;—it was not granted that the iron blade should help him in the strife. Too strong was the hand, as I have heard, which by its blow overtaxed all swords whatsoever; so that he fared none the better for it, when he bore into the fight a weapon wondrous hard.

Then the destroyer of people, the dread fire-dragon, for the third time was mindful of the feud. He rushed on the brave hero, when ground was yielded him. Hot and fierce, he seized upon Beowulf's whole neck with his sharp teeth. He was all bloodied over with his life-blood; the gore welled forth in streams.

Then I have heard men tell how, in the king's great need, Wiglaf, the hero, showed forth unceasing courage, skill and valor, as was natural to him; he heeded not the dragon's head (though the brave hero's hand was burned as he helped his kinsman), but the armed man smote the evil beast a little lower down, insomuch that that bright and plated sword drove into him, and the fire began to wane forthwith. Then the king recovered himself once more; he drew the short-sword, keen and sharp in battle, which he wore on his byrnie. The defence of the Weders cut the Serpent asunder in the middle. They struck down the foe; their might drove forth his life, and thus they twain, noble kinsmen, destroyed him. E'en such should a man be, a thane good at need. That was the king's last hour of victory by his own great deeds, the last of his worldly work.

But the wound which the earth-dragon had given him began to

burn and swell; presently he found that poison, deadly venom, was surging in his breast. Then the prince, still wise in mind, moved along so that he might seat him by the mound; he saw that work of giants, saw how the rocky arches standing firm on their pillars, upheld within the earth-hall everlasting. Then the thane, surpassing good, taking water, with his hands bathed the great king, his own dear lord, all gory and wearied with battle, and loosened his helmet.

Beowulf spoke and uttered words, despite his wound, his piteous battle-hurt; full well he knew that his life of earthly joy was spent, that the appointed number of his days was run, and Death exceeding near: "Now would I give my war-harness unto my son, had I been granted any heir, born of my body, to come after me. Fifty winters have I ruled this people; yet there was never a king of all the neighbor tribes who durst attack me with the sword or oppress me with terror. In my home I awaited what the times held in store for me, kept well mine own, sought out no wily quarrels, swore not many a false oath. In all this I can rejoice, though death-sick with my wounds, inasmuch as the Ruler of men cannot reproach me with murder of kinsmen, when my life parteth from my body. Now do thou, dear Wiglaf, lightly go and view the hoard 'neath the gray rock, now the dragon lieth low, sleepeth sore wounded, bereft of his treasure. Do thou make haste that I may behold the olden treasures, that store of gold, and look upon those bright and curious gems; and thus, having seen the treasured wealth, I may the easier quit life and the kingdom which long I have ruled."

And I have heard how the son of Weohstan, after these words, quickly obeyed his wounded lord, sick from the battle; he bore his ringèd mail-shirt, the woven battle-sark, 'neath the roof of the cave. And the brave thane, exultant victor, as he went by the seat, saw many precious jewels, much glistening gold lying upon the ground and wondrous treasures on the wall, and the den of the dragon, the old twilight-flier; bowls lay there, vessels of bygone men, with none to brighten them, their adornments fallen away. There was many a helmet old and rusty, many an arm-ring cunningly twisted. Treasure of gold found in the earth can easily puff with pride the heart of any man, hide it who will. Likewise he saw a banner all of gold standing there, high above the hoard, greatest of wonders, woven by skill of hand; from it there shone a ray of light, so that he could see the cavern floor, and examine the fair jewels. Naught was to be seen of the dragon there, for the sword had undone him!

Thus I have heard how one man alone at his own free will plundered the hoard within the cave, the old work of the giants, how he laid in his bosom beakers and dishes; he took the banner, too, that brightest of beacons. The old lord's blade, with its iron edge, had sorely injured him who long had been the owner of these treasures, who at midnight had borne about the fiery terror, dreadfully surging, hot before the hoard, until he died the death.

The messenger was in haste, eager to return, enriched with spoils. The great-hearted man was spurred with longing to know whether he would find alive the lord of the Weders, grievously sick, in the place where he had left him. And bringing the treasures, he found the great prince, his lord, bleeding, at the point of death; he began to sprinkle him again with water until the sword's point broke through the treasure of his heart, and Beowulf spoke, aged and sorrowful, as he gazed upon the gold: "I utter thanks unto the Ruler of all, King of Glory, the everlasting Lord, for these fair things, which here I look upon, inasmuch as ere my death-day I have been able to win them for my people. I have sold and paid mine aged life for the treasure-hoard. Fulfil ye now the needs of the people. Here can I be no more. Bid the brave warriors make a splendid mound at the sea-cape after my body is burned. There on Whale's Ness shall it tower high as a memorial for my people, so that seafarers, they who drive from far their great ships over the misty floods, may in aftertime call it 'Beowulf's Mound.'"

The great-hearted king took from his neck the ring of gold; gave to his thane, the youthful warrior, his helmet gold-adorned, his ring and his byrnie, bade him enjoy them well.

"Thou art the latest left of all our kin, the Waegmundings. Wyrd hath swept away all my kinsmen, heroes in their might, to the appointed doom. I must after them."

That was the old king's last word from the thoughts of his heart, ere he yielded to the bale-fire, the hotly surging flames. His soul departed from out his bosom unto the reward of the righteous.

Thus it went full hard with the young man to see his best-beloved friend lying lifeless on the ground, faring most wretchedly. His destroyer lay there too, the horrid earth-dragon, bereft of life, crushed in ruin. No longer could the coiled serpent rule over treasure-hoards, for the edge of the sword, the hard, battle-notched work of the hammer, had destroyed him, and he had fallen to the ground near his hoard-hall, stilled by the wounding. No more in play did he whirl through the air at midnight, and show himself forth, proud of his treasure, for he sank to earth by the mighty hand of the battle-chief.

Indeed, as I have heard, it hath prospered few men in the world, e'en though mighty, however daring in their every deed, to rush on against the breath of a venomous foe, or to disturb his treasure-hall, if they found the keeper waking, abiding in his mound. Beowulf paid with his death for his share in the splendid riches. Both of them had reached the end of this fleeting life.

It was not long thereafter that the cowards left the wood, those faint-hearted traitors, the ten of them together, e'en they who in their lord's great need had not dared to brandish the spear. But shamefully now they bore their shields, their war-armor, to where the old man lay. They looked upon Wiglaf. The wearied warrior was sitting by his lord's shoulder; he was trying to revive him with water, but it availed him naught. He could not stay the chieftain's life on earth, though dearly he wished it, nor change the will of God in aught. The judgment of the Lord was wont to rule the deeds of every man, e'en as still it doth.

And straightway the youth had a fierce and ready answer for those whose courage had failed them. Wiglaf, son of Weohstan, spoke, sad at heart, as he looked upon those hated men: "Lo! he who is minded to speak the truth may say that the liege lord, he who gave you these treasures, e'en the battle-armor in which ye are standing,—what time at the ale-bench the king gave oft unto his thanes, sitting in the hall, helms and byrnies, the choicest far or near which he could find,— that he utterly and wretchedly wasted that war-harness. Nowise did the king need to boast of his comrades in arms when strife overtook him; yet God, the Lord of victory, granted him unaided to avenge himself with the sword, when he had need of valor. Little protection could I give him in the fight; and yet I tried what was beyond my power,—to help my kinsman. It was ever the worse for the deadly foe when I smote him with the sword, the fire less fiercely flamed from his head. Too few defenders thronged about their lord when the dread moment fell. Now, all sharing of treasure, all gifts of swords, all hope, all rights of home, shall cease from your kin. Every man of your house shall roam, bereft of tribal rights, as soon as the princes in far countries hear of your flight, your inglorious deed. Death is better for every man than a life of shame!"

Then he bade announce the issue of the fight to the stronghold up over the sea-cliff, where the sad warrior-band had been sitting by their shields the morning long, looking either for the death or the return of their dear lord. Little did he keep silence of the new tidings, he who rode up the headland, but truthfully spoke before them all: "Now the chief of the Weder people, lord of the Geats, source of all our joy, is fast in the bed of the death; he lieth low in slaughter because of the Dragon's deeds. Beside him lieth his deadly adversary, slain by the wounding of the knife; for with the sword he could nowise wound the monster. Wiglaf, the son of Weohstan, sitteth over Beowulf, the living hero by the dead; over his head with weary heart he keepth watch for friend and foe.

"Now the people may look for a season of war as soon as the fall of the king is published abroad among the Franks and the Frisians. . . ."

13 / AMMIANUS MARCELLINUS: THE HUNS

The Germanic invasions began in the 370's when a Mongoloid people from Central Asia, called by Latin writers the Huns, invaded the Balkans, conquered the Ostrogoths, and pushed the Visigoths into the empire. One of the best of Roman historians, and a contemporary of these events, Ammianus Marcellinus, has given us a graphic description of the Huns.[26]

In the mean time the swift wheel of Fortune, which continually alternates adversity with prosperity, was giving Bellona the Furies for her allies, and arming her for war; and now transferred our disasters to the East, as many presages and portents foreshadowed by undoubted signs. . . .

The following circumstances were the original cause of all the destruction and various calamities which the fury of Mars roused up, throwing everything into confusion by his usual ruinous violence: the people called Huns, slightly mentioned in the ancient records, live beyond the Sea of Azov, on the border of the Frozen Ocean, and are a race savage beyond all parallel.

At the very moment of their birth the cheeks of their infant children are deeply marked by an iron, in order that the usual vigour of their hair, instead of growing at the proper season, may be withered by the wrinkled scars; and accordingly they grow up without beards, and consequently without any beauty, like eunuchs, though they all have closely-knit and strong limbs, and plump necks; they are of great size, and low legged, so that you might fancy them two-legged beasts, or the stout figures which are hewn out in a rude manner with an axe on the posts at the end of bridges.

They are certainly in the shape of men, however uncouth, but are so hardy that they neither require fire nor well-flavoured food, but live on the rots of such herbs as they get in the fields, or on the half-raw flesh of any animal, which they merely warm rapidly by placing it between their own thighs and the backs of their horses.

They never shelter themselves under roofed houses, but avoid them as people ordinarily avoid sepulchres as things not fitted for common use. Nor is there even to be found among them a cabin thatched with

[26] *The Roman History of Ammianus Marcellinus*, transl. C. D. Yonge (London: George Bell & Sons, 1887), pp. 576–79.

reed; but they wander about, roaming over the mountains and the woods, and accustom themselves to bear frost and hunger and thirst from their very cradles. And even when abroad they never enter a house unless under the compulsion of some extreme necessity; nor, indeed, do they think people under roofs as safe as others.

They wear linen clothes, or else garments made of the skins of field-mice: nor do they wear a different dress out of doors from that which they wear at home; but after a tunic is once put round their necks, however it becomes worn, it is never taken off or changed till, from long decay, it becomes actually so ragged as to fall to pieces.

They cover their heads with round caps, and their shaggy legs with the skins of kids; their shoes are not made on any lasts, but are so unshapely as to hinder them from walking with a free gait. And for this reason they are not well suited to infantry battles, but are nearly always on horseback, their horses being ill-shaped, but hardy; and sometimes they even sit upon them like women if they want to do anything more conveniently. There is not a person in the whole nation who cannot remain on his horse day and night. On horseback they buy and sell, they take their meat and drink, and there they recline on the narrow neck of their steed, and yield to sleep so deep as to indulge in every variety of dream.

And when any deliberation is to take place on any weighty matter, they all hold their common council on horseback. They are not under the authority of a king, but are contented with the irregular government of their nobles, and under their lead they force their way through all obstacles.

Sometimes when provoked, they fight; and when they go into battle, they form in a solid body, and utter all kinds of terrific yells. They are very quick in their operations, of exceeding speed, and fond of surprising their enemies. With a view to this, they suddenly disperse, then reunite, and again, after having inflicted vast loss upon the enemy, scatter themselves over the whole plain in irregular formations: always avoiding a fort or an entrenchment.

And in one respect you may pronounce them the most formidable of all warriors, for when at a distance they use missiles of various kinds tipped with sharpened bones instead of the usual points of javelin or arrow; but when they are at close quarters they fight with the sword, without any regard for their own safety; and often while their antagonists are warding off their blows they entangle them with twisted cords, so that, their hands being fettered, they lose all power of either riding or walking.

None of them plough, or even touch a plough-handle: for they have no settled abode, but are homeless and lawless, perpetually wandering with their waggons, which they make their homes; in fact they seem to be people always in flight. Their wives live in these waggons, and there weave their miserable garments; and here too they sleep with their husbands, and bring up their children till they reach the age of puberty; nor, if asked, can any one of them tell you where he was born, as he was conceived in one place, born in another at a great distance, and brought up in another still more remote.

In truces they are treacherous and inconstant, being liable to change their minds at every breeze of every fresh hope which presents itself, giving themselves up wholly to the impulse and inclination of the moment; and, like brute beasts, they are utterly ignorant of the distinction between right and wrong. They express themselves with great ambiguity and obscurity; have no respect for any religion or superstition whatever; are immoderately covetous of gold; and are so fickle and irascible, that they very often on the same day that they quarrel with their companions without any provocation, again become reconciled to them without any mediator.

This active and indomitable race, being excited by an unrestrainable desire of plundering the possession of others, went on ravaging and slaughtering all the nations in their neighbourhood. . . .

14 / JORDANES: THE VISIGOTHIC CONQUESTS

The Visigoths entered the empire in 376 as refugees from Hunnish attack, not as enemies or conquerors. They wanted to partake of Roman civilization, not to destroy it. But almost immediately there arose resentment and hostility on both sides, and the suspicious and treacherous attitudes of the emperors toward them, perhaps combined with duplicity on the part of Stilicho, the German head of the imperial army, brought ruin and destruction to imperial power in Western Europe. The Gothic History *by the early sixth-century churchman Jordanes is our fullest account of these sad but momentous events.*[27]

[27] *The Gothic History of Jordanes*, transl. C. C. Mierow (Princeton: Princeton University Press, 1915), pp. 89–90, 92, 93–6. Reprinted by permission of Dorothy Mierow.

That day put an end to the famine of the Goths and the safety of the Romans, for the Goths no longer as strangers and pilgrims, but as citizens and lords, began to rule the inhabitants and to hold in their own right all the northern country as far as the Danube.

When the Emperor Valens heard of this at Antioch, he made ready an army at once and set out for the country of Thrace. Here a grievous battle took place and the Goths prevailed.[28] The Emperor himself was wounded and fled to a farm near Hadrianople. The Goths, not knowing that an emperor lay hidden in so poor a hut, set fire to it (as is customary in dealing with a cruel foe), and thus he was cremated in royal splendor. Plainly it was a direct judgment of God that he should be burned with fire by the very men whom he had perfidiously led astray when they sought the true faith, turning them aside from the flame of love into the fire of hell. From this time the Visigoths, in consequence of their glorious victory, possessed Thrace and Dacia Ripensis as if it were their native land. . . .

After Theodosius,[29] the lover of peace and of the Gothic race, had passed from human cares, his sons began to ruin both empires by their luxurious living and to deprive their Allies, that is to say the Goths, of the customary gifts. The contempt of the Goths for the Romans soon increased, and for fear their valor would be destroyed by long peace, they appointed Alaric king over them. He was of famous stock, and his nobility was second only to that of the Amali, for he came from the family of the Balthi, who because of their daring valor had long ago received among their race the name *Baltha*, that is, The Bold. Now when this Alaric was made king, he took counsel with his men and persuaded them to seek a kingdom of their own exertions rather than serve others in idleness. In the consulship of Stilicho and Aurelian he raised an army and entered Italy, which seemed to be bare of defenders, and came through Pannonia and Sirmium along the right side. Without meeting any resistance, he reached the bridge of the river Candidianus at the third milestone from the royal city of Ravenna. This city lies amid the streams of the Po between swamps and the sea, and is accessible only on one side. . . .

When the army of the Visigoths had come into the neighborhood of this city, they sent an embassy to the Emperor Honorius, who dwelt within. They said that if he would permit the Goths to settle peaceably in Italy, they would so live with the Roman people that men might believe them both to be of one race; but if not, whoever prevailed in

[28] Battle of Hadrianople, 378 A.D.
[29] Theodosius I the Great died in 395 A.D., leaving his weak-minded son Honorius to succeed him in the west and to deal with the Visigoths.

war should drive out the other, and victor should henceforth rule unmolested. But the Emperor Honorius feared to make either promise. So he took counsel with his senate and considered how he might drive them from the Italian borders. He finally decided that Alaric and his race, if they were able to do so, should be allowed to seize for their own home the provinces farthest away, namely Gaul and Spain. For at this time he had almost lost them, and moreover they had been devastated by the invasion of Gaiseric, king of the Vandals. The grant was confirmed by an imperial rescript, and the Goths, consenting to the arrangement, set out for the country given them.

When they had gone away without doing any harm in Italy, Stilicho, the Patrician and father-in-law of the Emperor Honorius—for the Emperor had married both his daughters, Maria and Thermantia, in succession, but God called both from this world in their virgin purity—this Stilicho, I say, treacherously hurried to Pollentia, a city in the Cottian Alps. There he fell upon the unsuspecting Goths in battle, to the ruin of all Italy and his own disgrace. When the Goths suddenly beheld him, at first they were terrified. Soon regaining their courage and arousing each other by brave shouting, as is their custom, they turned to flight the entire army of Stilicho and almost exterminated it. Then forsaking the journey they had undertaken, the Goths with hearts full of rage returned again to Liguria whence they had set out. When they had plundered and spoiled it, they also laid waste Aemilia, and then hastened toward the city of Rome along the Flaminian Way, which runs between Picenum and Tuscia, taking as booty whatever they found on either hand. When they finally entered Rome by Alaric's express command they merely sacked it, and did not set the city on fire, as wild peoples usually do, nor did they permit serious damage to be done to the holy places. Thence they departed to bring like ruin upon Campania and Lucania, and then came to Bruttii. Here they remained a long time and planned to go to Sicily and thence to the countries of Africa.

Now the land of the Bruttii is at the extreme southern bound of Italy, and a corner of it marks the beginning of the Apennine mountains. It stretches out like a tongue into the Adriatic Sea and separates it from the Tyrrhenian waters. It chanced to receive its name in ancient times from a Queen Bruttia. To this place came Alaric, king of the Visigoths, with the wealth of all Italy which he had taken as spoil, and from there, as we have said, he intended to cross over by way of Sicily to the quiet land of Africa. But since man is not free to do anything he wishes without the will of God, that dread strait sunk several of his ships and threw all into confusion. Alaric was cast down by his reverse and, while deliberating what he should do, was suddenly overtaken by an untimely death and departed from human cares.

His people mourned for him with the utmost affection. Then turning from its course the river Busentius near the city of Consentia—for the stream flows with its wholesome waters from the foot of a mountain near that city—they led a band of captives into the midst of its bed to dig out a place for his grave. In the depths of this pit they buried Alaric, together with many treasures, and then turned the waters back into their channel. And that none might ever know the place, they put to death all the diggers. They bestowed the kingdom of the Visigoths on Athavulf his kinsman, a man of imposing beauty and great spirit; for though not tall of stature, he was distinguished for beauty of face and form.

When Athavulf became king, he returned again to Rome, and whatever had escaped the first sack his Goths stripped bare like locusts, not merely despoiling Italy of its private wealth, but even of its public resources. The Emperor Honorius was powerless to resist even when his sister Placidia, the daughter of the Emperor Theodosius by his second wife, was led away captive from the city. But Athavulf was attracted by her nobility, beauty and chaste purity, and so he took her to wife in lawful marriage at Forum Julii, a city of Aemilia. When the barbarians learned of this alliance, they were the more effectually terrified, since the Empire and the Goths now seemed to be made one. Then Athavulf set out for Gaul, leaving Honorius Augustus stripped of his wealth, to be sure, yet pleased at heart because he was now a sort of kinsman of his. Upon his arrival the neighboring tribes who had made cruel raids into Gaul—Franks and Burgundians alike—were terrified and began to keep within their own borders. Now the Vandals and the Alani, as we have said before, had been dwelling in both Pannonias by permission of the Roman Emperors. Yet fearing they would not be safe even here if the Goths should return, they crossed over into Gaul. But no long time after they had taken possession of Gaul they fled thence and shut themselves up in Spain, for they still remembered from the tales of their forefathers what ruin Geberich, king of the Goths, had long ago brought on their race, and how by his valor he had driven them from their native land. And thus it happened that Gaul lay open to Athavulf when he came. Now when the Goth had established his kingdom in Gaul, he began to grieve for the plight of the Spaniards and planned to save them from the attacks of the Vandals. So Athavulf left with a few faithful men at Barcelona his treasures and those who were unfit for war, and entered the interior of Spain. Here he fought frequently with the Vandals and, in this third year after he had subdued Gaul and Spain, fell pierced through the groin by the sword of Euervulf, a man whose short stature he had been wont to mock.

15 / CIVILITAS:
THE POLICY
OF THEODORIC
THE OSTROGOTH

The intention of the Goths to be supporters and not de-stroyers of Roman culture is demonstrated by the rule of the Ostrogothic king Theodoric the Great (496–526) in Italy. His program of civilitas, the restoration of Roman administration, economy, and culture, comes out clearly in the letters written in his behalf by his chief minister, the Roman aristocrat and Christian scholar Cassiodorus. In the end, however, the work of this greatest of Germanic kings before Charlemagne came to naught due to the combined opposition of the papacy, many of the Roman nobility, and the Byzantine emperor, whose armies began the reconquest of Italy shortly after Theodoric's death.[30]

KING THEODORIC TO MAXIMIAN, VIR ILLUSTRIS; AND ANDREAS, VIR SPECTABILIS

If the people of Rome will beautify their City we will help them.

Institute a strict audit (of which no one need be ashamed) of the money given by us to the different workmen for the beautification of the City. See that we are receiving money's worth for the money spent. If there is embezzlement anywhere, cause the funds so embez-zled to be disgorged. We expect the Romans to help from their own resources in this patriotic work, and certainly not to intercept our contributions for the purpose.

The wandering birds love their own nests; the beasts haste to their own lodgings in the brake; the voluptuous fish, roaming the fields of ocean, returns to its own well-known cavern. How much more should Rome be loved by her children!

---

[30] *Letters of Cassiodorus,* transl. Thomas Hodgkin (London: Henry Frowde, 1886), pp. 156, 160, 163, 183–4, 196, 201, 209, 210, 219, 229, 251, 280. Letters written by Cassiodorus in Theodoric's name.

KING THEODORIC TO ALL THE GOTHS
AND ROMANS

Most worthy of Royal attention is the rebuilding of ancient cities, an adornment in time of peace, a precaution for time of war.

Therefore, if anyone have in his fields stones suitable for the building of the walls, let him cheerfully and promptly produce them. Even though he should be paid at a low rate, he will have his reward as a member of the community, which will benefit thereby.

KING THEODORIC TO FAUSTUS, PRAEPOSITUS

It should be only the surplus of the crops of any Province, beyond what is needed for the supply of its own wants, that should be exported. Station persons in the harbours to see that foreign ships do not take away produce to foreign shores until the Public Providers have got all that they require.

KING THEODORIC TO THE SENATE OF THE
CITY OF ROME

We hear with sorrow, by the report of the Provincial Judges, that you the Fathers of the State, who ought to set an example to your sons (the ordinary citizens), have been so remiss in the payment of taxes that on this first collection nothing, or next to nothing, has been brought in from any Senatorial house. Thus a crushing weight has fallen on the lower orders, who have had to make good your deficiencies and have been distraught by the violence of the tax-gatherers.

Now then, . . . pay the taxes for which each one of you is liable, to the Procurators appointed in each Province, by three instalments. Or, if you prefer to do so—and it used to be accounted a privilege— pay all at once into the chest of the Vicarius. And let this following edict be published, that all the Provincials may know that they are not to be imposed upon and that they are invited to state their grievances.

AN EDICT OF KING THEODORIC

The King detests the oppression of the unfortunate, and encourages them to make their complaints to him. He has heard that the powerful houses are failing to pay their share of the taxes, and that a larger sum in consequence is being exacted from the *tenues*.

To "amputate" such wickedness for the future, the letter last preceding has been addressed to the Senate; and the "Possessores sive curiales" are now invited to state their grievances fully and frankly, or else ever after hold their peace and cultivate a habit of patience.

KING THEODORIC TO ALARIC, KING OF THE VISIGOTHS

Surrounded as you are by an innumerable multitude of subjects, and strong in the remembrance of their having turned back Attila, still do not fight with Clovis. War is a terrible thing, and a terrible risk. The long peace may have softened the hearts of your people, and your soldiers from want of practice may have lost the habit of working together on the battlefield. Ere yet blood is shed, draw back if possible. We are sending ambassadors to the King of the Franks to try to prevent this war between our relatives; and the ambassadors whom we are sending to you will go on to Gundibad, King of the Burgundians, to get him to interpose on behalf of peace. . . .

KING THEODORIC TO THE VENERABLE JANUARIUS, BISHOP OF SALONA

The lamentable petition of John says that you have taken sixty tuns of oil from him, and never paid him for them. It is especially important that preachers of righteousness should be righteous themselves. We cannot suppose that God is ignorant whence come the offerings which we make before Him [and He must therefore hate robbery for a burnt offering]. Pray enquire into this matter, and if the complaint be well founded remedy it promptly. You who preach to us our duty in great things should not be caught tripping in little ones.

KING THEODORIC TO COLOSSAEUS, VIR ILLUSTRIS AND COMES

We delight to entrust our mandates to persons of approved character. . . .

Show forth the justice of the Goths, a nation happily situated for praise, since it is theirs to unite the forethought of the Romans and the virtue of the Barbarians. Remove all ill-planted customs, and impress upon all your subordinates that we would rather that our Treasury lost a suit than that it gained one wrongfully, rather that we lost money than the taxpayer was driven to suicide.

KING THEODORIC TO ALL THE BARBARIANS AND ROMANS SETTLED IN PANNONIA

Intent on welfare of our subjects we are sending you Colossaeus for Governor. His name means a mighty man; and a mighty man he is, who has given many proofs of his virtue. Now we exhort you with patience and constancy to submit yourself to his authority. Do not excite that wrath before which our enemies tremble. Acquiesce in the rule of justice in which the whole world rejoices. Why should you, who have now an upright Judge, settle your grievances by single combat? What has man got a tongue for, if the armed hand is to settle all differences? Or where can peace be looked for, if there is fighting in a civilised State like ours? Imitate then our Goths, who have learned to practise war abroad, to show peaceable dispositions at home. We want you so to live as you see that our subjects have lived and flourished under the Divine blessing.

KING THEODORIC TO UNIGIS, THE SWORD-BEARER

We delight to live after the law of the Romans, whom we seek to defend with our arms; and we are as much interested in the maintenance of morality as we can possibly be in war. For what profit is there in having removed the turmoil of the Barbarians, unless we live according to law? . . . Let other kings desire the glory of battles won, of cities taken, of ruins made; our purpose is, God helping us, so to rule that our subjects shall grieve that they did not earlier acquire the blessing of our dominion.

KING THEODORIC TO FAUSTUS, PRAETORIAN PRAEFECT

. . . We are compelled to support this institution by the necessity of humouring the majority of the people, who are passionately fond of it; for it is always the few who are led by reason, while the many crave excitement and oblivion of their cares. Therefore, as we too must sometimes share the folly of our people, we will freely provide for the expenses of the Circus, however little our judgment approves of this institution.

KING THEODORIC TO ALL THE JEWS OF GENOA

The true mark of *civilitas* is the observance of law. It is this which makes life in communities possible, and which separates man from the brutes. We therefore gladly accede to your request that all the privileges which the foresight of antiquity conferred upon the Jewish customs shall be renewed to you, for in truth it is our great desire that the laws of the ancients shall be kept in force to secure the reverence due to us. Everything which has been found to conduce to *civilitas* should be held fast with enduring devotion.

KING THEODORIC TO ALL THE GOTHS SETTLED IN PICENUM AND SAMNIUM

The presence of the Sovereign doubles the sweetness of his gifts, and that man is like one dead whose face is not known to his lord. Come therefore by God's assistance, come all into our presence on the eighth day before the Ides of June [June 6], there solemnly to receive our royal largesse. But let there be no excesses by the way, no plundering the harvest of the cultivators nor trampling down their meadows, since for this cause do we gladly defray the expense of our armies that *civilitas* may be kept intact by armed men.

16 / GREGORY OF TOURS: FRANKISH GOVERNMENT AND SOCIETY

Among the many Germanic kingdoms established in continental Western Europe in the fifth and sixth centuries, only the kingdom of the Franks, founded in Gaul by Clovis I (d. 511), proved to have enduring qualities. But the Frankish Merovingian rulers were too primitive in their outlook and methods to make a successful effort at preserving Roman culture, law, political theory, and administration. A rapid barbarization of Gaul was the result. We have a detailed and extremely valuable account of sixth-century Gaul in the History *of the Franks by the late sixth-century bishop of Tours, Gregory, who came from an old Gallo-Roman family. While Gregory sympathized with the house of*

*Clovis on account of its championing of orthodox Catholicism,
he was not blind to the crude level of Frankish culture and the
disastrous consequences for civilization of Merovingian rule.*[31]

In these times when the practice of letters declines, nay, rather per-
ishes in the cities of Gaul, there has been found no scholar trained in
the art of ordered composition to present in prose or verse a picture
of the things that have befallen. Yet there have been done good things
many, and evil many; the peoples savagely raged; the fury of kings
grew sharp; churches were assailed by heretics and protected by
catholics; the faith of Christ that glowed in many hearts was lukewarm
in not a few; the faithful enriched the churches while the unbelievers
stripped them bare. Wherefore the voice of lament was oft-times raised,
and men said: "Alas! for these our days! The study of letters is perished
from us, nor is any found among our peoples able to set forth in a
book the events of this present time."

Now when I heard these and like complaints ever repeated, I was
moved, with however rude an utterance, to hand down the memory
of the past to future generations, in no wise leaving untold the conflicts
of the wicked and those who lived in righteousness. I was the more
encouraged because I often heard with surprise our people say that
while the accomplished writer is understood by few, it is the man
of plain speech who has the general ear.

Further, it seemed good to me for the better computation of the
years, that in this first book, of which the chapters follow, I should
begin from the foundation of the world.

. . . The streets were overshadowed with coloured hangings, the
churches adorned with white hangings, the baptistery was set in order,
smoke of incense spread in clouds, perfumed tapers gleamed, the
whole church about the place of baptism was filled with the divine
fragrance. And now the king [Clovis] first demanded to be baptized
by the bishop. Like a new Constantine, he moved forward to the
water to blot out the former leprosy, to wash away in this new stream
the foul stains borne from old days. As he entered to be baptized the
saint of God spoke these words with eloquent lips: "Meekly bow thy
proud head, Sicamber; adore that which thou hast burned, burn that
which thou hast adored." For the holy Remigius, the bishop, was of
excellent learning, and above all skilled in the art of rhetoric, and so
exemplary in holiness that his miracles were equal to those of the holy
Silvester; there is preserved to us a book of his life, in which it is

[31] Gregory of Tours, *History of the Franks,* transl. O. M. Dalton (Oxford: The
Clarendon Press, 1927), Vol. II, pp. 1, 69–70, 160, 167, 194–5, 200–1, 263–4,
321. Reprinted by permission of The Clarendon Press.

related how he raised a man from the dead. The king therefore, confessing Almighty God, three in one, was baptized in the name of the Father, the Son, and the Holy Ghost, and anointed with holy chrism, with the sign of the Cross of Christ. Of his army were baptized more than three thousand; . . .

. . . Sigibert, after taking the cities situated south of Paris, pushed on as far as Rouen, intending to abandon these places to their enemies; but his own men prevented him from doing this. On this return, he entered Paris, where he was rejoined by Brunhild and his sons. Those Franks who were formerly subject to Childebert the elder now sent an embassy to Sigibert, proposing that they should transfer their allegiance from Chilperic, and that he should come among them to be made king. At this news he sent a force to besiege his brother in the aforesaid city, and proposed himself to follow it with all speed. Thereupon the holy bishop Bermanus said to him: "If thou departest with the intent not to slay thy brother, thou shalt return living and victorious; but if thou hast in thy heart aught else, thou shalt surely die. For so hath the Lord spoken by the mouth of Solomon; 'If thou preparest a ditch for thy brother, thou shalt fall therein thyself.' " But the king, because of his sinfulness, would not hearken. And when he came to the royal villa named Vitry, the whole army was assembled, and placing him upon a shield, they elected him their king. Then two servitors whom Fredegund had bewitched came armed with the strong knives commonly called *scramasaxes* smeared with poison, and making as though they would speak with him on some matter, struck him from both sides. He uttered a cry, and fell, not long after giving up the ghost. There, too, fell his chamberlain Charegisel, and there was sorely wounded Sigila, who came long before from the country of the Goths. At a later time he fell into the hands of King Chilperic, when all his joints were burned with red-hot irons, and he ended his life torn limb from limb in cruel torture.

. . . My heart is mournful as I recount the divers civil wars which so grievously wear down the race and the dominion of the Franks. Herein, worst sign of all, we seem even now to perceive the time begin which the Lord foretold as the beginning of sorrows: "The father shall rise up against the son, and the son against the father; brother shall rise up against brother, and kinsman against kinsman." Yet the examples of former kings should have affrighted them, who, through their divisions, were slain by their enemies. How oft fell the city of cities and great head of all the world through her civil wars; but when these ended, she arose once more as out of the ground! Would that you, O kings, were practised in such wars as those in which your fathers toiled in the sweat of their brows, that so the peoples, in awe of your unity, might be subjected by your might! Remember all that Clovis did, the beginner of your victories, who slew enemy kings, shattered the dangerous outland nations, and subdued the races of Gaul, over whom he handed down to you a dominion whole and unimpaired. And when he accomplished this, he had neither silver nor gold, such as ye now have in your treasuries. What deeds are yours, what desires? Wherein have you not abundance? For in your houses too much abound things of delight, your store-houses are overfilled with corn, wine, and oil; in your treasuries gold and silver are heaped in piles. But one thing lacks: because you keep not peace you have not the grace of God. Wherefore does each one of you despoil his brethren of their own? Wherefore does the brother lust after the brother's goods? Listen, I beseech you, to the warning of the apostle: "But if ye bite and devour one another, take heed that ye be not consumed one of another." Search diligently that which was written by the ancients, and you shall see what issue comes of civil wars. . . .

Now the people rose against the bishops Salonius and Sagittarius. These brothers had been brought up by the holy Nicetius, bishop of Lyons; under him they received the rank of deacon, and in his lifetime both were made bishops, Salonius of Embrun, Sagittarius of Gap. But the episcopal dignity once theirs, they were carried away by the joy of doing as they pleased, and began abandoning themselves to a very fury of mad wickedness, robbing, wounding, slaying, committing adulteries, and all manner of crimes, to such a point that one day when Victor, bishop of Saint-Paul-Trois-Chateaux, was celebrating his birthday, they fell upon him with a troop armed with swords and arrows. They came and rent his garments, beat his attendants, carried off all the vessels and furnishings of the feast, and left him thus grossly outraged. When news of this reached King Guntram, he commanded a council to assemble at Lyons. The bishops met, together with their patriarch, the blessed Nicetius, and after investigating the affair and finding the accused plainly convicted of the crimes laid to their charge, ordered that men who had committed such acts should be deprived of the episcopal dignity. But the two, aware that the king still regarded them with favour, sought his presence, urging that the deprivation was unjust, and asking his permission to go before the pope of Rome. The king granted their petition, gave them a letter, and his permission to depart. When they came before the pope John they set forth to him that they had been deprived without reasonable cause assigned, and he addressed a letter to the king, directing that they should be restored to their former rank. The king straightway did as he desired, not without first reprimanding them at great length. But the worst of the matter was that no amendment followed, though they sought to make their peace with Bishop Victor by handing over to him the men whom they had sent to do him that outrage. But Victor, remembering the Lord's commandment not to render to our enemies evil for evil, did the men no hurt, and suffered them to depart in freedom. For this he was afterwards suspended from communion on the ground that, privily and without consulting his brethren, he had spared the enemies whom he had publicly accused before them; but by royal favour he was received into communion again.

. . . Now King Chilperic ordered heavy new tax-assessments to be made in all his kingdom. For which cause many left their cities and their own possessions, and sought other kingdoms, deeming it better to migrate than to remain exposed to such risk of oppression. For it was enacted that each proprietor should pay one amphora of wine for every half-acre of land. Further taxes were imposed on other lands and on serfs, which it was impossible to meet. The people of Limoges, perceiving with what a burden they were to be laden, assembled on the first of March, and would have slain Mark the referendary, who had been ordered to carry out the plan; nor could they have been prevented, had not Bishop Ferreolus delivered him from his imminent peril. The mob seized the tax collector's lists and burned them all to ashes. Whereat the king was exceeding wroth, and dispatched thither men from about his person; through these he inflicted immense losses upon the people, crushed them with punishments, and freely inflicted the penalty of death. It is said that these envoys of the king falsely accused even priests and abbots of having incited the people to burn the lists during the riot, stretched them on posts, and subjected them to divers tortures. Afterwards yet severer tributes were imposed.

. . . But when the king and queen came out from the holy church, Leudast followed them into the street, without suspecting what should befall him. He went about among the merchants' houses, examined the precious things, had silver weighed, and caused divers ornaments to be shown him, saying: "This and this will I buy, for I have yet good store of gold and silver." While the words were yet in his mouth, the queen's servants came up, and would have put him in chains. But he unsheathed his sword, and wounded one of them; whereupon the rest, in their fury, seized the sword and shield, and rushed upon him.

. . . In those days a merchant, Christopher by name, journeyed to Orleans, having heard that a large quantity of wine had been brought there. He went, bought the wine, and had it transported in boats; he himself with two Saxon servants travelled on horseback; he had on him a large sum of money received from his father-in-law.

17 / THE JUSTINIAN CODE

While the west Roman Empire was disintegrating, the east Roman Empire, centered on the great fortress and port of Constantinople, was affirming its Roman traditions by codifying the great corpus of Roman law. This work was brought to a most successful conclusion in the Corpus Iuris Civilis of the emperor Justinian I (527–565), the greatest of the Byzantine emperors. While Justinian's attempt to reconquer the western empire had only limited success, in that he so exhausted the east Roman state that it suffered great losses of territory to the Lombards immediately after his death and, much more extensively, to the Arabian Moslem invaders in the seventh century, his direction of the final codification of the Roman law remains his monument to the present day. The Justinian Code is the greatest legal achievement of Western civilization; in a few volumes it sums up, along principles of reason, equity, and absolutism, the legal doctrines and practices of a whole civilization. Unknown in the early medieval West, it began to be intensively studied in the European world in the eleventh century and became the basis of the legal doctrines and system of all of continental Europe by the end of the fourteenth century. The Corpus of the Civil Law is the last product of east Roman culture to be written in Latin; after the Islamic expansion, Byzantium was cut off from the West and became more and more an Eastern culture outside the province of Western civilization. In the following selections are presented first a discussion of the importance of the Justinian Code by the great early-nineteenth-century German legal historian Carl von Savigny (A),[32] and then extracts from the Justinian Code itself (B), revealing the political and legal conceptions fundamental to the work.[33]

A. CARL VON SAVIGNY: THE ACHIEVEMENTS OF THE JUSTINIAN CODE

When the Western Empire ceased, in A.D. 476, the following Law-Sources were known in practice.

1. The works of the Jurists, according to the rule contained in the Constitution of Valentinian III.
2. The Gregorian and Hermogenian Collection of Rescripts.
3. The Code of Theodosius II.

---

[32] C. von Savigny, *The History of Roman Law during the Middle Ages*, transl. E. Cathcart (Edinburgh: Adam Black, 1829), Vol. I, pp. 10, 11–12, 13–15.

[33] *The Civil Law*, transl. S. P. Scott, 17 vols. (Philadelphia: The Jefferson Medical College of Philadelphia, 1932), Vol. II, pp. 179–80, 181–2, 5–6, 7, Vol. XII, pp. 88–9, Vol. XVI, pp. 30, 38, Vol. XII, pp. 152–3. Reprinted by permission of The Jefferson Medical College of Philadelphia.

4. The separate Novellae, which formed, as it were, a supplement to this last Code. . . .

The necessity of a second Reform was urgent and general; and, soon after the dissolution of the Western Empire, four different attempts to supply this defect were made within thirty years;—each, in a different kingdom, and independent of the others.

1. The Edict of the East-Goth, Theodoric (A.D. 500).
2. The West-Gothic Breviarium of Alaric II (A.D. 506).
3. The Papian, among the Burgundians (soon after A.D. 500).
4. The Laws promulgated by Justinian, at first only for the Eastern Empire (A.D. 528–534). . . .

The Edict, the Papian, and the Breviarium are perfect, as abridgements of a subject become unwieldy from its extent; but their poverty is incredible, when viewed in connexion with the richness of the material, from which they were formed. In them all, the whole Roman Law, Jurists and Constitutions, are collected into a single book of small magnitude. . . .

It is impossible to compare the laws of Justinian with these compilations, without being filled with astonishment; although, even without such a comparison, we could not refuse to them our admiration and gratitude. Original genius was indeed denied to this age, and the Law-Sources to be consulted by Justinian's compilers, belonged to a foreign and cultivated people, and were not to be found in the original literature of the Eastern Empire. Under these adverse circumstances, the compilations were begun, and the selections made with so much discernment and regard for the subject, that, notwithstanding our great want of historical information, the spirit of the Roman Law has been made comprehensible to us, after the lapse of 1300 years, by these books as almost our only guides, and its influence insured in every country, in which the people were unprejudiced, and possessed minds open to instruction. He who still maintains, that accident alone guided the compilers in their selection, and that they were devoid both of system and of knowledge of the subject, may convince himself of the contrary, by a comparison with the above mentioned laws of the Gothic and Burgundian kingdoms. To reply, that the compilers of these were barbarians, and that Justinian's assistants were Romans, is to state what is historically erroneous; for the authors of the former in the West were not Goths or Burgundians, but Romans settled in Rome and in Gaul. The merit which is here claimed for the Justinian Law may be called literary; but still, the object in making the compilation was not literary, but practical; although no doubt, Justinian's own Constitutions had a more intimate connexion with practice. These must indeed be admitted to possess different degrees of merit. A great part of them are unquestionably distinguished by the fullest comprehension of the subject, and by the most perfect adaptation of means to ends. Many of the ordinances also, which appear to us to be mere disfiguration of the old law, are only the judicious promulgation of changes, already spontaneously introduced and valid without any legislative interference. Regarding these also, a comparison may be made much to the honour of Justinian. If the Edicts in the Theodosian Code, or the Novellae at the end of it, be contrasted with the Constitutions of Justinian, particularly with those in the Code, the latter, both in subject and form, will be almost universally acknowledged to be the most valuable, and the most easily understood.

Justinian's plan embraced the two principal objects of abridging, in separate works, the Jurists, and the Constitutions. The first, or the Pandects, was very properly intended to contain the fundamental principles of the law; and it was the only work since the Twelve Tables, which, in itself complete, and without reference to another, might be considered as a centre point, from which the whole law emanated. In this respect, it may be called a Code of Laws, and the first full comprehensive Code since the Twelve Tables: although, a great part of its contents is not properly legislative, but dogmatic and illustrative of particular cases. In place of the inadequate rules of Valentinian III, numerous excerpts from the writings of the Jurists are quoted at length, and classed in the order of the subjects. The plan of Justinian's Code, which included both Rescripts and Edicts, was more comprehensive than any which had preceded it. These two works completely fulfilled the purpose of Justinian. The Institutes cannot be considered as a third, and as independent of the other two, but rather as an introduction and preparatory work to them. Finally, the Novellae are separate and posterior additions and changes; and it is quite accidental, that a third edition of the Code, containing the Novellae still in use, had not been prepared towards the end of the reign of Justinian.

B. THE CORPUS OF THE CIVIL LAW

The Making of the Corpus Iuris Civilis

THE EMPEROR CAESAR, FLAVIUS, JUSTINIANUS, PIOUS, FORTUNATE, RENOWNED, CONQUEROR AND TRIUMPHER, EVER AUGUSTUS, TO TRIBONIANUS HIS QUAESTOR: GREETING.

With the aid of God governing Our Empire which was delivered to Us by His Celestial Majesty, We carry on war successfully. We adorn peace and maintain the Constitution of the State, and have such confidence in the Protection of Almighty God that We do not depend upon Our arms, or upon Our soldiers, or upon those who conduct Our Wars, or upon Our own genius, but We solely place Our reliance upon the providence of the Holy Trinity, from which are derived the elements of the entire world and their disposition throughout the globe.

1. Therefore, since there is nothing to be found in all things so worthy of attention as the authority of the law, which properly regulates all affairs both divine and human, and expels all injustice; We have found the entire arrangement of the law which has come down to Us from the foundation of the City of Rome and the times of Romulus, to be so confused that it is extended to an infinite length and is not within the grasp of human capacity; and hence We were first induced to begin by examining what had been enacted by former most venerated princes, to correct their constitutions, and make them more easily understood; to the end that being included in a single Code, and having had removed all that is superfluous in resemblance and all iniquitous discord, they may afford to all men the ready assistance of their true meaning.

2. After having concluded this work and collected it all in a single volume under Our illustrious name, raising Ourself above small and comparatively insignificant matters, We have hastened to attempt the most complete and thorough amendment of the entire law, to collect and revise the whole body of Roman jurisprudence, and to assemble in one book the scattered treatises of so many authors; which no one else has herebefore ventured to hope for or to expect, and it has indeed been considered by Ourselves a most difficult undertaking, nay, one that was almost impossible; but with Our hands raised to heaven and having invoked the Divine aid, We have kept this object in Our mind, confiding in God who can grant the accomplishment of things which are almost desperate, and can Himself carry them into effect by virtue of the greatness of His power.

3. We have also taken into consideration your marked integrity as disclosed by your labors, and have committed this work to you, after having already received the evidence of your talents in the preparation of Our Code; and We have ordered you in the prosecution of your task, to select as your assistants whomever you might approve of from among the most eloquent professors of law, as well as from the most learned men belonging to the bar of this great city. These, therefore, having been collected and introduced into Our palace, and accepted by Us upon your statements, We have permitted the entire work to be accomplished; it being provided, however, that it should be conducted under the supervision of your most vigilant mind.

4. Therefore We order you to read and revise the books relating to the Roman law drawn up by the jurists of antiquity, upon whom the

most venerated princes conferred authority to write and interpret the same; so that from these all the substance may be collected, and, as far as may be possible, there shall remain no laws either similar to or inconsistent with one another, but that there may be compiled from them a summary which will take the place of all. And while others have written books relating to the law, for the reason that their writings have not been adopted by any authorities, or made use of in practice, We do not deem their treatises worthy of Our consideration.

5. Since this compilation is to be ascribed to the extraordinary liberality of Our Imperial will, it ought to constitute a most excellent work and, as it were, be revered as a peculiar and most holy temple of justice. You shall divide the entire law into fifty books, and into a certain number of titles following, as far as may be convenient for you, the arrangement of Our Code, as well as that of the Perpetual Edict, so that nothing may be omitted from the above mentioned collection; and that all the ancient law which has been in a confused condition for almost fourteen hundred years shall be embraced in the said fifty books, and this ancient law, purified by Us, shall be, so to speak, surrounded by a wall, and shall have nothing beyond it. All legal authors shall possess equal authority, and no preference shall be given to any, because all of them are neither superior nor inferior to one another in every respect, but some are of greater or less weight as far as certain subjects are concerned. . . .

7. We desire you to be careful with regard to the following: if you find in the old books anything that is not suitably arranged, superfluous, or incomplete, you must remove all superfluities, supply what is lacking, and present the entire work in regular form, and with as excellent an appearance as possible. You must also observe the following, namely: if you find anything which the ancients have inserted in their old laws or constitutions that is incorrectly worded, you must correct this, and place it in its proper order, so that it may appear to be true, expressed in the best language, and written in this way in the first place; so that by comparing it with the original text, no one can venture to call in question as defective what you have selected and arranged. Since by an ancient law, which is styled the *Lex Regia*, all the rights and power of the Roman people were transferred to the Emperor, We do not derive Our authority from that of other different compilations, but wish that it shall all be entirely Ours, for how can antiquity abrogate Our laws?

We wish that all these matters after they have been arranged in place shall be observed to such an extent that, although they may have been written by the ancients in a different way than appears in Our collection, no blame shall be imputed the text, but it shall be ascribed to our selection. . . .

10. However, by no means do We allow you to insert into your treatise laws that appearing in ancient works have now fallen into desuetude; since We only desire that legal procedure to prevail which has been most frequently employed, or which long custom has established in this benign City; in accordance with the work of Salvius Julianus which declares that all states should follow the custom of Rome, which is the head of the world, and not that Rome should follow the example of other states; and by Rome is to be understood not only the ancient city, but Our own royal metropolis also, which by the grace of God was founded under the best auguries.

11. Therefore We order that everything shall be governed by these two works, one that of the Imperial Constitutions, the other, that of the law to be interpreted and compiled in a future Code; so that if anything else should be promulgated by Us in the form of an elementary treatise, the uninstructed mind of the student, being nourished by simple matters, may the more readily be conducted to a knowledge of the higher principles of jurisprudence. . . .

14. Let it be your earnest desire, therefore, to do all these things, God willing, by the aid of your own wisdom and that of those other most eloquent men, and bring the work to as excellent and rapid a conclusion as possible; so that it having been completed and digested into fifty books may remain a monument to the great and eternal memory of the undertaking, a proof of the wisdom of Almighty God, to the glory of Our Empire and of your service. Given on the eighteenth day before the *Kalends* of January [December 15], during the Consulship of those most illustrious men Lampadius and Orestes, 530.

General Legal Conceptions

CONCERNING JUSTICE AND LAW

Justice is the constant and perpetual desire to give to each one that to which he is entitled.

1. Jurisprudence is the knowledge of matters divine and human, and the comprehension of what is just and what is unjust.

2. These divisions being generally understood, and We being about to explain the laws of the Roman people, it appears that this may be most conveniently done if separate subjects are at first treated in a clear and simple manner, and afterwards with greater care and exactness; for if We, at once, in the beginning, load the still uncultivated and inexperienced mind of the student with a multitude and variety of details, We shall bring about one of two things; that is, We shall either cause him to abandon his studies, or, by means of excessive labor—

and also with the distrust which very frequently discourages young men—conduct him to that point to which, if led by an easier route, he might have been brought more speedily without much exertion and without misgiving.

3. The following are the precepts of the Law: to live honestly, not to injure another, and to give to each one that which belongs to him.

4. There are two branches of this study, namely: public and private. The Public Law is that which concerns the administration of the Roman government; Private Law relates to the interests of individuals. Thus Private Law is said to be threefold in its nature, for it is composed of precepts of Natural Law, of those of the Law of Nations, and of those of the Civil Law.

CONCERNING NATURAL LAW, THE LAW OF NATIONS, AND THE CIVIL LAW

Natural Law is that which nature has taught to all animals, for this law is not peculiar to the human race, but applies to all creatures which originate in the air, on the earth, and in the sea. Hence arises the union of the male and the female which we designate marriage; and hence are derived the procreation and the education of children; for we see that other animals also act as though endowed with knowledge of this law.

1. The Civil Law and the Law of Nations are divided as follows. All peoples that are governed by laws and customs make use of the law which is partly peculiar to themselves and partly pertaining to all men; for what each people has established for itself is peculiar to that State, and is styled the Civil Law; being, as it were, the especial law of that individual commonwealth. But the law which natural reason has established among all mankind and which is equally observed among all peoples, is called the Law of Nations, as being that which all nations make use of. . . .

6. Whatever is approved by the sovereign has also the force of law, because by the *Lex Regia*, from whence his power is derived, the people have delegated to him all their jurisdiction and authority. Therefore, whatever the Emperor establishes by means of a Rescript or decrees as a magistrate, or commands by an Edict, stands as law, and these are called Constitutions. Some of these are personal and are not considered as precedents, because the sovereign does not wish them to be such; for any favor he grants on account of merit, or where he inflicts punishment upon anyone or affords him unusual assistance, this affects only the individual concerned; the others, however, as they are of general application unquestionably are binding upon all.

Imperial Authority

The Emperor Justinian to Demosthenes, Praetorian Prefect.

When His Imperial Majesty examines a case for the purpose of deciding it, and renders an opinion in the presence of the parties in interest, let all the judges in Our Empire know that this law will apply, not only to the care with reference to which it was promulgated, but also to all that are similar. For what is greater or more sacred than the Imperial Majesty? Or who is swollen with so much pride that he can despise the royal decisions, when the founders of the ancient law have decided that the constitutions which have emanated from the Imperial Throne have plainly and clearly the force of law?

1. Therefore, as We have found that a doubt existed in the ancient laws as to whether a decision of the Emperor should be considered a law, We have come to the conclusion that this vain subtlety is not only contemptible, but should be suppressed.

For this reason We hold that every interpretation of the laws by the Emperor, whether in answer to requests made to him, or whether given in judgment, or in any other way whatsoever, shall be considered valid, and free from all ambiguity; for if, by the present enactment, the Emperor alone can make laws, it should also be the province of the Imperial Dignity alone to interpret them. For when any doubt arises in Litigation on account of the conflicting opinions of the legal authorities, and they do not think that they are either qualified or able to decide the question, why should they have recourse to Us? And wherefore should all the ambiguities which may exist with reference to the laws be brought to Our ears, if the right to interpret them does not belong to Us? Or who appears to be capable of solving legal enigmas, and explaining them to all persons, unless he who alone is permitted to be legislator? Therefore, these ridiculous doubts having been cast aside, the Emperor shall justly be regarded as the sole maker and interpreter of the laws; and this provision shall in no way prejudice the founders of ancient jurisprudence, because the Imperial Majesty conferred this privilege upon them.

Given on the sixth day before the *Kalends* of November [October 27], during the Consulate of Decius, 529.

The Church

The priesthood and the Empire are the two greatest gifts which God, in His infinite clemency, has bestowed upon mortals; the former has reference to Divine matters, the latter presides over and directs human affairs, and both, proceeding from the same principle, adorn the life of mankind; hence nothing should be such a source of care to the emperors as the honor of the priests who constantly pray to God for their salvation. For if the priesthood is everywhere free from blame, and the Empire full of confidence in God is administered equitably and judiciously, general good will result, and whatever is beneficial will be bestowed upon the human race. Therefore We have the greatest solicitude for the observance of the divine rules and the preservation of the honor of the priesthood, which, if they are maintained, will result in the greatest advantages that can be conferred upon us by God, as well as in the confirmation of those which We already enjoy, and whatever We have not yet obtained We shall hereafter acquire. For all things terminate happily where the beginning is proper and agreeable to God. We think that this will take place if the sacred rules of the Church which the just, praiseworthy, and adorable Apostles, the inspectors and ministers of the Word of God, and the Holy Fathers have explained and preserved for Us, are obeyed. . . .

The holy patriarchs of every diocese, the metropolitans and the remaining reverend bishops and clergy, shall observe inviolate and in conformity with the sacred canons the rules which We have above established, and shall, for the future, observe the worship of God and the discipline of the Church unimpaired, under the penalty of being rejected by God, and excluded from the sacred order of the priesthood as being unworthy of it. We, however, grant permission to everyone, no matter what may be his office or to what order he may belong, when he becomes aware of any of these breaches of discipline, to notify Us, or the government; so that We, who have established the said rules, in accordance with the sacred apostolic canons of the Church, may inflict the proper penalty upon those who are guilty. . . .

If, for the general welfare, We have taken measures to render the civil laws more effective, with whose execution, God, through His good will towards men, has entrusted Us, how much more reason is there not for Us to compel the observance of the sacred canons, and Divine Laws, which have been promulgated for the safety of Our souls? For those who observe the sacred canons become worthy of the assistance of Our Lord God, while those who disobey them render themselves liable to be punished by Him. Therefore, the most holy bishops who are charged with the enforcement of these laws are liable to severe penalties when they allow any breaches of them to remain unpunished. And, indeed, as the sacred canons have not been, up to this time, strictly observed, various complaints have been made to Us of clerks, monks, and certain bishops, on the ground that they do not live in accordance with the divine canons; and indeed there are even some among them who are either ignorant of, or do not perform the holy service of the mass, or of the ceremony of baptism.

Therefore We, understanding and being deeply impressed with the spirit of God, do hereby order that proceedings shall be instituted at the same time to inquire into and correct the matters which have been submitted to Us. For if the general laws do not suffer crimes committed by laymen to go unpunished, even when investigated, how can We permit the rules canonically established by the Holy Apostles and the Holy Fathers with reference to the salvation of all men to be treated with contempt?

We are perfectly aware that the principal reason why so many persons are guilty of sin is because the episcopal synods are not held in accordance with the regulations established by the Holy Apostles and Fathers of the Church. If this was done, as every ecclesiastic would then apprehend being subjected to a serious accusation, all would exert themselves to master the sacred liturgies, and live temperately through fear of being rendered liable to condemnation under the divine canons.

18 / GERMANIC LAW: THE ANGLO-SAXON DOOMS

In sharp contrast to the Justinian Code in every respect are the early medieval collections of Germanic laws, which reveal a far inferior concept of law as oral, customary, without any general principles of reason or equity. The aim of the Germanic law court was not to provide justice, but simply to provide alternatives to the blood feud. In only one respect, but an important one, was the Germanic legal concept a contribution to Western civilization: law resided in the folk or community, not in the will of an absolute monarch. The greater part of Germanic law was oral and customary; the so-called Germanic law codes are not really codes at all, but merely statements of novel or confusing points of law, such as the amount of compensation (the wergild) to be paid to the kinsmen of a slain person. The best examples of Germanic law are the Anglo-Saxon dooms. In England there was no legacy of Roman law whatsoever, and Germanic law con-

tinued in operation in its pristine form until the eleventh century.[34]

I. FROM THE LAWS OF KING ALFRED (871–899)

I, then, Alfred, king, gathered these together, and commanded many of those to be written which our forefathers held, those which to me seemed good; and many of those which seemed to me not good I rejected them, by the counsel of my "witan" ["wise men," i.e. magnates], and in otherwise commanded them to be holden; for I durst not venture to set down in writing much of my own, for it was unknown to me what of it would please those who should come after us. But those things which I met with, either of the days of Ine my kinsman, or of Offa king of the Mercians, or of Æthelbryht, who first among the English race received baptism, those which seemed to me the rightest, those I have here gathered together, and rejected the others.

I, then, Alfred, king of the West-Saxons, showed these to all my "witan," and they then said that it seemed good to them all to be holden.

In Case a Man Fight in the King's Hall

7. If any one fight in the king's hall, or draw his weapon, and he be taken; be it in the king's doom, either death, or life, as he may be willing to grant him. If he escape, and be taken again, let him pay for himself according to his "wer-gild," and make "bōt" [compensation] for the offence. . . .

Of Those Men Who Fight Before a Bishop

15. If a man fight before an archbishop or draw his weapon, let him make "bōt" with one hundred and fifty shillings. If before another bishop or an ealdorman this happen, let him make "bōt" with one hundred shillings.

Of Kinless Men

27. If a man, kinless of paternal relatives, fight, and slay a man, and then if he have maternal relatives, let him pay a third of the "wēr"; his gild-brethren [kindred] a third part; for a third let him flee. If he have no maternal relatives, let his gild-brethren pay half, for half let him flee.

[34] G. C. Lee, *Source Book of English History* (New York: Holt, 1900), pp. 87–93, from B. Thorpe, transl., *Ancient Laws and Institutes.*

Of Feuds

42. We also command: that the man who knows his foe to be home-sitting fight not before he demand justice of him. If he have such power that he can beset his foe, and besiege him within, let him keep him within for VII. days, and attack him not, if he will remain within. And then, after VII. days, if he will surrender, and deliver up his weapons, let him be kept safe for XXX. days, and let notice of him be given to his kinsmen and his friends. If, however, he flee to a church, then let it be according to the sanctity of the church. . . . But if he have not sufficient power to besiege him within, let him ride to the "ealdorman," and beg aid of him. If he will not aid him, let him ride to the king before he fights. In like manner also, if a man come upon his foe, and he did not before know him to be home-staying; if he be willing to deliver up his weapons, let him be kept for XXX. days, and let notice of him be given to his friends; if he will not deliver up his weapons, then he may attack him. . . . We also declare, that with his lord a man may fight without incurring the bloodfeud, if any one attack the lord: thus may the lord fight for his man. After the same wise, a man may fight with his born kinsman, if a man attack him wrongfully, except against his lord; that we do not allow.

Of Various Limbs

If the shooting [i.e. fore] finger be struck off, the "bōt" is XV. shillings; for its nail it is IV. shillings.

If a man's thigh be pierced, let XXX. shillings be paid him as "bōt"; if it be broken, the "bōt" is likewise XXX. shillings.

If the great toe be struck off, let XX. shillings be paid him as "bōt"; if it be the second toe, let XV. shillings be paid as "bōt"; if the middle-most toe be struck off, there shall be IX. shillings as "bōt"; if it be the fourth toe, there shall be VI. shillings as "bōt"; if the little toe be struck off, let V. shillings be paid him.

If a man's arm, with the hand, be entirely cut off before the elbow, let "bōt" be made for it with LXXX. shillings.

For every wound before the hair, and before the sleeve, and beneath the knee, the "bōt" is two parts more.

19 / POPE LEO I
THE GREAT:
THE PETRINE DOCTRINE

With the disintegration of the Roman empire and the weakness and crudity of most of the Germanic kings, the Church remained the only institution which could provide leadership in Western Europe from the fifth to the middle of the eighth century. In the middle of the fifth century the bishop of Rome began the long task of organizing the Church, asserting his supreme authority and imposing Latin Christian culture on barbarian Europe. This development was inaugurated by clear assertion of the Pope's authority as vicar of Christ on earth by Pope Leo I the Great (440–461) on the basis of the Petrine Doctrine. Leo's formulation of this doctrine became authoritative for the Catholic Church, and reflects the new consciousness on the part of the bishop of Rome of his potential role as the leader of Europe.[35]

FROM CHRIST AND THROUGH ST. PETER THE PRIESTHOOD IS HANDED ON IN PERPETUITY

Although, therefore, dearly beloved, we be found both weak and slothful in fulfilling the duties of our office, because, whatever devoted and vigorous action we desire to do, we are hindered by the frailty of our very condition; yet having the unceasing propitiation of the Almighty and perpetual Priest, who being like us and yet equal with the Father, brought down His Godhead even to things human, and raised His Manhood even to things Divine, we worthily and piously rejoice over His dispensation, whereby, though He has delegated the care of His sheep to many shepherds, yet He has not Himself abandoned the guardianship of His beloved flock. And from His overruling and eternal protection we have received the support of the Apostles' aid also, which assuredly does not cease from its operation: and the strength of the foundation, on which the whole superstructure of the Church is reared, is not weakened by the weight of the temple that rests upon it. For the solidity of that faith which was praised in the chief of the Apostles is perpetual: and as that remains which Peter be-

[35] *Library of the Nicene and Post-Nicene Fathers*, Vol. XII, transl. J. Barmby (New York: Christian Literature Co., 1895), p. 117.

lieved in Christ, so that remains which Christ instituted in Peter. For when, as has been read in the Gospel lesson, the LORD had asked the disciples whom they believed Him to be amid the various opinions that were held, and the blessed Peter had replied, saying, "Thou art the Christ, the Son of the living GOD," the LORD says, "Blessed art thou, Simon Bar-Jona, because flesh and blood hath not revealed it to thee, but My Father, which is in heaven. And I say to thee, that thou art Peter, and upon this rock will I build My church, and the gates of Hades shall not prevail against it. And I will give unto thee the keys of the kingdom of heaven. And whatsoever thou shalt bind on earth, shall be bound in heaven; and whatsoever thou shalt loose on earth, shall be loosed also in heaven."

ST. PETER'S WORK IS STILL CARRIED OUT BY HIS SUCCESSORS

The dispensation of Truth therefore abides, and the blessed Peter persevering in the strength of the Rock, which he has received, has not abandoned the helm of the Church, which he undertook. For he was ordained before the rest in such a way that from his being called the Rock, from his being pronounced the Foundation, from his being constituted the Doorkeeper of the kingdom of heaven, from his being set as the Umpire to bind and to loose, whose judgments shall retain their validity in heaven, from all these mystical titles we might know the nature of his association with Christ. And still to-day he more fully and effectually performs what is entrusted to him, and carries out every part of his duty and charge in Him and with Him, through Whom he has been glorified. And so if anything is won from the mercy of GOD by our daily supplications, it is of his work and merits whose power lives and whose authority prevails in his See. For this, dearly beloved, was gained by that confession, which, inspired in the Apostle's heart by GOD the Father, transcended all the uncertainty of human opinions, and was endued with the firmness of a rock, which no assaults could shake. For throughout the Church Peter daily says, "Thou art the Christ, the Son of the living GOD," and every tongue which confesses the LORD, accepts the instruction his voice conveys. This Faith conquers the devil, and breaks the bonds of his prisoners. It uproots us from this earth and plants us in heaven, and the gates of Hades cannot prevail against it. For with solidity is it endued by GOD that the depravity of heretics cannot mar it nor the unbelief of the heathen overcome it.

20 / POPE GELASIUS I: THE DOCTRINE OF CHURCH-STATE RELATIONS

Following suggestions made by Ambrose, Augustine, and Leo I, Pope Gelasius I (492–496) asserted, against the Caesaropapist claims of the Byzantine emperor to rule the Church and decide dogma by imperial decree, the papal doctrine on Church-state relations. This Gelasian doctrine became the authoritative political theory of the early medieval Church and was frequently cited by Church theorists for many centuries—in fact, to the present day. It is one of the most important pronouncements in the history of political thought.[36]

Two things there are indeed, August Emperor, by which this world is principally ruled: the consecrated authority of priests and royal power. Of these, the burden of the priests is so much the heavier, because they will answer even for the kings of men at the divine judgment. Know therefore most merciful son, that, although you may take precedence over the human race with your dignity, nevertheless you obediently bow your head to the leaders of divine affairs and look to them for the means of your salvation. In partaking of the heavenly sacraments, when they are properly dispensed, you recognize that you ought to be obedient to the religious orders rather than rule them. In these matters, therefore, you ought to rely on their judgment and not wish that they be brought to your opinion. For if the ministers of religion, realizing that governance, insofar as it pertains to the keeping of public discipline, was given to you by divine disposition, obey your laws, lest they seem to obstruct the proper course of worldly affairs; with what good will ought you to obey those, who have been charged with the dispensation of holy mysteries? Just as a heavy judgment lies on priests who have omitted what is necessary for the service of God, in the same way there is grave danger to those who are scornful—which God forbid—when they ought to be obedient. And if it is proper for the hearts of the

[36] C. Mirbt, ed., *Quellen zur Geschichte des Papsttums* (Tübingen: J. C. B. Mohr (Paul Siebeck), 1924), pp. 85–6. Translated by permission of J. C. B. Mohr (Paul Siebeck).

faithful to be submitted to all priests in general who correctly administer divine matters, how much the more is it necessary to respect the opinion of the bishop of that seat, which the Most High wished to be placed above all priests, and which is, therefore, constantly honored by the devotion of the whole Church? . . .

As your Reverence has evidently observed: no one can ever elevate himself, by any purely human means, to the recognized position of him, whom the voice of Christ has preferred before all others, and the venerable Church has always acknowledged and worshipped as her primate. Those things which were founded by divine ordinance can be assailed by human presumption, they cannot, however, be conquered by any human power. . . . Let those men, therefore, desist, I pray you, who are using the perturbance of the Church as a pretext, rashly seeking things which are forbidden: let them not attain those things for which they are evilly striving, nor maintain any standing among God and men.

But if emperors fear to essay these things, and recognize that they do not pertain to the measure of their power, because they are permitted to judge human affairs alone, and are not also given preeminence in divine affairs: how then do they presume to judge these men, through whom divine affairs are administered? It occurred before the coming of Christ that certain men, although until that event they were ordained for carnal activities, were both kings and priests, and Holy Writ tells us that the blessed Melchisedek was such a man.[37] This the devil also imitated among his people, since he always sought to arrogate unto himself those things which occurred through divine institution. Thus it happened that pagan emperors were also called High Priests. But when He came, Who was truly both King and Priest, the emperor, of his own free will, no longer assumed the name of priest, nor did the priest any longer seek the royal insignia (although His people, that is, of the true King and Priest, are said to have assumed, out of sacred generosity, both natures, because of their participation in His divine nature, so that they are simultaneously of both royal and sacerdotal stock): since Christ, mindful of human fragility, governed what pertained to the well-being of His flock with an excellent disposition. Thus He differentiated the functions of each power by its appropriate activities and separate dignities, wishing that His flock be saved by a healthful humility and not be carried off again through human pride. It thus happened that the Christian emperors depended on the priests for .

---

[37] The Book of Genesis mentions a certain Melchisedek ("king of righteousness," literally) who was both king and priest for his people. Early medieval theorists, especially in the Greek church, interpreted this to be a foreshadowing of the Archtype of Christ, the Archking and Archpriest. The Emperor claimed to be the vice-regent of God, and like Melchisedek, both king and high priest.

their eternal life, and the priests made use of imperial dispositions in the course of temporal affairs; in this manner the spiritual activity would stand apart from carnal onslaughts and "the soldier of God" would not be involved in secular affairs. He, in turn, who was involved in secular affairs, would not seem to preside over divine matters. Thus the purity of each order would be preserved, and not unduly increased by the subservience of the other; and thus each profession would be especially provided with its suitable function.

21 / ST. BENEDICT: THE RULE

The assertion of papal authority was one of the two important aspects of the growth of ecclesiastical leadership in Western Europe in the fifth and sixth centuries; the other was the emergence of the Benedictine monastic order. By the eighth century the Benedictine Rule had become universal in the Latin monastic world, and the black monks were taking such a leading role in the new European civilization—not only in the affairs of the Church, but also in government, education, and economy—that the period between 550 and 1050 has, with considerable justice, been called the Benedictine centuries. All this depended on the excellence of the Rule itself, drawn up by St. Benedict of Nursia (d. 543), a Roman aristocrat drawn to the monastic life and the founder of Monte Cassino. His Rule reflects not only the ascetic impulse to assure salvation through withdrawal from secular temptations, but also the organizing skill and balanced, judicious consideration of the strength and weaknesses of human nature of a great statesman and administrator. The Rule is one of the most successful examples of constitution drafting in the history of Western civilization. It so finely balances Christian ascetic ideals with a Roman sense of good order that it created an institution perfectly adapted to the needs of early medieval society, which lacked effective institutions. Hence many social obligations were grafted onto the original religious purposes of the Benedictine monastery in the early Middle Ages. The Benedictine Rule stands in sharp contrast to the eremitic asceticism of the Fathers of the Desert; it emphasizes the value of communal religious life.

It has served as a model and guide to most of the later religious orders of the Church, and continues to be the constitution of the Benedictine order to the present day.[38]

PROLOGUE

Listen, my son, to the precepts of your Master, and incline the ear of your heart unto them. Freely accept and faithfully fulfil the advice of a loving father, so that you may, by the labor of obedience, return to Him, Whom you abandoned through the sloth of disobedience. To you, therefore, whoever you are, my words are directed, who, renouncing your own will, takes up the strong and excellent arms of obedience to fight for the true King, our Lord Christ.

In the first place, beg with most earnest prayer that He may perfect whatever good work you begin, so that He Who has seen fit to count us among the number of His sons may never be grieved by our evil deeds. For we must always so serve Him with the gifts He has given us, that He will not, as an angry father, disinherit His sons, nor, as a dread lord, be provoked by our sins to consign to perpetual punishment His most wicked servants, who did not wish to follow Him to glory.

Let us, therefore, arise at last, for the Scripture arouses us, saying: "It is now the hour to arise from sleep." And with our eyes opened to the divine light, let us hear with awe-filled ears the warning which the divine voice daily calls out to us: "Today if you will hear His voice, harden not your ears"; and again: "He who has ears to hear, let him hear what the Spirit says to the Churches." And what does He say? "Come My sons, harken unto Me, and I will teach you the fear of the Lord. Run while you have the light of life, lest the darkness of death overtake you."

And our Lord, seeking His workman among the multitude of people to whom He thus calls, says again: "Who is the man who longs for life and desires to see good days?" And if you hear this and answer: "I am he"; God says to you: "If you wish to have true and everlasting life, restrain your tongue from evil, and let not your lips speak guile. Turn away from evil and do good, inquire after peace and pursue it." And when you have done these things My eyes shall be upon you and My ears shall be open to your prayers; and before you call Me, I will say unto you; "Behold, I am here." What can be sweeter to us, dearest brothers, than this voice of the Lord inviting us? Behold, in His loving kindness, the Lord shows us the way of life.

[38] St. Benedict, *Rule for Monks*, D. P. Schmitz, ed. (Namur, Belgium: Abbaye de Maredsous, 1955), prologue, and chapters 1, 2, 33, 34, 37, 39, 40, 48, 58, 60, 63, 64. Translated by permission of D. P. Schmitz, O.S.B.

Let us, therefore, with our loins girt up by faith and the performance of good works, follow the guidance of His Gospel and walk in His path, so that we may deserve to see Him, Who has called us into His Kingdom. If we wish to dwell in the tabernacle of His Kingdom, we shall not reach it unless we run thither with good works.

But let us, with the Prophet, question the Lord, saying to Him: "Lord, who shall dwell in Your tabernacle, and who shall rest on Your holy hill?" After this question, my brothers, let us hear the Lord answer and show us the way to His tabernacle, saying: "he who walks without blemish and works justice; he who speaks truth in his heart; he who has used no guile on his tongue; he who has done no evil to his neighbor, and has believed no evil of his neighbor." He who takes the evil demon who tempts him and casts him and his temptation from the sight of his heart and brings them to naught. He who takes his evil thoughts as they arise and dashes them against the rock which is Christ. They who, fearing the Lord, do not exalt themselves because of their good works, but know that what is good in them is not performed by them but by the Lord, and magnify the Lord working in them, saying with the Prophet: "Not unto us, O Lord, not unto us, but to Your Name give glory." Thus the apostle Paul imputed nothing of his preaching to himself, saying: "By the grace of God I am what I am." And he says again: "He who glorifies, let him glory in the Lord."

Wherefore the Lord also says in the Gospel: "He who hears these My words and does them, I will make him like unto a wise man who has built his house upon a rock; the floods came and the winds blew, they beat upon that house and it did not fall, because it was founded upon a rock."

Having answered us in full, the Lord daily expects us to make our deeds correspond with these His holy instructions. Therefore the days of this life are lengthened to give us respite in which to mend our evil ways. For the Apostle says: "Do you not know that the patience of the Lord leads you to repentance?" And our merciful Lord says: "I do not desire the death of the sinner, but that he be converted and live."

So, my brothers, we have asked the Lord about the dwellers in His tabernacle, and have heard the duties of him who would dwell therein; but we can only attain our goal if we fulfil these duties.

Therefore must our hearts and bodies be prepared to fight under the holy obedience of His commands. Let us beg the Lord to grant us the aid of His grace where our own natures are powerless. And if, fleeing the pains of hell, we wish to attain to perpetual life, then we must—while there is till time, while we are in this body and can fulfil all these precepts by the light of this life—hasten to do now what will profit us in eternity.

Therefore must we establish a school for the service of the Lord, in which we hope to ordain nothing harsh or burdensome. But if, for some sound reason, for the amendment of vices or the preservation of charity, we proceed somewhat severely at times, do not immediately become frightened and flee the path of salvation, whose entrance is always narrow. But as we progress in our life and faith, our hearts shall be enlarged and we shall follow the path of God's commandments with the unspeakable sweetness of love: so that, never departing from His rule, and persevering in His teaching in the monastery until our deaths, we may participate in the sufferings of Christ by our patience, and thus deserve to be partakers of His Kingdom. Amen.

CHAPTER 1. ON THE TYPES OF MONKS

It is evident that there are four types of monks. The first are the Cenobites: that is, those who live in monasteries, serving under a rule and an abbot.

The second type is that of the Anchorites, or Hermits: that is, those who, not in the first fervor of conversion, but after long probation in a monastery, having been taught by the example of many brothers, have learned to fight against the devil and are well prepared to go forth from the ranks of their brothers to solitary combat in the desert. They are now able, with God's assistance, to fight against the vices of the flesh and evil thoughts without the encouragement of a companion, using only their own strength.

The third and worst type of monks is that of the Sarabites, who have not been tested by any rule or the lessons of experience, as gold is in the furnace, but are as soft as lead. They still follow the standards of the world in their works and are known to lie to God by their tonsure. They live in twos or threes, or even singly, without a shepherd, not in the Lord's sheepfold, but in their own. Their desires are their law: whatever they think of or choose to do, they call holy, and they consider what they do not like as unlawful.

The fourth type of monks are called the Gyrovagues. These spend their whole lives moving from one province to the next, staying as guests for three or four days in different monasteries, always wandering and never stable. They obey their own wills and the entirements of gluttony, and are in all ways inferior to the Sarabites.

It is better to pass over the wretched observances of all these men in silence than to speak of them. Let us omit these, therefore, and proceed, with God's help, to provide for the Cenobites, the strongest type of monks.

CHAPTER 2. WHAT KIND OF MAN THE ABBOT OUGHT TO BE

The abbot who is worthy to rule over a monastery should always remember what he is called and suit his actions to his high calling. For he is believed to take the place of Christ in the monastery, and therefore is he called by His title, in accordance with the words of the Apostle: "Ye have received the spirit of the adoption of sons, whereby we cry: Abba, Father."

Therefore the abbot ought not to teach, ordain, or command anything which is against the law of the Lord; but he should infuse the leaven of divine justice into the minds of his disciples through his commands and teaching. Let the abbot always remember that there will be an inquiry both as to his teachings and as to the obedience of his disciples at the dread Judgment of God. Let the abbot know that whatever lack of profit the Father of the family may find in His sheep will be accounted the fault of the shepherd. However, if the shepherd has used all his diligence on an unruly and disobedient flock, and has devoted all his care to amending their corrupt ways, he shall be acquitted at the Judgment of the Lord and may say to Him with the Prophet: "I have not hidden Your justice in my heart, I have declared Your truth and Your salvation; but they have scorned and despised me." And then at last, death itself shall be the penalty for the sheep who have not responded to his care.

When, therefore, any one receives the name of abbot, he ought to rule his disciples with a two-fold doctrine—that is, he should display all that is good and holy by his deeds rather than by his words. To his intelligent disciples, let him expound the commands of the Lord in words, but to those of harder hearts and simpler minds, let him demonstrate the divine precepts by his example. All things which he teaches his disciples to be contrary to God's law, let him show in his deeds that they are not to be done, lest while preaching to others he himself should become a castaway and God should some day say to him as he sins: "Why do you declare My justice and take My testament in your mouth? For you have hated My discipline and cast My words behind you"; and: "You saw the mote in your brother's eye and did not see the beam in your own."

Let him make no distinction of persons in the monastery. Let no one be loved more than another, unless it be him who is found better in good works or obedience. Let not the free-born monk be put before the man who was born in slavery unless there is some good reason for it. But if the abbot, for some reason, shall see fit to do so, he may fix anyone's rank as he will; otherwise let all keep their own places, because whether slave or freeman, we are all one in Christ and we must all alike bear the burden of service under the same Lord. "There is no respect of persons with God." In this regard alone are we distinguished in His sight, if we are found better than others in good works and humility. Therefore let him show equal love for all; and let one discipline be imposed on all in accordance with their deserts.

In his teaching, the abbot should always observe the apostolic rule which says: "Reprove, entreat, rebuke." That is, he ought to adapt himself to the circumstances and mingle encouragements with his reproofs. Let him show the sternness of a master and the devoted affection of a father. He ought to reprove the undisciplined and unruly severely, but should exhort the obedient, meek, and patient to advance in virtue. We warn him to rebuke and punish the negligent and scornful.

Let him not blind himself to the sins of offenders, but let him cut them out by the roots as soon as they begin to appear. . . . He should use words of warning to punish, for the first and second time, those who are of gentle disposition and good understanding; but he ought to use the lash and corporal punishment to check the bold, hard, proud, and disobedient even at the very beginning of their wrongdoing, in accordance with the text: "The fool is not corrected by words"; and again: "Beat your son with a rod, and you will free his soul from death."

The abbot should always remember what he is and what he is called, and he should know that from him, to whom more is entrusted, more is also required. Let him know how difficult and arduous a task he has taken upon himself, to govern the souls and cater to the different dispositions of many men. One must be encouraged, the second rebuked, the third one persuaded; in accordance with the disposition and understanding of each. He must so adapt and accommodate himself to all that not only will he endure no loss in the flock entrusted to his care, but even rejoice in the increase of his good sheep.

Above all else, let him not slight or undervalue the salvation of the souls entrusted to him by giving more attention to transitory, earthly, and perishable matters. Let him always remember the souls he has undertaken to govern, for which he will also have to render an account. Let him not complain of lack of means, but let him remember that it is written: "Seek first the Kingdom of God, and His justice, and all things shall be given unto you"; and again: "Nothing is lacking to those who fear Him."

Let him know that they who undertake to govern souls must prepare themselves to give answer for them. Let him understand that, however great the number of brothers he has under his care, on the Day of Judgment he will have to answer to God for the souls of all of them, as well as for his own. And so, fearing always the inquiry which the shepherd must face for the sheep entrusted to him, and anxious about the answers which he must give for the others, he becomes solicitous for his own sake also. Thus, while his admonitions help others to amend, he himself is freed of all his faults.

CHAPTER 33. WHETHER THE MONKS OUGHT TO HAVE ANYTHING OF THEIR OWN

This vice especially ought to be cut out of the monastery by its roots. Let no one presume to give or receive anything without the permission of the abbot or to keep anything whatever for his own, neither book, nor tablets, nor pen, nor anything else, because monks should not even have their own bodies and wills at their own disposal. Let them look to the father of the monastery for whatever is necessary and let it be forbidden for them to have anything he has not given them or allowed them to possess.

Let all things be common to all, as it is written, lest anyone should say that anything is his own or arrogate it to himself. If anyone shall be found to indulge in this most wicked vice, let him be admonished for the first and second time. If he does not amend let him undergo punishment.

CHAPTER 34. WHETHER ALL SHOULD RECEIVE EQUAL MEASURE OF NECESSARY THINGS

It is written: "Distribution was made to each according to his need." By this, we do not mean that there should be—which God forbid— respect of persons, but rather consideration of infirmities. Therefore, he who needs less should give thanks to God and not be discontented; but he that needs more should be humble because of his infirmity, not exalted by the pity shown him. In this way will all members be in peace.

Before all things, let not the sin of murmuring for any reason show itself in any word or sign. If anyone shall be found guilty of this, let him undergo severe punishment.

CHAPTER 37. OF OLD MEN AND CHILDREN

Although human nature is drawn towards pity for these two ages, that is, for old men and children, nevertheless let them also be cared for by the authority of the Rule. Their weakness should always be taken into account, and in no way should the severity of the Rule in regard to food be applied to them. Let them receive, on the contrary, loving consideration, and let them eat before the regularly established hours.

CHAPTER 39. THE AMOUNT OF FOOD

We believe it to be sufficient for the daily meal, whether it be at the sixth or ninth hour, that every table have two cooked dishes, on account of the individual weaknesses of the brothers, so that he who, by chance, cannot eat out of the one, may eat from the other. Therefore, let two cooked dishes suffice for all the brothers, and if there are fruits or young vegetables available, let a third dish be added.

CHAPTER 40. THE AMOUNT OF DRINK

"Every man has his proper gift from God, one after this manner, another after that." And therefore it is with some misgiving that we determine the amount of food for someone else. Still, having regard for the weakness of some brothers, we believe that a hemina of wine per day will suffice for all. Let those, however, to whom God gives the gift of abstinence, know that they shall have their proper reward.

But if either the circumstances of the place, the work, or the heat of summer necessitates more, let it lie in the discretion of the abbot to grant it. But let him take care in all things lest satiety or drunkenness supervene. We do read that wine is not a proper drink for monks; but since in our days monks cannot at all be persuaded of this, let us at least agree to drink sparingly and not unto satiety: for "wine makes even the wise to fall away."

CHAPTER 48. OF THE DAILY MANUAL LABOR

Idleness is the enemy of the soul. The brothers, therefore, ought to be engaged at certain times in manual labor, and at other hours in divine reading. Therefore do we think this arrangement should be ordained for both times: that is, from Easter until the Kalends of October [October 1] they shall begin early in the morning, from the first until about the fourth hours, to do the necessary tasks. Let the time from the fourth until about the sixth hour be spent on reading.

After the sixth hour, let them rise from the table and rest on their beds in perfect silence. If anyone may wish to read to himself, let him do so in such a way as not to disturb the others. Let None be said early, about the middle of the eighth hour, and then let them do the work which has to be done until Vespers. If the circumstances of the place or poverty forces them to gather the harvest by themselves, let them not be saddened on this account: because then they are truly monks, if they live by the labor of their own hands like our Fathers or the Apostles. Let all things, however, be done in moderation because of the faint-hearted. . . .

CHAPTER 58. THE MANNER OF THE RECEPTION OF BROTHERS

Let not anyone, newly coming to the religious life, be granted an easy entrance; but, as the Apostle says: "Test the spirits to see whether they are of God." If, therefore, anyone perseveres in his knocking at the door, and if he is seen, after four or five days, to bear patiently the harsh treatment inflicted on him and the difficulty of admission and to persist in his petition, let admittance be granted to him, and let him stay in the guest-house for a few days. Afterwards let him stay in the novitiate, where the novices study, eat, and sleep.

And let a senior, who is skilled at the winning of souls, be appointed to watch over them with the utmost care. Let him be diligent to learn whether the novice is truly seeking God, whether he is eager for the Work of God, for obedience, and for humiliations. Let the novices be told of all the hardships and difficulties through which we journey to God.

If he promises to persevere in his purpose, at the end of two months let this Rule be read to him from beginning to end, and let him be told: "Behold the law under which you wish to serve; if you can observe it enter; but if you cannot, depart freely." If he remains there still, then let him be led back into the above-mentioned room and let him again be tested in all patience.

After the lapse of six months let the Rule be read to him so that he may know upon what he is entering. If he still abides, let this same Rule be read to him again after four months. And if, after having deliberated with himself, he promises to observe all its provisions and to obey all commands given him, then let him be received into the congregation. But let him know that from that day forth he shall not be allowed to leave the monastery nor to withdraw his neck from under the yoke of the Rule, which it was open to him, during that long period of deliberation, either to reject or accept.

When the novice is ready to be received, let him, in the oratory, in the presence of all, and in the sight of God and His Saints; promise stability, the conversion of his life, and obedience. Let him know that, if he behaves otherwise, he shall be condemned by Him, Whom he mocks. . . .

If he has any property, let him either give it beforehand to the poor, or offer it to the monastery in a formal donation. Let him keep back nothing for himself, since he knows that from that day forth he will not even have power over his own body.

In the oratory, therefore, let him be immediately stripped of his own clothes, which he is wearing, and be attired in the clothes of the monastery. The garments which he had worn, however, should be stored and preserved in the clothes-room. Then, if he ever consents to any persuasion of the devil—which God forbid—and determines to leave the monastery, he may be stripped of the clothing of the monastery before being dismissed. Let him not receive, however, his petition, which the abbot placed above the altar, but let it be preserved in the monastery.

CHAPTER 60. OF PRIESTS WHO MAY WISH TO DWELL IN THE MONASTERY

If anyone of the priestly order requests to be received into the monastery, let him not obtain this permission too quickly. If, nevertheless, he still perseveres in this petition, give him to understand that he will have to observe the entire discipline of the Rule and that none of it will be lightened for him. For Scripture says: "Friend, for what purpose have you come?"

Let him be allowed, however, to stand behind the abbot in rank, to say the blessing, and to celebrate masses, if the abbot permits him to do so. If not, let him not presume to do anything, knowing that he is subject to the discipline of the Rule, and that he, especially, ought to set an example for others by his humility.

If he entered the monastery in hopes of obtaining special station or privilege, let him know that he shall achieve his rank in accordance with the length of time which he has spent in the monastery and not because of the respect for his priesthood.

Likewise, if any clerics should wish to be admitted into the monastery, let them be placed in a middle rank; but only if they promise to observe the Rule and to be stable in this observance.

CHAPTER 63. THE ORDER OF THE COMMUNITY

Let all keep their order in the community according to the date of their conversion, the merit of their lives, or as the abbot shall determine. Yet let not the abbot disturb the flock entrusted to him, nor ordain any thing unjustly by making arbitrary use of his power; but let him always consider that he will have to answer to God for all his decisions and deeds.

In accordance, therefore, with the order which the abbot has determined, or the one which the brothers themselves hold, let them receive the kiss of peace, go to Communion, intone the psalms, and stand in the choir. And in no place whatsoever should age distinguish or predetermine their order, since Samuel and Daniel, although boys, judged the priests.

Except for those, therefore, whom, as we have said, the abbot has promoted by a special decision, or degraded for a definite reason, let all the rest take their rank from the date of their conversion. Thus, for example, he who came at the second hour of the day should know that he is younger than he who came at the first hour—no matter what his age or dignity may be. Boys, however, are to be kept under discipline in all things and by every one.

Let the juniors, therefore, honor their seniors; let the seniors love their juniors. In addressing each other, let no one be permitted to use the bare name: let the seniors call the juniors "Brother," and let the juniors call the seniors "Nonnus," which means "Reverend Father."

The abbot, however, because he is believed to hold the place of Christ, should be called "Lord" and "Abbot," not because of his own pretensions, but out of honor and love for Christ. Let the abbot himself remember this, and so deport himself that he may be worthy of such honor.

Whenever brothers meet each other, let the younger ask the older for his blessing. When a senior passes by, let the junior rise and give him his seat; and let not the junior presume to sit unless his senior so instructs him, in order to fulfill what is written: "Outdo one another in showing honor."

Small boys and youths shall keep strictly to their order in the oratory and at the table. Outside, however, or anywhere else, let them be supervised and disciplined, until they come to the age of discretion.

CHAPTER 64. THE APPOINTMENT OF THE ABBOT

In the appointment of the abbot, let this rule always be observed: he should be made abbot whom the whole community, unanimously, and in the fear of God, or even a minority, however small, acting more wisely, has chosen. Let him who is to be appointed be chosen for the merit of his life and for his wisdom, even if he is the last in order of the community.

But if the whole congregration—which God forbid—should agree to choose a person who supports them in their vices, and this depravity somehow comes to the knowledge of the bishop, to whose diocese the monastery pertains, or to the knowledge of the neighboring abbots and Christians, let them annul the choice of the wicked, and set up a worthy steward for the house of God. Let them know that they will receive a good reward, if they do this with pure intention and out of zeal for God, just as they will, on the contrary, incur sin, if they neglect their duty.

After he has been appointed, let the abbot always consider how weighty a burden he has undertaken, and to Whom he will have to answer for his stewardship. Let him understand that he ought to profit his brothers rather than to preside over them. He ought, therefore, to be learned in Divine Law, so that he may know whence to bring forth things both new and old; and to be chaste, sober, and merciful. Let him always exalt mercy above justice, so that he himself may obtain mercy. Let him hate vice and love the brothers.

Let him proceed prudently in the administration of correction, lest, being too anxious to remove the rust, he break the vessel. Let him always distrust his own frailty, and remember that the bruised reed must not be broken. By this we do not mean to imply that he should allow vice to thrive; but, as we have already said, that he should remove it prudently and with charity, in the way which seems best for each case. Let him study more to be loved than to be feared. Let him not be turbulent, or anxious, or too exacting, or obstinate, or jealous, or over-suspicious, for then he will never be at rest.

He should be prudent and considerate in all his commands; and whether the task he enjoins concerns God or the world, let him be discreet and temperate, remembering the discretion of holy Jacob, who said: "If I cause my flocks to be over-driven, they shall all die in one day."

Imitating, therefore, these and other examples of discretion, the mother of virtues, let him so arrange all things that the strong shall have something to strive for, and the weak shall not be put to flight.

And, especially, let him keep the present Rule in all things, so that, having administered it well, he may hear from the Lord what was heard by the good servant, who gave wheat to his fellow-servents in due season: "Amen, I say unto you, he will set him over all his goods."

22 / CASSIODORUS: TRANSMISSION OF THE CLASSICAL LEGACY

St. Benedict's contemporary Cassiodorus (d. 575), who had formerly served as the chief minister of Theodoric the Ostrogoth, already envisioned the monastery as the best institution for Christian education and learning. This necessitated not only a school but also a library and scriptorium in the monastery where the literature necessary for the education of churchmen could be copied and preserved. Cassiodorus founded a new monastery for this purpose and prepared a handbook for his monastic scholars setting forth his educational curriculum and methods. Along the lines set down by St. Jerome and St. Augustine, he favored the use in his monastic school of whatever aspects of the classical heritage were necessary for the education of churchmen. By the middle of the eighth century Cassiodorus' program of preserving and transmitting the classical texts through the medium of the monastic school was widely adopted, first in England and Ireland, then in France. While his educational guide is arid and difficult for the modern reader, it is one of the most important works in the development of education.[39]

Perceiving that the schools were swarming with students because of a great longing for secular letters (a great part of mankind believed that through these schools it attained worldy wisdom), I was, I confess, extremely sorry that the Divine Scriptures had no public teachers, since worldly authors were rich in instruction beyond doubt most distinguished. I strove with the most holy Agapetus, bishop of the city of Rome, to collect subscriptions and to have Christian rather than secular schools receive professors in the city of Rome, just as the custom is said to have existed for a long time at Alexandria and is said even

[39] Cassiodorus, *An Introduction to Divine and Human Readings*, transl. in L. W. Jones, *Records of Civilization*, Vol. 40 (New York: Columbia University Press, 1946), pp. 67–8, 110–11, 140, 204, 205, 207. Reprinted by permission of Columbia University Press.

now to be zealously cultivated by the Hebrews in Nisibis, a city of the Syrians, that thereby the soul might obtain eternal salvation and the tongue of the faithful might be adorned with a holy and completely faultless eloquence. But although my ardent desire could in no way have been fulfilled because of the struggles that seethed and raged excessively in the Italian realm, inasmuch as a peaceful affair has no place in anxious times, I was driven by divine charity to this device, namely, in the place of a teacher to prepare for you under the Lord's guidance these introductory books; through which, in my opinion, the unbroken line of the Divine Scriptures and the compendious knowledge of secular letters might with the Lord's beneficence be related— books not at all fluent, perhaps, since in them is found, not studied eloquence, but indispensable narration; to be sure, they are extremely useful, since through them one learns the indicated origin of both the salvation of the soul and secular knowledge. In them I commit to you, not my own learning, but the words of men of former times, which it is right to praise and glorious to proclaim for future generations, for whatever is said about men of former times by way of praise of the Lord is not considered hateful display. Add to this the fact that one is pleased with a venerable teacher if one consults him frequently; moreover, whenever one desires to have recourse to such teachers, one will find no harshness in them. . . .

We must now speak about the manner in which we ought to emend texts other than the Holy Scriptures. Let every corrector read commentaries on the divine law, epistles, sermons, and books of the ancients in such a way as to associate their correction with the works of teachers of secular letters, and wherever errors are found in excellent writers, let the corrector intrepidly set the mistakes right again, since the aforesaid writers should be thought of as having written their words in such manner as to have observed the grammatical rules which they had learned. Let the epistles of the Fathers too, the words and books of various writers, and the homilies and disputes of the faithful with heretics be read with great zeal, since they reveal the conflicting passages in the Sacred Scripture pleasantly and diligently, in order that with certain lamps properly lighted, as it were, in the Church of the Lord the whole may with His help shine clearly and brightly. If anything is discovered in them suitable for the expounding of the Sacred Scriptures, do not hesitate to associate it with the divine books, as we have done in the books of Kings. Many rather extensive remarks on the divine books are found to have been made by very excellent writers when opportunity offered in another work, and these remarks are of course properly accommodated to the sacred authority. Hence I beg you, when you have fully read not merely those codices which we leave you but also those which you will have the good fortune to discover, to finish more perfectly in Christ's name that which we have by no means been able to expound because of our scant reading.

I also beseech you who venture to make corrections to form the added letters so beautifully that they may be thought to be the product of scribes. It is surely inappropriate for anything unsightly to be found in this glorious work to offend the eyes of students hereafter. Consider, then, the nature of the cause entrusted to you, the serving of Christians, the guarding of the Church's treasure, the lighting of souls. And consequently take pains lest there be any residue of faultiness in its truth, of alteration in its purity, of erroneous letters in its correctness. . . .

The preceding book, completed with the aid of the Lord, contains, as you have seen, the principles of instruction for divine readings. It is comprised of thirty-three chapters, a number acknowledged to correspond with the age of the Lord when he offered eternal life to the world laid low by sin and granted rewards without end to those who believed. It is now the time for us to present in seven additional chapters the text of the second book, on secular readings; this number, continuously repeated throughout the weeks as they succeed one another, is ever being extended to the very end of the world. . . .

Since, then, our promises have, we believe been fulfilled with the Lord's aid according to the measure of our ability, we shall consider the reason why this regular succession of sciences has been extended as far as the stars; clearly, in order to lead from earthly affairs minds which have been devoted to secular wisdom and have been purified by training in the sciences and to place these minds in laudable fashion in the celestial regions created by God. . . .

But let us who sincerely long to enter heaven through intellectual exertions believe that God disposes all things in accordance with his will, and let us, as stated in Book I, reject and condemn the vanities of the present life and carefully investigate the books of the Divine Scriptures in their normal order, so that by referring all things to the glory of the Creator we may profitably assign to the celestial mysteries that which those men have seemed to seek vainly for the sake of mortal praise. And therefore, as the blessed Augustine and other very learned Fathers say, secular writings should not be spurned. It is proper, however, as the Scripture states, to "meditate in the (divine) law day and night," for, though a worthy knowledge of some matters is occasionally obtained from secular writings, this law is the source of eternal life. . . .

In these matters and others like them all wonder is inadequate, all human investigation fails, and yet these are the delights of Christians; this is the great consolation of those who sorrow, since so long as we ponder such things reverently and intently, through Christ's bounty we put the devil and his works to flight. These things, however, should be regarded with such admiration as to cause them to be believed immovably and indisputably; they should be admitted to be beyond our understanding in such a way that they may remain wholly fixed in our minds. For our senses may retire from such contemplations; our faith, however, is not permitted to waver and hesitate at all. But nevertheless, that which we cannot attain on this earth (although we have seen the Lord through his own indulgence) we unhesitatingly recognize, insofar as he has granted us the power and insofar as our slight ability allows; just as the Apostle says "Now we see through a glass, darkly, but then face to face."

23 / POPE GREGORY I THE GREAT: ECCLESIASTICAL LEADERSHIP

Pope Gregory the Great (590–604) delineated the program which the papacy was to follow in the succeeding three centuries. This involved the furtherance of the Christianization of Europe, an alliance with the Frankish monarchy, and the assertion of ecclesiastical leadership in all aspects of social, political, and moral life. Gregory, the fourth and last of the Latin Church fathers, exercised a strong influence on the shaping of the new European civilization.[40]

THE DUTIES OF A PRELATE

The conduct of a prelate ought so far to transcend the conduct of the people as the life of a shepherd is wont to exalt him above the flock. For one whose estimation is such that the people are called his flock is bound anxiously to consider what great necessity is laid upon him to maintain rectitude. It is necessary, then, that in thought he should be pure, in action chief; discreet in keeping silence, profitable in speech; a near neighbour to every one in sympthy, exalted above all in

[40] *Library of Nicene and Post-Nicene Fathers,* Vols. XII and XIII, transl. J. Barmby (New York: Christian Literature Co., 1895–1896), Vol. XII, pp. 9, 27, 176, Vol. XIII, pp. 105–6, Vol. XII, pp. 190, 205, 202–3, Vol. XIII, pp. 69, 23, 79.

contemplation; a familiar friend of good livers through humility, unbending against the vices of evildoers through zeal for righteousness; not relaxing in his care for what is inward from being occupied in outward things, nor neglecting to provide for outward things in his solicitude for what is inward. . . .

THE DUTIES OF SUBJECTS

. . . Subjects are to be admonished that they judge not rashly the lives of their superiors, if perchance they see them act blamably in anything, lest whence they rightly find fault with evil they thence be sunk by the impulse of elation to lower depth. They are to be admonished that, when they consider the faults of their superiors, they grow not too bold against them, but, if any of their deeds are exceedingly bad, so judge of them within themselves that, constrained by the fear of God, they still refuse not to bear the yoke of reverence under them. Which thing we shall show the better if we bring forward what David did. For when Saul the persecutor had entered into a cave to ease himself, David, who had so long suffered under his persecution, was within it with his men. And, when his men incited him to smite Saul, he cut them short with the reply, that he ought not to put forth his hand against the Lord's anointed. And yet he rose unperceived, and cut off the border of his robe. For what is signified by Saul but bad rulers, and what by David but good subjects? Saul's easing himself, then, means rulers extending the wickedness conceived in their hearts to works of woeful stench, and their showing the noisome thoughts within them by carrying them out into deeds. Yet him David was afraid to strike, because the pious minds of subjects, withholding themselves from the whole plague of backbiting, smite the life of their superiors with no sword of the tongue, even when they blame them for imperfection. And when through infirmity they can scarce refrain from speaking, however humbly, of some extreme and obvious evils in their superiors, they cut as it were silently the border of their robe; because, to wit, when, even though harmlessly and secretly, they derogate from the dignity of superiors, they disfigure as it were the garment of the king who is set over them; yet still they return to themselves, and blame themselves most vehemently for even the slightest defamation in speech. Hence it is also well written in that place, "Afterward David's heart smote him, because he had cut off the border of Saul's robe." For indeed the deeds of superiors are not to be smitten with the sword of the mouth, even when they are rightly judged to be worthy of blame. But if ever, even in the least, the tongue slips into censure of them, the heart must needs be depressed by the affliction of penitence, to the end that it may return to itself, and, when it has offended against the power set over it, may dread the judgment against itself of Him by whom it was set over it. For, when we offend against those who are set over us, we go against the ordinance of Him who set them over us. Whence also Moses, when he had become aware that the people complained against himself and Aaron, said, "For what are we? Not against us are your murmurings, but against the Lord."

THE POSITION OF THE PRIESTHOOD

. . . Ecclesiastical history also testifies that, when accusations in writing against bishops had been offered to the Prince Constantine of pious memory, he received indeed the bills of accusation, but, calling together the bishops who had been accused, he burnt before their eyes the bills which he had received, saying, "Ye are gods, constituted by the true God. Go, and settle your causes among you, for it is not fit that we should judge gods." Yet in this sentence, my pious Lord, he conferred more on himself by his humility than on them by the reverence paid to them. For before him there were pagan princes in the republic, who knew not the true God, but worshipped gods of wood and stone; and yet they paid the greatest honour to their priests. What wonder then if a Christian emperor should condescend to honour the priests of the true God, when pagan princes, as we have already said, knew how to bestow honour on priests who served gods of wood and stone?. . .

ATTITUDE TO THE EMPEROR

Gregory to Boniface, Deacon at Constantinople. . . .

We have though it right to deliver our sentence to no one, lest we should seem to do anything contrary to the order of our most clement lord the Emperor, or (which God forbid) in contempt of him. Wherefore let thy Love diligently represent the whole matter to his Piety, and steadily insist that the thing is altogether unlawful, altogether bad, altogether unjust, and greatly opposed to the sacred canons. And so may he not allow a sin of this sort to be introduced in his times to the prejudice of the Church. But represent to him what is contained in the judgment of the aforesaid late metropolitan on the business, and in what manner his decision had been confirmed by us, and endeavour so to act that our sentence, with an order from him, may be sent to those parts, to the end that we may be seen to have paid due deference to his Serenity, and to have corrected reasonably what had been presumptuously done amiss. In this affair pains must by all means be taken that, if it can be effected, he may contribute also his own order, enjoining the observance of what has been decided by us. For if this is done, all place for subornation hereafter will be shut out. Make haste, then, so to exercise thy vigilance, with the help of Almighty God, for abating these wrongs, that neither may the will of those who attempt perverse things obtain any advantage now against the ancient settlement of ecclesiastical usage, nor a nefarious proceeding gain ground for example afterwards. . . .

THE FRANKISH KINGDOM AND THE CHRISTIANIZATION OF EUROPE

1. Gregory to Childebert, King of the Franks.

As much as royal dignity is above that of other men, so much in truth does the high position of your kingdom excel that of the kingdoms of other nations. And yet to be a king is not extraordinary, there being others also; but to be a Catholic, which others are not counted worthy to be, this is enough. For as the splendour of a great lamp shines by the clearness of its light in the darkness of earth's night, so the clear light of your faith glitters and flashes amid the dark perfidy of other nations. Whatever the other kings glory in having you have. But they are in this regard exceedingly surpassed, because they have not the chief good thing which you have. In order, then, that they may be overcome in action as well as in faith, let your Excellence always show yourself kind to your subjects. And, if there are any things such as to offend your mind, punish them not without enquiry. For then you will the more please the King of kings, that is the Almighty Lord, if restraining your power, you feel that you may not do all that you can.

Now that you keep purity of faith both in mind and deed, the love that is in you of the blessed Peter, Prince of apostles, evidently shews, whose property has been so far well governed and preserved under the sway of your supremacy. . . .

Moreover we have sent to your Excellency Saint Peter's keys, containing a portion of his chains, to protect you from all evils, when hung on your neck.

2. Gregory to Theodoric and Theodebert, Brethren, Kings of the Franks.

Since Almighty God has adorned your kingdom with rectitude of faith, and has made it conspicuous among other nations by the purity of its Christian religion, we have conceived great expectations of you, that you will by all means desire that your subjects should be converted to that faith in virtue of which you are their kings and lords. This being so, it has come to our knowledge that the nation of the Angli is desirous, through the mercy of God, of being converted to the Christian faith, but that the priests in their neighbourhood neglect them, and are remiss in kindling their desires by their own exhortations. On this account therefore we have taken thought to send them the servant of God Augustine, the bearer of these presents, whose zeal and earnestness are well known to us, with other servants of God. And we have also charged them to take with them some priests from the neighbouring parts, with whom they may be able to ascertain the disposition of the Angli, and, as far as God may grant it to them, to aid their wishes by their admonition. Now, that they may have it in their power to show themselves efficient and capable in this business, we beseech your Excellency, greeting you with paternal charity, that these whom we have sent may be counted worthy to find the grace of your favour. And, since it is a matter of souls, let your power protect and aid them; that Almighty God, who knows that with devout mind and with all your heart you take an interest in His cause, may propitiously direct your causes, and after earthly dominion bring you to heavenly kingdoms. . . .

THE CONVERSION OF ENGLAND

To the Brethren Going to England.

Gregory, servant of the servants of God, to the servants of our Lord Jesus Christ.

Since it had been better not to have begun what is good than to return back from it when begun, you must, most beloved sons, fulfil the good work which with the help of the Lord you have begun. Let, then, neither the toil of the journey nor the tongues of evil-speaking men deter you; but with all instancy and all fervour go on with what under God's guidance you have commenced, knowing that great toil is followed by the glory of an eternal reward. Obey in all things humbly Augustine your provost, who is returning to you, whom we also appoint your abbot, knowing that whatever may be fulfilled in you through his admonition will in all ways profit your souls. May Almighty God protect you with His grace, and grant to me to see the fruit of your labour in the eternal country; that so, even though I cannot labour with you, I may be found together with you in the joy of the reward; for in truth I desire to labour. God keep you safe, most beloved sons. Given the tenth day before the Kalends of August [July 23], the fourteenth year of the Emperor our lord Mauricius Tiberius, the most pious Augustus, the thirteenth year of the consulship of our said lord, Indiction 14.

THE CLASSICAL HERITAGE

Gregory to Desiderius, Bishop of Gaul.

Many good things have been reported to us with regard to your pursuits, such joy arose in our heart that we could not bear to refuse what your Fraternity had requested to have granted to you. But it afterwards came to our ears, what we cannot mention without shame, that thy Fraternity is in the habit of expounding grammar to certain persons. This thing we took so much amiss, and so strongly disapproved it, that we changed what had been said before into groaning and sadness, since the praises of Christ cannot find room in one mouth with the praises of Jupiter.

THE NATURE OF RELIGIOUS IMAGES

Gregory to Serenus, Bishop of Massilia.

. . . We notify you that it has come to our ears that your Fraternity, seeing certain adorers of images, broke and threw down these same images in Churches. And we commend you indeed for your zeal against anything made with hands being an object of adoration; but we signify to you that you ought not to have broken these images. For pictorial representation is made use of in Churches for this reason; that such as are ignorant of letters may at least read by looking at the walls what they cannot read in books. Your Fraternity therefore should have both preserved the images and prohibited the people from adoration of them, to the end that both those who are ignorant of letters might have wherewith to gather a knowledge of the history, and that the people might by no means sin by adoration of a pictorial representation.

SEXUAL INTERCOURSE

. . . Lawful copulation of the flesh ought therefore to be for the purpose of offspring, not of pleasure; and intercourse of the flesh should be for the sake of producing children, and not a satisfaction of frailties. If, then, any one makes use of his wife not as seized by the desire of pleasure, but only for the sake of producing children, he certainly, with regard to entering the church or taking the mystery of the body and blood of the Lord, is to be left to his own judgment, since by us he ought not to be prohibited from receiving it who knows no burning though in the midst of fire. But, when not the love of producing offspring but pleasure dominates in the act of intercourse, married persons have something to mourn over in their intercourse. For holy preaching concedes them this, and yet in the very concession shakes the mind with fear. . . .

24 / THE KORAN: THE PRINCIPLES OF ISLAM

In the second half of the seventh century the old centers of Christianity on the eastern and southern shores of the Mediterranean were conquered by Arabic peoples united by the new religion of Islam, and in the early eighth century Visigothic Spain was also conquered by the Moslems. The expansion of Islam was a crippling blow to Byzantine power and it also had the effect of driving the centers of Latin Christianity away from the Mediterranean toward northern France, the Rhine Valley, and southern England. The Islamic world rapidly disintegrated as a political entity and several Moslem states emerged, but this new third civilization bordering on the Mediterranean was united by the Arabic language and the Islamic faith that had been propounded by the prophet Mohammed. The main doctrines of Islam are illustrated in the following selection from the Moslem bible, the Koran, which was supposedly dictated to Mohammed by the archangel Gabriel.[41]

> SAY: He is ONE God;
> God the Eternal.
> He begetteth not, nor is begotten;
> Nor is there one like unto Him.

. . . .

MAGNIFY the name of thy LORD, THE MOST HIGH,
Who created, and fashioned,
And decreed, and guided,

[41] Stanley Lane-Poole, *The Speech and Table-Talk of the Prophet Mohammed* (London: Macmillan and Co., 1882), pp. 32, 15, 129, 127, 137, 133, 140–1, 83.

Who bringeth forth the pasturage,
Then turneth it dry and brown.

We will make thee cry aloud, and thou shalt not forget,
Except what God pleaseth; verily He knoweth the plain and the hidden.
And we will speed thee to ease.
Admonish, therefore,—verily admonishing profiteth,—
Who so feareth God will mind;
And there will turn away from it only the wretch
Who shall broil upon the mighty fire;
And then shall neither die therein, nor live.
Happy is he who purifieth himself,
And remembereth the name of his Lord, and prayeth.

.   .   .   .

Mohammed is the Apostle of God, and those of his party are vehement
against the infidels, but compassionate to one another. Thou mayest
see them bowing down, worshipping, seeking grace from God, and
His approval; their tokens are on their faces—the traces of their
prostrations. This is their likeness in the Torah, and their likeness in
the Gospel, like a seed which putteth forth its stalk, and strengthen-
eth it, and it groweth stout, and standeth up upon its stem, rejoicing
the sowers—to anger unbelievers thereby. To those among them who
believe, and do the things that are right, God hath promised forgiveness and a mighty reward.

.   .   .   .

Well-pleased was God with the believers, when they sware fealty to
thee under the tree; and He knew what was in their hearts: therefore did He send down tranquility upon them, and rewarded them
with a victory near at hand,
And many spoils to take, for God is Mighty and Wise!
God promised you many spoils to take, and sped this for you; (and He
held back men's hands from you, that it might be a sign to the faithful, and that He might guide you on the straight way;)
And other spoils which ye could not take: but now hath God compassed it, for God is powerful over all.
If the unbelievers had fought against you, they would assuredly have
turned their backs; then would they have met with no protector or
helper.
This is God's way which prevailed before: and no changing wilt thou
find in God's way.

.   .   .   .

Fight in the path of God with those who fight with you;—but exceed not; verily God loveth not those who exceed.—And kill them wheresoever ye find them, and thrust them out from whence they thrust you out; for dissent is worse than slaughter; but fight them not at the Sacred Mosque, unless they fight you there: but if they fight you, then kill them: such is the reward of the infidels! But if they desist, then verily God is forgiving and merciful.—But fight them till there be no dissent, and the worship be only to God;—but, if they desist, then let there be no hostility save against the transgressors.

. . . .

Say: We believe in God, and what hath been sent down to thee, and what was sent down to Abraham, and Ishmael, and Isaac, and Jacob, and the tribes, and what was given to Moses, and to Jesus, and the prophets from their Lord,—we make no distinction between any of them,—and to Him are we resigned: and whoso desireth other than Resignation [Islām] for a religion, it shall certainly not be accepted from him, and in the life to come he shall be among the losers.

It is not righteousness that ye turn your face towards the east or the west, but righteousness is [in] him who believeth in God and the Last Day, and the Angels, and the Scripture, and the Prophets, and who giveth wealth for the love of God to his kinsfolk and to orphans and the needy and the son of the road and them that ask and for the freeing of slaves, and who is instant in prayer, and giveth the alms; and those who fulfil their covenant when they covenant, and the patient in adversity and affliction and in time of violence, these are they who are true, and these are they who fear God.

. . . .

He who slayeth a soul, unless it be for another soul, or for wickedness in the land, is as though he had slain all mankind; and he who saveth a soul alive is as though he had saved the lives of all mankind.

. . . .

The reward of those who war against God and His apostle, and work evil in the earth, is but that they shall be killed or crucified, or that their hands and feet shall be cut off alternately, or that they shall be banished from the land—that is their disgrace in this world, and in the next they shall have a mighty torment.

The man thief and the woman thief, cut off the hands of both in requittal for what they have done; an example from God, for God is mighty and wise.

. . . .

They who devour usury shall not rise again, save as he riseth whom the Devil hath smitten with his touch; that is because they say, "Selling is only like usury:" but God hath allowed selling, and forbidden usury.

. . . .

If ye fear that ye cannot do justice between orphans, then marry such women as are lawful to you, by twos or threes or fours; and if ye fear ye cannot be equitable, then only one, or what [slaves] your right hands possess: that is the chief thing—that ye be not unfair.

. . . .

Verily the Hour is assuredly coming: there is no doubt of it;—but most men do not believe.
And your Lord saith, "Call upon me;—I will hearken unto you: but as to those who are too puffed up for my service, they shall enter Hell in contempt."

. . . .

Verily we will help our apostles and those who believe, both in the life of this world and on the day when the witness shall stand forth;—
A day whereon the excuse of the wicked shall not profit them; but they shall have the curse and the abode of woe.
And of old gave we Moses the guidance, and the Children of Israel made we heirs of the Book,—a guidance and a warning to those who have understanding.
Be patient, therefore; verily the promise of God is true; and seek pardon for thy sins, and magnify the praises of thy Lord at eve and early morn.
Verily those who dispute about the signs of God, without proof reaching them, there is naught in their breasts but pride: and they shall not win. But seek refuge with God; verily, He heareth and seeth.

25 / BEDE: MEDIEVAL RELIGIOSITY

European religious thought of the medieval period is remarkable for the widespread belief in miracles and for very graphic conceptions of purgatory, heaven, and hell. The Christianization of European society, inaugurated by the work of the papacy and the Benedictine order, involved not only the spreading of the dogmas of the faith but also these more popular kinds of religious conceptions, which were much easier for ordinary people to understand than Augustinian theology, and which therefore occupied a central place in medieval piety. Bede, the learned eighth-century English scholar, teacher, and historian, describes this kind of religiosity.[42]

At this time a memorable miracle, and like to those of former days, was wrought in Britain; for, to the end that the living might be saved from the death of the soul, a certain person, who had been some time dead, rose again to life, and related many remarkable things he had seen; some of which I have thought fit here briefly to take notice of.

There was a master of a family in that district of the Northumbrians which is called Cunningham, who led a religious life, as did also all that belonged to him. This man fell sick, and his distemper daily increasing, being brought to extremity, he died in the beginning of the night; but in the morning early he suddenly came to life again, and sat up, upon which all those that sat about the body weeping fled away in a great fright: only his wife, who loved him best, though in a great consternation and trembling, remained with him. He, comforting her, said, "Fear not, for I am now truly risen from death, and permitted again to live among men; however, I am not to live hereafter as I was wont, but from henceforward after a very different manner."

Then rising immediately, he repaired to the oratory of the little town and, continuing in prayer till day, immediately divided all his substance into three parts, one whereof he gave to his wife, another to his children, and the third, belonging to himself, he instantly distributed among the poor. Not long after he repaired to the monastery of Melrose, which is almost inclosed by the winding of the river Tweed, and having been shaven, went into a private dwelling which the abbot had provided, where he continued till the day of his death in such extraordinary contrition of mind and body that, though his tongue had been silent, his life declared that he had seen many things, either to be dreaded or coveted, which others knew nothing of.

Thus he related what he had seen: "He that led me had a shining countenance and a bright garment, and we went on silently, as I thought, towards the northeast. Walking on, we came to a vale of great breadth and depth, but of infinite length; on the left it appeared full of dreadful flames; the other side was no less horrid for violent

---

[42] Bede, *Ecclesiastical History of England*, transl. in J. H. Robinson, *Readings in European History* (Boston: Ginn & Co., 1904), Vol. I, pp. 93–7.

hail and cold snow flying in all directions; both places were full of men's souls, which seemed by turns to be tossed from one side to the other, as it were by a violent storm; for when the wretches could no longer endure the excess of heat, they leaped into the middle of the cutting cold; and finding no rest there, they leaped back again into the middle of the unquenchable flames.

"Now whereas an innumerable multitude of deformed spirits were thus alternately tormented far and near, as far as could be seen, without any intermission, I began to think that this perhaps might be hell, of whose intolerable flames I had often heard talk. My guide, who went before me, answered to my thought, saying, 'Do not believe so, for this is not hell, as you imagine.'

"When he had conducted me, much frightened with that horrid spectacle, by degrees, to the farther end, on a sudden I saw the place begin to grow dusk and filled with darkness. When I came into it, the darkness, by degrees, grew so thick that I could see nothing besides it and the shape and garment of him that led me. As we went on through the shades of night, on a sudden there appeared before us frequent globes of black flames, rising, as it were, out of a great pit, and falling back again into the same.

"When I had been conducted thither, my leader suddenly vanished, and left me alone in the midst of darkness and this horrid vision, whilst those same globes of fire, without intermission, at one time flew up and at another fell back into the bottom of the abyss; and I observed that all the flames, as they ascended, were full of human souls, which, like sparks flying up with smoke, were sometimes thrown on high, and again, when the vapor of the fire ceased, dropped down into the depth below. Moreover, an insufferable stench came forth with the vapors, and filled all those dark places.

"Having stood there a long time in much dread, not knowing what to do, which way to turn, or what end I might expect, on a sudden I heard behind me the noise of a most hideous and wretched lamentation, and at the same time a loud laughing, as of a rude multitude insulting captured enemies. When that noise, growing plainer, came up to me, I observed a gang of evil spirits dragging the howling and lamenting souls of men into the midst of the darkness, whilst they themselves laughed and rejoiced.

"Among those men, as I could discern, there was one shorn like a clergyman, also a layman, and a woman. The evil spirits that dragged them went down into the midst of the burning pit; and as they went down deeper, I could no longer distinguish between the lamentation of the men and the laughing of the devils, yet I still had a confused sound in my ears.

"In the meantime some of the dark spirits ascended from that flaming abyss, and, running forward, beset me on all sides, and much perplexed me with their glaring eyes and the stifling fire which proceeded from their mouths and nostrils; and they threatened to lay hold on me with burning tongs, which they had in their hands; yet they durst not touch me, though they frightened me. Being thus on all sides inclosed with enemies and darkness, and looking about on every side for assistance, there appeared behind me, on the way that I came, as it were, the brightness of a star shining amidst the darkness, which increased by degrees, and came rapidly towards me: when it drew near, all those evil spirits that had sought to carry me away with their tongs dispersed and fled.

"He whose approach put them to flight was the same that had led me before; who, turning then towards the right, began to lead me, as it were, towards the southeast, and having soon brought me out of the darkness, conducted me into an atmosphere of clear light.

"While he thus led me in open light, I saw a vast wall before us, the length of height of which, in every direction, seemed to be altogether boundless. I began to wonder why we went up to the wall, seeing no door, window, or path through it. When we came to the wall, we were presently, I know not by what means, on the top of it, and within it was a vast and beautiful field, so full of fragrant flowers that the odor of its delightful sweetness immediately dispelled the stench of the dark furnace, which had penetrated me through and through.

"So great was the light in this place that it seemed to exceed the brightness of the day, or of the sun in its meridian height. In this field were innumerable assemblies of men in white and many companies seated together rejoicing. As he led me through the midst of these happy people, I began to think that this might, perhaps, be the kingdom of heaven, of which I had often heard so much. He answered to my thought, saying, 'This is not kingdom of heaven, as you imagine.'

"When we had passed those mansions of blessed souls and gone farther on, I discovered before me a much more beautiful light, and heard therein sweet voices of persons singing; and so wonderful a fragrancy proceeded from the place that the other, which I had before thought most delicious, then seemed to me but very indifferent, even as that extraordinary brightness of the flowery field, compared with this, appeared mean and inconsiderable. When I began to hope we should enter that delightful place, my guide on a sudden stood still; and then, turning round, led me back by the way we came.

"When we returned to those joyful mansions of the souls in white, he said to me, 'Do you know what all these things are which you have seen?' I answered that I did not; and then he replied, "That vale you saw, so dreadful for its consuming flames and cutting cold, is the place in which the souls of those are tried and punished who, delaying to confess and amend their crimes, at length have recourse to repentance at the point of death, and so depart this life; but nevertheless because they, even at their death, confessed and repented, they shall all be received into the kingdom of heaven at the day of judgment by the prayers, alms, and fasting of the living, and more especially by masses.

" 'That fiery and stinking pit which you saw is the mouth of hell, into which whosoever falls shall never be delivered to all eternity. This flowery place, in which you see these most beautiful young people, so bright and gay, is that into which the souls of those are received who depart the body in good works, but who are not so perfect as to deserve to be immediately admitted into the kingdom of heaven; yet they shall all, at the day of judgment, see Christ and partake of the joys of his kingdom; for whoever are perfect in thought, word, and deed, as soon as they depart the body immediately enter into the kingdom of heaven; in the neighborhood whereof that place is, where you heard the sound of sweet singing, with the fragrant odor and bright light.

" 'As for you, who are now to return to your body and live among men again, if you will endeavor nicely to watch your actions, and to direct your speech and behavior in righteousness and simplicity, you shall, after death, have a place of residence among these joyful troops of blessed souls; for when I left you for a while, it was to know how you were to be disposed of.' When he had said this to me I much abhorred returning to my body, being delighted with the sweetness and beauty of the place I beheld and with the company of those I saw in it. However, I durst not ask him any questions; but in the meantime, on a sudden, I found myself alive among men."

26 / THE LIFE OF ST. STURMI: ST. BONIFACE AND THE CONVERSION OF GERMANY

The conversion of the Anglo-Saxons to the Roman faith, which Gregory the Great had inaugurated, had far-reaching results which not even that far-seeing pope could envision. In the

seventh and early eighth centuries the English Benedictine mon-
asteries had the best schools in Europe, and in the second, third,
and fourth decades of the eighth century the English Benedictine
missionary St. Boniface (originally Wynfrith) carried on the work
which won him the title of apostle to the Germans. The great
abbeys established in Germany by Boniface and his English
companions became the nucleus of a new German Church, and
Boniface, working under the close direction of the papacy and
with the support of the Carolingians, the new Frankish rulers,
became the first archbishop of Mainz. This account from the Life
of St. Sturmi, *one of Boniface's disciples, describes the founding*
of Fulda Abbey, which became one of the greatest monasteries
in Europe with a reputation for both wealth and learning. The
selection also illustrates the literary form of the saint's life;
hagiography was by far the most popular literary form in West-
ern Europe from the sixth century to the end of the eleventh.[43]

[The holy and venerable archbishop Boniface came to Bavaria, and
turned many people to the gospel of Christ. Among them a certain
boy, Sturmi, son of noble and Christian parents, followed the teaching
of Boniface and was ordained priest.] For almost three years he fulfilled the duties of the priesthood, preaching and baptizing among
the people. Then by the inspiration of God the purpose came into his
soul to chasten himself by the straiter life and the hardships of the
wilderness. He sought counsel thereupon from Boniface—his master
in the spirit,—who, when he understood Sturmi, knew that this purpose was inspired of God and rejoiced that God had designed to lead
him by his grace. He gave Sturmi two companions, and when he had
prayed and blessed them all he said: "Go forth into that solitude which
is called Bochonia and seek a place meet for the servants of God to
dwell in. For God is able to prepare for his servants a place in the
wilderness."

And so those three went forth into the wilderness and entered into
places solitary and rough, and saw almost nothing but heaven and
earth and great trees; and they prayed Christ fervently that he would
direct their feet in the path of peace. On the third day they came to
the place which even to this day is called Hersfeld; and when they
had seen and explored the region round about, they asked Christ

[43] *Vita Sancti Sturmis abbatis,* MGH Scriptores, Vol. II, p. 367 ff., transl. in
J. H. Robinson, *Readings in European History* (Boston: Ginn & Co., 1904), Vol. I,
pp. 107–11.

that the place might be blest to the dwellers therein. On the very spot where the monastery now stands they built poor huts of the bark of trees. There they tarried many days, serving God with holy fasts and watching and prayer. . . .

Then after some time spent in holy meditation Sturmi returned to the bishop, and described the lay of the land and the course of the streams, and the hills and valleys. . . . Boniface heard him attentively, and answered: "I fear to have you dwell in this place which ye have found because a barbarous race lives close by, for, as thou knowest, the fell Saxons are near at hand. Wherefore seek a dwelling in the wilderness farther away and higher up the stream, where ye may remain without danger."

Then the holy man Sturmi returned to his companions. With two brethren he entered a boat and traveled along the river Fulda, spying out the land, but they found no place which pleased them. So Sturmi went again to Boniface and said, "For many days did we sail along the river Fulda, but we found nothing that we would dare to praise to you." And the holy bishop saw that God had not yet revealed the place which he had chosen.

Sturmi returned to the cell which had now been built in a place above Hersfeld. Here he saluted the brethren and reported to them what the holy bishop had counseled. Then after resting a little he mounted his ass and set forth alone, commending his journey to Christ, who is the way, the truth, and the life. All alone, sitting upon his ass, he began his journey through the vast places of the wilderness. He eagerly explored the region and observed with quick eye the mountains and the hills and the plains, the springs and torrents and rivers. With psalms always upon his lips, he prayed to God with groaning, his soul lifted up to heaven. And wherever night found him, there he rested; and he hewed wood with the sword which he bore in his hand, and laid it in a circle, and set it on fire to protect his ass, lest the wild beasts which were there in great numbers might devour him. For himself, he made on his forehead the sign of the cross of Christ, in the name of God, and rested in safety. . . .

Once as he had paused at sunset, and was busied with preparing for the night, he heard a sound as of a living creature, but whether it was man or beast he knew not. . . . Then because the man of God did not wish to cry out, he struck a hollow tree with the sword he bore in his hand. And verily when the man had heard the sound of the blow he came thither, and spoke to Sturmi. And when the man of God asked him whence he came, he answered that he came from Wetteran and led in his hand the horse of Ortis, his lord. So they talked together and stayed there together that night. Now the man had a full acquaintance with the solitudes of the forest, and when the man of

God made known to him what was in his mind and what he would fain do, he began to tell him the names of the places, and to show him how the torrents and springs did flow. . . . At sunrise they blessed each the other, and straightway the secular man went upon his way to Grapfelt. . . .

[And Sturmi also went on his way till he reached the torrent that even to this day is called Grezzibach.] He saw how the land lay, and what was the nature of the soil, and he tarried there a little space. And then he went back a little way and came to the place already made ready and blessed by God, even the place where the holy monastery [of Fulda] now stands. When he had come thither straightway the holy man Sturmi was filled with exceeding great joy, for he knew that through the merits and prayers of the holy bishop Boniface the place had been revealed to him by God.

Then on the second day the man of God came again to Hersfeld and found his brethren there calling upon God with fervent prayers. He told them of the place he had found and bade them make ready to go thither with him. But Sturmi went straightway to the holy bishop Boniface to tell him how he had found a place for the brethren to dwell in. Together they rejoiced and gave God thanks and held sweet converse about the life and conversation of monks. Then did the bishop let Sturmi go back to his wilderness, while he went to the palace of Carloman, the king, to gain from him a grant of the place Sturmi had chosen.

When Boniface came before the king, he said to him: "We have found in the wilderness called Bochonia, beside the river named Fulda, a place meet for the servants of God to dwell in, where before us no man has dwelt. It is under your sway, and we do beg of your beneficence to give us this place, so that we may be enabled to serve God under your protection." . . . Then did the king before all the lords of his palace give over to the bishop the place he had asked for, saying, "This place which thou seekest on the bank of the river Fulda I give over whole and entire from my law to the law of God—from that place in all directions in a circle four thousand paces toward east and west and north and south, we shall hold the region."

Then the king gave command that a charter be written to this end, and he sealed it with his own hand.

In the year of the incarnation of Christ 744, in the first month, the twelfth day of the month, while the brothers Carloman and Pippin were reigning over the Frankish people, did Sturmi arise, in the name of God, and with seven brethren he did go to the place where now the monastery stands. They prayed to the Lord Christ that he would ever protect and defend them by his power; and, serving God in sacred psalms and in fasts, vigils, and prayers by day and by night, they did busy themselves cutting down the forests and clearing the ground by their own labor so far as strength was given them.

When two months had passed by, and a multitude of men were gathered together, the reverend archbishop Boniface came unto them; and when he looked and saw the convenience and great resources of the place, he exulted in the Holy Spirit, giving thanks and praising Christ because he had deigned to bestow upon his servants such a lodge in the wilderness. . . .

And the brethren decided to follow the rule of the holy father Benedict. They spent many years in holy pursuits; and the number of brethren in the monastery grew greater, for many men gave themselves and all that they had to serve God there. And the holy bishop was zealous to visit them from time to time; and he had compassion upon their poverty, and gave them some lands to furnish them necessary food.

27 / THE DONATION OF CONSTANTINE

The great strides made by Benedictine scholars and missionaries, working under papal direction, toward the achievement of the Christianization of Europe, and the assistance which the new Carolingian dynasty sought from Rome to sanction their seizure of the Frankish throne in the early 750's, encouraged the papacy to assert fully its claims to authority over Europe. This assertion took the form of the most famous forgery in history, the Donation of Constantine, by which the emperor Constantine was supposed to have resigned his crown and the empire into the hands of Pope Sylvester I as compensation for being cured of leprosy by the pope. It was common practice in the early Middle Ages, given the Germanic legal conception that old law was the best law, to assert new claims through a forged document purporting to give the prescriptive rights of ancient law and practice as support for the new aim. The ideology of the Donation of Constantine can be traced back to the Gelasian doctrine and its justifying historical account to the legend of St. Sylvester, which was known at least as early as the time of Gregory of Tours (see No. 16) and probably originated in the late fifth century, contemporaneous with the promulgation of the Gelasian doctrine. The form in which the Donation comes down to us dates probably from the mid-ninth century, but the original version was probably drafted in the papal court in the early 750's for use in negotiations with the Frankish king Pippin III, who confirmed it. The Donation was branded a forgery about 1000 A.D. by the German emperor Otto III, acting on the advice of Pope Sylvester II (the great French scholar Gerbert of Aurillac), and its genuineness was again questioned in the fourteenth century, but it was not proved a forgery until the mid-fifteenth century. The Donation became a powerful weapon in the spiritual armory of the medieval papacy and the foundation of papal ideology. Its existence was greatly regretted by kings, heretics, and even by some churchmen, but, with the exceptions noted, it was accepted as a genuine document until the Renaissance scholar Lorenzo Valla proved that it was fraudulent seven centuries after its manufacture.[44]

I

In the name of the sacred and indivisible Trinity of Father, Son, and Holy Spirit. The emperor in Christ Jesus, one Member of the Holy Trinity, our Savior and our Lord God, Caesar Flavius Constantine, faithful, gentle, supreme, beneficent, lord of the Alemannians, Goths, Sarmatians, Germans, Britains, Huns, pious, fortunate victorious, triumphant, and always august, wishes grace, peace, love, joy, long-suffering, and mercy from omnipotent God the Father, His Son, Jesus Christ, and the Holy Spirit to the most holy and blessed father of fathers Sylvester, bishop of the city of Rome and pope, and to all his successors who shall ever sit on the seat of St. Peter until the end of time, and to all the most reverend and righteous catholic bishops in the world, who are subject to the sacrosanct Roman church, now and for all the times to come, because of this, our imperial constitution.

II

Our most gracious serenity has been zealous to preserve those things which our Savior and Redeemer, the Lord Jesus Christ, Son of the most High Father, has most wonderfully deemed worthy to perform through His sacred apostles Peter and Paul, and through our father Sylvester,

[44] C. Mirbt, ed. *Quellen zur Geschichte des Papsttums* (Tübingen: J. C. B. Mohr (Paul Siebeck), 1924), pp. 107–12. By permission of J. C. B. Mohr (Paul Siebeck).

highest pontiff and universal pope. To this end have we set them forth
clearly in the charter of this our imperial decree for the information
of all the peoples in the whole world. The first of these is our creed,
which we were taught by the most blessed prelate, our father and confessor Sylvester, the universal pope. This we confess from the bottom
of our heart so that we might teach it to all of you and so, at length,
announce the mercy of God which has been poured down upon us.

III

For we wish you to know, as we have set forth earlier in our holy
legislative decree, that we have abandoned the worship of idols, hand-
made images both deaf and dumb, diabolical contrivances, and all
the displays of Satan; and that we have joined the pure faith of the
Christians, which is the true light and perpetual life. We believe in
that which we learned from our great and saintly father and teacher,
the aforesaid pontiff Sylvester: in God the Father, omnipotent creator
of heaven and earth, of all things visible and invisible, and in Jesus
Christ, His only Son, our Lord God, by Whom all things were created,
and in the Holy Spirit, Lord and life-giver to all creation. We confess
these, the Father, Son, and Holy Spirit: that They are in perfect
Trinity, and they have fulness of divinity and unity of power. The
Father is God, the Son is God, the Holy Spirit is God, and these Three
are One in Jesus Christ. . . .

V

For this is our orthodox creed, made known to us by our most
blessed father Sylvester, the supreme pontiff. Therefore do we exhort
all peoples and nations to hold this faith, to cherish it, and to attain
the grace of baptism in the name of the Holy Trinity. We exhort them
adore with devout hearts the Lord Jesus Christ, our Savior, Who, with
the Father and the Holy Spirit, lives and reigns through infinite ages,
Whom Sylvester, our most blessed father, the universal pontiff,
preaches.

VI

For He Himself, our Lord God, took pity on me, a sinner. He sent
His blessed apostles to visit us, and caused the light of His splendor
to shine upon us. Do ye rejoice that I, withdrawn from the shadows,
have arrived at the true light and the perception of truth. For when a
powerful and filthy leprosy invaded all the flesh of my body, I was
treated by many doctors who had gathered at my bedside and I gained

health from none of them. Then the priests of the Capitol came and said that I ought to have a font built on the Capitol and fill it with the blood of innocent babes. They said that I might be cleansed in that warm bath. And, in accordance with their words, many innocent babes were gathered, because the sacrilegious pagan priests wished them to be slaughtered and the font to be filled with their blood. But our serenity perceived the tears of their mothers and straightway I was horrified at my crime. We, taking pity on them, ordered that their own sons be restored to them. We gave them vehicles and gifts, and sent them off, rejoicing, to their homes.

VII

When that same day had passed, the silence of night came upon us and the time for sleep arrived. Then came the apostles Peter and Paul, saying to me: "Since you have put an end to your crimes, and have shuddered at the shedding of innocent blood, we have been sent by Christ, our Lord God, to give you counsel so that you may recover your health. Hear therefore our warnings and do whatever we indicate to you. Sylvester, the bishop of the city of Rome, fleeing with his clergy from your persecutions to Mount Serapte, has a hiding-place there in the caverns of stone. He, when you have brought him to you, shall show you a pool of piety. When he has dipped you in this pool for the third time, all the virulence of your leprosy shall desert you. When this has been done, make this return to your Savior: have all the churches in the whole world rebuilt at your command. Moreover, purify yourself in this way: abandon all the superstition of idolatry, so that you may adore and cherish the living and true God, and devote yourself to doing His will."

VIII

Immediately arising from sleep, I did what I had been advised to do by the holy apostles. When I had summoned the aforesaid excellent and gracious father, our enlightener Sylvester, the universal pope, I told him all that had been taught me by the holy apostles, and asked him who were those gods Peter and Paul? He answered that they were not really called gods, but the apostles of our Savior, the Lord Jesus Christ. And we began again to ask this same most blessed pope whether he had a clear image of these apostles so that we might learn from the picture if they were the same as those whom the revelation had shown to us. Then the same venerable father ordered his deacon to show the images of those apostles to us. When I had looked at them and had recognized, represented in the images, those same countenances which I had seen in my dream, I, with a loud voice, confessed before all my satraps that the countenances were those which I had seen in my dreams.

IX

Hereupon, this same most blessed Sylvester, our father, the bishop of the city of Rome, imposed a period of penance upon us, to be spent inside our Lateran Palace, and in a hairshirt, in order that we might obtain by vigils, fasts, tears, and prayers, pardon from the Lord God, our Savior Jesus Christ for all those things which were impiously and unjustly done by us. Then, through the laying on of hands of the clergy, I came even unto the bishop himself, and there renouncing the displays of Satan, his works, and all his hand-made idols, I, of my own free will, proclaimed before all the people that I believed in God the Father, the omnipotent creator of heaven and earth, of all things visible and invisible, and in Jesus Christ His only Son, our Lord, Who was born of the Holy Spirit and the Virgin Mary. When the font had been blessed, the wave of salvation purified me through triple immersion. For there, after I had been placed at the bottom of the font, I saw with my own eyes a hand from Heaven touching me. Know that I, arising clean from the font, was cleansed of all the squalor of leprosy. When I had been lifted from the venerable font and dressed in pure white raiment, the bishop applied the unction of holy oil to me as the sign of the seven-fold Holy Spirit, and he traced the standard of the Holy Cross on my forehead saying: "God marks you with the seal of His faith in the name of the Father, and of the Son, and of the Holy Spirit, in token of your faith." All the clergy responded: "Amen." The bishop added: "Peace be with you." . . .

XI

And when, with the blessed Sylvester as my teacher, I had learned that I had been restored to full health through the kindness of St. Peter himself, we, together with all the people of Rome who are subject to the glory of our rule, considered it appropriate that just as Peter seems to have been constituted as the vicar of the Son of God on earth, in the same way the pontiffs, who represent the prince of the apostles, should obtain a greater power of supremacy than that which the earthly beneficence of our serenity is seen to have. We thought that this should be conceded to him from us and from our empire, and that we should choose this same prince of the apostles, or his vicars, to be our constant intercessors with God. We decreed that his sacrosanct Roman church should be honored with veneration to the extent of our power, and that the most sacred seat of St. Peter is gloriously exalted above our empire and earthly throne. We gave it imperial power, the dignity of glory, strength, and honor.

XII

We ordain and decree that he should have dominion over the four principal dioceses of Antioch, Alexandria, Constantinople, and Jerusalem, as well as over all the churches of God in the world. And the pontiff who, for the time being, is head of the sacrosanct Roman church is more exalted than and chief of all the priests in the whole world. All those things which pertain to the worship of God or the stability of the Christian faith are to be administered according to his judgment. It is just indeed that the holy law should have the source of its dominion where the founder of holy laws, our Savior, ordered St. Peter to build the cathedral of the apostles; where the latter, holding the yoke of the cross, drained the cup of blessed death, and appeared as the imitator of his Lord and Master. It is just that the people should bend their necks in the confession of the name of Christ where their teacher, St. Paul the Apostle, with neck bent for Christ, was crowned with martyrdom. Let them, until the end of time, seek their teacher there, where the holy corpse of their teacher rests. Let them, prone and with humility, perform the service of the Heavenly King, our God and Savior Jesus Christ, there where the haughty used to serve under the rule of an earthly king.

XIII

Meanwhile, we want all the people of every race and nation through the whole world to know that we have built, within our Lateran Palace, a church and a baptistry to this same Savior, our Lord God, Jesus Christ. Know that we have carried on our own shoulders, from its foundations, twelve baskets loaded with earth, in accordance with the number of the twelve apostles. We order that this church be spoken of, cherished, venerated, and preached as the source and summit of all churches in the whole world, just as we have ordained through our other imperial decrees. We have also built the churches of St. Peter and St. Paul, chiefs of the apostles, which we have enriched with gold and silver. In these churches we have constructed caskets of electrum, against which no force of the elements can prevail, and we have placed their bodies in them with great ceremony. We have also placed a cross of the purest gold and precious jewels on each of their caskets, and we have fastened them with golden nails. We have conferred estates upon these churches so that they might be provided with lights, and we have enriched them with various objects. Through our sacred imperial decrees we have given them our gift of land in the east and west, and in the northern and southern regions: namely in Judaea, Greece, Asia, Thrace, Africa, Italy, and the various islands. This grant is made on the condition that all estates be administered by the hand of our most blessed father Pope Sylvester and his successors.

XIV

Let all the peoples and nations of the whole world rejoice with us as we exhort you all to give endless thanks to our Lord and Savior Jesus Christ. For He Who, visiting us through His holy apostles, made us worthy to receive the holy sacrament of baptism and bodily health, is God in Heaven above and on earth below. In return for this we do concede, and by this gift confer our imperial Lateran Palace, which excels all other palaces in the world, upon these same holy apostles, my masters, St. Peter and St. Paul, and through them upon the blessed Sylvester, our father, and upon all the succeeding popes, who shall ever sit upon the throne of Peter even until the end of the world. We give them next a diadem, that is the crown of our head; a miter; a shoulder band, that is, the collar which usually surrounds our imperial head; a purple mantle, a scarlet tunic, and all the other imperial garments; the rank of the leaders of the imperial cavalry. We give them also the imperial sceptre, spears, standards, banners, various other imperial ornaments, all the advantage of our high imperial rank, and the glory of our power.

XV

We decree that these most reverend men in the various orders of clergy which serve the Roman church, shall have the same advantage, distinction, power, and excellence, by the glory of which our most illustrious senate is adorned. We command that they are to be made patricians and consuls, and are to be decorated with all other imperial dignities. We decree that the clergy of the sacrosanct Roman church be adorned in the same way as the imperial army; and even as the imperial power is embellished with different offices, namely those of chamberlain, doorkeeper, and watchman, so do we wish the holy Roman church to be adorned. . . . Before all other things, we give to our most blessed father Sylvester, bishop of the city of Rome, and pope, and to all the most blessed pontiffs who shall ever follow him, the right to receive into the ranks of the monastic clergy any member of our senate who may, of his own choice, wish to become a clerk. But let no one presume to act haughtily on this account.

XVI

We have also decreed that our most venerable father Sylvester, supreme pontiff, and all his successors, ought to wear the diadem, that is, the crown of purest gold and jewels, which we have given him from off of our own head, for the glory of God and the honor of St. Peter. The most holy pope, however, did not at all wish to use the golden crown above the clerical crown which he wore for the glory of St. Peter. But we, with our own hands, placed a miter of gleaming splendor on his head in token of the glorious resurrection of our Lord. Then, holding the bridle of his horse, we did him the office of groom out of reverence for St. Peter and decreed that all succeeding pontiffs, and they alone, could use that miter in processions.

XVII

Behold, in imitation of our power, in order that the supreme pontificate should not deteriorate, but should rather be adorned with more power and glory than the earthly empire, we do give and relinquish to the power and dominion of the oft-mentioned most blessed pontiff, our father Sylvester, the universal pope, and to his successors, our palace, as we have said before, the city of Rome, all the provinces, districts, and cities of Italy and the western regions. We make this inviolable gift, through this our sacred imperial charter, and decree that all these things shall permanently remain within the holy Roman church.

XVIII

Therefore have we deemed it fitting to have our empire and the power of our kingdom transferred to the eastern regions; to have a city erected in our name in the most suitable spot in the province of Byzantium; and to have our empire established there. For it is not right that the earthly ruler should have his power in that place where the supreme priest and head of the Christian religion has been established by the heavenly Ruler.

XIX

We do decree that all these things which we have ordained and confirmed through this our imperial charter, and through other imperial decrees, shall remain uninjured and unshaken even unto the end of the world. Therefore, before the living God, Who commanded us to rule, and before His terrible tribunal, we do swear by this imperial constitution that all succeeding emperors, all nobles, satraps, the most illustrious senate, and all people in the whole world who are now, ever were, or ever will be subject to our rule, are forbidden to oppose, destroy, or diminish in any way these things, which through our imperial sanction, have been granted to the sacrosanct Roman church and to all its pontiffs. If anyone, which we do not believe possible, scorns or despises this decree, he shall be bound by eternal damnation. He shall know that the holy chiefs of the apostles of God, Peter and Paul, will oppose him in the present and future life, and that having been burned in deepest Hell, he shall perish with the devil and all impious men.

XX

We, confirming it with our own hands, placed the page of this our imperial decree above the venerable body of St. Peter, the chief of the apostles. We promised this same apostle of God that we would leave instruction for its preservation in our commands to all succeeding emperors. Then we did give it into the eternal and happy possession of our most blessed father, Sylvester, supreme pontiff and universal pope, and, through him, to all succeeding pontiffs. May the Lord God and our Savior Jesus Christ approve.

The imperial subscription: May the Divinity preserve you, O most holy and blessed fathers, for many years.

Given at Rome on the third day before the Kalends of April [March 30], in the fourth consulship of our master the august Flavius Constantine, and in that of Gallicanus, both very illustrious men.

28 / CHARLEMAGNE AND THE CHRISTIAN EMPIRE

The papacy, in its great expectation of establishing a Christian world system with Roman hegemony, was immediately disappointed. The leadership of the new European civilization was rapidly taken up by the Frankish king Charlemagne (774–814). With his military prowess, his quasi-sacred position as the anointed of the Lord, and his eagerness to support the educational and devotional work of the Frankish churchmen, Charles the Great possessed all the characteristics which both churchmen and laymen of the period admired. Not even a desperate attempt by the pope on Christmas day of 800 to place Charlemagne in his debt by crowning him emperor of the Romans was able to detract from Charles' supreme position in Western Europe. In the following selections are illustrated the major aspects of Charlemagne's leadership: the imposing personality of the king revealed in his biography by his secretary, the monastic scholar Einhard, who, while he was not above lifting an occasional phrase from Suetonius' Lives of the Twelve Caesars, nevertheless was moved by admiration for his master to write the best early medieval royal life (A); [45] the ideology of Carolingian rule—the idea of the Christian empire—propounded by the English scholar Alcuin, whom Charlemagne had brought to his court as a sort of chief minister for ecclesiastical and educational affairs, and who played the leading role in the heightened respect for the classical heritage which is sometimes called the Carolingian Renaissance (B); [46] and finally Charlemagne's capitularies (decrees) directing improvements in government, economy, and the Church, revealing for the first time a Germanic king with sufficient intelligence and education to attempt a conscious policy of social melioration (C). [47]

A. EINHARD: LIFE OF CHARLEMAGNE

Chapter 4

I pass by the birth, infancy, and childhood of Karl, because there is no written record concerning them, nor is any one now known to survive who can speak from personal knowledge. I have therefore thought it foolish to write about them, and have given my attention to relating and explaining those actions, habits, and other portions of his

[45] Life of the Emperor Karl the Great by Eginhard, transl. W. Glaister, (London: George Bell & Sons, 1877), pp. 25–6, 26–31, 32–4, 35–7, 39–42, 43–6, 51–2, 53, 55, 56–7, 59–63, 64–85, 85–90.

[46] Monumenta Germaniae Historica, Epistolarum Karolini Aevi, Vol. II, E. Duemmler, ed. (Berlin: Weidmann, 1895), pp. 136–8, 556, 205–9, 288–9, 292–3.

[47] J. H. Robinson, Readings in European History (Boston: Ginn & Co., 1904), Vol. I, pp. 137–45.

life which are not matters of uncertainty; first narrating his military exploits at home and abroad, then his domestic habits and occupations, then his administration of the kingdom, and lastly, about his death, omitting nothing that is worthy and necessary to be narrated.

Chapter 5

Karl was engaged in many wars. The first he undertook was the Aquitanian, because there seemed to be good hope of quickly bringing it to an end. It had been begun by his father, but not finished. . . .

Chapter 6

When the war was finished and affairs settled in Aquitaine—his partner in the government being now dead—Karl was induced by the prayer and entreaty of Adrian, Bishop of the city of Rome, to undertake a war against the Lombards. . . .

Chapter 7

The Lombard war being thus finished, the Saxon war, which seemed for the time to have been neglected, was again renewed. No war undertaken by the Franks was so protracted or so fierce, or so full of toil and hardship, since the Saxons, like most of the nations inhabiting Germany, were naturally brave, and being addicted to heathenism, were hostile to our religion, and thought it no disgrace to dishonour divine laws or violate human ones.

Causes, too, daily arose which contributed to disturb the peace. The boundaries of their country and ours were in the open and almost everywhere contiguous. It was only in a few places that large forests, or ranges of mountains coming between, formed a well-defined and natural boundary line to both countries. On the borders therefore, plundering, burning, and bloodshed never ceased.

The Franks were so enraged at this that they judged it now to be no longer a matter of making reprisals, but so important that it warranted them in undertaking an avowed war against them. War therefore was declared, and was carried on continuously during thirty-three years, with much bitterness on both sides, but with greater loss to the Saxons than to the Franks. It was the bad faith of the Saxons which prevented a more speedy termination. It is hard to say how often they were beaten, and humbly surrendered to the king, promising to obey his orders, giving up at once the hostages he asked, and acknowledging the ambassadors sent to them; how sometimes they were so tamed and compliant as even to promise to give up their idolatry, declaring they wished to embrace Christianity. But ready as they were at times to undertake all these things, they were always far readier to renounce them. It is difficult to state correctly to which failing they were more prone, since it is certainly the fact that, after the war was begun, scarcely a single year passed in which they did not pursue this shifty course.

But the magnanimity of the King, and the unwavering firmness of his disposition, alike in adversity and prosperity, could not be shaken by any faithlessness on their part, nor could they divert him from his purpose by tiring him out.

He never allowed any act of insincerity to be done with impunity; either taking the command in person, or despatching an army under his counts, he took vengeance on their perfidy and exacted from them a commensurate penalty.

He pursued this course until all who continued to resist him were overcome and brought into submission. He then transported ten thousand men, taken from both banks of the Elbe, together with their wives and children, and distributed them here and there, in very small groups, in Gaul and Germany.

It was on the following terms, offered by the King and accepted by the Saxons, that this war, which had lasted so many years, was brought to a close. The Saxons were to put away their heathen worship and the religious ceremonies of their fathers; were to accept the articles of the Christian faith and practice; and, being united to the Franks, were to form with them one people.

Chapter 8

. . . During those years many great wars sprang up against the Franks in different parts, which were, by the skill of the King, so well managed that it was not without reason that men were perplexed whether to admire more the patience with which the King pursued his undertakings, or the good fortune which attended them.

This war was begun two years before the Italian war, and although it was carried on at the same time without any intermission, there was no relaxation anywhere. In both places the campaign was equally carried on without diminution of effort, for, of all contemporary sovereigns, King Karl took the highest rank for his good administration, and was most distinguished for his ability. In all his undertakings and enterprises there was nothing he shrank from because of the toil, and nothing he feared because of the danger; but, skilful in weighing everything at its true value, he was neither yielding in adversity nor deceived by the smiles of fortune in prosperity.

Chapter 9

It was during the time that the Saxon war was being vigorously and incessantly carried on, garrisons having been placed in all the most suitable places on the borders, that Karl marched into Spain with the best-appointed army possible. Having crossed the Pyrenean mountains, he reduced all the fortified towns and castles he came to, and was on his march home with his army safe and sound, when in the very pass of the Pyrenees on his way back, he had a slight experience of Gascon treachery.

The army was moving in column, and its formation was much extended, as the narrowness of the pass required, when the Gascons, who had placed ambuscades on the highest ledges of the mountains—the abundant thick cover of wood making the place most suitable for the disposal of an ambush—rushed down from their vantage ground into the valley below, and threw themselves upon the extreme section of the baggage, and on those who were marching with it for its protection. The Gascons attacked them in a hand-to-hand fight, killed them all to a man, and destroyed the baggage; and being protected by the darkness of the night, which was then coming on, they quickly dispersed in all directions.

In this exploit the Gascons were much favoured by the lightness of their weapons and the nature of the place where the attack was made, while the Franks, impeded by their heavy arms and the unevenness of the ground, were at a great disadvantage.

There were killed in this fight, Eggihard the King's Sewer; Anselm, the Pfalsgraf; Roland, Count of the British March, and many others. No revenge could be taken at the time for this defeat, for the enemy immediately dispersed, and so secretly that no trace was left by which they could be followed. . . .

Chapter 13

The greatest of all the wars waged by the King, except the Saxon, was that which now followed, against the Avars or Huns. He set about it with far more ardour and preparation than was bestowed upon any of the others. The King himself only made one expedition into Pannonia—it was that province which the Avar race then inhabited; the others he entrusted to the direction of his son Pippin, and to the prefects of the provinces, and to the counts and lieutenants. Although these commanders used the greatest exertions, it was not until the eighth year that the war was finished. . . .

In this war the whole nobility of the Avars perished, and the glory of their nation was destroyed. All their riches and treasures, which they had long been accumulating, were carried away, nor can memory recall any war of the Franks in which they have gained greater booty or by which they have been more enriched. Indeed, we may confess that, up to this time, the Franks appeared to be a poor nation; but so much gold and silver was found in the palace, and such a quantity of valuable spoil was taken in the battles, as can scarcely be believed.

The Franks justly spoiled the Huns (Avars) of this booty, for the Huns themselves had no right to it, it being the plunder they had carried off from other nations. . . .

The war was almost a bloodless one for the Franks, and although it lasted longer than its magnitude seemed to warrant, its result was most successful.

Chapter 14

. . . The last war undertaken was against the Northmen who are called Danes, who, at first as pirates, and afterwards with a larger fleet, were ravaging the coasts of Gaul and Germany. . . .

Chapter 15

Such were the wars waged by the most potent prince with the greatest skill and success in different countries during the forty-seven years of his reign. Great and powerful as was the realm of the Franks, which Karl had received from his father Pippin, he nevertheless so splendidly enlarged it by these wars that he almost doubled it. . . .

Chapter 16

The renown of his Kingdom was also much increased by the friendly alliances he cultivated with different kings and nations. . . .

Haroun, king of the Persians, who, with the exception of India, ruled over nearly all the East, was held by the King in such hearty friendship, that he valued Karl's esteem above that of all other Kings and princes of the world, and thought that he alone was worthy to be honoured by his regard and munificence. When the officers sent by King Karl with offerings to the most sacred sepulchre and place of the resurrection of our Lord and Saviour came to Haroun and announced the pleasure of their master, he not only gave them permission to do as they desired, but granted that that revered and sacred spot should be considered as belonging to King Karl. When the ambassadors set out on their return, he sent with them his own envoys, who conveyed to the King strange and curious gifts, with garments and spices and other rich products of the East, just as he had sent him a few years before, upon his request, the only elephant he then possessed.

The Constantinopolitan Emperors, Nicephorus, Michael, and Leo, of their own accord, also sought his friendship and alliance, and sent to him several embassies; and since by assuming the Imperial title he had laid himself open to the grave suspicion of wishing to deprive them of Empire, he made with them the most binding treaty possible, that there might be no occasion of offence between them. But the Romans and Greeks always viewed with distrust the power of the Franks; hence arose the Greek proverb, "Have a Frank for a friend but not for a neighbour."

Chapter 17

Illustrious as the King was in the work of enlarging his Kingdom and in conquering foreign nations, and though so constantly occupied with such affairs, he nevertheless began in several places very many works for the advantage and beautifying of his Kingdom. Some of these he was able to finish. Chief among them may be mentioned, as deserving of notice, the Basilica of the Holy Mother of God, built at Aachen, a marvel of workmanship; and the bridge over the Rhine at Mainz, five hundred paces in length, so broad is the river at that place. . . .

Chapter 19

The King thought so much about the education of his children that he caused both sons and daughters to be early instructed in those liberal studies which attracted his own attention. As soon as his sons were old enough he caused them to ride on horseback, as was the Frankish custom, and to practice themselves in arms and hunting. He bade his daughters should learn wool-spinning and the use of the distaff and spindle, and be taught to employ themselves industriously in every virtuous occupation, that they might not be enervated by idleness.

Of this large family, two sons and one daughter died before him— Karl, the eldest, and Pippin, whom he had made King of Italy, and Hruodrud, his eldest girl, who had been betrothed to Constantine VI, the Emperor of the Greeks. Pippin left surviving one son, Bernhard, and five daughters, Adalhaid, Atula, Guntrada, Berthaid, and Theodorada. The King showed marked tokens of his affection toward them, allowing his grandson to succeed to his father's Kingdom, and bringing up his grand-daughters with his own daughters. He bore the deaths of his sons and daughters with that greatness of soul for which he was distinguished; but his resignation was not greater than his affection, for he mourned for them with tears. So also, when the death of Adrian, the Roman Pontiff, was announced to him, regarding him as his chief friend, he wept for him as if he had lost the son or brother that was dearest to him. For he was most sincere in his friendships, being readily open to form them and most constant in retaining them, cherishing with the most sacred regard those whom he united to himself in ties of affection.

He was so careful in the bringing up of his sons and daughters that when at home he never dined without them, and they always accompanied him on his journeys, his sons riding by his side, and his daughters following close behind, attended by a train of servants appointed for that purpose. His daughters were very fair, and he loved them passionately. Strange to say, he would never consent to give them in marriage, either to any of his own nation or to foreigners; but he kept them all at home and near his person at all times until his death, for he used to say that he could not deprive himself of their society. On account of this, although happy in all else, he here experienced the malignity of fortune; but he concealed his vexation, and conducted himself as if they had never given rise to injurious suspicions, and as if no reports had ever gone abroad concerning them.

Chapter 22

The person of Karl was large and robust, and of commanding stature, though not exceeding good proportions, for it appears that he measured seven feet in height. The top of his head was round, his eyes large and animated, his nose somewhat long, his hair white, and his face bright and pleasant; so that, whether standing or sitting, he showed very great presence and dignity. Although his neck was thick and rather short, and his belly too prominent, still the fair proportions of his limbs concealed these defects. His walk was firm, and the whole carriage of his body was manly. His voice was clear, but not so strong as his frame would have led one to expect. His health was good until the last four years of his life, when he was attacked with frequent fevers, and latterly walked lame on one foot. Even in illness he leaned more on his own judgment than on the advice of physicians, whom he greatly disliked, because they used to recommend him to leave off roasted meats, which he preferred, and to accustom himself to boiled.

He took constant exercise in riding and hunting, which was natural for a Frank, since scarcely any nation can be found to equal them in these pursuits. He also delighted in the natural warm baths, frequently exercising himself by swimming, in which he was very skilful, no one being able to outstrip him. It was on account of the warm baths that he built the palace at Aachen, living there constantly during the last years of his life and until his death. He not only invited his sons to bathe with him, but also his chief men and friends, and occasionally even a crowd of his attendants and guards, so that at times one hundred men or more would be bathing together.

Chapter 23

He wore the dress of his native country—that is, the Frankish; on his body a linen shirt and linen drawers; then a tunic with a silver border, and stockings. He bound his legs with garters and wore shoes on his feet. In the winter he protected his shoulders and chest with a vest made of the skins of otters and sable. He wore a blue cloak, and was always girt with his sword, the hilt and belt being of gold and silver. Sometimes he wore a jewelled sword, but only on great festivals, or when receiving foreign ambassadors. He thoroughly disliked the dress of foreigners, however fine, and he never put it on except at Rome—once at the request of Pope Adrian, and again a second time, to please his successor, Pope Leo. He then wore a long tunic, chlamys, and shoes made after the Roman fashion. On festivals he used to walk in processions clad in a garment woven with gold, and shoes studded with jewels, his cloak fastened with a golden clasp, and wearing a crown of gold set with precious stones. At other times his dress differed little from that of a private person.

Chapter 24

In his eating and drinking he was temperate; more particularly so in his drinking, since he had the greatest abhorrence of drunkenness in anybody, but more especially in himself and his companions. He was unable to abstain from food for any length of time, and often complained that fasting was injurious to him. He very rarely feasted, only on great festive occasions, when there were very large gatherings. The daily service of his table was only furnished with four dishes, in addition to the roast meat, which the hunters used to bring in on spits, and of which he partook more freely than of any other food.

While he was dining he listened to music or reading. History and the deeds of men of old used to be read. He derived much pleasure from the works of St. Augustine, especially from his book called "Civitas Dei." He took very sparingly of wine and other drinks, rarely taking at meals more than two or three draughts. In summer, after the mid-day repast, he would take some fruit and one draught, and then, throwing aside his clothes and shoes as at night, he would repose for two or three hours. He slept at night so lightly that he would break his rest four or five times, not merely by awaking, but even getting up.

While he was dressing and binding on his sandals, he would receive his friends; and also, if the Count of the palace announced that there was any cause which could only be settled by his decree, the suitors were immediately ordered into his presence, and, as if sitting in court, he heard the case and gave judgment. And this was not the only business that used to be arranged at that time, for orders were then given for whatever had to be done on that day by any officer or servant.

Chapter 25

He was ready and fluent in speaking, and able to express himself with great clearness. He did not confine himself to his native tongue, but took pains to learn foreign languages, acquiring such knowledge of Latin that he used to repeat his prayers in that language as well as in his own. Greek he could better understand than pronounce. In speaking he was so voluble that he almost gave one the impression of a chatterer. He was an ardent admirer of the liberal arts, and greatly revered their professors, whom he promoted to high honours. In order to learn grammar, he attended the lectures of the aged Peter of Pisa, a deacon; and for other instruction he chose as his preceptor Albinus, otherwise called Alcuin, also a deacon—a Saxon by race, from Britain, the most learned man of the day, with whom the King spent much time in learning rhetoric and logic, and more especially astronomy. He learned the art of computation, and with deep thought and skill very carefully calculated the courses of the planets.

Karl also tried to write, and used to keep his tablets and writing-book under the pillow of his couch, that when he had leisure he might practice his hand in forming letters; but he made little progress in a task too long deferred, and begun too late in life.

Chapter 26

The Christian religion, in which he had been brought up from infancy, was held by Karl as most sacred, and he worshipped in it with the greatest piety. For this reason he built at Aachen a most beautiful church, which he enriched with gold and silver, and candlesticks, and also with lattices and doors of solid brass. When columns and marbles for the building could not be obtained from elsewhere, he had them brought from Rome and Ravenna.

As long as his health permitted, he was most regular in attending the church at matins and evensong, and also during the night, and at the time of the Sacrifice; and took especial care that all the services of the church should be performed in the most fitting manner possible, frequently cautioning the sacristans not to allow anything improper or unseemly to be brought into, or left in, the building.

He provided for the church an abundance of sacred vessels of gold and silver, and priestly vestments, so that when service was celebrated it was not necessary even for the doorkeepers, who are the lowest order of ecclesiastics, to perform their duties in private dress. He carefully revised the order of reading and singing, being well skilled in both, though he did not read in public, nor sing, except in a low voice and only in the chorus.

Chapter 27

He was most devoted in providing for the poor, and in charitable gifts, which the Greeks call almsgiving. In this matter he took thought not only for those of his own country and kingdom, but also for those whom he heard were living in poverty beyond the seas, in Africa, Egypt, and Syria, at Carthage, Alexandria, and Jerusalem, to whom he used to send money in compassion for their wants. It was on this account especially that he courted the friendship of foreign princes, that he might be able to become a solace and comfort to those Christians who were living under their rule.

He held the church of the blessed Peter the Apostle, at Rome, in far higher regard than any other place of sanctity and veneration, and he enriched its treasury with a great quantity of gold, silver, and precious stones.

To the Pope he made many and rich presents; and nothing lay nearer his heart during his whole reign than that the city of Rome should attain to its ancient importance by his zeal and patronage, and that the church of St. Peter should, through him, not only be in safe keeping and protection, but should also by his wealth be ennobled and enriched beyond all other churches. Although he thought so much of this, it was only four times, during the forty-seven years of his reign, that he had leisure to go to Rome for prayer and supplication.

Chapter 28

The last visit he paid to Rome was not only for the above reasons, but also because the Romans had driven Pope Leo to ask his assistance —for they had grievously ill-treated him; indeed, his eyes had been plucked out and his tongue cut off.

Karl therefore went to Rome, and stayed there the whole winter in order to reform and quiet the Church, which was in a most disturbed state. It was at this time that he received the title of Emperor and Augustus, to which at first he was so averse that he remarked that had he known the intention of the Pope, he would not have entered the church on that day, great festival though it was.

He bore very quietly the displeasure of the Roman Emperors, who were exceedingly indignant at his assumption of the Imperial title, and overcame their sullenness by his great magnanimity, in which, without doubt, he greatly excelled them, sending them frequent embassies, and styling them his brothers in his letters to them.

Chapter 29

After he had taken the Imperial title, he turned his attention to the laws of his people, which seemed greatly to need it, since the Franks have two laws, which differ much in many places.

Karl's intention was to add what was wanting in each, to assimilate discrepancies, and to correct what was mischievous and wrongly expressed. In the end, however, he did nothing more than add a few capitularies, and those imperfect ones.

He, however, caused the unwritten laws, of all the nations under his rule, to be tabulated and reduced to writing. He also wrote out and committed to memory the rude and very ancient songs which told of the exploits and wars of the kings of old. He also began a grammar of the speech of his country. He also gave names in the national tongue to the months of the year, for up to this time the Franks had distinguished them partly by Latin and partly by barbarian names. He likewise gave the proper names to the twelve winds, for previously names were known for hardly four. . . .

Chapter 30

Towards the close of his life, when bowed down by disease and old age, he summoned to him his son, Ludwig, the King of Aquitaine, who alone survived of the sons of Hildegard, and in a solemn assembly of the chief men of the whole realm of the Franks, and with their unanimous consent, appointed Ludwig his partner in the whole Kingdom and and bade that he be saluted as Emperor and Augustus.

This proposal was received by all who were present with great approbation. It seemed to them as if Heaven inspired the King in advancing the prosperity of the Kingdom, for this arrangement increased his own dignity and struck foreign nations with no slight awe.

The King then dismissed his son into Aquitaine, and, although weakened by age, went on his usual hunting expedition in the neighbourhood of the palace at Aachen. In this pursuit he passed the remainder of the autumn, and returned to Aachen early in November. During the winter, in the month of January, he was confined to his bed by a sharp attack of fever. He at once prescribed for himself a lesser diet, which was his usual treatment of fever, thinking that by this means he could throw off the disease, or at least control it; but inflammation of the side, which the Greeks call pleurisy, supervened. He still continued to starve himself, only keeping himself up by occasionally taking liquids; and on the seventh day after he had been confined to his bed he received the Holy Communion, and died soon after, at nine o'clock, on the 28th January, in the seventy-third year of his age and forty-seventh of his reign.

Chapter 31

His body was reverently washed and tended, and then carried into the church and buried, to the great grief of all his people. There was some doubt at first where was the most proper place for his burial, for during his life he had given no orders on this matter. At last it was agreed by all that he could be buried in no more fitting place than in the church which he had built at his own cost at Aachen, out of love to God and our Lord Christ, and to the honour of the ever blessed Virgin, His Mother. So he was buried there on the same day that he died. Above his tomb was erected a gilded monument, with his effigy and title upon it.

B. LETTERS OF ALCUIN

Letters Written by Alcuin in Charlemagne's Behalf

I

Charles, by the grace of God king of the Franks and Lombards, and Patrician of the Romans, wishes everlasting blessedness in Christ to Pope Leo.

. . . Just as I entered into an alliance of holy fatherhood with the most blessed father, your predecessor, in the same way I do desire to form an inviolable alliance of the same faith and love with your blessedness, since the prayers of your apostolic sanctity have called down divine grace for me, your apostolic benediction follows me everywhere, and, God granting, the most holy see of the Roman church is always defended by our devotion. This is our duty: to defend the holy Church of Christ against the incursions of pagans and the devastations of the unfaithful from without, making use of our arms in accordance with divine aid; and to fortify the Church from within with the knowledge of the Catholic faith. This is your duty, most holy father: to aid our soldiery, raising your hands to God with Moses, so that through your intercession the Christian people, with God as their leader and source of strength, may always have the victory of His holy Name over their enemies everywhere and the Name of our Lord Jesus Christ may be famous throughout the whole world. . . .

II

In the name of the Father, and of the Son, and of the Holy Spirit. Charles, by the gift of divine grace Emperor and Augustus, king of the Franks and Lombards, wishes eternal salvation in our Lord Jesus Christ to his honorable brother Michael, the glorious and august Emperor.

We bless the Lord Jesus Christ, our true God, and give thanks to Him with all our heart in accordance with the possibilities of our strength and intelligence, because He has seen fit to make us so rich by the gift of His ineffable kindness, so that He might establish the long-sought and always wished-for peace between the eastern and western empires in our day. He has also seen fit to unify and pacify His holy and immaculate Catholic Church, which is spread throughout the whole world, so that it might always be ruled and protected in accordance with His daily commands. We speak of this as of a deed accomplished because we, for our part, have done whatever must be done, and we do not doubt that you, for your part, will wish to act likewise. We have faith in Him Who has commanded this task, that is, to make peace, which we have in hand, because He is faithful and truthful, and is the co-laborer to all engaged in good work. We are also confident that He will bring what has been well-begun by us to its completion. . . .

Letters Written by Alcuin in his own Name

I

Flaccus Albinus sends greetings in faith and affection to his venerable and beloved lord, King David.[48]

I have received the letters of your most noble piety, in which I recognized your exceedingly friendly state of mind towards our health and the very necessary prosperity of the whole empire of Christianity. I have, therefore, poured out thanks to Christ, the most merciful King; and I, along with all those who share our devotion, have beseeched His piety with earnest prayers that He deem it worthy for your peaceful and friendly power to protect, rule, and expand the boundaries of His most sacred empire in long-lasting prosperity, for the exaltation of His holy Church. . . .

The main point of the question you proposed, as I found it in the

---

[48] I.e., Charlemagne. David was the archetype of the anointed king.

letters of your excellency, went like this, and I shall use the same words as in the letter: "There is a place in the Gospel According to Luke where the Lord Christ, on His way to His Passion, orders His disciples to sell their mantles and purses, and to buy a sword. When He was told that there were two swords, He said that it was enough. We think that it was one of these swords that Peter used in cutting off the ear of Malchus; after which the Lord said to him: 'Put your sword back in its sheath; for all who take the sword shall perish by the sword.' How does it come about that He Who just ordered His disciples to sell their mantles to buy swords, could then immediately say that those who took the sword would perish by the sword? If the sword is the word of God, and the Lord, when he instructed them to buy a sword, meant thereby the word of God; how can it be that all who take the word of God shall perish by the word of God?"

But the solution is easy, if you will consider the circumstances in which each evangelist uses the word, and comprehend the different meanings of "sword." For "sword" does not have the same meaning in all places, just as "lion" means one thing where it is said: "Behold, the lion of the tribe of Judah has conquered," and another where it is said: "He prowls around like a lion, seeking someone to devour"—the former lion is Christ, the latter is the devil. Although "lion" is written with the same letters in each case, nevertheless they do not have the same meaning. . . .

Therefore it is with one meaning that the Lord said in Matthew: "All who take the sword shall die by the sword;" but with another meaning that He said in Luke: "but now, let him who has a bag, take it, and likewise a purse; and let him who has no sword sell his mantle and buy one." For the latter sword seems to have been pleasing to Him, and the former displeasing; wherefore He ordered the one to be put back in its sheath, and the other to be purchased. We must, therefore, diligently consider what each one signifies. And first we must cite the sacred opinions of the holy fathers, lest we, insignificant as we are, should seem to say anything presumptuously.

According to Matthew, the sword is understood to mean revenge for our injuries. He who seeks this shall perish for his crimes, as the Truth itself says: "If you do not forgive men for their sins, your Father in heaven will not forgive you for your trespasses." Wherefore He orders this sword to be put back into the sheath of the heart. . . .

But let us see what the sword can mean in the Gospel of Luke, about which the whole series of questions arose. Here it indisputably means the word of God, which we, selling all secular impediments to life, must buy, in order to use it to fight against all the snares of the old serpent. This sword our Savior, when He was returning to His Father's throne in the triumph of His glory, gave to His disciples, saying: "Go and teach all the nations. . . ."

What signifies the purchase of a sword? What signifies the bag, the purse, and the mantle? Why were two swords later said to be enough? . . . The purchase of this sword symbolized the renunciation of the world. On this subject the Lord said: "He who does not renounce all that he has cannot be My disciple"; that is: he who seeks to satisfy his avarice cannot be a preacher, since he destroys in his deeds what he preaches with his mouth. In the bag, hidden riches can be understood; in the purse, public riches. Carnal pleasure is sybolized in the mantle. All these must be sold, that is, utterly cast away, so that the soldier may become worthy to accept the sword of the word of Christ the God. But when the disciples said: "behold, here are two swords," and the Lord replied: "It is enough," the two swords meant the body and the soul, armed with which each one of us, in accordance with the grace given to him by God, ought to do battle for the will of the Lord God. And it will be enough for the will of God if His instructions are fulfilled by the body and the soul. . . .

If this sword is, as we said, the word of God, why did it cut off the ear of the adversary, since the word of God is wont to go from the hearing to the secret chambers of the heart so that there it may bring forth increase, a hundredfold, sixtyfold, or thirtyfold? What can this cutting off signify, I ask, unless it be that the ear of infidelity shall be cut off, so that it may be healed by a new touch of divine grace? Therefore that slave was called Malchus. In the Latin language Malchus may mean either king or prince. How could a man be both king and slave, unless in our old selves we were the slaves of sin, and in our new selves, healed by the grace of the Lord God, we shall be kings and princes with Christ? Why is it that the Lord Himself healed His persecutor, if not to show that every preacher in the Church of Christ should not stop healing his enemies with the word of piety? . . .

We have said that the two swords signify the body and soul. Both of these ought to work with one faith, so that the faith, which lies hidden in the soul, may be shown to the world outside in the deeds of the body. "Out of the abundance of the heart the mouth speaks." The disciples, therefore, when they had received the gifts of the Holy Spirit in their fiery tongues, are said to have spoken of the great works of God. And it is for this reason: when holy love burns deep within the soul, it will soon, through the gift of the Holy Spirit, become well-known outside in the words of preaching. The two swords can also, without much inconvenience, be understood to mean faith and good works: the former lying hidden within the heart, the latter manifesting itself publicly in deeds. This explanation can also be discovered if one diligently examines the earlier meaning, since faith is of the soul, and good works of the body. Let each and every man, therefore, search out the depths of his heart to learn how much he loves God, and let him manifest this same love of God in good works.

And let the ministers of the Church of Christ, especially, show the charity of our Redeemer to the people through the words of their earnest sermons. Let them be burning lamps in the house of God. Let them be strong cities founded on mountains of virtue. Let them be wise shepherds, leading the flock of Christ to the pastures of life everlasting; so that, along with their great flock of souls, they may deserve to enter into the pleasures of their Lord God. Let your most excellent dignity and your will, most holy in its love of Christ, always encourage these things; nay rather, urge them to the ranks of priests with your most loving exhortation. Thus, on the great day of our Lord Jesus Christ, you also will be worthy to hear the loving words: "Well done, good and faithful servant, since you have been faithful over little, I will set you over much; enter into the joy of your Lord God." For do not imagine that this shall be heard only by priests and clerks. Know that it will also be said to good laymen, who labor hard in the work of God, especially to those who have been placed in the more sublime ranks of this world: those whose good observance, sanctity of life, and instructive words about eternal life can be as a sermon to their subjects. For each and every man shall have to answer for the property which he has received from his Lord on the Day of Judgment; and he who labors more shall receive a greater reward. Therefore, most beloved and honorable defender and ruler of the churches of Christ, let the venerable zeal of your most holy wisdom encourage some with admonitions, chastise others with punishment, and instruct others with the learning of life. Thus, when all has been done, you, among the rest, shall deserve to have a perpetual reward; and thus you, along with the great and praiseworthy multitude of peoples, shall appear glorious in the sight of your Lord God. . . .

II

Flaccus Albinus sends greetings to the peaceful lord, King David.

. . . If I were present I should have used many words to persuade your venerable dignity, had you the opportunity to listen, or I the eloquence to speak. For the pen is often wont to stimulate the secrets of the love of my heart to write of your excellence, of the stability of the kingdom given to you by God, and of the progress of the holy Church of Christ. She is disturbed greatly by the manifold wickedness of evil men, and tainted by the audacious crimes of the worst of men, not only among low-born persons, but even among the greatest and highest. All this is greatly to be feared.

For three persons have hitherto been the highest in the world: that is, the apostolic sublimity, which is accustomed to rule the throne of St. Peter, the prince of the Apostles, as its vicar. Your venerable goodness has informed me of what should be done in the case of him, who was the ruler of the aforesaid seat. Another is the imperial dignity and secular power of the second Rome, whose governor was impiously deposed, not by foreigners, but by his own relatives and fellow-citizens, as the story was everywhere spread by rumor. The third is the royal dignity, in which the dispensation of our Lord Jesus Christ placed you, as ruler of the Christian people, more excellent in power than the others mentioned above, more renowned for your wisdom, more sublime in the dignity of your realm. Behold, on you alone rests the entire safety of the churches of Christ. You are the avenger of crimes, you are the guide of the erring, you are the consoler of the grieving, you are the exaltation of good men. . . .

Nothing can be concealed from your wisdom: for we know that you are exceedingly well-learned both in the holy Scriptures and in secular histories. In all these things you have been given full knowledge by God, so that through you the holy Church of God might be ruled, exalted, and preserved for the Christian people. Who can describe the magnitude of the reward which God will give you for your greatest devotion? For eye has not seen, nor ear heard, nor the heart of man conceived what God has prepared for those who love Him. . . .

III

Flaccus, the faithful orator, sends wishes for eternal blessedness in Christ to his most beloved lord of lords, King David.

. . . O most sweet [Charles], glory of the Christian people, O defense of the churches of Christ, consolation of this present life. Because of these virtues, it is necessary that all men should exalt your blessedness in their prayers and aid you by their intercessions, since it is through your prosperity that the Christian Empire may be protected, that the Catholic faith may be defended, and that the rule of justice may become known to all. . . .

And would that you, whenever divine grace grants you enough freedom from the wicked Saxon people, might travel on the roads, govern your realms, do justice, repair churches, discipline the people, decree laws for individual persons and classes, to defend the oppressed, to ordain laws, to comfort pilgrims, and to show the way of righteousness and heavenly life to everyone everywhere. Thus the arrival of your piety would be a consolation to all; and blessings would come to the most famous sons of your nobility through your copious blessings, just as it is read that through the sanctity of your namesake David alone, a king most pleasing to God, the power of the royal throne was preserved for all his descendants. In such exercises of this religion the exaltation of your sons, the felicity of your realm, the well-being of your people, the abundance of harvests, the delight of all good men, and the blessings which the heavenly kingdom holds in store for you shall increase and be augmented through all eternity, with the help of Christ the God, O most sweet David. . . .

IV

Flaccus, the old soldier, sends eternal greetings in Christ to his most beloved lord, most worthy of every honor, King David.

. . . Let God do this and more. Let Him subject enemy nations to the triumph of your terror. Let Him subject the fiercest minds to the most gentle yoke of His love in the Christian faith, so that God alone and our Lord Jesus Christ may be believed in, worshipped, and loved. Your most famous power and most holy will labor in this task with all zeal so that the name of Christ may be made famous and His divine power may be well-known to the many kingdoms of the world through the triumphs of your courage. Thus, not only does the magnitude of your power show you to be a king, but your perseverance in disseminating the word of God in praise of the name of our Lord Jesus Christ makes you a preacher. Divine grace has, therefore, wondrously enriched you with these two gifts: that is, with the power of earthly felicity and with the breadth of spiritual wisdom, so that you may advance in both until you arrive at the felicity of everlasting blessedness.

Be merciful to your Christian people and defend the churches of Christ, so that the blessing of the heavenly King may make you strong against the pagans. We read that one of the ancient poets, when he sang, if I remember rightly, of the praises of the Roman emperors, described what kind of men they should have been, saying: "Spare the lowly, and humble the proud." The blessed Augustine expounded this verse with great praise in his book *The City of God*. It would be more proper, however, for us to attend to the precepts of the Gospel than to the verse of Vergil. For the Truth itself says: "Blessed are the merciful, for they shall obtain mercy"; and elsewhere: "Be merciful, even as your heavenly Father is merciful. . . ."

But Rome, which began with fraternal discord, does not cease to hold the ingrown poison of dissension even now. It compels the power of your venerable dignity to hasten from the sweet lands of Germany to root out the calamity of this plague.

We follow your absence with tears and your course with continuous prayers, humbly begging for divine clemency to lead you and your men there in safety and with all prosperity, and to lead you back rejoicing. I shall in no way consent to have the letters of your piety forget me. But let them come often, in the spirit of consolation, so that I may kiss them, reread them again and again, and preserve them, with perpetual sweetness, in the treasury of my heart.

> May Christ grant happy times to you,
> In this and in the eternal kingdom, beloved David.

C. ROYAL CAPITULARIES

Capitulary on the Management of Royal Estates

We desire that each steward shall make an annual statement of all our income, giving an account of our lands cultivated by the oxen which our own plowmen drive and of our lands which the tenants of farms ought to plow; of the pigs, of the rents, of the obligations and fines; of the game taken in our forests without our permission; of the various compositions; of the mills, of the forest, of the fields, of the bridges and ships; of the free men and the districts under obligations to our treasury; of markets, vineyards, and those who owe wine to us; of the hay, firewood, torches, planks, and other kinds of lumber; of the waste lands; of the vegetables, millet, panic; of the wool, flax, and hemp; of the fruits of the trees; of the nut trees, larger and smaller; of the grafted trees of all kinds; of the gardens; of the turnips; of the fish ponds; of the hides, skins, and horns; of the honey and wax; of the fat, tallow, and soap; of the mulberry wine, cooked wine, mead, vinegar, beer, and wine, new and old; of the new grain and the old; of the hens and eggs; of the geese; of the number of fishermen, workers in metal, sword makers, and shoemakers; of the bins and boxes; of the turners and saddlers; of the forges and mines,—that is, of iron, lead, or other substances; of the colts and fillies. They shall make all these known to us, set forth separately and in order, at Christmas, so that we may know what and how much of each thing we have.

The greatest care must be taken that whatever is prepared or made with the hands,—that is, bacon, smoked meat, sausage, partially salted meat, wine, vinegar, mulberry wine, cooked wine, garum, mustard, cheese, butter, malt, beer, mead, honey, wax, flour,—all should be prepared and made with the greatest cleanliness.

Each steward on each of our domains shall always have, for the sake of ornament, peacocks, pheasants, ducks, pigeons, partridges, and turtle-doves.

In each of our estates the chambers shall be provided with counterpanes, cushions, pillows, bedclothes, coverings for the tables and benches; vessels of brass, lead, iron, and wood; andirons, chains, pothooks, adzes, axes, augers, cutlasses, and all other kinds of tools, so that it shall never be necessary to go elsewhere for them, or to borrow them. And the weapons which are carried against the enemy shall be well cared for, so as to keep them in good condition; and when they are brought back they shall be placed in the chamber.

For our women's work they are to give at the proper time, as has been ordered, the materials,—that is, the linen, wool, woad, vermilion, madder, wool combs, teasels, soap, grease, vessels and the other objects which are necessary.

Of the kinds of food not forbidden on fast days, two thirds shall be sent each year for our own use,—that is, of the vegetables, fish, cheese, butter, honey, mustard, vinegar, millet, panic, dried and green herbs, radishes, and, in addition, of the wax, soap and other small products; and let it be reported to us, by a statement, how much is left, as we have said above; and this statement must not be omitted as in the past, because after those two thirds we wish to know how much remains.

Each steward shall have in his district good workmen, namely, blacksmiths, a goldsmith, a silversmith, shoemakers, turners, carpenters, sword makers, fishermen, foilers, soap makers, men who know how to make beer, cider, perry, or other kind of liquor good to drink, bakers to make pastry for our table, net makers who know how to make nets for hunting, fishing, and fowling, and other sorts of workmen too numerous to be designated.

Capitulary on the "Missi" [49]

The most serene and most Christian lord emperor Charles has chosen from his nobles the wisest and most prudent men, archbishops and some of the other bishops also, together with venerable abbots and pious laymen, and has sent them throughout his whole kingdom; through them he would have all the various classes of persons mentioned in the following sections live strictly in accordance with the law. Moreover, where anything which is not right and just has been enacted in the law, he has ordered them to inquire into this most diligently and to inform him of it; he desires, God granting, to reform it.

And let no one, through cunning craft, dare to oppose or thwart the written law, as many are wont to do, or the judicial sentence passed upon him; or to do injury to the churches of God, or the poor, or the widows, or the wards, or any Christian. But all shall live entirely in accordance with God's precept, justly and under a just rule, and each one shall be admonished to live in harmony with his fellows in his business or profession. The canonical clergy ought to observe in every respect a canonical life without heeding base gain; nuns ought to keep diligent watch over their lives; laymen and the secular clergy ought

[49] Inspectors sent out from the royal court to supervise the work of the counts and other local officials.

rightly to observe their laws without malicious fraud; and all ought to live in mutual charity and perfect peace.

And let the *missi* themselves make a diligent investigation whenever any man claims that an injustice has been done to him by any one, just as they desire to deserve the grace of omnipotent God and to keep their fidelity pledged to him, so that in all cases, everywhere, they shall, in accordance with the will and fear of God, administer the law fully and justly in the case of the holy churches of God and of the poor, of wards and widows, and of the whole people. And if there shall be anything of such a nature that they, together with the provincial counts, are not able of themselves to correct it and to do justice concerning it, they shall, without any reservations, refer this, together with their reports, to the judgment of the emperor. The straight path of justice shall not be impeded by any one on account of flattery or gifts, or on account of any relationship, or from fear of the powerful.

Concerning the fidelity to be promised to the lord emperor: he has commanded that every man in his whole kingdom, whether ecclesiastic or layman, each according to his vow and occupation, shall now pledge to him as emperor the fidelity which he has previously promised to him as king; and all of those who have not yet taken any oath shall do likewise, down to those who are twelve years old.

And that it shall be announced to all in public, so that each one may know, how great and how many things are comprehended in that oath; not merely, as many have thought hitherto, fidelity to the lord emperor as regards his life, and not introducing any enemy into his kingdom out of enmity, and not consenting to, or concealing another's faithlessness to him; but that all may know that this oath contains in itself the following meaning:

First, that each one voluntarily shall strive, in accordance with his knowledge and ability, to live entirely in the holy service of God in accordance with the precept of God and in accordance with his own promise, because the lord emperor is unable to give to all individually the necessary care and discipline.

Secondly, that no man, either through perjury or any other wile or fraud, or on account of the flattery or gift of any one, shall refuse to give back or dare to abstract or conceal a serf of the lord emperor, or a district, or land, or anything that belongs to him; and that no one shall presume, through perjury or other wile: to conceal or abstract his fugitive serfs belonging to the fisc, who wrongly and fraudulently claim that they are free.

That no one shall presume to rob or in any way do injury fraudulently to the churches of God, or to widows or orphans or pilgrims; for the lord emperor himself, after God and his saints, has constituted himself their protector and defender.

That no one shall dare to lay waste a benefice of the lord emperor, or to make it his own property.

That no one shall presume to neglect a summons to war from the lord emperor; and that no one of the counts shall be so presumptuous as to dare to excuse any one of those who owe military service, either on account of relationship, or flattery, or gifts from any one.

That no one shall presume to impede in any way a ban or command of the lord emperor, or to dally with his work, or to impede or to lessen or in any way to act contrary to his will or commands. And that no one shall dare to neglect to pay his dues or tax.

That no one, for any reason, shall make a practice in court of defending another unjustly, either from any desire of gain when the cause is weak, or by impeding a just judgment by his skill in reasoning, or by a desire of oppressing when the cause is weak. . . .

The oath to the emperor should include the observance of all those things mentioned above.

Bishops and priests shall live according to the canons and shall teach others to do the same.

Bishops, abbots, and abbesses, who are in charge of others, shall strive with the greatest devotion to surpass those subject to them in this diligence and shall not oppress those subject to them with a harsh rule of tyranny, but with sincere love shall carefully guard the flock committed to them with mercy and charity and by the examples of good works. . . .

The monks shall live sincerely and strictly in accordance with the rule, because we know that any one whose good will is lukewarm is displeasing to God; as John bears witness in the Apocalypse: "I would thou wert cold or hot. So then because thou art lukewarm, and neither cold nor hot, I will spew thee out of my mouth." Let them in no way usurp to themselves secular business. They shall not have leave to go outside of their monastery at all, unless compelled by a very great necessity; but the bishop in whose diocese they are shall take care in every way that they do not get accustomed to wandering outside of the monastery. But if it shall be necessary for a monk to go outside in obedience to a command this shall be done with the counsel and consent of the bishop. Such persons shall be sent out with a certificate, that there may be no suspicion of evil in them and that no evil report may arise from them.

To manage the property and business outside of the monastery, the abbot, with the permission and counsel of the bishop, shall appoint some person who is not a monk, but another of the faithful. Let the monks wholly shun secular gain or a desire for worldly affairs; for avarice or a desire for this world ought to be avoided by all Christians, but especially by those who claim to have renounced the world and its lusts. Let no one presume in any way to incite strife or controversies, either within or without the monastery. But if any one shall have presumed to do so, he shall be corrected by the most severe discipline of the rule, and in such a manner that others shall fear to commit such actions. Let them entirely shun drunkenness and feasting, because it is known to all that these give rise to lust. . . .

Let no bishops, abbots, priests, deacons, or other members of the clergy presume to keep dogs for hunting, or hawks, falcons, and sparrow hawks, but each shall observe fully the canons or rule of his order. If any one shall presume to violate this order, let him know that he shall lose his office; and in addition he shall suffer such punishment for his offense that the others will be afraid to appropriate such things for themselves. . . .

And we command that no one in our whole kingdom shall dare to deny hospitality either to rich or poor, or to pilgrims; that is, no one shall deny shelter and fire and water to pilgrims traversing our country in God's name, or to any one traveling for the love of God or for the safety of his own soul. If, moreover, any one shall wish to serve them farther, let him expect the best reward from God, who himself said, "And whoso shall receive one such little child in my name receiveth me"; and elsewhere, "I was a stranger, and you took me in."

Concerning messengers coming from the lord emperor: the counts and *centenarii* shall provide most carefully, as they desire the grace of the lord emperor, for the *missi* who are sent out, so that they may go through their provinces without any delay. The emperor commands all, everywhere, to see to it that the *missi* are not hindered anywhere, but are sent forward with the utmost dispatch and provided with such things as they may require. . . .

In our forests no one shall dare to steal our game. This has already been many times forbidden; we now again strictly forbid it for the future. If one would keep his fidelity pledged to us, let him take heed to his conduct. . . .

Finally, we desire that all our commands should be made known throughout our whole realm by means of the *missi* now sent forth, whether these commands be directed to those connected with the Church—bishops, abbots, priests, deacons, canons, monks or nuns—with a view of securing the observance of our ban or decrees, or whether we would duly thank the citizens for their good will, or request them to furnish aid, or to correct some matter. . . .

29 / THE SAGA OF GUNNLAUG AND HRAFN: VIKING SOCIETY

The Carolingian empire disintegrated in the late ninth and early tenth centuries partly because the forces of localism were too strong for the embryonic central institutions of the period, partly because of the personal inadequacies of the later Carolingians, and partly because of the incursions of new barbarian invaders, of whom the Scandinavian Vikings were the most important. The Viking way of life can best be studied in the Icelandic sagas of the twelfth century which recall, in a mixture of history and legend, the deeds of the great Scandinavian warlords. The Saga of Gunnlaug and Hrafn *is typical of this epic literature.*[50]

Now it is to be said of Hrafn that he fitted out his ship in the bay called Leiruvág. Two men are mentioned who traveled with Hrafn, both of them sons of his father's sister: the one was called Grím and the other was Oláf, and they were both worthy men. It seemed a great loss to all Hrafn's kinsmen when he went away, but he told them that he had challenged Gunnlaug to a duel since he had no pleasure with Helga. And he said that one of them must fall before the other. Then Hrafn put to sea when they got a fair wind, and he brought his ship into Thrándheim and stayed there for the winter without hearing anything of Gunnlaug. He remained there throughout the summer waiting for Gunnlaug, and he was yet another winter in Thrándheim, at the place called Lifanger.

Gunnlaug took ship with Hallfred Troublesome Poet in the north at Slétta, and they were very late sailing. But they set sail when they got a fair wind, and they reached the Orkneys a little before winter. Earl Sigurd, son of Hladvir, then ruled the Islands, and Gunnlaug went to him and remained there for the winter. The Earl showed him great honour.

[50] *Three Icelandic Sagas*, transl. M. Schlauch and M. H. Scargill (Princeton: Princeton University Press and American-Scandinavian Foundation, 1950), pp. 40–44. Reprinted by permission of the American-Scandinavian Foundation.

In the spring the Earl prepared to go raiding, and Gunnlaug made ready to go with him. Throughout the summer they plundered widely in the Hebrides and Scotland and engaged in many fights. Wherever they went Gunnlaug proved himself the most valiant and bravest of men and the boldest retainer. Earl Sigurd returned early after the summer, and then Gunnlaug shipped with merchants who were sailing to Norway. Earl Sigurd and he parted in great friendship.

Gunnlaug journeyed north to Thrándheim, to Hladir, to meet Earl Eric, and he was there at the beginning of winter. The Earl received him well and invited him to stay with him, and Gunnlaug agreed. The Earl had learned earlier of the dealings between Hrafn and Gunnlaug, and he knew just how matters stood. He told Gunnlaug that he forbade them to fight there in his kingdom; Gunnlaug said he had the say in such things, and all through the winter he remained there Gunnlaug was continually aloof.

One day in the spring Gunnlaug went out, and Thorkell, his kinsman, was with him. They went away from the dwellings and into the open fields, and in front of them there was a circle of men. In the circle there were two fellows with weapons, and they were fencing. One called himself Hrafn, and the other said he was Gunnlaug. Those standing in the circle said that Icelanders struck small blows and were slow to remember their boasts. Gunnlaug saw that much mockery accompanied the sport and that great ridicule was shown, and he went away in silence.

A short time after this Gunnlaug told the Earl that he was no longer inclined to endure the mockery and ridicule of his retainers about the dispute between him and Hrafn, and he asked the Earl to give him a guide into Lifanger. The Earl had been informed previously that Hrafn had left Lifanger and had gone eastwards to Sweden, and therefore he gave Gunnlaug permission to go and granted him two guides for the journey.

Now Gunnlaug went from Hladir with six men to Lifanger. In the evening he reached the very place which Hrafn, together with four men, had left that same morning. From there Gunnlaug went on into Veradale, and each evening he came to the very place where Hrafn had spent the previous night. Gunnlaug continued until he came to the highest house in the dales, and this was at the place called Súla. Hrafn had gone thence that morning. Gunnlaug did not break his journey, but he traveled away that night, and next morning at sunrise each party saw the other.

Hrafn had reached the place where there were two great rivers, and there were level plains between them. The place was called the Plains of Gleipnir, and a little headland went out into one of the rivers, and it was called Dinganess. Hrafn and his company took their stand on this headland, and they were five in number, including Hrafn and his kinsmen Grím and Oláf.

And when they met, Gunnlaug said, "Now is it well that we have come together."

Hrafn said that there was no blame for this. "And there is now a choice. Which way will you have it: that we should all fight or just the two of us? For there is an equal number on each side."

Gunnlaug said that it would please him very well either way. Then Hrafn's kinsmen, Grím and Oláf, said that they had no desire to stand aside when they were fighting, and so said Thorkell the Black, Gunnlaug's kinsman.

Then said Gunnlaug to the Earl's guides, "You shall stand on one side and help neither of us. And you must tell the story of our meeting."

And the men did this.

Then the fight began, and all bore themselves valiantly. Grím and Oláf both attacked Gunnlaug alone, and the outcome of their dealings was that Gunnlaug slew them both, but he himself was not wounded. Thord, Kolbein's son, affirms this in the poem which he made about Gunnlaug:

> Dyed anew in red blood's stain,
> With shining sword he clove his way
> To kill three foemen in that fray,
> Oláf and Grím before him slain.

In the meantime Hrafn and Thorkell the Black, Gunnlaug's kinsman, fought together, and Thorkell fell before Hrafn and gave up his life. So, finally, all their companions fell, and then Gunnlaug and Hrafn fought on with great blows. Each was fearless in the attack which he made on the other, and they fought incessantly and vehemently. And Gunnlaug had the sword which Ethelred had given him, and it was the best of weapons. Then Gunnlaug finally struck a great blow at Hrafn and cut his leg from under him. Nevertheless Hrafn did not fall down, but he drew back to a hewn tree and supported himself on the stump.

Then Gunnlaug said, "Now you are not fit for battle, and I will fight no longer with you, a wounded man."

Hrafn replied, "It is true that I have got the worst of it. Yet I have a mind to fight further, if I could get something to drink."

Gunnlaug answered, "If I fetch you water in my helmet, do not then deceive me."

Hrafn replied, "I will not deceive you."

And Gunnlaug went down to a stream and dipped in his helmet and carried it back to Hrafn. Hrafn took hold of the helmet with his left hand, but holding his sword in his right hand, he struck Gunnlaug on the head and gave him a great wound.

Then said Gunnlaug, "You have evilly deceived me now, and you have behaved unmanfully when I trusted you."

Hrafn replied, "That is true, but the fact that I grudge you the embrace of Helga the Fair goaded me to it."

So they fought on again fiercely, and it finally came about that Gunnlaug overcame Hrafn, and there Hrafn died.

Then the Earl's guides came forward and bound up the wound in Gunnlaug's head, and he sat there meanwhile and spoke this verse:

> No coward he who Hrafn hight,
> Ever foremost in the fight.
> Many a blow was struck this morn,
> Many a life from body torn,
> On Dinganess.

Then they buried the dead men, and after that they lifted Gunnlaug onto his horse and came with him all the way down to Lifanger. There he lay for three days, and he received all the sacraments from a priest. And there he died and was buried at the church.

And to everybody it seemed a great loss that Gunnlaug and Hrafn should die thus.

30 / LIUDPRAND OF CREMONA: AN EMBASSY TO CONSTANTINOPLE

The Carolingian rulers were succeeded in Germany by the Ottonian dynasty in the tenth century. The most effective of these Saxon rulers, Otto I the Great (936–973), asserted his authority over northern Italy and, regarding himself as the heir of Charlemagne, whom he resembled in personality, aims, and methods, took the imperial title. As recognition of his imperial status Otto attempted to obtain a Byzantine princess as his son's wife, and was eventually successful in this endeavor. But his ambassador to Constantinople, the Lombard bishop of Cremona, was initially met with hostility and suspicion by the Greeks. Liudprand's report of this first unsuccessful embassy, addressed to the emperor Otto, reveals both the growing separation between the western and Byzantine worlds and the aggressive self-consciousness of the new German Roman emperor and his supporters.[51]

On the fourth of June we arrived at Constantinople, and after a miserable reception, meant as an insult to yourselves, we were given the most miserable and disgusting quarters. The palace where we were confined was certainly large and open, but it neither kept out the cold nor afforded shelter from the heat. Armed soldiers were set to guard us and prevent my people from going out, and any others from coming in. This dwelling, only accessible to us who were shut inside it, was so far distant from the emperor's residence that we were quite out of breath when we walked there—we did not ride. To add to our troubles, the Greek wine we found undrinkable because of the mixture in it of pitch, resin and plaster. The house itself had no water and we could not even buy any to quench our thirst. All this was a serious "Oh dear me!", but there was another "Oh dear me" even worse, and that was our warden, the man who provided us with our daily wants. If you were to seek another like him, you certainly would not find him on earth; you might perhaps in hell. Like a raging torrent he poured upon us every calamity, every extortion, every expense, every grief and every misery that he could invent. In our hundred and twenty days not one passed without bringing to us groaning and lamentation.

On the fourth of June, as I said above, we arrived at Constantinople and waited with our horses in heavy rain outside the Carian gate until five o'clock in the afternoon. At five o'clock Nicephorus ordered us to be admitted on foot, for he did not think us worthy to use the horses with which your clemency had provided us, and we were escorted to the aforesaid hateful, waterless, draughty stone house. On the sixth of June, which was the Saturday before Pentecost, I was brought before the emperor's brother Leo, marshal of the court and chancellor; and there we tired ourselves with a fierce argument over your imperial title. He called you not emperor, which is Basileus in his tongue, but insultingly Rex, which is king in yours. I told him that the thing meant was the same though the word was different, and he then said that I had come not to make peace but to stir up strife. Finally he got up in a rage, and really wishing to insult us received your letter not in his

[51] *The Works of Liudprand of Cremona*, transl. F. A. Wright (London: Routledge & Kegan Paul Ltd., 1930), pp. 235–8, 240–1, 244–5. Reprinted by permission of Routledge & Kegan Paul Ltd.

own hand but through an interpreter. He is a man commanding enough in person but feigning humility: whereupon if a man lean it will pierce his hand.

On the seventh of June, the sacred day of Pentecost, I was brought before Nicephorus himself in the palace called Stephana, that is, the Crown Palace. He is a monstrosity of a man, a dwarf, fat-headed and with tiny mole's eyes; disfigured by a short, broad, thick beard half going gray; disgraced by a neck scarcely an inch long; piglike by reason of the big close bristles on his head; in colour an Ethiopian and, as the poet says, "you would not like to meet him in the dark"; a big belly, a lean posterior, very long in the hip considering his short stature, small legs, fair sized heels and feet; dressed in a robe made of fine linen, but old, foul smelling, and discoloured by age; shod with Sicyonian slippers; bold of tongue, a fox by nature, in perjury and falsehood a Ulysses. My lords and august emperors, you always seemed comely to me; but how much more comely now! Always magnificent; how much more magnificent now! Always mighty; how much more mighty now! Always clement; how much more clement now! Always full of virtues; how much fuller now! At his left, not on a line with him, but much lower down, sat the two child emperors, once his masters, now his subjects. He began his speech as follows:—

It was our duty and our desire to give you a courteous and magnificent reception. That, however, has been rendered impossible by the impiety of your master, who in the guise of an hostile invader has laid claim to Rome; has robbed Berengar and Adalbert of their kingdom contrary to law and right; has slain some of the Romans by the sword, some by hanging, while others he has either blinded or sent into exile; and furthermore has tried to subdue to himself by massacre and conflagration cities belonging to our empire. His wicked attempts have proved unsuccessful, and so he has sent you, the instigator and furtherer of this villainy, under pretence of peace to act *comme un espion,* that is, as a spy upon us.

To him I made this reply: "My master did not invade the city of Rome by force nor as a tyrant; he freed her from a tyrant's yoke, or rather from the yoke of many tyrants. Was she not ruled by effeminate debauchers, and what is even worse and more shameful, by harlots? Your power, methinks, was fast asleep then; and the power of your predecessors, who in name alone are called emperors of the Romans, while the reality is far different. If they were powerful, if they were emperors of the Romans, why did they allow Rome to be in the hands of harlots? Were not some of the holy popes banished, others so distressed that they could not procure their daily supplies nor money wherewith to give alms? . . ."

As Nicephorus, like some crawling monster, walked along, the singers began to cry out in adulation: "Behold the morning star approaches: the day star rises: in his eyes the sun's rays are reflected: Nicephorus our prince, the pale death of the Saracens." And then they cried again: "Long life, long life to our prince Nicephorus. Adore him, ye nations, worship him, bow the neck to his greatness." How much more truly might they have sung:—"Come, you miserable burnt-out coal; old woman in your walk, wood-devil in your look; clodhopper, haunter of byres, goat-footed, horned, double-limbed; bristly, wild, rough, barbarian, harsh, hairy, a rebel, a Cappadocian!" So, puffed up by these lying ditties, he entered St. Sophia, his masters the emperors following at a distance and doing him homage on the ground with the kiss of peace. His armour bearer, with an arrow for pen, recorded in the church the era in progress since the beginning of his reign. So those who did not see the ceremony know what era it is. . . .

They began their discourse as follows: "Tell us, brother, the reason that induced you to take the trouble to account of the marriage which was to be the ground for a lasting peace," they said:—"It is unheard of that a daughter born in the purple of an emperor born in the purple should contract a foreign marriage. Still, great as is your demand, you shall have what you want if you give what is proper: Ravenna, namely, and Rome with all the adjoining territories from thense to our possessions. If you desire friendship without the marriage, let your master permit Rome to be free, and hand over to their former lord the princes of Capua and Benevento, who were formerly slaves of our holy empire and are now rebels."

To this I answered:—"Even you cannot but know that my master rules over Slavonian princes who are far more powerful than Peter king of the Bulgarians who has married the daughter of the emperor Christopher." "Ah," said they, "but Christopher was not born in the purple."

"As for Rome," I went on, "for whose freedom you are so noisily eager; who is her master? To whom does she pay tribute? Was she not formerly enslaved to harlots? And while you were sleeping, nay powerless, did not my master the august emperor free her from that foul servitude? Constantine, the august emperor who founded this city and called it after his name, as being ruler of the world made many offerings to the holy Roman apostolic church, not only in Italy, but in almost all the western kingdoms as well as those in the east and south, in Greece, Judaea, Persia, Mesopotamia, Babylonia, Egypt, Libya, as his own special regulations testify, preserved in our country. In Italy, in Saxony, in Bavaria, and in all my master's realms, everything that belongs to the church of the blessed apostles has been handed over to those holy apostles' vicar. And if my master has kept back a single city, farm, vassal or slave, then I have denied God. Why does not your emperor do the same? Why does he not restore to the apostolic church what lies in his kingdoms and thereby himself increase the richness and freedom which it already owes to my master's exertions and generosity?" . . .

31 / ROSWITHA: COSMOLOGY AND THE LIBERAL ARTS IN THE TENTH CENTURY

Europe, by the middle of the tenth century, exhibits an expanding economy, growing population, and slow but steady improvement in the achievement of peace and order. It was a world in which there was new leisure and opportunity for higher thought. One of the plays of the German nun Roswitha well illustrates the level of understanding of cosmology and attitudes to the liberal arts in the tenth century.[52]

PAPHNUTIUS. You know that the greater world is composed of four elements which are contraries, yet by the will of the Creator these contraries are adjusted in harmonious arrangement. Now, man is composed of even more contrary parts.

DISCIPLES. What can be more contrary than the elements?

PAPHNUTIUS. The body and the soul. The soul is not mortal like the body, nor the body spiritual as is the soul.

DISCIPLES. That is true. But what did you mean, father, when you spoke of "harmonious arrangement"?

PAPHNUTIUS. I meant that as low and high sound harmoniously united produce a certain music, so discordant elements rightly adjusted make one world.

DISCIPLES. It seems strange that discords can become concords.

PAPHNUTIUS. Consider. No thing is composed of "likes"—neither can it be made up of elements which have no proportion among themselves, or which are entirely different in substance and nature.

[52] *The Plays of Roswitha*, transl. C. St. John (London: Chatto & Windus, 1923), pp. 96–100. Reprinted by permission of Chatto & Windus.

DISCIPLES. What is music, master?

PAPHNUTIUS. One of the branches of the "quadrivium" of philosophy, my son. Arithmetic, geometry, music, and philosophy form the quadrivium.

DISCIPLES. I should like to know why they are given that name.

PAPHNUTIUS. Because just as paths branch out from the quadrivium, the place where four roads meet, so do these subjects lead like roads from one principle of philosophy.

DISCIPLES. We had best not question you about the other three, for our slow wits can scarcely follow what you have told us about the first.

PAPHNUTIUS. It is a difficult subject.

DISCIPLES. Still you might give us a general idea of the nature of music.

PAPHNUTIUS. It is hard to explain to hermits to whom it is an unknown science.

DISCIPLES. Is there more than one kind of music?

PAPHNUTIUS. There are three kinds, my son. The first is celestial, the second human, the third is produced by instruments.

DISCIPLES. In what does the celestial consist?

PAPHNUTIUS. In the seven planets and the celestial globe.

DISCIPLES. But how?

PAPHNUTIUS. Exactly as in instruments. You find the same number of intervals of the same length, and the same concords as in strings.

DISCIPLES. We do not understand what intervals are.

PAPHNUTIUS. The dimensions which are reckoned between planets or between notes.

DISCIPLES. And what are their lengths?

PAPHNUTIUS. The same as tones.

DISCIPLES. We are none the wiser.

PAPHNUTIUS. A tone is composed of two sounds, and bears the ratio of nine to eight.

DISCIPLES. As soon as we get over one difficulty, you place a greater one in our path!

PAPHNUTIUS. That is inevitable in a discussion of this kind.

DISCIPLES. Yet tell us something about concord, so that at least we may know the meaning of the word.

PAPHNUTIUS. Concord, harmony, or symphonia may be defined as a fitting disposition of modulation. It is composed sometimes of three, sometimes of four, sometimes of five sounds.

DISCIPLES. As you have given us these three distinctions, we should like to learn the name of each.

PAPHNUTIUS. The first is called a fourth, as consisting of four sounds, and it has the proportion of four to three. The second is called a fifth.

It consists of five sounds and bears the ratio of one and a half. The third is known as the diapason; it is double and is perfected in eight sounds.

DISCIPLES. And do the spheres and planets produce sounds, since they are compared to notes?

PAPHNUTIUS. Undoubtedly they do.

DISCIPLE. Why is the music not heard?

DISCIPLES. Yes, why is it not heard?

PAPHNUTIUS. Many reasons are given. Some think it is not heard because it is so continuous that men have grown accustomed to it. Others say it is because of the density of the air. Some assert that so enormous a sound could not pass into the mortal ear. Others that the music of the spheres is so pleasant and sweet that if it were heard all men would come together, and, forgetting themselves and all their pursuits, would follow the sounds from east to west.

DISCIPLES. It is well that it is not heard.

PAPHNUTIUS. As our Creator foreknew.

DISCIPLES. We have heard enough of this kind of music. What of "human" music?

PAPHNUTIUS. What do you want to know about that?

DISCIPLES. How is it manifested?

PAPHNUTIUS. Not only, as I have already told you, in the combination of body and soul, and in the utterance of the voice, now high, now low, but even in the pulsation of the veins, and in the proportion of our members. Take the finger-joints. In them, if we measure, we find the same proportions as we have already found in concord; for music is said to be a fitting disposition not only of sounds, but of things with no resemblance to sounds.

DISCIPLES. Had we known the difficulty that such a hard point presents to the ignorant, we would not have asked you about your "lesser world." It is better to know nothing than to be bewildered.

PAPHNUTIUS. I do not agree. By trying to understand you have learned many things you did not know before.

DISCIPLES. That is true.

II / THE HIGH MIDDLE AGES

The early medieval struggle to develop institutions which would realize the ecclesiastical ideals coming from the papacy and the Benedictine order was largely resolved by the middle of the eleventh century. The outcome was the remarkable achievements in government, law, and economy, and the flowering of European art, literature, and philosophy in the period from 1050 to 1300, the period which historians call the high Middle Ages. But this creativity and improvement brought with it many problems: conflicts between the leaders of Church and state, between the spirit of individualism and the spirit of organization, between piety and secularism, and between dogma and science. By the thirteenth century, following on the optimism and achievements of the previous hundred and fifty years, the consensus on the nature of a Christian world order began to break down. Discrepancies between old ideals and new practices, which fatally give evidence of a disintegrating civilization, made their appearance. The high Middle Ages begin with the conflicts over the right order in the world resulting from the Gregorian reform; they end with even deeper and more violent disputes.

32 / FEUDAL INSTITUTIONS AND IDEALS

The great political and social upheavals of the early Middle Ages gave birth to a group of institutions—lordship, vassalage, fiefs—which, since the eighteenth century, has been called feudalism. In a strict sense feudalism was a form of decentralized government in which administrative, military, and legal power passed into the hands of the lords. In a broader sense feudalism involved the mores and ideals of the ruling class of medieval society; it was the way of life of the European nobility from at least

173

the ninth century (if not earlier) until at least the thirteenth century (if not later). The following selections illustrate feudalism in both the narrow and broad sense. We have first a feudal act of homage from early twelfth-century France (A); this is followed by the classic statement of the mutual obligations of lord and vassal made by bishop Fulbert of Chartres in 1020 (B).[1] The third selection is a fascinating account of the beginnings of one of those violent and seemingly endless feudal wars which were, at least until the early twelfth century, the chief occupation of most of the European nobility; the account is taken from the great French epic Raoul de Cambrai *which, while written in its present form in the early twelfth century, is based on historical incidents of the later Carolingian period and can be accepted as a reliable picture of the conduct and attitudes of the European nobility in the heyday of feudalism (C).[2] Finally we have the proclamation of the Truce of God in the diocese of Cologne in 1083 (D).[3] The Truce of God was one of the devices by which the Church sought to limit war in feudal society and impose its ideals on the European nobility; the Truce of God was never particularly successful as an institution, but by the early twelfth century the general consequences of the spread of lay piety were helping to tame the rough warlords in Western Europe.*

A. AN ACT OF HOMAGE IN 1110

[The viscount of Carcassonne does homage to the abbot of St. Mary of Grasse]

In the name of the Lord, I, Bernard Atton, viscount of Carcassonne, in the presence of my sons, Roger and Trencavel, and of Peter Roger of Barbazan, and William Hugo, and Raymond Mantellini, and Peter de Vitry, nobles, and of many other honorable men, who had come to the monastery of St. Mary of Grasse in honor of the festival of the august St. Mary. Since Lord Leo, abbot of the said monastery, asked me, in the presence of all those above mentioned, to acknowledge to him the fealty and homage for the castles, manors, and places which

---

[1] J. H. Robinson, *Readings in European History* (Boston: Ginn & Co., 1904), Vol. I, pp. 180–2, 184.

[2] *Raoul de Cambrai*, transl. J. Crossland (London: Chatto & Windus, 1926), pp. 4–10, 11, 17–20, 22–6. Reprinted by permission of Chatto & Windus.

[3] D. C. Munro, *Translations and Reprints* (Philadelphia: University of Pennsylvania Press), Vol. I, No. 2.

the patrons, my ancestors, held from him and his predecessors and from the said monastery as a fief, and which I ought to hold as they held, I have made to the Lord Abbot Leo acknowledgment and done homage as I ought to do.

Therefore, let all present and to come know that I, the said Bernard Atton, lord and viscount of Carcassonne, acknowledge verily to thee, my Lord Leo, by the grace of God abbot of St. Mary of Grasse, and to thy successors, that I hold and ought to hold as a fief, in Carcassonne, the following: that is to say, the castles of Confoles, of Léocque, of Capendes (which is otherwise known as St. Martin of Sussagues); and the manors of Mairac, of Albars, and of Musso; also, in the valley of Aquitaine, Rieux, Traverina, Hérault, Archas, Servians, Villatroitoes, Tansiraus, Presler, and Cornelles.

Moreover, I acknowledge that I hold from thee and from the said monastery, as a fief, the castle of Termes in Narbonne; and in Minèrve, the castle of Ventaion, and the manors of Cassanolles, and of Ferral and Aiohars; and in Le Rogès, the little village of Longville; for each and all of which I render homage and fealty with hands and mouth to thee, my said Lord Abbot Leo and to thy successors; and I swear upon these four gospels of God that I will always be a faithful vassal to thee and to thy successors and to St. Mary of Grasse in all things in which a vassal is required to be faithful to his lord; and I will defend thee, my lord, and all thy successors, and the said monastery, and the monks present and to come, and the castles and manors and all your men and their possessions against all malefactors and invaders, of my own free will and at my own cost, and so shall my successors do after me; and I will give to thee power over all the castles and manors above described, in peace and in war, whenever they shall be claimed by thee or by thy successors.

Moreover, I acknowledge that, as a recognition of the above fiefs, I and my successors ought to come to the said monastery at our own expense, as often as a new abbot shall have been appointed, and there do homage and return to him the power over all the fiefs described above. And when the abbot shall mount his horse, I and my heirs, viscounts of Carcassonne, and our successors ought to hold the stirrup for the honor of the dominion of St. Mary of Grasse; and to him and all who come with him, to as many as two hundred beasts, we should make the abbot's purveyance in the borough of St. Michael of Carcassonne, the first time he enters Carcassonne, with the best fish and meat, and with eggs and cheese, honorably, according to his will, and pay the expense of shoeing the horses, and for straw and fodder as the season shall require.

And if I or my sons or their successors do not observe towards thee or thy successors each and all the conditions declared above, and should come against these things, we desire that all the aforesaid fiefs should by that very fact be handed over to thee and to the said monastery of St. Mary of Grasse and to thy successors.

I, therefore, the aforesaid Lord Leo, by the grace of God abbot of St. Mary of Grasse, receive the homage and fealty for all fiefs of castles and manors and places which are described above, in the way and with the agreements and understandings written above; and likewise I concede to thee and thy heirs and their successors, the viscounts of Carcassonne, all the castles and manors and places aforesaid, as a fief, along with this present charter. . . . And I promise by the religion of my order to thee and thy heirs and successors, viscounts of Carcassonne, that I will be a good and faithful lord concerning all those things described above. . . .

Made in the year of the Incarnation of the Lord 1110, in the reign of Louis [VI]. Seal of Bernard Atton, viscount of Carcassonne, seal of Raymond Mantellini, seal of Peter Roger of Barbazan, seal of Roger, son of the said viscount of Carcassonne, seal of Peter de Vitry, seal of Trencavel, son of the said viscount of Carcassonne, seal of William Hugo, seal of Lord Abbot Leo, who has accepted this acknowledgment of the homage of the said viscount.

And I, the monk John, have written this charter at the command of the said lord Bernard Atton, viscount of Carcassonne, and of his sons, on the day and year given above, in the presence and witness of all those named above.

B. FULBERT OF CHARTRES ON THE DUTIES OF LORD AND VASSAL

To William, most glorious duke of the Aquitanians, Bishop Fulbert, the favor of his prayers:

Asked to write something concerning the forms of fealty, I have noted briefly for you, on the authority of the books, the things which follow. He who swears fealty to his lord ought always to have these six things in memory: what is harmless, safe, honorable, useful, easy, practicable. *Harmless*, that is to say, that he should not injure his lord in his body; *safe*, that he should not injure him by betraying his secrets or the defenses upon which he relies for safety; *honorable*, that he should not injure him in his justice or in other matters that pertain to his honor; *useful*, that he should not injure him in his possessions; *easy* and *practicable*, that that good which his lord is able to do easily he make not difficult, nor that which is practicable he make not impossible to him.

That the faithful vassal should avoid these injuries is certainly proper, but not for this alone does he deserve his holding; for it is not sufficient to abstain from evil, unless what is good is done also. It remains, therefore, that in the same six things mentioned above he should faithfully counsel and aid his lord, if he wishes to be looked upon as worthy of his benefice and to be safe concerning the fealty which he has sworn.

The lord also ought to act toward his faithful vassal reciprocally in all these things. And if he does not do this, he will be justly considered guilty of bad faith, just as the former, if he should be detected in avoiding or consenting to the avoidance of his duties, would be perfidious and perjured.

C. RAOUL DE CAMBRAI: THE ORIGINS OF A FEUDAL WAR

You shall now hear of the distress and disorder caused by the great interminable war. The King of France had a noble youth in his service whom the French called Gibouin of Mans. He served the king with his good sword, and made many an orphan in the course of his wars. He served our noble king so well and in such knightly fashion that he was entitled to a full reward. Those from beyond the Rhine counselled that he should be given the fief of Cambrai which was held by Aalais, conqueror of men's hearts, of the family of Geoffroy of Lavardin. Now, if God who turned the water into wine prevent it not, a fief is about to be given and bestowed by reason of which many a knight will lie prone in death.

Our emperor listened to the barons talking and advising him to give the fair Aalais to the baron of Mans who had served him so well. He took their counsel, for which he is to be blamed; he gave the glove to Gibouin, who thanked him for it and stooped and kissed his shoe. Then said the King of France: "Gibouin, my brother, I deserve thy thanks, for it is a great gift that I give thee here. But on one condition I grant it: I wish not to disinherit the boy Raoul. He is yet young, now protect him well until such time that he can carry arms. He shall hold Cambrai; no one can refuse it to him and I shall give you some other land." Said Gibouin: "I accept it on condition that you bid me marry the lady." But he acted like a fool in daring to expect this, for it afterwards caused the overthrow of many a valiant knight, for the fair lady would not accept him though she were cut to pieces for it.

King Louis did a very foolish thing when he took the heritage away from his nephew; and Gibouin on his side acted like a felon when he desired the land of another as his fief. It caused him afterwards to die a shameful death. Then the emperor called his messenger: "Go, saddle the Arab steed, and tell my fair sister in her heritage of Cambrai, that she take to husband the brave Gibouin of Mans. Between here and Carthage there is not such a knight to be found, and I give him all the land as a marriage portion. Tell her to come without delay to my court and bring her escort with her, and I will summon many of my kinsmen. But if she fails me because of her pride, I will seize both the land and the inheritance."

The messenger took his leave and mounted the saddle of his horse; then he left Paris and rode straight for Cambrai. He entered the city by the main gate and halted by the church of St. Geri. He found the noble lady in the open space before the church with several knights in her company. He reined in his horse and dismounted, and greeted the lady in the king's name: "The king, our protector, prays God who created heaven and earth and all things therein to save the countess and all those she loves"—"May God the Creator protect thee, brother! Tell me the king's bidding and hide it not"—"In God's name, lady, I will tell you. The king's message is that he will give you Gibouin for a husband. Know of a truth, that is the king's command." Dame Aalais sank down to the earth, tears fell from her eyes and she gave a deep sigh. Then she called her counsellors. "Ah, God!" said she, "Here is an evil message. . . ."

"Just Emperor," said the baron Guerri, "Are you minded to disinherit your nephew because as yet he can neither walk nor ride? By the faith that I owe you, you shall see a thousand knights over-turned ere this Knight of Mans can vaunt himself in court. Just Emperor, I declare to you that if he lets himself be seen in Cambrai he may be certain of losing his head. And you too, foolish king, deserve blame for this. The child is your nephew, and you should never have thought of such a thing." But the king replied: "Let all this be! The gift is given and I cannot go back on it now." So Guerri departed, for he had no desire to remain, and ill-omened was the leave that he took! The good steeds were ready at the foot of the steps and the barons mounted. And Guerri cried at the top of his voice: "Now make ready, you young warriors who desire hard knocks! For I swear by Him who allowed Himself to suffer, I would rather be cut to pieces than fail my nephew as long as I live."

Guerri the Red was full of anger. He returned to Cambrai and dismounted before the church. Dame Aalais saw the knight coming and spoke to him as you may now hear: "Sir Guerri, without fail now, will you tell me the truth?" "Lady," said he, "I wish not to lie to you. The king is determined to seize your heritage for Gibouin, God curse him! —Take him for thy husband, for only so canst thou make thy peace with Louis, the ruler of France." "God!" said the lady, "I could die of grief! I would rather be burnt alive than that the king should force a greyhound to lie with a watchdog. God will allow me to bring up my child till such time as he can carry arms." Then said Guerri: "Lady, a blessing on you for daring to say it; I will not desert you in your great need."

Guerri the stout-hearted speaks again: "Lady Aalais, I swear by God the Redeemer that I will not fail you as long as I live. Where is my nephew? Bring him here, I pray you." Up rose two young lords and brought the child to the fore-court. He was three years old, I tell you for a fact, and he was dressed in bright silk with a tunic of crimson cloth. A more beautiful child could not be found. Guerri takes him in his arms at once and sighs deeply from his heart: "Child," said he, "you are scarce grown yet, and the knight of Mans has evil intent towards you, since he deprives you of your land." "Uncle," said the child, "I shall get it back, if I live long enough to carry arms seated on my charger." "Truly," said Guerri, "you shall not lose a foot of it, unless twenty thousand warriors die for it first." Then the knights call for water and seat themselves at the table.

Dame Aalais and the vassal Guerri and the barons are seated at table. The seneschals have done their duty well, for they have been well trained to serve. After the meal the lady gives costly garments to the barons. Then the powerful Guerri takes his leave; he kisses the lady and departs. Straight to Arras he goes at full speed. After this many years and days passed and there was no sound of war or of discord in the land. When Raoul of Cambrai was fifteen years old he was an exceedingly courteous and noble youth and greatly beloved by his men and his nobles.

Fifteen years have now passed and gone and dame Aalais sees her son tall and broad and well-formed. There was a nobleman in that kingdom, Ybert by name, a man of dauntless spirit. He had a son who was christened Bernier when he was small. He was grown now and well-favoured, and at fifteen years he too was both tall and strong. Count Raoul loved him dearly, and the dame Aalais out of goodness of heart had fostered him from an early age. Together they went to Paris to acquaint themselves with noble knighthood, and he waited on Raoul with the wine and the spiced cup. Better had it been for him, I can tell you, had his head been severed from his body, for grievously and shamefully he slew him in the end.

Count Raoul, the courteous youth, had a great affection for young Bernier. Bernier was the son of Ybert of Ribemont and there was no fairer youth in any land nor any that knew better the use of shield and spear, nor of wise speech in a king's court, albeit he was called a bastard. Raoul loved him and gladly made him his squire, but ill-mated comrades they proved to be.

Dame Aalais has watched her son grow up and now she sees that he is fit to bear arms, and thus she addressed him as you may hear: "Call the ban and summon your men, so that you may see them assembled at Cambrai, and we shall soon see who is loth to serve." Raoul summoned them and spoke his mind to them: "You must not fail me when I need you." . . .

The emperor has knighted the boy and now he calls his seneschals and says: "Bring hither arms, for so I bid you.". . . Then the emperor spoke to his nephew: "Nephew Raoul, I see that you have grown up tall and strong, thanks be to God the Father omnipotent." . . .

Then the king girded him with a strong sword. Its pommel and hilt were of gold and it was forged in a gloomy valley by Galant, who had put into it of his best. Except Durendal, which was the choicest sword of all, this sword was better than all others and no arm in the world could stand against it. Such were the arms which became him. For Raoul was fair and of noble form and, but for the immoderateness that was in him, a better vassal than he had never ruled his land. But because of his excess the outcome was grievous, for an unbridled man passes his days in sorrow. . . .

Raoul, who was full of wrath, spoke thus: "Just emperor, by St. Amant I swear that I have served you ever since I carried arms and you have never given me the amount of a farthing. Now at least give me the glove as a pledge that I may hold my own land as my valiant father held it before me." "I cannot grant it," replied the king; "I have given it to the Knight of Mans, and for all the wealth of Milan I would not take it from him." Guerri listened, then he shouted: "I will fight for it first, fully armed on my steed, against that mercenary Gibouin of Mans." And Raoul, ill-tempered now and sullen, cried: "By the apostle whom the penitents seek, if now thou dost not take possession of thy land, this very day or to-morrow ere the sun set, never again will I nor my men fight in thy defence." These are the words that Raoul kept so well and which caused the untimely death of many a baron. "Just emperor, I tell you all this first: every one knows that the land of the father ought by right to pass to the child. By St. Amant, every one, both small and great, will scorn me henceforth, if I do violence to my pride any longer when I see another man holding my land. By God who made the firmament, if ever I find that mercenary of Mans, no ordinary death shall he die by my sword." The king was heavy at heart when he heard these words.

The Knight of Mans was sitting at a table in the palace. He heard these threats and was filled with fear. He put on his cloak of ermine and came to the king: "Just emperor," said he, "now am I in a sorry plight. You gave me Cambresis by Artois; and now you cannot guarantee the possession of it to me. Here now is this arrogant Count Raoul with his fine equipment (he is your nephew, as the Frenchmen know

well), and Guerri the Red, his loyal friend. I have no friend so good
in all this land who would be worth anything to me against these two.
I have served thee long with my Viennese blade, and never have I
obtained the worth of a farthing. I shall go forth on my good Nor-
wegian steed poorer than I came, and the Alemans and the Germans,
the men of Burgundy, of Normandy and France will all talk of it,
and all my service will not have earned me a doit." Sorrow filled the
heart of King Louis and he beckoned Raoul to him with his broidered
glove and said: "Fair nephew, by God, the giver of laws, I pray you
let him hold it for two or three years on such terms as I will tell you:
if any count dies between here and Vermandois, or between Aix-la-
Chapelle and Senlis, or from Monillon to Orleans, you shall inherit the
rights and the land. You shall not lose a fraction of a penny by the
exchange." Raoul listened and did not hesitate: at the advice of Guerri
of Artois he accepted the pledge—it was by reason of it that he lay
cold in death at last.

Count Raoul called Guerri to speak of the matter! "Uncle," said he,
"I count on your support. I will accept this gift and there shall be no
drawing back from it." It was a great thing that he demanded in
exchange for his father's fief, and fatal to many a baron in the end.
Then they demanded hostages from King Louis; and the king harkened
to bad advice and allowed Raoul to choose some of the highest in the
land. . . .

Hostages he had now; as many as he wanted, and for some time
things remained thus—for a year and a fortnight at any rate, I know
and Raoul returned to Cambrai. But during the time of which I have
been speaking Herbert, a powerful count, died; he was a loyal man
and wise and had a great many friends. All Vermandois was his territory, also Roie, Péronne, Origny, Ribemont, St. Quentin and Clairy.
He is a fortunate man who possesses many friends! Raoul heard of his
death and bestirred himself. He quickly mounted his steed and summoned his hostages; his uncle Guerri the Red of Arras accompanied
him and with a hundred and forty men and much costly clothing he
rode straight without stopping to demand from King Louis the fatal
gift. Raoul was in his right, as I have told you; it was the king of St.
Denis who was in the wrong. When the king is bad many a loyal man
suffers for it. The barons arrived at the court at Paris and dismounted
beneath the olive trees. Then they went up the palace steps and demanded to see the king. They found King Louis sitting upon his throne;
he looked and saw all these nobles coming, headed by the eager Raoul;
"Salutations to the great king Louis," said he, "on behalf of God who
suffered on the cross." The emperor replied slowly: "May God, who
made paradise, protect thee, nephew!"

Raoul, the noble baron, spoke: "Just emperor. I desire to speak only to you; I am your nephew and you must not act unfairly towards me. I have heard of the death of Herbert, lord and suzerain of Vermandois. Now invest me at once with his land, for thus you swore that you would do, and you pledged it to me by hostages." "I cannot, brother," said the baron Louis. "This noble count of whom thou speakest has four valiant sons, than whom no better knights can be found. If now I handed their land over to you, every right-minded person would blame me for it and I could not summon them to my court, for they would refuse to serve or honour me. Besides, I tell thee, I have no desire to disinherit them: I do not wish to vex four men on account of one." Raoul listened and thought he would go mad. He cannot think, he is so enraged, but he turns away in a fury and does not stop till he reaches his palace and finds the hostages waiting there, whereupon he calls them to him upon their oath.

Count Raoul was very angry. He called upon Droon and Geoffroy the bold of Anjou, who was much dismayed at the news, Herbert of the Maine and Gerard and Henry, Samson and the aged Bernard. "Come hither, barons, I bid you, as you have pledged and sworn to do. To-morrow at daybreak I summon you upon your oath to my tower and, by St. Geri, you will be filled with despair." Geoffroy shuddered when he heard these words and said: "Friend, why do you alarm me thus?" "I will tell you" replied Raoul. "Herbert who owned Origny and St. Quentin, Péronne and Clairy, Ham and Roie, Nesle and Falévy, is dead. Do you think that I have been invested with this rich fief? I tell you no, for the emperor has failed toward me completely." And the barons all replied: "Give us time: for we will go to Louis and learn from his own lips how he means to protect us." "I grant it, by my faith," said Raoul, and Bernier goes to the palace and all the hostages go straightway to the king. Geoffroy speaks first and implores the mercy of the king: "Just emperor, we are in an evil plight; why has thou given us as hostages to this devil, the greatest felon that ever donned a hauberk? Herbert, the best of barons, is dead, and he wishes to be invested with the whole of his fief."

Geoffroy the bold spoke again: "Just emperor, you committed great folly when you gave your nephew such a heritage and the title deed to some one else's land. Count Herbert is dead and he ruled a large estate. Raoul is in the right; the outrage is yours. You will have to invest him with it—we are the hostages therefor." "God," said the king, "it nearly makes me mad to think that four men should lose their heritage on account of one! By the one who caused the statue to speak, I swear this gift will turn out to his undoing. Unless some pact of marriage stays his hand there will be grief in many a noble home."

The king speaks, and he is sad at heart: "Fair nephew Raoul, come hither. I give you the glove, but the land is yours on such terms as I shall tell you: to wit that neither I nor my men will help thee in any way." "I ask for nothing better," Raoul replies. But Bernier heard his words and leapt up, and he speaks out so that all can hear: "The sons of Herbert are valiant knights, rich and possessed of many friends and never will they suffer any loss through you." The Frenchmen in the palace, both old and young, talk of the matter, and they say: "The boy Raoul has the mind of a man. He is demanding a fair exchange for his father's land. The king is stirring up a great war which will bring a sad heart to many a fair lady."

Bernier, who does not lack courage, speaks out loudly again: "Just emperor, consider whether there be not unreason in all this. The sons of Herbert have done no wrong, and they should not be misjudged in your court. Why do you surrender their land like this? May the Lord God not forgive them if they defend not their lands against Raoul!" "So be it," said the king straightway; "since against my will he has accepted the gift, never shall the pennon float from my lance on his behalf."

Bernier speaks to Raoul of Cambrai: "I am your man, I deny it not, but for my part I will never advise you to seize their lands, for I know that Ernaut of Douai alone has fifty followers and there are no such warriors in all the land. Go now to law before any wrong is committed. If they have wronged thee, I will make amends for them. I will be surety for them out of love to thee." "By my faith," replied Raoul, "I will not think of it. The grant is made and I will not give it up at any price." Said Bernier: "Then, Sire, I will say no more until such time as I see their strong defence."

D. THE TRUCE OF GOD

[Proclamation of the Truce of God by the bishop of Cologne, late eleventh century]

Inasmuch as in our own times the church, through its members, has been extraordinarily afflicted by tribulations and difficulties, so that tranquillity and peace were wholly despaired of, we have endeavored by God's help to aid it, suffering so many burdens and perils. And by the advice of our faithful subjects we have at length provided this remedy, so that we might to some extent re-establish, on certain days at least, the peace which, because of our sins, we could not make enduring. Accordingly we have enacted and set forth the following: Having called together our parishioners to a legally summoned council, which was held at Cologne, the chief city of our province, in the Church of St. Peter, in the 1083rd year of our Lord's Incarnation, in the sixth indiction, on the XII day before the Kalends of May [April

20], after arranging other business, we have caused to be read in public what we proposed to do in this matter. After this had been for some time fully discussed "pro and con" by all, it was unanimously agreed upon, both the clergy and the people consenting, and we declared in what manner and during what parts of the year it ought to be observed:

Namely, that from the first day of the Advent of our Lord through Epiphany, and from the beginning of Septuagesima to the eighth day after Pentecost and through that whole day, and throughout the year on every Sunday, Friday and Saturday, and on the fast days of the four seasons, and on the eve and the day of all the apostles, and on all days canonically set apart—or which shall in the future be set apart—for fasts or feasts, this decree of peace shall be observed; so that both those who travel and those who remain at home may enjoy security and the most entire peace, so that no one may commit murder, arson, robbery or assault, no one may injure another with a sword, club or any kind of weapon, and so that no one irritated by any wrong, from the Advent of our Lord to the eighth day after Epiphany, and from Septuagesima to the eighth day after Pentecost, may presume to carry arms, shields, sword or lance, or moreover any kind of armor. On the remaining days indeed, viz., on Sundays, Fridays, apostles' days and the vigils of the apostles, and on every day set aside, or to be set aside, for fasts or feasts, bearing arms shall be legal, but on this condition that no injury shall be done in any way to anyone. If it shall be necessary for anyone in the time of the decreed peace—*i.e.*, from the Advent of our Lord to the eighth day after Epiphany, and from Septuagesima to the eighth day after Pentecost—to go from one bishopric into another in which the peace is not observed, he may bear arms, but on the condition that he shall not injure anyone, except in self-defence if he is attacked; and when he returns into our diocese he shall immediately lay aside his arms. If it shall happen that any castle is besieged during the days which are included within the peace the besiegers shall cease from attack unless they are set upon by the besieged and compelled to beat the latter back.

And in order that this statute of peace should not be violated by anyone rashly or with impunity, a penalty was fixed by the common consent of all: if a free man or noble violates it, *i.e.*, commits homicide or wounds anyone or is at fault in any manner whatever, he shall be expelled from our territory without any indulgence on account of the payment of money or the intercession of friends, and his heirs shall take all his property; if he holds a fief, the lord to whom it belongs shall receive it again. Moreover, if it is learned that his heirs after his expulsion have furnished him any support or aid, and if they are convicted of it, the estate shall be taken from them and given to the king.

But if they wish to clear themselves of the charge against them, they shall take oath with twelve who are equally free or equally noble. If a slave kills a man, he shall be beheaded; if he wounds a man, he shall lose a hand; if he does an injury in any other way with his fist or a club, or by striking with a stone, he shall be shorn and flogged. If, however, he is accused and wishes to prove his innocence, he shall clear himself by the ordeal of cold water, but he must himself be put into the water and no one else in his place; if, however, fearing the sentence decreed against him, he flees, he shall be under a perpetual excommunication; and if he is known to be in any place, letters shall be sent thither, in which it shall be announced to all that he is excommunicate, and that it is unlawful for anyone to associate with him. In the case of boys who have not yet completed their twelfth year, the hand ought not to be cut off; but only in the case of those who are twelve years or more of age. Nevertheless if boys fight, they shall be whipped and deterred from fighting.

It is not an infringement of the peace, if anyone orders his delinquent slave, pupil, or anyone in any way under his charge to be chastised with rods or cudgels. It is also an exception to this constitution of peace, if the Lord King publicly orders an expedition to attack the enemies of the kingdom or is pleased to hold a council to judge the enemies of justice. The peace is not violated if, during the time, the duke or other counts, advocates or their substitutes hold courts and inflict punishment legally on thieves, robbers and other criminals.

The statute of this imperial peace is especially enacted for the security of those engaged in feuds; but after the end of the peace, they are not to dare to rob and plunder in the villages and houses, because the laws and penalties enacted before the institution of the peace are still legally valid to restrain them from crime, moreover because robbers and highwaymen are excluded from this divine peace and indeed from any peace.

If anyone attempts to oppose this pious institution and is unwilling to promise peace to God with the others or to observe it, no priest in our diocese shall presume to say a mass for him or shall take any care for his salvation; if he is sick, no Christian shall dare to visit him; on his death-bed he shall not receive the Eucharist, unless he repents. The supreme authority of the peace promised to God and commonly extolled by all will be so great that it will be observed not only in our time, but forever among our posterity, because if anyone shall presume to infringe, destroy or violate it, either now or ages hence, at the end of the world, he is irrevocably excommunicated by us.

The infliction of the above mentioned penalties on the violators of the peace is not more in the power of the counts, centenaries or officials, than in that of the whole people in common; and they are to be especially careful not to show friendship or hatred or do anything contrary to justice in punishing, and not to conceal the crimes, if they can be hidden, but to bring them to light. No one is to receive money for the release of those taken in fault, or to attempt to aid the guilty by any favor of any kind, because whoever does this incurs the intolerable damnation of his soul; and all the faithful ought to remember that this peace has not been promised to men, but to God, and therefore must be observed so much the more rigidly and firmly. Wherefore we exhort all in Christ to guard inviolably this necessary contract of peace, and if anyone hereafter presumes to violate it, let him be damned by the ban of irrevocable excommunication and by the anathema of eternal perdition.

In the churches however, and in the cemeteries of the churches, honor and reverence are to be paid to God, so that if any robber or thief flees thither, he is by no means to be killed or seized, but he is to remain there until by urgent hunger he is compelled to surrender. If any person presumes to furnish arms or food to the criminal or to aid him in flight, the same penalty shall be inflicted on him as on the criminal. Moreover by our ban we interdict laymen from punishing the transgressions of the clergy and those living under this order; but if seized in open crime they shall be handed over to their bishop. In cases in which laymen are to be executed, the clergy are to be degraded; in cases in which laymen are to be mutilated, the clergy are to be suspended from office and with the consent of the laymen they are to suffer frequent fasts and floggings until they atone.

33 / MANORIAL LIFE

The major feudal lords derived a great part of their income, and minor lords nearly all their revenue, from their manorial estates on which the labor was provided by dependent serfs. By no means all medieval peasants were manorial serfs bound to the land; in southern France, eastern England, and eastern Germany the free peasant was very common. But from at least the sixth century until the later Middle Ages, more than half of the European peasantry were bound to the land and required to provide services and rents to the lord. In return the manorial serf received a small amount of land and the opportunity to earn a living. He also possessed certain limited rights under the law, but since he had to seek justice in the lord's court, his chances of winning a lawsuit against his lord were rather slim.

The life of the medieval peasant has often been pictured as a jolly one. Whether it was in fact the reader may judge from the following selections: first, an extract from the records of one of the manors of Battle Abbey in England in 1307 (A); [4] *then an assessment by a modern authority, H. S. Bennett, of the economic problems of the manorial peasant (B).* [5]

A. A MANOR IN 1307

Extent of the manor of Bernehorne, made on Wednesday following the feast of St. Gregory the pope, in the thirty-fifth year of the reign of King Edward, in the presence of Brother Thomas, keeper of Marley, John de la More, and Adam de Thruhlegh, clerks, on the oath of William de Gocecoumbe, Walter le Parker, Richard le Knyst, Richard the son of the latter, Andrew of Estone, Stephen Morsprich, Thomas Brembel, William of Swynham, John Pollard, Roger le Glide, John Syward, and John de Lillingewist, who say that there are all the following holdings: . . .

The total of the acres of woods is 12 acres.

The total of the acres of arable land is 444 acres and 3 roods, of which 147 acres 4 roods are maritime land, 101 acres marshy land, and 180 acres waste ground.

The total of the acres of meadow is 13 acres 1 rood.

The total of the whole preceding extent 18£. 10s. 4d.

John Pollard holds a half acre in Aldithewisse and owes 18d. at the four terms, and owes from it relief and heriot.

John Suthinton holds a house and 40 acres of land and owes 3s. 6d. at Easter and Michaelmas.

William of Swynhamme holds 1 acre of meadow in the thicket of Swynhamme and owes 1d. at the feast of Michaelmas.

Ralph of Leybourne holds a cottage and 1 acre of land in Pinden and owes 3s. at Easter and Michaelmas, and attendance at the court in the manor every three weeks, relief and heriot.

Richard Knyst of Swynham holds two acres and a half of land and owes yearly 4s.

William at Knelle holds 2 acres of land in Aldithewisse and owes yearly 4s.

Roger le Glede holds a cottage and 3 roods of land and owes 2s. 6d. at Easter and Michaelmas.

---

[4] A. *Custumals of Battle Abbey*, transl. D. C. Munro, *Translations and Reprints*, Vol. III, No. 5 (Philadelphia: University of Pennsylvania Press), pp. 7–11.

[5] H. S. Bennett, *Life on the English Manor* (Cambridge: Cambridge University Press, 1960), pp. 77–8, 95–6. Reprinted by permission of Cambridge University Press.

Alexander Hamound holds a little piece of land near Aldithewisse and owes 1 goose, of the value of 2d.

The sum of the whole rent of the free tenants, with the value of the goose, is 18s. 9d.

They say moreover that John of Cayworth holds a house and 30 acres of land, and owes yearly 2s. at Easter and Michaelmas; and he owes a cock and two hens at Christmas, of the value of 4d.

And he ought to harrow for 2 days at the Lenten sowing with one man and his own horse and his own harrow, the value of the work being 4d.; and he is to receive from the lord on each day 3 meals, of the value of 5d., and then the lord will be at a loss of 1d. Thus his harrowing is of no value to the service of the lord.

And he ought to carry the manure of the lord for 2 days with 1 cart, with his own 2 oxen, the value of the work being 8d.; and he is to receive from the lord each day 3 meals of the price as above. And thus the service is worth 3d. clear.

And he shall find 1 man for 2 days for mowing the meadow of the lord, who can mow, by estimation 1 acre and a half, the value of the mowing of an acre being 6d.; the sum is therefore 9d.; and he is to receive each day 3 meals of the value given above; and thus that mowing is worth 4d. clear.

And he ought to gather and carry that same hay which he has cut, the price of the work being 3d.

And he shall have from the lord 2 meals for 1 man, of the value of 1½d. Thus the work will be worth 1½d. clear.

And he ought to carry the hay of the lord for 1 day with a cart and 3 animals of his own, the price of the work being 6d. And he shall have from the lord 3 meals of the value of 2½d. And thus the work is worth 3½d. clear.

And he ought to carry in autumn beans or oats for 2 days with a cart and 3 animals of his own, the value of the work being 12d. And he shall receive from the lord each day 3 meals of the value given above; and thus the work is worth 7d. clear.

And he ought to find 1 man for 2 days to cut heath, the value of the work being 4d., and he shall have 3 meals each day of the value given above: and thus the lord will lose, if he receives the service, 3d. Thus that mowing is worth nothing to the service of the lord.

And he ought to carry the heath which he has cut, the value of the work being 5d. And he shall receive from the lord 3 meals at the price of 2½d. And thus the work will be worth 2½d. clear.

And he ought to carry to Battle, twice in the summer season, each time half a load of grain, the value of the service being 4d. And he shall receive in the manor each time 1 meal of the value of 2d. And thus the work is worth 2d. clear.

The totals of the rents, with the value of the hens, is 2s. 4d.

The total of the value of the works is 2s. 3½d., owed from the said John yearly.

William of Cayworth holds a house and 30 acres of land and owes at Easter and Michaelmas 2s. rent. And he shall do all customs just as the aforesaid John of Cayworth.

William atte Grene holds a house and 30 acres of land and owes in all things the same as the said John.

Alan atte Felde holds a house and 16 acres of land (for which the sergeant pays to the court of Bixley 2s.), and he owes at Easter and Michaelmas 4s., attendance at the manor court, relief, and heriot.

John Lyllingwyst holds a house and 4 acres of land and owes at the two terms 2s., attendance at the manor court, relief, and heriot.

The same John holds 1 acre of land in the fields of Hoo and owes at the two periods 2s., attendance, relief, and heriot.

Reginald atte Denne holds a house and 18 acres of land and owes at the said periods 18d., attendance, relief, and heriot.

Robert of Northehou holds 3 acres of land at Saltcoat and owes at the said periods attendance, relief, and heriot.

Total of the rents of the villeins, with the value of the hens, 20s.

Total of all the works of these three villeins, 6s. 10½d.

And it is to be noted that none of the above-named villeins can give their daughters in marriage, nor cause their sons to be tonsured, nor can they cut down timber growing on the lands they hold, without license of the bailiff or sergeant of the lord, and then for building purposes and not otherwise. And after the death of any one of the aforesaid villeins, the lord shall have as a heriot his best animal, if he had any; if, however, he have no living beast, the lord shall have no heriot, as they say. The sons or daughters of the aforesaid villeins shall give, for entrance into the holding after the death of their predecessors, as much as they give of rent per year.

Sylvester, the priest, holds 1 acre of meadow adjacent to his house and owes yearly 3s.

Total of the rents of tenants for life, 3s.

Petronilla atte Holme holds a cottage and a piece of land and owes at Easter and Michaelmas _____; also, attendance, relief, and heriot.

Walter Herying holds a cottage and a piece of land and owes at Easter and Michaelmas 18d., attendance, relief, and heriot.

Isabella Mariner holds a cottage and owes at the feast of St. Michael 12d., attendance, relief, and heriot.

Jordan atte Melle holds a cottage and 1½ acres of land and owes at Easter and Michaelmas 2s., attendance, relief, and heriot.

William of Batelesmere holds 1 acre of land with a cottage and owes at the feast of St. Michael 3d., and 1 cock and 1 hen at Christmas of the value of 3d., attendance, relief, and heriot.

John le Man holds half an acre of land with a cottage and owes at the feast of St. Michael 2s., attendance, relief, and heriot.

John Werthe holds 1 rood of land with a cottage and owes at the said term 18d., attendance, relief, and heriot.

Geoffrey Caumbreis holds half an acre and a cottage and owes at the said term 18d., attendance, relief, and heriot.

William Hassok holds 1 rood of land and a cottage and owes at the said term 18d., attendance, relief, and heriot.

The same man holds 3½ acres of land and owes yearly at the feast of St. Michael 3s. for all.

Roger Doget holds half an acre of land and a cottage, which were those of R. the miller, and owes at the feast of St. Michael 18d., attendance, relief, and heriot.

Thomas le Brod holds 1 acre and a cottage and owes at the said term 3s., attendance, relief, and heriot.

Agnes of Cayworth holds half an acre and a cottage and owes at the said term 18d., attendance, relief, and heriot. . . .

Total of the rents of the said cottagers, with the value of the hens, 34s. 6d.

And it is to be noted that all the said cottagers shall do as regards giving their daughters in marriage, having their sons tonsured, cutting down timber, paying heriot, and giving fines for entrance, just as John of Cayworth and the rest of the villeins above mentioned.

Note: Fines and penalties, with heriots and reliefs, are worth yearly 5s.

B. H. S. BENNETT: ECONOMIC PROBLEMS OF THE MANORIAL PEASANT

Let us now turn to the actual day-to-day operations which medieval agriculture made necessary, and let us consider for convenience the task confronting a manorial peasant, who, as we have seen, had his strips in the common fields. In those parts of England where the two-field system prevailed he found himself working on one field during one year while the other field lay fallow for most of the year, but was ploughed from time to time, and the next year vice versa. In those areas where the three-field system was in vogue, one field was planted in the autumn with wheat (and perhaps rye) as its main crop, another with oats, vetches, or barley in the following spring, while the third field was fallow. The next year the fallow field was used for wheat, the first for oats, etc., while the second field rested. The third year completed the cycle, and in this elementary fashion men sought to keep their land fertile. It was a wellnigh impossible task, for the number of species they had at their command was very limited: wheat, oats, rye, barley, vetches, beans and peas were the main crops; roots and artificial grasses were unknown, so that any serious rotation of crops which would give the ground a chance to recover was impossible.

The peasants were even worse off than their lords in this respect, for not only had the lord the unrestricted right to the manure of his own herds, but he had also a *jus faldae*—a right of folding all the manorial sheep (and sometimes all cattle) on his own lands. This privilege he sometimes was able to exercise for a limited period only, but on some manors he could exercise it throughout the year. The lord's shepherd, therefore, was expected to see to it that his master's fold was moved about from place to place on the demesne, and also to report any peasants who were so bold as to keep their sheep on their own holdings. The privilege to do this could be got only by a cash payment. Cattle markets and fairs were also a welcome aid in fertilising the ground, but here also the lord usually insisted that these were held on his land, and even that the dung in the streets of the vill should be reserved for his own use.

All this evidence clearly indicates that medieval farmers understood quite well the need for constant manuring, and yet at the same time it was very difficult for the peasant to accomplish this on his own holding. When we recall the slender resources which were at his command the reasons for his constant defeat are obvious. First, as we have seen, the lord had the *jus faldae*. Secondly we must bear in mind that the peasant could not keep any large number of animals himself owing to the difficulty of feeding them throughout the winter. He had great difficulty in keeping the comparatively limited numbers he owned, and was forced to feed them on what would now be considered very scanty rations. The amount of manure, therefore, he could hope for from animals fed in this way was limited. The peasant was caught: he had neither the number of animals, the unrestricted use of them, nor adequate fodder to produce the quantity of manure that soil, cultivated under the medieval cropping system, required if it were not to lose its productive power. He did what he could: he worked to get his land manured, and even at times went to the great labour of carrying marl or lime and treating his land with this, but it was an uphill task. . . .

Our rapid examination of the 30-acre holder's resources leaves the impression that, given reasonable harvests, he had no difficulty in producing enough corn and livestock to keep himself and his family, and to leave something over for sale or exchange. But we have constantly to be reminding ourselves that no manor was made up of the "typical" villein—the virgater or 30-acre holder. As we have seen, every manor had a number of *undermanni*—men holding anything from a little "close" of a rood or two to seven or eight acres, as well as others who held as much as half a virgate and so on. The manorial holdings were capable of innumerable grades, and the resources of the lowest of these grades must have been slender. If we assume that some 36–40 bushels of corn were a minimum requirement for a normal family, it is clear that this required a holding of between five and ten acres—and probably nearer ten than five—on which it could be grown. Those who held less than this were forced to adopt a lower standard of living, or to seek auxiliary means of augmenting their incomes by helping on wealthier men's holdings, or by working as manorial servants, or as communal shepherds or swineherds, or in one of the village trades.

But whatever means were employed, it seems that a considerable number of peasants in the medieval village lived very near the border line of actual want. For them, as for the poor man in *Piers Plowman*, there was many a "winter time when they suffered much hunger and woe."

34 / THE GREGORIAN REFORM AND THE DEBATE ON THE NATURE OF A CHRISTIAN SOCIETY

The world order of the eleventh century, based on feudalism, manorialism, and theocratic monarchy, included the Church within its institutional nexus to the extent that the areas of Church and state were intertwined and interdependent. Theocratic kings such as the German emperors of the Salian dynasty were the leaders and patrons of their territorial churches, and churchmen were feudal and manorial lords and the chief ministers of kings. Beginning in the 1050's, a group of very able and brilliant cardinals at Rome began to protest against this world order and to advocate instead the "liberty of the Church," which meant not only the freedom of the Church from secular control but also the assertion of papal authority over all of Christian society and the subjection of kings, from whom they removed sacred qualities, to papal authority. In the pontificate of Gregory

VII (1073–1085) *an attempt was made to realize these ideas. The result was the great investiture controversy between pope and emperor, which takes its name from Gregory's claim that the German ruler Henry IV (1056–1106) had no right to invest bishops and abbots with the symbols of their office and thereby to control their appointments.*

The investiture controversy did not end until 1122. It involved civil war in Germany, the deposition of the emperor by the pope, the emperor's attempt to regain his authority through self-humiliation before Gregory at Canossa in 1077, the renewal of the struggle, the weakening of the institutions of the central royal government and the rise of powerful territorial princes in the empire, a short-lived investiture dispute between 1103 and 1107 with Anglo-Norman king Henry I (1100–1135), and a great public debate on the nature of Christian society. Neither side won in this momentous struggle over right order in the world. The exhausted parties resorted to formal compromise by the Concordat of London of 1107 and the Concordat of Worms in 1122, by which the English and German rulers conceded they had no right to invest churchmen and thereby admitted that their theocratic claims had been wrong, and the pope allowed the kings to continue to demand feudal homage from ecclesiastics as a way of maintaining their authority over bishops and abbots and of controlling Church appointments. The English kings found their domination over their territorial church virtually undiminished, but the central institutions of the German monarchy had in any case suffered severe damage.

The papacy of the twelfth and thirteenth centuries did not abandon Gregory's aims, but devoted itself to the more limited policy of creating a great and complex international legal, financial, and political institution centered on Rome through the obtaining of agreements, concessions, and compromises with particular kings. The spirit of the Gregorian papacy was revolutionary, puritanical, uncompromising; the spirit of the twelfth- and thirteenth-century papacy was legalistic, political, and diplomatic. The Gregorian reformers had, however, put forward ideas in the heat of argument, such as the Donatist heretical idea of a saintly, purified priesthood and the necessity of ecclesiastical poverty in imitation of the apostolic Church, which were to inspire the great heretical movements of the high and late Middle Ages and which would eventually play a leading role in undermining the authority and unity of the medieval Church. In the following selections are presented the main lines of argument during the investiture controversy: Gregory VII on church and kingship (A); [6] *the negation of the Donatist doctrine that the personal morality of priests affected the validity of their ordained powers of ministering the sacraments, made by the saintly mystic, theologian, and devotional leader Cardinal Peter Damiani (d. 1072) against the heretical opinions of his brilliant colleague Cardinal Humbert (d. 1061) (B);* [7] *Henry IV's impassioned defense of theocratic monarchy (C);* [8] *a defense of royal authority from a moderate, conservative, position made by Hugh, a monk in the French abbey of Fleury, an affiliate of the great monastery of Cluny, which stood for the conservative view of Church-state relations as they existed in the Carolingian and German empires (D);* [9] *the extreme royalist position in the so-called* Anonymous of York *tractates, probably written by Archbishop Gerard of York to defend Henry I's position in the English investiture dispute (E);* [10] *and finally the radical pronouncement in 1111 by Pope Paschal II (1099–1116), the most revolutionary of the Gregorian reformers, that he had ended the investiture controversy by abandoning to the German king all the wealth and secular power of the German Church, a solution which neither the German bishops nor the Roman cardinals would accept, but which had a great influence on the origins of the doctrine of apostolic poverty of the Church, declared a heresy by the papacy in the early fourteenth century (F).* [11]

[6] Parts I, II, and III from *Das Register Gregors VII, Monumenta Germaniae Historica*, E. Caspar, ed. (Berlin: Weidmannische Buchhandlung, 1920), pp. 202–8, 270–1, 312–4. By permission of Monumenta Germaniae Historica.

Part IV from J. H. Robinson, *Readings in European History* (Boston: Ginn & Co., 1904), Vol. I, pp. 284–7.

[7] *Libelli de Lite, Monumenta Germaniae Historica* (Hanover: Impensis Bibliopoli, 1891), Vol. I, pp. 21, 24.

[8] E. F. Henderson, *Select Historical Documents of the Middle Ages* (London: G. Bell & Sons, 1925), pp. 372–3. Reprinted by permission of G. Bell & Sons.

[9] N. F. Cantor, *Church, Kingship and Lay Investiture in England 1089–1135* (Princeton, N. J.: Princeton University Press, 1958), pp. 228–9, 230–1. Reprinted by permission of Princeton University Press.

[10] N. F. Cantor, *Church, Kingship and Lay Investiture in England 1089–1135* (Princeton, N. J.: Princeton University Press, 1958), pp. 191–2. Reprinted by permission of Princeton University Press.

[11] J. H. Robinson, *Readings in European History* (Boston: Ginn & Co., 1904), Vol. I, 290–2.

A. GREGORY VII ON CHURCH AND KINGSHIP

I. *Dictatus Papae* [12]

1. That the Roman Church was founded by God alone.
2. That the Roman pontiff alone can by right be called universal.
3. That he alone can depose and reinstate bishops.
4. That his legate should take precedence over all bishops in a council, even if he is of lower rank, and can pronounce the sentence of deposition against them.
5. That the Pope may depose those who are absent.
6. That, among other things, we ought not to remain in the same house with those who have been excommunicated by him.
7. That to him alone is it granted, in accordance with the needs of the time, to establish new laws, to assemble new congregations, to make an abbey out of a canonry and vice versa, and to divide a wealthy bishopric and unite poor ones.
8. That he alone may use the imperial insignia.
9. That all princes should kiss the feet of the pope alone.
10. That his name alone should be recited in the churches.
11. That his name is unique in the world.
12. That he ought to be allowed to depose emperors.
13. That, when necessity forces him to it, he should be allowed to transfer bishops from diocese to diocese.
14. That he has the power to ordain a clerk from any church whensoever he shall wish it.
15. That the man ordained by him can preside over another church, but he cannot serve it in an inferior capacity; and that he ought not to accept a higher rank from any other bishop.
16. That no synod ought to be called general without his command.
17. That no chapter and no book shall be considered canonical without his authority.
18. That his sentence ought to be retracted by nobody, and he alone, of all men, can retract it.
19. That he ought to be judged by no man.
20. That no man should dare to condemn a man who is an appellant to the Apostolic Throne.
21. That the more important cases of each and every church should be referred to that See.

---

[12] Most, and perhaps all, of these statements were extracted from early medieval canon-law collections.

22. That the Roman Church has never erred, nor, as Scripture proclaims, will it ever err, through all eternity.

23. That the Roman pontiff, if he was canonically ordained, has undoubtedly been sanctified by the merits of the blessed Peter, as St. Ennodius, bishop of Pavia, tells us and many saintly fathers believe; just as it is stated in the decrees of the blessed Pope Symmachus.

24. That by his command and permission subordinates may be allowed to bring accusations.

25. That he can depose and reinstate bishops without calling a synod.

26. That he who does not agree with the Church of Rome should not be considered a Catholic.

27. That he can absolve vassals from their allegiance to iniquitous men.

II. Excommunication of Henry IV

Oh St. Peter, prince of the apostles, incline, we pray, your holy ears to us, and hear me, your servant, whom you have nourished from infancy, and whom you have, even unto this day, freed from the hands of wicked men who did hate me, and hate me still, for my faithfulness to you. You, as well as my mistress the Mother of God, and your brother St. Paul, are my witness among all the saints that your holy Roman Church dragged me unwilling to its helm; that I did not think to ascend your seat through violence; and that I would rather have wished to end my life in pilgrimage, than to have seized your place by secular means for the sake of the glory of this world. And therefore do I believe that it is because of your grace, and not because of my own good works, that it did please you, and does please you now, that the Christian people, who were especially entrusted to you, should obey me, because your office has been especially entrusted to me. And mine also is your God-given power of binding and loosing, in heaven and on earth. And so, placing my confidence in this belief, for the honor and protection of your Church, and in the name of Almighty God, Father, Son, and Holy Spirit, I do withdraw, through your power and authority, the government of the whole kingdom of Germany and Italy from King Henry, son of Emperor Henry, because he has risen against your Church with unheard of insolence. I absolve all Christians from the bond of any oath which they have sworn or will swear unto him, and I forbid anyone to serve him as a king. For it is meet that he who strives to diminish the honor of your Church should himself lose that honor which he seems to possess. And since he has scorned to obey as a Christian, and has not returned to God Whom he abandoned by associating with the excommunicated; by spurning the warnings which I, as you are my witness, sent him for his own salvation; and by separating himself from your Church and trying to sunder it: I, in your place, do bind him with the chain of anathema. On the strength of your faith, I do bind him thus that all the nations may know and confirm that you are Peter, and on this rock the Son of the living God has built His Church and the gates of Hell shall not prevail against it.

III. Canossa

Bishop Gregory, servant of the servants of God, sends greetings and apostolic benediction to all the archbishops, bishops, dukes, counts, and other rulers of the kingdom of the Germans who are defending the Christian faith.

Since for the love of justice you have undertaken common cause and danger with us in the struggle of Christian warfare, we have taken care to describe to you, beloved, in what manner the king, humbled unto repentance, obtained the grace of absolution, and how the whole affair has proceeded from the time of his entry into Italy until this day.

As it had been decided with the legates, who had been sent to us in your names, we came to Lombardy about twenty days before the date on which one of the dukes was supposed to have met us at the pass, and we awaited his arrival so that we might cross over into that region. But when that date had passed, we were told—and well do we believe it—that because of many difficulties, no escort could, at this time be sent to meet us. And since we had no other way of going across to you, we were troubled by no small anxiety as to what should be the best thing for us to do.

Meanwhile, we received certain information that the king was arriving. And he, before entering Italy, offered through the suppliant legates whom he sent on to us, to render satisfaction in all things to God, to St. Peter, and to us. Once again he promised to amend his life and observe all obedience if only he might deserve to obtain the grace of absolution and apostolic favor from us. After we had long deferred this by holding many consultations, and had bitterly reproached him, through all the messengers who passed between us, for his excesses, he, with a few of his followers, came of his own free will, and without displaying any hostility or haughtiness, to the town of Canossa in which we were staying. And there, in a pathetic manner, having cast aside all his royal apparel, unshod and clothed in wool, he remained before the gate of the town for three days. Nor did he cease to implore with many tears the aid and consolation of apostolic mercy until he had moved all who were there, and all who had heard the story, to such pity and merciful compassion that they interceded for him with many prayers and tears. Indeed, all were amazed at the unwonted hardness of our heart, and some even declared that we were displaying not the austerity of apostolic severity, but, as it were, the cruelty of tyrannical ferocity.

At last, having been overcome by the sincerity of his compunction, and the persistent supplication of those who were there, we loosed the chain of anathema and received him back into the grace of communion and the bosom of Holy Mother Church. We also accepted guarantees through the hands of the Abbot of Cluny, of our daughters Mathilda and the Countess Adelaide, and of other princes, episcopal and lay, who seemed to us useful for this purpose.

And when all these things had been accomplished, we wanted to cross over into your territories at the first opportunity possible, so that, with the aid of God, we might more fully arrange all matters for the peace of the Church and the harmony of the kingdom, just as we have long desired. For, beloved, we wish you to know for certain that, as you can recognize in the attached guarantees, the outcome of the whole affair is still suspended, and our arrival and the unanimity of your counsel are therefore most imperative. And so, do you all strive to continue in that faith in which you have begun and in the love of justice, and know that we are not bound to the king except by our word alone, as is our custom. For we have told him that he might hope that, in those matters which are conducive to his salvation and honor, we might be able to aid him, without danger either to our soul or to his, either through justice or through mercy.

THE OATH OF HENRY, KING OF THE GERMANS

I, King Henry, shall, within the term which the lord Pope Gregory has set, render satisfaction and restore harmony, in accordance with his judgment and counsel, for the murmuring and dissension of which the archbishops, bishops, dukes, counts, and other princes of the kingdom of the Germans, and those others who follow them in the matter of this dissension, now accuse me—unless a specific impediment shall prevent either me or him from doing so. And when this has been accomplished, I shall be prepared to fulfil all the arrangements.

Likewise, if the same lord Pope Gregory shall wish to go beyond the mountains, or to other parts of the world, he, as well as those in his escort or following, or those who have been sent by him, or who have come to him from any part of the world whatsoever, shall be secure, while going, remaining, and returning, from any injury to life or limbs, and from capture, by me or by those over whom I can exercise control. Nor shall he, by my consent, suffer any other impediment contrary to his dignity. And, if anyone shall offer such hindrance, I shall aid him, in good faith, and in accordance with my power.

Given at Canossa on the fifth day before the Kalends of February [January 28], in the fifteenth Indiction.

IV. From the Treatise on Royal and Sacerdotal Power in the Form of a Letter to Bishop Hermann of Metz

Shall not an office instituted by laymen—by those even who did not know God—be subject to that office which the providence of God Almighty has instituted for his own honor, and in compassion given to the world? For his Son, even as he is unquestioningly believed to be God and man, so is he considered the chief of priests, sitting on the right hand of the Father and always interceding for us. Yet he despised a secular kingdom, over which the men of this world swell with pride, and came of his own will to the priesthood of the cross. Whereas all know that kings and princes are descendants of men who were ignorant of God, and who, by arrogance, robbery, perfidy, murder,—in a word by almost every crime,—at the prompting of the prince of this world, the devil, strove with blind avarice and intolerable presumption to gain the mastery over their equals, that is, over mankind.

To whom, indeed, can we better compare them, when they seek to make the priests of God bend to their feet, than to him who is chief of all the sons of pride and who tempted the highest Pontiff himself, the chief of priests, the Son of the Most High, and promised to him all the kingdoms of the world, saying, "All these will I give thee, if thou wilt fall down and worship me"?

Who doubts that the priests of Christ should be regarded as the fathers and masters of kings and princes, and of all the faithful? Is it not evidently hopeless folly for a son to attempt to domineer over his father, a pupil over his master, or for any one, by iniquitous exactions, to claim power over him by whom he himself, as he acknowledges, can be bound and loosed both on earth and in heaven? . . .

In short, any good Christian whatsoever might far more properly be considered as a king than might a bad prince; for the former, seeking the glory of God, strenuously governs himself, whereas the latter, seeking the things which are his own and not the things of God, is an enemy to himself and a tyrannical oppressor of others. Faithful Christians constitute the body of the true king, Christ; evil rulers, that of the devil. The former rule themselves in the hope that they will eternally reign with the Supreme Emperor, but the sway of the latter ends in their destruction and eternal damnation with the prince of darkness, who is king over all the sons of pride.

It is certainly not strange that wicked bishops are of one mind with a bad king, whom they love and fear for the honors which they have wrongfully obtained from him. Such men, simoniacally ordaining whom they please, sell God even for a paltry sum. As even the elect are indissolubly united with their Head, so also the wicked constitute a pertinacious league with him who is the head of evil, with the special purpose of resisting the good. But surely we ought not so much to inveigh against them as to mourn for them with tears and lamentations, beseeching God Almighty to snatch them from the snares of Satan in which they are held captive, and after their peril to bring them at last to a knowledge of the truth.

We refer to those kings and emperors who, too much elated by worldly glory, rule not for God but for themselves. Now, since it belongs to our office to admonish and encourage everyone as befits the special rank or dignity which he enjoys, we endeavor, by God's grace, to implant in emperors and kings and other princes the virtue of humility, that they may be able to allay the gusts of passion and the floods of pride. For we know that mundane glory and worldly cares usually foster pride, especially in those who are in authority, and that, in consequence, they forget humility and seek ever their own glory, and dominion over their brethren. Wherefore it is well for kings and emperors, particularly when they grow haughty in spirit and delight in their own pomp, to discover a means by which they may be humbled and be brought to realize that the cause of their complacency is the very thing that they should most fear.

Let them, therefore, diligently consider how dangerous and how much to be dreaded are the royal and imperial offices. For in them very few are saved, and those who, through the mercy of God, do attain to salvation are not so glorified in the holy Church by the will of the Holy Spirit as are many of the poor. From the beginning of the world to this our own day, in the whole extent of recorded history, we do not find seven emperors or kings whose lives were as distinguished for piety and as beautified by the gift of miracles as were those of an innumerable multitude who despised the world; yet, notwithstanding this, we believe that many of them achieved salvation through the almighty God of mercy.

B. PETER DAMIANI: AGAINST DONATISM

Therefore does sincere and perfect faith hold that sacerdotal consecration, just as baptism, is in no way polluted by the taint of corrupt ministrants, is in no way violated by the offenses of another man. But let him who consecrates be ever so villainous, let him be entangled by ever so many crimes, he who is consecrated does not, on this account, suffer any damage to his sacred office, or any diminution of heavenly grace. For it is not from the merit of the priest, but from the office which he discharges, that the mystery of consecration is transmitted at the altar. Nor is it useful to consider the consecrator's manner of life, for it is only necessary to pay attention to the ministry which he has accepted. . . .

Undoubtedly, it must therefore be believed that if the consecration of any ecclesiastical office takes place within the Catholic Church, that is to say, in harmony with the orthodox Faith, the sacrament is truly valid for both participants: whatever is given by a good man to a good man is just as effectively given by a bad man to a bad man, because this sacrament does not depend on the merit of the consecrator or consecrated, but on the office of the ecclesiastical institution and on the invocation of the divine Name. And without doubt He Who consecrates is one and the same as He Who baptizes. For Christ, in His great beneficence, grants that a man may receive this sacrament without deserving it.

C. HENRY IV'S DEFENSE OF THEOCRATIC MONARCHY [13]

Henry, king not through usurpation but through the holy ordination of God, to Hildebrand, at present not pope but false monk.

Such greeting as this hast thou merited through thy disturbances, inasmuch as there is no grade in the church which thou hast omitted to make a partaker not of honour but of confusion, not of benediction, but of malediction. For, to mention few and especial cases out of many, not only hast thou not feared to lay hands upon the rulers of the holy church, the anointed of the Lord—the archbishops, namely, bishops and priests—but thou has trodden them under foot like slaves ignorant of what their master is doing. Thou hast won favour from the common herd by crushing them; thou hast looked upon all of them as knowing nothing, upon thy sole self, moreover, as knowing all things. This knowledge, however, thou hast used not for edification but for destruction; so that with reason we believe that St. Gregory, whose name thou hast usurped for thyself, was prophesying concerning thee when he said: "The pride of him who is in power increases the more, the greater number of those subject to him; and he thinks that he himself can do more than all." And we, indeed, have endured all this, being eager to guard the honour of the apostolic see;

---

[13] It should be remembered that Henry's letter was actually written by German churchmen in his service, although the opinions expressed are certainly those of the king himself.

thou, however, hast understood our humility to be fear, and hast not, accordingly, shunned to rise up against the royal power conferred upon us by God, daring to threaten to divest us of it. As if we had received our kingdom from thee! As if the kingdom and the empire were in thine and not in God's hand! And this although our Lord Jesus Christ did call us to the kingdom, did not, however, call thee to the priest-hood. For thou hast ascended by the following steps. By wiles, namely, which the profession of monk abhors, thou hast achieved money; by money, favour; by the sword, the throne of peace. And from the throne of peace thou hast disturbed the peace, inasmuch as thou hast armed subjects against those in authority over them; inasmuch as thou, who wert not called, hast taught that our bishops called of God are to be despised; inasmuch as thou hast usurped for laymen the ministry over their priests, allowing them to depose or condemn those whom they themselves had received as teachers from the hand of God through the laying on of hands of the bishops. On me also who, although unworthy to be among the anointed, have nevertheless been anointed to the kingdom, thou hast lain thy hand; me who—as the tradition of the holy Fathers teaches, declaring that I am not to be deposed for any crime unless, which God forbid, I should have strayed from the faith—am subject to the judgment of God alone. For the wisdom of the holy Fathers committed even Julian the apostate not to themselves, but to God alone, to be judged and to be deposed. For himself the true pope, Peter, also exclaims: "Fear God, honour the king." But thou who dost not fear God, dost dishonour in me His appointed one. Wherefore St. Paul, when he has not spared an angel of Heaven if he shall have preached otherwise, has not excepted thee also who dost teach other-wise upon earth. For he says: "If any one, either I or an angel from Heaven, should preach a gospel other than that which has been preached to you, he shall be damned." Thou, therefore, damned by this curse and by the judgment of all our bishops and by our own, descend and relinquish the apostolic chair which thou hast usurped. Let an-other ascend the throne of St. Peter, who shall not practise violence under the cloak of religion, but shall teach the sound doctrine of St. Peter. I, Henry, king by the grace of God, do say unto thee, together with all our bishops: Descend, descend, to be damned throughout the ages.

D. HUGH OF FLEURY: THE INVESTITURE QUESTION

Considering lord King [Henry I of England], the crisis of discord, in which the holy church is directed concerning the royal power and sacerdotal dignity, which indeed separate and divide from one an-other in turn, goaded by pious care and fraternal love I have determined to write this pamphlet, in which this dispute may be somewhat laid to rest, and the error, which is spreading far and wide, may be equally alleviated: the error, I say, of those who rashly separating the priestly dignity from the royal dignity, overturn the order arranged by God, while they imagine that they know what they do not know. For they think that the arrangement of the earthly kingdom should be ordered and arranged not by God, but by men. And therefore they place the sacerdotal dignity above the royal majesty, when the former ought to be subject to the latter on account of order, not on account of dignity. . . . Our maker and savior the Lord Jesus Christ was worthy to be called at once king and priest by most holy mystery, in order that it might be shown to us, by how much the king and priest ought to join to each other in turn by compact and union. . . . I know certain men in our times [i.e. Gregory VII in his letter to Hermann of Metz] who assert that kings had their origin not from God but from those who ignoring God, strove by pride, rapine, perfidy, murder, and finally almost universal crimes, at the devil's instigation in the beginning of the world, to dominate men who were their equals with blind cupidity and indescribable presumption and temerity. How frivolous this opinion is, is made clear by the apostolic document, which said: "There is no power but of God. The powers that be are ordained of God." By this opinion, therefore, it is certain that not by men but by God the royal power was ordained and arranged on earth. . . . "The two principal powers, by which this world is ruled, are the royal and priestly." These two powers the Lord Jesus, who was king and priest at the same time, decreed to bear in his own person only by most sacred mystery. . . . The king in the body of his kingdom is seen to obtain the image of the Omnipotent Father, and the bishop that of Christ. Whence as the Son is discovered to be subject to the Father not by nature but on account of order, all bishops of the kingdom are rightly seen to be subject to the king, so that the community of the kingdom might be reduced to one origin. . . . The office of the king is to amend from error the people subjected to him and recall them to the narrow path of equity and justice. . . . Omnipotent God is known to have preferred the king to other men, with whom he has one condition of being born and dying, in order that by his terror he may restrain from evil the people subject to himself and in order that he may subdue them rightly by laws. . . . What the priest does not prevail to achieve through the word of doctrine, the royal power achieves and commands through the terror of discipline. . . .

By the inspiration of the Holy Spirit the King can, I believe, bestow the honor of the prelacy upon a religious cleric. But the archbishop ought to give him [the bishop-elect] the care of souls. . . . Where, however, the bishop was elected by clergy and people according to ecclesiastical custom, the king ought reasonably to inflict no force or disturbance on the electors through tyranny, but he should aid his consent to the legitimate ordination. . . . After the election, the elected bishop ought to receive from the royal hand not the ring or staff, but the investiture of secular things, and from his archbishops he ought to receive, through the ring or staff, among his [ecclesiastical] orders, the care of souls, so that a matter of this kind may be accomplished without dispute, and the privilege of his authority may be preserved by both earthly and spiritual powers.

E. ANONYMOUS OF YORK: DIVINE RIGHT OF KINGS

By divine authority and the institution of the holy fathers, kings are consecrated in God's Church before the sacred altar and are anointed with holy oil and sacred benediction to exercise the ruling power over Christians, the Lord's people, . . . the Holy Church of God. . . . The power of the king is the power of God, but it is God's through nature, the king's through grace, and whatever he does is not simply as a man, but as one who has been made God and Christ through grace. . . . No one by right ought to take precedence over the king, who is blessed with so many and such great benedictions, who is consecrated and deified by so many and such great sacraments. No one receives greater or better blessings or is consecrated and dedicated to God with greater or higher sacraments, not even indeed with as many and equal sacraments, and because of this no one is the king's equal. Wherefore he is not to be called a layman, since he is the anointed of the Lord [Christus Domini] and through grace he is God. He is the supreme ruler, the chief shepherd, master, defender and instructor of the Holy Church, lord over his brethren and worthy to be "adored" by all, since he is chief and supreme prelate. Nor is he to be spoken of as inferior to the bishop, because the bishop consecrates him, since it often happens that superiors are consecrated by their inferiors. . . .

It is manifest that kings have the sacred power of ecclesiastical rule over the bishops of God and power over them. . . . Therefore it is not against the rule of sanctity, if kings confer on bishops the signs of holy rule, that is the staff and ring of honor. . . .

F. PASCHAL II: ECCLESIASTICAL POVERTY

Bishop Paschal, servant of the servants of God, to his beloved son Henry [V] and his successors forever:

It is forbidden by the provisions of divine law, and interdicted by the holy canons, that priests should busy themselves with secular concerns or should attend the public tribunals except to rescue the condemned or bear aid to those who are suffering wrong. Wherefore, also, the apostle Paul says, "If ye have judgments of things pertaining to this life, set them to judge who are least esteemed in the church." Nevertheless in portion of your kingdom bishops and abbots are so absorbed in secular affairs that they are obliged regularly to appear at court and to perform military service, pursuits rarely, if ever, carried on without plunder, sacrilege, or arson.

Ministers of the altar are become ministers of the king's court, inasmuch as they receive cities, duchies, margravates, mints, and other things which have to do with the king's service. Hence the custom has grown up, intolerable for the Church, that bishops should not receive consecration until they have first been invested by the hand of the king. From this have sprung the prevalent vices of simoniacal heresy and ambition, at times so strong that episcopal sees were filled without any previous election. Occasionally investiture has even taken place while the bishop holding the office was still alive. . . .

So, most beloved son, King Henry,—now through our sanction, by the grace of God, emperor of the Romans,—we decree that those royal appurtenances are to be restored to thee and to thy kingdom which clearly belonged to that kingdom in the time of Charles, Louis, and of thy other predecessors. We forbid and prohibit, under penalty of anathema, any bishop or abbot, present or future, from intruding upon these same royal appurtenances; in which are included the cities, duchies, margravates, counties, mints, tolls, market rights, manors, rights of royal bailiffs, and rights of the judges of the courts of the hundreds, which manifestly belong to the king, together with what pertains to them, the military posts and camps of the kingdom. Nor shall they henceforth, unless by favor of the king, have aught to do with these royal appurtenances. Neither shall it be allowable for our successors, who shall follow us in the apostolic chair, to disturb thee or thy kingdom in this matter.

In addition we decree that the churches, with their offerings and hereditary possessions which plainly do not belong to the kingdom, shall remain free. . . .

35 / THE FIRST CRUSADE

The crusading movement against the Moslems, which had roots in the Spanish Christian reconquest of northern Spain, the Norman invasion of southern Italy, and the interests of north Italian merchants in Mediterranean trade, was launched by the

*First Crusade of 1095–1096. It was succeeded by six more cru-
sades in the following two centuries, the only one of which to
have any marked success was the notorious Fourth Crusade of
1204 against Constantinople. The crusading movement, as illustrated by these records of the First Crusade, was in many ways a
microcosm of high medieval civilization; it shows medieval men
at their best and at their worst; it reveals their piety and idealism,
their materialism and violence.*[14]

ROBERT THE MONK: SPEECH OF POPE URBAN II
AT THE COUNCIL OF CLERMONT 1095

O, race of the Franks, race from across the mountains, race beloved
and chosen by God! As is clear from your many works you are a race
set apart from all other nations by the situation of your country as
well as by your catholic faith and the honor which you render to the
holy church. To you our discourse is addressed and for you our
exhortations are intended. . . .

From the confines of Jerusalem and from the city of Constantinople
has gone forth a horrible tale which has very frequently been brought
to our ears. It has been reported that a race from the kingdom of the
Persians, an accursed race, a race wholly alienated from God . . . has
violently invaded the lands of those Christians and has depopulated
them by pillage and fire. They have led away a part of the captives
into their own country, and a part they have destroyed by cruel tortures. They have either destroyed the churches of God or appropriated
them for the rites of their own religion. They destroy the altars, after
having defiled them with their uncleanness. They circumcise the
Christians, and the blood of the circumcision they either spread upon
the altars or pour into the baptismal vases.

When they wish to torture anyone by a base death, they perforate
his navel and dragging forth the extremity of the intestines, bind it
to a stake; then by blows they compel the victim to run around the
stake, until the viscera gush forth and the victim falls prostrate on the
ground. Others they bind to a post and pierce with arrows. Others they
compel to extend their necks and then, attacking them with naked
swords, attempt to cut through the neck with a single blow. What
shall I say of the abominable rape of the women? To speak of it is
worse than to be silent. The kingdom of the Greeks is now dismem-
bered by them and deprived of territory so vast in extent that it could
not be traversed in two month's time.

[14] D. C. Munro, *Translation and Reprints* (Philadelphia: University of Pennsylvania Press), Vol. I, No. 2, pp. 5–8, 13–14, No. 4, pp. 5–8, 8–10.

On whom therefore is the labor of avenging these wrongs and of recovering this territory incumbent, if not upon you? You, upon whom above all other nations God has conferred remarkable glory in arms, great courage, bodily activity, and strength to humble the heads of those who resist you. Let the deeds of your ancestors encourage you and incite your minds to manly achievements; the glory and greatness of king Charlemagne, and of his son Louis, and of your other monarchs, who have destroyed the kingdoms of the Turks and have extended the sway of the holy church over the lands of the pagans. Let the holy sepulchre of our Lord and Saviour, which is possessed by the unclean nations, especially incite you, and the holy places which are now treated with ignominy and irreverently polluted with the filth of the unclean. O, most valiant soldiers and descendants of invincible ancestors, be not degenerate, but recall the valor of your progenitors.

But if you are hindered by love of children, parents or wife, remember what the Lord says in the Gospel, "He that loveth father or mother more than me, is not worthy of me." "Everyone that hath forsaken houses, or brethren, or sisters, or father, or mother, or wife, or children, or lands for my name's sake shall receive an hundred-fold and shall inherit everlasting life." Let none of your possessions retain you nor solicitude for your family affairs. For this land which you inhabit, shut in on all sides by the seas and surrounded by mountain peaks, is too narrow for your large population; nor does it abound in wealth; and it furnishes scarcely food enough for its cultivators. Hence it is that you murder and devour one another, that you wage war, and that very many among you perish in intestine strife.

Let therefore hatred depart from among you, let your quarrels end, let wars cease, and let all dissensions and controversies slumber. Enter upon the road to the Holy Sepulchre; wrest that land from the wicked race, and subject it to yourselves. That land which as the Scripture says "floweth with milk and honey," was given by God into the power of the children of Israel. Jerusalem is the centre of the earth; the land is fruitful above all others, like another paradise of delights. This the Redeemer of mankind has made illustrious by His advent, has beautified by His residence, has consecrated by His passion, has redeemed by His death, has glorified by His burial.

This royal city, however, situated at the centre of the earth, is now held captive by the enemies of Christ, and is subjected by those who do not know God, to the worship of the heathens. She seeks therefore and desires to be liberated and does not cease to implore you to come to her aid. From you especially she asks succor, because, as we have already said, God has conferred upon you above all other nations great glory in arms. Accordingly undertake this journey for the remission of your sins, with the assurance of the imperishable glory of the kingdom of heaven.

When Pope Urban had said these and very many similar things in his urbane discourse, he so influenced to one purpose the desires of all who were present, that all cried out, "It is the will of God! It is the will of God!" When the venerable Roman pontiff heard that, with eyes uplifted to heaven he gave thanks to God and, with his hand commanding silence, said:

Most beloved brethren, to-day is manifest in you what the Lord says in the Gospel, "Where two or three are gathered together in my name there am I in the midst of them." For unless God had been present in your spirits, all of you would not have uttered the same cry. For, although the cry issued from numerous mouths, yet the origin of the cry was one. Therefore I say to you that God, who implanted this in your breasts, has drawn it forth from you. Let that then be your war-cry in combats, because it is given to you by God. When an armed attack is made upon the enemy, let this one cry be raised by all the soldiers of God: it is the will of God! It is the will of God!

And we do not command or advise that the old or feeble, or those incapable of bearing arms, undertake this journey. . . .

Whoever, therefore, shall determine upon this holy pilgrimage and shall make his vow to God to that effect and shall offer himself to Him for sacrifice, as a living victim, holy and acceptable to God, shall wear the sign of the cross of the Lord on his forehead or on his breast. When, truly, in fulfillment of his vow he wishes to enter upon his journey, let him place the cross on his back between his shoulders. This two-fold action will fulfill the precept of the Lord, as He commands in the Gospel, "He that taketh not his cross and followeth after me, is not worthy of me."

WILLIAM OF TYRE: PETER THE HERMIT

A certain priest named Peter, from the kingdom of the Franks and the bishopric of Amiens, a hermit both in deed and name, led by the same ardor, arrived at Jerusalem. He was small in stature and his external appearance contemptible. But great valor ruled in his slight frame. For he was sharp-witted, his glance was bright and captivating, and he spoke with ease and eloquence. Having paid the tax which was exacted from all Christians who wished to enter, he went into the city and was entertained by a trusty man who was also a confessor of Christ. He diligently questioned his host, who was also a zealous man, and learned from him not only of the existing perils, but also of the persecutions which the former Christians had suffered long before. And if in what he heard any details were lacking, he completed the account from the witness of his own eyes. For remaining in the city and visiting the churches he learned more fully the truth of what had been told to him by others.

Hearing also that the Patriarch of the city was a devout and God-fearing man, he wished to confer with him and to learn more fully from him the truth concerning some matters. Accordingly he went to him and, having been presented by a trustworthy man, both he and the Patriarch mutually enjoyed their conferences.

The name of the Patriarch was Simeon. As he learned from Peter's conversation that the latter was prudent, able and eloquent, and a man of great practical experience, he began to disclose to him more confidentially all the evils which the people of God had suffered while dwelling in Jerusalem.

To whom Peter replied: "You may be assured, holy father, that if the Roman Church and the princes of the West should learn from a zealous and reliable witness the calamities which you suffer, there is not the slightest doubt that they would hasten to remedy the evil, both by words and deeds. Write then zealously both to the Lord Pope and the Roman Church and to the kings and princes of the West and confirm your letter by the authority of your seal. I truly, for the sake of the salvation of my soul, do not hesitate to undertake this task. And I am prepared under God's guidance to visit them all, to exhort them all, zealously to inform them of the greatness of your sufferings and to urge them to hasten to your relief."

Of a truth, Thou art great, O Lord our God, and to Thy mercy there is no end! Of a truth, blessed Jesus, those who trust in Thee shall never be brought to confusion! How did this poor pilgrim, destitute of all resources and far from his native land, have so great confidence that he dared to undertake an enterprise so much beyond his strength and to hope to accomplish his vow? Unless it was that he turned all his thoughts to Thee, his protector, and filled with charity, pitying the misfortunes of his brethren, loving his neighbor as himself, he was content to fulfill the law? Strength is a vain thing, but charity over-cometh. What his brethren prescribed might appear difficult and even impossible, but the love of God and of his neighbor rendered it easy for him, for love is strong as death. Faith which worketh by love availeth with Thee and the good deeds which Thou receivest do not remain without fruit. Accordingly Thou didst not permit Thy servant long to remain in doubt. Thou didst manifest Thyself to him. Thou didst fortify him by Thy revelation that he might not hesitate, and breathing into him Thy hidden spirit, Thou madest him arise with greater strength to accomplish the work of charity.

Therefore, after performing the usual prayers, taking leave of the Patriarch and receiving his blessing, he went to the sea-coast. There he found a vessel belonging to some merchants who were preparing to cross to Apulia. He went on board and after a successful journey arrived at Bari. Thence he proceeded to Rome and found the lord Pope Urban in the vicinity. He presented the letters of the Patriarch and of the Christians who dwelt at Jerusalem and showed their misery and the abominations which the unclean races wrought in the holy places. Thus faithfully and prudently he performed the commission entrusted to him.

COUNT STEPHEN OF BLOIS: EXPERIENCES OF A CRUSADER

Count Stephen to Adele, his sweetest and most amiable wife, to his dear children, and to all his vassals of all ranks—his greeting and blessing.

You may be very sure, dearest, that the messenger whom I sent to give you pleasure, left me before Antioch safe and unharmed, and through God's grace in the greatest prosperity. And already at that time, together with all the chosen army of Christ, endowed with great valor by Him, we had been continuously advancing for twenty-three weeks toward the home of our Lord Jesus. You may know for certain, my beloved, that of gold, silver and many other kind of riches I now have twice as much as your love had assigned to me when I left you. For all our princes with the common consent of the whole army, against my own wishes, have made me up to the present time the leader, chief and director of their whole expedition.

You have certainly heard that after the capture of the city of Nicaea we fought a great battle with the perfidious Turks and by God's aid conquered them. Next we conquered for the Lord all Romania and afterwards Cappadocia. And we learned that there was a certain Turkish prince Assam, dwelling in Cappadocia; thither we directed our course. All his castles we conquered by force and compelled him to flee to a certain very strong castle situated on a high rock. We also gave the land of that Assam to one of our chiefs and in order that he might conquer the above-mentioned Assam, we left there with him many soldiers of Christ. Thence, continually following the wicked Turks, we drove them through the midst of Armenia, as far as the great river of Euphrates. Having left all their baggage and beasts of burden on the bank, they fled across the river into Arabia.

The holder of the Turkish soldiers, indeed, entering Syria, hastened by forced marches night and day, in order to be able to enter the royal city of Antioch before our approach. The whole army of God learning this gave due praise and thanks to the omnipotent Lord. Hastening with great joy to the aforesaid chief city of Antioch, we besieged it and very often had many conflicts there with the Turks; and seven times with the citizens of Antioch and with the innumerable troops coming to its aid, whom we rushed to meet, we fought with the fiercest courage under the leadership of Christ. And in all these seven battles, by the aid of the Lord God, we conquered and most assuredly killed an innumerable host of them. In those battles, indeed, and in very many attacks made upon the city, many of our brethren and followers were killed and their souls were borne to the joys of Paradise.

We found the city of Antioch very extensive, fortified with incredible strength and almost impregnable. In addition, more than 5000 bold Turkish soldiers had entered the city, not counting the Saracens, Publicans, Arabs, Turcopolitans, Syrians, Armenians and other different races of whom an infinite multitude had gathered together there. In fighting against these enemies of God and of our own we have, by God's grace, endured many sufferings and innumerable evils up to the present time. Many also have already exhausted all their resources in this very holy passion. Very many of our Franks, indeed, would have met a temporal death from starvation, if the clemency of God and our money had not succoured them. Before the above-mentioned city of Antioch indeed, throughout the whole winter we suffered for our Lord Christ from excessive cold and enormous torrents of rain. What some say about the impossibility of bearing the heat of the sun throughout Syria is untrue, for the winter there is very similar to our winter in the west.

When truly Caspian, [Bagi Seian] the Emir of Antioch—that is Prince and Lord—perceived that he was hard pressed by us, he sent his son Sensadolo [Chems Eddaulah] by name, to the prince who holds Jerusalem, and to the Prince of Calep Rodoam [Rodoanus], and to Docap [Deccacus Ibn Toutousch], Prince of Damascus. He also sent into Arabia to Bolianuth and to Carathania to Hamelnuth. These five emirs with 12,000 picked Turkish horsemen suddenly came to aid the inhabitants of Antioch. We, indeed, ignorant of all this, had sent many of our soldiers away to the cities and fortresses. For there are one hundred and sixty-five cities and fortresses throughout Syria which are in our power. But a little before they reached the city, we attacked them at three leagues distance with 700 soldiers, on a certain plain near the "Iron Bridge." God, however, fought for us, his faithful, against them. For on that day, fighting in the strength that God gives, we conquered them and killed an innumerable multitude—God continually fighting for us—and we also carried back to the army more than two hundred of their heads, in order that the people might rejoice on that account. The Emperor of Babylon also sent Saracen messengers to our army with letters and through these he established peace and concord with us.

RAYMOND OF ST. GILES, COUNT OF TOULOUSE: THE CAPTURE OF JERUSALEM BY THE CRUSADERS

To lord Paschal, pope of the Roman church, to all the bishops, and to the whole Christian people, from the archbishop of Pisa, Duke Godfrey, now, by the grace of God, defender of the church of the Holy Sepulchre, Raymond, count of St. Giles, and the whole army of God, which is in the land of Israel, greeting.

Multiply your supplications and prayers in the sight of God with joy and thanksgiving, since God has manifested His mercy in fulfilling by our hands what He had promised in ancient times. . . .

And after the army had suffered greatly in the siege, especially on account of the lack of water, a council was held and the bishops and princes ordered that all with bare feet should march around the walls of the city, in order that He who entered it humbly in our behalf might be moved by our humility to open it to us and to exercise judgment upon His enemies. God was appeased by this humility and on the eighth day after the humiliation, He delivered the city and His enemies to us. It was the day indeed on which the primitive church was driven thence and on which the festival of the dispersion of the apostles is celebrated. And if you desire to know what was done with the enemy who were found there, know that in Solomon's Porch and in his temple our men rode in the blood of the Saracens up to the knees of their horses.

Then when we were considering who ought to hold the city, and some moved by love for their country and kinsmen, wished to return home, it was announced to us that the King of Babylon had come to Ascalon with an innumerable multitude of soldiers. His purpose was, as he said, to lead the Franks, who were in Jerusalem, into captivity, and to take Antioch by storm. But God had determined otherwise in regard to us.

Therefore, when we learned that the army of the Babylonians was at Ascalon, we went down to meet them, leaving our baggage and the sick in Jerusalem with a garrison. When our army was in sight of the enemy, upon our knees we invoked the aid of the Lord, that He who in our other adversities had strengthened the Christian faith, might in the present battle break the strength of the Saracens and of the devil, and extend the kingdom of the Church of Christ from sea to sea, over the whole world. There was no delay; God was present when we cried for His aid and furnished us with so great boldness, that one who saw us rush upon the enemy would have taken us for a herd of deer hastening to quench their thirst in running water. It was wonderful, indeed, since there were in our army not more than 5000 horsemen and 15,000 foot-soldiers, and there were probably in the enemy's army 100,000 horsemen and 400,000 foot-soldiers. Then God appeared wonderful to His servants. For before we engaged in fighting, by our very onset alone, He turned this multitude in flight and scattered all their weapons, so that if they wished afterward to attack us, they did not have the weapons in which they trusted. There can be no question how great the spoils were, since the treasures of the King of Babylon were captured. More than 100,000 Moors perished there by the sword. Moreover, their panic was so great that about 2000 were suffocated at the gate of the city. Those who perished in the sea were innumerable. Many were entangled in the thickets. The whole world was certainly fighting for us, and if many of ours had not been detained in plundering the camp, few of the great multitude of the enemy would have been able to escape from the battle.

And although it may be tedious, the following must not be omitted: on the day preceding the battle the army captured many thousands of camels, oxen and sheep. By the command of the princes these were divided among the people. When we advanced to battle, wonderful to relate, the camels formed in many squadrons and the sheep and oxen did the same. Moreover, these animals accompanied us, halting when we halted, advancing when we advanced, and charging when we charged. The clouds sheltered us from the heat of the sun and cooled us.

Accordingly, after celebrating the victory, the army returned to Jerusalem. Duke Godfrey remained there, the Count of St. Giles, Robert, Count of Normandy, and Robert, Count of Flanders, returned to Laodicea. There they found the fleet belonging to the Pisans and to Bohemond. After the Archbishop of Pisa had established peace between Bohemond and our leaders, Raymond prepared to return to Jerusalem for the sake of God and his brethren.

Therefore, we call upon you of the Catholic Church of Christ and of the whole Latin Church to exult in the so admirable bravery and devotion of your brethren, in the so glorious and very desirable retribution of the omnipotent God, and in the so devoutly hoped for remission of all our sins through the grace of God. And we pray that He may make you—namely, all bishops, clergy and monks who are leading devout lives, and all the laity—to sit down at the right hand of God, who liveth and reigneth God for ever and ever. And we ask and beseech you in the name of our Lord Jesus, who has ever been with us and aided us and freed us from all our tribulations, to be mindful of your brethren who return to you, by doing them kindnesses and by paying their debts, in order that God may recompense you and absolve you from all your sins and grant you a share in all the blessings which either we or they have deserved in the sight of the Lord. Amen.

36 / ST. ANSELM: PROOF OF THE EXISTENCE OF GOD

The late decades of the eleventh century not only witnessed the Gregorian reform controversies and the First Crusade; they also mark the inauguration of one of the most fertile, original, and energetic centuries in the history of human thought. This great intellectual revolution, frequently referred to with considerable inaccuracy as the twelfth-century Renaissance, was marked by great advances in every aspect of higher thought and culture, by a vastly improved knowledge of the classical heritage, by the application of science and intelligence to both Church doctrine and the needs of lay society. One of the most significant developments was the attempt to show that science and religion were not incompatible, that the truths of faith could be supported by conclusions attained by reason, and that consequently Christian doctrine was founded on both revelation and reason. The pioneer in this important intellectual development (although precedents are found in the patristic writers), which is usually called scholasticism, was St. Anselm (d. 1109), an Italian aristocrat turned Norman monastic leader, who ended his career as archbishop of Canterbury. The following ontological proof for the existence of God, which he presented, is based on the assumption of the reality of universals or general concepts which we have in our minds, and reveals him as one of the chief advocates of realism, which was one of the leading schools of medieval philosophy.[15]

[15] St. Anselm, *Proslogium, Monologium,* transl. S. N. Deane, with an introduction by Charles Hartshorne (La Salle, Illinois: Open Court Publishing Company, 1962), pp. 37–41. Reprinted by permission of the publisher.

THERE IS A BEING WHICH IS BEST, AND GREATEST, AND HIGHEST OF ALL EXISTING BEINGS

If any man, either from ignorance or unbelief, has no knowledge of the existence of one Nature which is the highest of all existing beings, which is also sufficient to itself in its eternal blessedness, and which confers upon and effects in all other beings, through its omnipotent goodness, the very fact of their existence, and the fact that in any way their existence is good; and if he has no knowledge of many other things, which we necessarily believe regarding God and his creatures, he still believes that he can at least convince himself of these truths in great part, even if his mental powers are very ordinary, by the force of reason alone.

And, although he could do this in many ways, I shall adopt one which I consider easiest for such a man. For, since all desire to enjoy only those things which they suppose to be good, it is natural that this man should, at some time, turn his mind's eye to the examination of that cause by which these things are good, which he does not desire, except as he judges them to be good. So that, as reason leads the way and follows up these considerations, he advances rationally to those truths of which, without reason, he has no knowledge. And if, in this discussion, I use any argument which no greater authority adduces, I wish it to be received in this way: although, on the grounds that I shall see fit to adopt, the conclusion is reached as if necessarily, yet it is not, for this reason, said to be absolutely necessary, but merely that it can appear so for the time being.

It is easy, then, for one to say to himself: Since there are goods so innumerable, whose great diversity we experience by the bodily senses, and discern by our mental faculties, must we not believe that there is some one thing, through which all goods whatever are good? Or are they good, one through one thing, and another through another? To be sure, it is most certain and clear, for all who are willing to see, that whatsoever things are said to possess any attribute in such a way that in mutual comparison they may be said to possess it in greater, or less, or equal degree, are said to possess it by virtue of some fact, which is not understood to be one thing in one case and another in another, but to be the same in different cases, whether it is regarded as existing in these cases in equal or unequal degree. For, whatsoever things are said to be *just*, when compared one with another, whether equally, or more, or less, cannot be understood as just, except through the quality of *justness*, which is not one thing in one instance, and another in another.

Since it is certain, then, that all goods, if mutually compared, would prove either equally or unequally good, necessarily they are all good by virtue of something which is conceived of as the same in different goods, although sometimes they seem to be called good, the one by virtue of one thing, the other by virtue of another. For, apparently it is by virtue of one quality, that a horse is called *good*, because he is strong, and by virtue of another, that he is called *good*, because he is swift. For, though he seems to be called good by virtue of his strength, and good by virtue of his swiftness, yet swiftness and strength do not appear to be the same thing.

But if a horse, because he is strong and swift, is therefore good, how is it that a strong, swift robber is bad? Rather, then, just as a strong, swift robber is bad, because he is harmful, so a strong, swift horse is good, because he is useful. And, indeed, nothing is ordinarily regarded as good, except either for some utility—as, for instance, safety is called good, and those things which promote safety—or for some honorable character—as, for instance, beauty is reckoned to be good, and what promotes beauty.

But, since the reasoning which we have observed is in no wise refutable, necessarily, again, all things, whether useful or honorable, if they are truly good, are good through that same being through which all goods exist, whatever that being is. But who can doubt this very being, through which all goods exist, to be a great good? This must be, then a good through itself, since every other good is through it.

It follows, therefore, that all other goods are good through another being than that which they themselves are, and this being alone is good through itself. Hence, this alone is supremely good, which is alone good through itself. For it is supreme, in that it so surpasses other beings, that it is neither equalled nor excelled. But that which is supremely good is also supremely great. There is, therefore, some one being which is supremely good, and supremely great, that is, the highest of all existing beings. . . .

But, just as it has been proved that there is a being that is supremely good, since all goods are good through a single being, which is good through itself; so it is necessarily inferred that there is something supremely great, which is great through itself. But I do not mean physically great, as a material object is great, but that which, the greater it is, is the better or the more worthy,—wisdom, for instance. And since there can be nothing supremely great except what is supremely good, there must be a being that is greatest and best, i.e., the highest of all existing beings.

37 / RUDOLPH SOHM:
ROMAN LAW
IN MEDIEVAL EUROPE

The intellectual history of the late eleventh and early twelfth centuries is marked not only by advances in literature and philosophy but also by the application of the classical heritage to meet the needs of society. The rediscovery of Roman law in the form of the Justinian Code (No. 17) and its absorption into the continental legal systems is the most obvious example of this development; it had far-reaching consequences for the political as well as legal life of western Europe. In the following selection, the development of Roman law from the eleventh to the fourteenth century is surveyed by the early twentieth-century German legal historian, Rudolph Sohm.[16]

The credit of having founded the School of Glossators has been assigned to Irnerius, who flourished about 1100 A.D. The most distinguished among his successors were the "quattuor doctores," Martinus, Bulgarus, Jacobus, and Hugo (who were contemporaries of Frederick Barbarossa) and, in the first half of the thirteenth century, Azo, Accursius, and Odofredus. The jurists of the earlier school of Ravenna . . . had taught Roman law by means of comprehensive epitomes and manuals. The Glossators of Bologna, on the other hand—and it is this that distinguishes them from the teachers of the earlier school—adopted the exegetic method practised by the Lombard jurists; that is to say, they dealt with the provisions of the Corpus juris *in detail* by means of *glossae*, or explanatory notes appended to the text of the Code. The most fruitful part of the work done alike by the Lombard jurists in dealing with the Liber Papiensis and by the Glossators in explaining the several passages of the Corpus juris consisted in the searching out of what are known as "parallel" passages, that is, the various other passages connected with the particular passage under discussion. It is remarkable how much light the Glossators were able by this means to throw on the provisions of Roman law. Their explanations went far deeper than any mere elucidation of the letter of the

[16] R. Sohm, *The Institutes of Roman Law*, 3rd ed., transl. J. C. Ledlie (Oxford: The Clarendon Press, 1907), pp. 135–50, *passim*. Reprinted by permission of The Clarendon Press.

law; they served to reconcile contradictions and to bring such parts as were mutually related into vital connexion; they took account of the system of Roman law as a whole without neglecting any single detail. The need for a compendious survey of the results achieved gave rise to the so-called Summae which were also apparently modelled on similar works by the Lombard jurists. The strength of the school lay in the before-mentioned *glossae*. Undeterred by the difficulties of the task, Irnerius and his followers boldly set themselves to analyze the countless provisions of the Corpus juris, and by the use of genuinely scientific methods they were able to bring to light the wealth of legal treasure that lay embedded there. They accomplished what nobody had accomplished before, for it is to their efforts that the modern world owes its intellectual mastery over the vast materials of the Corpus juris. By dint of unremitting labour they succeeded in bringing out the full significance of the priceless work contained in the Digest, and in revealing the noble fabric of Roman law, not merely in separate sections, but as a great whole. The Glossators re-discovered the Digest in the sense that they brought home its meaning—and, with it, the meaning of Roman jurisprudence—to the minds of men once more, and at the same time, by means of a magnificent exegetical apparatus, they secured all future generations in the enjoyment of the fruits of their labours. What the Glossators have thus accomplished is work done once and for all, and it entitles the School of Bologna to rank for all time to come as one of the mightiest forces in the history of Roman law.

The "Glossa ordinaria" of Accursius (about 1250 A.D.), in which the results achieved by the Glossators were finally and comprehensively summed up, marked the completion of the special work of their school: there is necessarily a point at which a scientific process working exclusively on exegetic lines must come to an end. The Glossators had succeeded in showing once more what the provisions of pure Roman law, of the Corpus juris, actually were, so far as it was possible to do so by a method of inquiry and explanation which confined itself strictly to the contents of the code itself.

But in order to place pure Roman law in a position to exercise an influence on practical life a mere re-discovery of its provisions was not sufficient. It would be the greatest mistake to suppose that any sudden reform in the application of law took place at the time of the Glossators. In Italy as elsewhere the law continued for the present to be administered on the old lines, and the importance of the results effected by the Glossators was at first rather theoretical than practical. The law of the Corpus juris had to undergo a process of modification and adaptation before it could be actually applied in the Courts and resume the commanding position in the civilized world that had once belonged to it: ancient Roman law had to be suited to the altered conditions of mediaeval life.

One step in this direction was taken by the Glossators themselves. Among the "authenticae," or excerpts from the laws of the later Roman emperors which they inserted in the text of the Codex . . . , we find some that are based on laws of the German Emperors Frederick I and Frederick II. . . . What the Glossators were aiming at was to re-establish the authority of Roman Law as *living* law. Hence the unexpected appearance of the mediaeval German emperors in their Corpus juris. . . .

. . . Roman procedure and Roman criminal law were in fact transformed into the procedure and the criminal law of the Canon law. It was in the altered form given to them in the Corpus juris canonici that Western Europe, at a subsequent date, received not only the law of procedure and the criminal law of the Corpus juris civilis, but also, in the main, the private law of Rome. The Papal Code represented a kind of revised version of the ancient Imperial Code in which the law of the Roman emperors was made intelligible to the Middle Ages and was fitted for practical application.

It must, however, be borne in mind that the Canon law as such was not recognized in the secular, but only in the ecclesiastical courts. The Church was not strong enough to effect unaided such a reform of Roman law as would have enabled it to be applied in the secular courts.

In this instance again it was from the scientific jurists that the development of Roman law received its decisive impulse.

From the middle of the thirteenth century onwards the School of Glossators was replaced by the School of Post-Glossators or Commentators, whose ablest representatives—Cinus, Bartolus, Baldus—lived in the fourteenth century. The School of Post-Glossators, which had its principal seats at Perugia, Padua, and Pavia, represents the second phase in the evolution of Italian jurisprudence. The importance of this phase has been largely misjudged owing to a tendency to measure the services of the Post-Glossators merely by what they have contributed towards a better understanding of the Corpus juris civilis. Judged by this test it is quite true that the jurists in question can claim little merit of their own; they are mere imitators, fitly described as "Post-Glossators"; distinguished—and very unfavourably distinguished—from their predecessors solely by the fact that, instead of writing short explanatory notes (glossae) on the several passages of the Corpus juris, they indulge—as their name "Commentators" betokens—in long-winded commentaries teeming with scholastic "distinctions,"—commentaries, moreover, which do not even comment on the passage upon which they profess to be founded, but are really exhaustive disquisitions on doctrines having no inner connexion whatever with the text (or the gloss on the text) to which they are appended.

We cannot, however, accept this estimate as correct. The work which the Commentators were called upon to perform, and did in fact perform, was in truth of quite a different kind. These men never set themselves to explain the Corpus juris at all; in their view indeed, after what the gloss had done, there was nothing more to explain in Roman law. The task to which they addressed themselves was a new one, and a greater one than anything attempted by their predecessors, the task namely of building up, on the foundations furnished by the Glossators, a Roman law which might be applied in actual life and which, as such, might serve (in the first instance for Italy) as the living *common* law.

The time had arrived—it was the fourteenth century—for fusing the various elements, Lombard and Romance, that constituted the population of Italy into a national unity. Dante, Petrarch, and Boccaccio created a national Italian literature. At the same time Cinus, Bartolus, and Baldus created a body of national Italian law. . . .

. . . Just as the growth of a common national art and literature tended to reduce the differences of language and national character in Italy, so the success of the new scientific movement tended to reduce the existing differences in the law and to bring unity into the legal ideas and habits of the people.

The new common law which had grown up under the hands of the Commentators had proved itself capable of serving as a common law for Italy. But its importance was not to be confined to Italy. It was—as the events proved—strong enough to exercise a dominant influence throughout the civilized world. And in this instance again it was the Commentators from whose labours the historical development of the law received its decisive impulse. For it was the Commentators who introduced scholasticism into the science of law. . . .

. . . No science will ever rest content with mere matters of fact: what the schoolmen attempted will be attempted again and again as long as a science exists, and men will endeavour to grasp the world of reality through the universal and the abstract, and, having observed the phenomena presented to them, they will seek to bring these phenomena under the mastery of an idea. In its essence scholasticism contains a portion of the essential nature of all science whatsoever, including the science of our own times.

It was from France that scholasticism had found its way to Italy, and in the fourteenth century the Italian Commentators applied the scholastic methods to the science of law. The foundations of modern Continental jurisprudence were thus laid. The Commentators were no longer satisfied with merely ascertaining and elucidating the actual provisions of Roman law as set forth in the authorities. Their endeavour was to trace back the rules of law to general conceptions. This way of treating the subject-matter of law had not occurred to the Roman jurists. Throughout their writings they exhibit an astonishing skill in dealing with definite legal conceptions, but their skill was, to a very considerable extent, the skill of the artist who instinctively applies unalterable aesthetic laws without being intellectually conscious of them. The saying "feeling is everything" is true more especially of art, including the particular art in which the Roman jurists were pre-eminent above all others, the art namely of developing a legal system through the casuistic method, by a clear-sighted adjustment of conflicting principles. . . . Modern jurisprudence is quite different in character. It is reflective, it is, so to speak, "sicklied o'er with the pale cast" of general conceptions, though, on the other hand, it is just these general conceptions that constitute its real power and enable it to exert a direct influence on practical life. Jurisprudence of this modern type, of which German jurisprudence offers a particularly instructive example, owes its origin to the scholastic science of the Commentators. The legal science of modern Germany is, to a considerable extent, an inheritance from the schoolmen of the Middle Ages.

The jurisprudence expounded by the Commentators in the fourteenth and fifteenth centuries has been described as a "jurisprudence of abstract conceptions." The description is appropriate enough, but it must not be taken to imply that the Commentators ever sacrificed the realities of life to the fetish of an abstract idea. For it was precisely by means of this "jurisprudence of abstract conceptions" that the Commentators were able to build up a body of law which obtained *practical* force throughout the Western Continent.

It would not be difficult to show that the doctrines of the Commentators are already foreshadowed in the Gloss at every, or at least almost every, point. It is natural enough that this should have been the case, considering that the influence of scholasticism had been steadily in the ascendant ever since the early part of the twelfth century. In the main, however, the work of the Glossators was in its nature rather humanistic than scholastic. Their principal achievement was the revival of the spirit of antiquity, and Roman law remained, in their hands, to a large extent divorced from practical life. It was the Commentators who brought about a complete union between jurisprudence and life, and, at the same time, a union between jurisprudence and the scholasticism of the Middle Ages, for scholasticism was an integral part of mediaeval life. The Commentators transformed Roman law into a different law, viz. Mediaeval law, and they effected this transformation, not merely by fusing Roman law with the Canon law and German law in the manner we have previously described, but rather, first and foremost, by successfully applying the speculative methods of scholastic jurisprudence and thereby permeating the whole fabric of the law with the spirit of mediaeval scientific thought. . . .

While in the Eastern Empire Roman law was degenerating into a mere provincial law for the Greeks and, as such, was maintaining but a precarious existence, in the West it was gathering force for a fresh period of power. In the main it was the labours of the Commentators that had fitted Roman law for its new career. By working out their scientific conceptions in immediate connexion with the doctrines of Roman law, they were able to present Roman law (in the shape which it assumed under their hands) in the light of a natural law founded on scientific principles, a law, therefore, which claimed to be recognized as a common law valid not only for Italy, but for all countries. In a word, the Commentators raised Roman law for the second time in history to the rank of a universal law. The path was now clear for the reception of Roman law in Germany.

38 / JOHN OF SALISBURY: THE BEGINNINGS OF THE UNIVERSITIES

The intellectual revolution of the twelfth century brought with it a new institution for higher thought and learning—the university (literally "corporation" of masters or students), which grew out of the municipal legal and medical school of Italy and the cathedral school of France, and which rapidly took away from the monastic school the educational leadership of Europe. John of Salisbury (d. 1180), humanist and political theorist, who closed his career as bishop of Chartres, was a young English student at the French universities in 1136, when they were in their formative stage. In these selections he describes the teachers, curriculum, and methods of the first French universities. It should be noted that John believed in the value of the classical belletristic literature in education as the inculcator of moral values; he was suspicious of the value of dialectic (logic), the characteristic scientific method of the period.[17]

[17] C. H. Haskins, *Renaissance of the Twelfth Century* (Cambridge: Harvard University Press, 1928), pp. 135–6, 373–4. Reprinted by permission of Harvard University Press.

Bernard of Chartres, the most abounding spring of letters in Gaul in modern times, followed this method, and in the reading of authors showed what was simple and fell under the ordinary rules; the figures of grammar, the adornments of rhetoric, the quibbles of sophistries; and where the subject of his own lesson had reference to other disciplines, these matters he brought out clearly, yet in such wise that he did not teach everything about each topic, but in proportion to the capacity of his audience dispensed to them in time the due measure of the subject. And because the brilliancy of discourse depends either on propriety (that is, the proper joining of adjective or verb with the substantive) or on metathesis (that is, the transfer of an expression for a worthy reason to another signification), these were the things he took every opportunity to inculcate in the minds of his hearers.

And since the memory is strengthened and the wits are sharpened by exercise, he urged some by warnings and some by floggings and punishments to the constant practice of imitating what they heard. Every one was required on the following day to reproduce some part of what he had heard the day before, some more, some less, for with them the morrow was the disciple of yesterday. Evening drill, which was called declension, was packed with so much grammar that one who gave a whole year to it would have at his command, unless unusually dull, a method of speaking and writing and could not be ignorant of the meaning of expressions which are in common use. [The material, however, of the evening lesson was chosen for moral and religious edification, closing with the sixth penitential psalm and the Lord's prayer.]

Before those for whom the preliminary exercises of boys in imitating prose or poetry were prescribed, he held up the poets or orators, and bade them follow in their footsteps, pointing out their combinations of words and the elegance of their phrasing. But if any one had sewed on another's raiment to make his own work brilliant, he detected and exposed the theft, though very often he inflicted no punishment. But if the poorness of the work had so merited, with indulgent mildness he ordered the culprit to embark on the task of fashioning a real likeness of the ancient authors; and he brought it about that he who imitated his predecessors became worthy of imitation by his successors.

The following matters, too, he taught among the first rudiments and fixed them in the students' minds: the value of order; what is praiseworthy in embellishment and in the choice of words; where there is tenuity and, as it were, emaciation of speech; where a pleasing abundance; where excess; and where the limit due in all things. History and poetry, too, he taught, should be diligently read, without the spur of compulsion; and he insistently required that each pupil should commit something to memory every day; but he taught them to avoid superfluity and be content with what they found in famous writers. . . . And since in the entire preliminary training of pupils there is nothing more useful than to grow accustomed to that which must needs be done with skill, they wrote prose and poetry daily, and trained themselves by mutual comparisons.

When as a lad I first went into Gaul for the cause of study (it was the next year after that the glorious king of the English, Henry the Lion of Righteousness, departed from human things) I addressed myself to the Peripatetic of Palais [Abaelard], who then presided upon Mount Saint Genovefa, an illustrious teacher and admired of all men. There at his feet I acquired the first rudiments of the dialectical art, and snatched according to the scant measure of my wits whatever passed his lips with entire greediness of mind. Then, when he had departed, all too hastily, as it seemed to me, I joined myself to master Alberic, who stood forth among the rest as a greatly esteemed dialectician, and verily was the bitterest opponent of the nominal sect.

Being thus for near two whole years occupied on the Mount I had to my instructors in the dialectical art Alberic and master Robert of Melun (that I may designate him by the surname which he hath deserved in the governing of schools; howbeit by nation he is of England): whereof the one was in questions subtil and large, the other in responses lucid, short, and agreeable. [They were in some sort counterparts of one another; if the analytical faculty of Alberic had been combined in one person with Robert's clear decision] our age could not have shown an equal in debate. For they were both men of sharp intellect, and in study unconquerable. . . . Thus much for the time that I was conversant with them: for afterwards the one went to Bologna and unlearned that which he had taught; yea, and returned and untaught the same; whether for the better or no, let them judge who heard him before and since. Moreover the other went on to the study of divine letters, and aspired to the glory of a nobler philosophy and a more illustrious name.

With these I applied myself for the full space of two years, to practice in the commonplaces and rules and other rudimentary elements, which are instilled into the minds of boys and wherein the aforesaid doctors were most able and ready; so that methought I knew all these things as well as my nails and fingers. This at least I had learned, in the lightness of youth to account my knowledge of more worth than it was. I seemed to myself a young scholar, because I was quick in that which I heard. Then returning unto myself and measuring my powers, I advisedly resorted, by the good favour of my preceptors, to the Grammarian of Conches [William], and heard his teaching by the space of three years; the while teaching much: nor shall I ever regret that time. [While at Chartres John also studied with Richard l'Évêque] a man whose training was deficient almost in nothing, who had more heart even than speech, more knowledge than skill, more truth than vanity, more virtue than show: and the things I had learned from others I collected all again from him, and certain things too I learned which I had not before heard and which appertain to the Quadrivium, wherein formerly I had for some time followed the German Hardwin. I read also again rhetoric, which aforetime I had scarce understood when it was treated of meagerly by master Theodoric. The same I afterwards received more plenteously at the sand of Peter Helias.

Since I received the children of noble persons to instruct, who furnished me with living—for I lacked the help of friends and kinsfolk, but God assuaged my neediness,—the force of duty and the instance of my pupils moved me the oftener to recall what I had learned. Wherefore I made closer acquaintance with master Adam [du Petit-Pont], a man of exceeding sharp wits and, whatever others may think, of much learning, who applied himself above the rest to Aristotle: in such wise that, albeit I had him not to my teacher, he gave me kindly of his, and delivered himself openly enough; the which he was wont to do to none or to few others than his own scholars, for he was deemed to suffer from jealousy. . . .

From hence I was withdrawn by the straitness of my private estate, the instance of my companions, and the counsel of my friends, that I should undertake the office of a teacher. I obeyed: and thus returning at the expiration of three years, I found master Gilbert [de la Porrée] and heard him in logic and divinity; but too quickly was he removed. His successor was Robert Pullus, whom his life and knowledge alike recommended. Then I had Simon of Poissy, a trusty lecturer, but dull in disputation. But these two I had in theologics alone. Thus, engaged in diverse studies near twelve years passed by me.

And so it seemed pleasant to me to revisit my old companions on the Mount [at Paris], whom I had left and whom dialectic still detained, to confer with them touching old matters of debate; that we might by mutual comparison measure together our several progress. I found them as before, and where they were before; nor did they appear to have reached the goal in unravelling the old questions, nor had they added one jot of a proposition. The aims that once inspired them, inspired them still: they only had progressed in one point, they had unlearned moderation, they knew not modesty; in such wise that one might despair of their recovery. And thus experience taught me a manifest conclusion, that, whereas dialectic furthers other studies, so if it remain by itself it lies bloodless and barren, nor does it quicken the soul to yield fruit of philosophy, except the same conceive from elsewhere.

39 / PETER ABELARD: AUTOBIOGRAPHY

John of Salisbury tells us (No. 38) that when he first came to Paris as a student, he found Abelard (d. 1142) to be "an illustrious teacher and admired of all men." Abelard was, in fact, the greatest philosopher of the twelfth century and a pioneer in the application of Aristotelian logic to the ultimate problems of theology and philosophy. As such, he was bound not to be admired universally for long, for he was penetrating into new regions of thought and subjecting dogmas of the faith to dialectical scrutiny in a bold manner disturbing to many churchmen. Furthermore, in his philosophical views he leaned, although in a moderate way, toward nominalism, the second great medieval philosophical school, which contradicted Anselm's realism by insisting that universals were not res, things, *but rather,* nomina, *merely names or terms, or as Abelard said, confused general images. This seemed to cast grave doubt on the possibility of demonstrating the compatibility of revelation and science.*

Finally, Abelard's egoism and rather scandalous private life helped to ruin him. In this respect Abelard is also significant; he plays a leading role in the twelfth-century discovery of real, individual personality, as compared with the indistinct types of early medieval culture, and his History of My Calamities *is one of the very first autobiographies written since Augustine's* Confessions. *Abelard was condemned by a Church council and forced to recant some opinions on the nature of the Trinity, which he had been so bold as to try to analyze with his dialectical methods. Through his pioneering philosophical and theological work, and his contribution to the rediscovery of personality, he deserves to be regarded as one of the most important and influential of medieval thinkers.*[18]

[18] *Historia Calamitatum*, by Peter Abélard, transl. H. A. Bellows (St. Paul: Thomas A. Boyd, 1920), pp. 1–2, 16–22, 29–30, 33–5.

CHAPTER I. OF THE BIRTHPLACE OF PIERRE ABELARD AND OF HIS PARENTS

Know, then, that I am come from a certain town which was built on the way into lesser Brittany,[19] distant some eight miles, as I think, eastward from the city of Nantes, and in its own tongue called Palets. Such is the nature of that country, or, it may be, of them who dwell there—for in truth they are quick in fancy—that my mind bent itself easily to the study of letters. Yet more, I had a father who had won some smattering of letters before he had girded on the soldier's belt. And so it came about that long afterwards his love thereof was so strong that he saw to it that each son of his should be taught in letters even earlier than in the management of arms. Thus indeed did it come to pass. And because I was his first born, and for that reason the more dear to him, he sought with double diligence to have me wisely taught. For my part, the more I went forward in the study of letters, and ever more easily, the greater became the ardour of my devotion to them, until in truth I was so enthralled by my passion for learning that, gladly leaving my brothers the pomp of glory in arms, the right of heritage and all the honours that should have been mine as the eldest born, I fled utterly from the court of Mars that I might win learning in the bosom of Minerva. And since I found the armory of logical reasoning more to my liking than the other forms of philosophy, I exchanged all other weapons for these, and to the prize of victory in war I preferred the battle of minds in disputation. Thenceforth, journeying through many provinces, and debating as I went, going withersoever I heard that the study of my chosen art most flourished, I became such an one as the Peripatetics.

CHAPTER IV. OF THE PERSECUTION HE HAD FROM HIS TEACHER ANSELM [OF LAON]

Now this venerable man of whom I have spoken was acutely smitten with envy, and straightway incited, as I have already mentioned, by the insinuation of sundry persons, began to persecute me from my lecturing on the Scriptures no less bitterly than my former master, William, had done for my work in philosophy. At that time there were in this old man's school two who were considered far to excel all the others: Alberic of Rheims and Lotulphe the Lombard. The better opinion these two held of themselves, the more they were incensed against me. Chiefly at their suggestion, as it afterwards transpired,

---

[19] A wild frontier region in the twelfth century.

yonder venerable coward had the impudence to forbid me to carry on any further in his school the work of preparing glosses which I had thus begun. The pretext he alleged was that if by chance in the course of this work I should write anything containing blunders—as was likely enough in view of my lack of training—the thing might be imputed to him. When this came to the ears of his scholars, they were filled with indignation at so undiguised a manifestation of spite, the like of which had never been directed against any one before. The more obvious this rancour became, the more it redounded to my honour, and his persecution did nought save to make me more famous.

CHAPTER V. OF HOW HE RETURNED TO PARIS AND FINISHED THE GLOSSES WHICH HE HAD BEGUN AT LAON

And so, after a few days, I returned to Paris, and there for several years I peacefully directed the school which formerly had been destined for me, nay even offered to me, but from which I had been driven out. At the very outset of my work there, I set about completing the glosses on Ezekiel which I had begun at Laon. These proved so satisfactory to all who read them that they came to believe me no less adept in lecturing on theology than I had proved myself to be in the field of philosophy. Thus my school was notably increased in size by reason of my lectures on subjects of both these kinds, and the amount of financial profit as well as glory which it brought to me cannot be concealed from you, for the matter was widely talked of. But prosperity always puffs up the foolish, and worldly comfort enervates the soul, rendering it an easy prey to carnal temptations. Thus I, who by this time had come to regard myself as the only philosopher remaining in the whole world, and had ceased to fear any further disturbance of my peace, began to loosen the rein on my desires, although hitherto I had always lived in the utmost continence. And the greater progress I made in my lecturing on philosophy or theology, the more I departed alike from the practice of the philosophers and the spirit of the divines in the uncleanness of my life. For it is well known, methinks, that philosophers, and still more those who have devoted their lives to arousing the love of sacred study, have been strong above all else in the beauty of chastity.

Thus did it come to pass that while I was utterly absorbed in pride and sensuality, divine grace, the cure for both diseases, was forced upon me, even though I, forsooth, would fain have shunned it. First was I punished for my sensuality, and then for my pride. For my sensuality I lost those things whereby I practiced it; for my pride, engendered in me by my knowledge of letters—and it is even as the

Apostle said: "Knowledge puffeth itself up" (I Cor. viii, 1)—I knew the humiliation of seeing burned the very book in which I most gloried. And now it is my desire that you should know the stories of these two happenings, understanding them more truly from learning the very facts than from hearing what is spoken of them, and in the order in which they came about. Because I had ever held in abhorrence the foulness of prostitutes, because I had diligently kept myself from all excesses and from association with the women of noble birth who attended the school, because I knew so little of the common talk of ordinary people, perverse and subtly flattering chance gave birth to an occasion for casting me lightly down from the heights of my own exaltation. Nay, in such case not even divine goodness could redeem one who, having been so proud, was brought to such shame, were it not for the blessed gift of grace.

CHAPTER VI. OF HOW, BROUGHT LOW BY HIS LOVE FOR HÉLOÏSE, HE WAS WOUNDED IN BODY AND SOUL

Now there dwelt in that same city of Paris a certain young girl named Héloïse, the niece of a canon who was called Fulbert. Her uncle's love for her was equalled only by his desire that she should have the best education which he could possibly procure for her. Of no mean beauty, she stood out above all by reason of her abundant knowledge of letters. Now this virtue is rare among women, and for that very reason it doubly graced the maiden, and made her the most worthy of renown in the entire kingdom. It was this young girl whom I, after carefully considering all those qualities which are wont to attract lovers, determined to unite with myself in the bonds of love, and indeed the thing seemed to me very easy to be done. So distinguished was my name, and I possessed the advantages of youth and comeliness, that no matter what woman I might favour with my love, I dreaded rejection of none. Then, too, I believed that I could win the maiden's consent all the more easily by reason of her knowledge of letters and her zeal therefor; so, even if we were parted, we might yet be together in thought with the aid of written messages. Perchance, too, we might be able to write more boldly than we could speak, and thus at all times could we live in joyous intimacy.

Thus, utterly aflame with my passion for this maiden, I sought to discover means whereby I might have daily and familiar speech with her, thereby the more easily to win her consent. For this purpose I persuaded the girl's uncle, with the aid of some of his friends, to take me into his household—for he dwelt hard by my school—in return for the payment of a small sum. My pretext for this was that the care of my own household was a serious handicap to my studies, and likewise burdened me with an expense far greater than I could afford. Now, he was a man keen in avarice, and likewise he was most desirous for his niece that her study of letters should ever go forward, so, for these two reasons, I easily won his consent to the fulfillment of my wish, for he was fairly agape for my money, and at the same time believed that his niece would vastly benefit by my teaching. More even than this, by his own earnest entreaties he fell in with my desires beyond anything I had dared to hope, opening the way for my love; for he entrusted her wholly to my guidance, begging me to give her instruction whensoever I might be free from the duties of my school, no matter whether by day or by night, and to punish her sternly if ever I should find her negligent of her tasks. In all this the man's simplicity was nothing short of astounding to me; I should not have been more smitten with wonder if he had entrusted a tender lamb to the care of a ravenous wolf. When he had thus given her into my charge, not alone to be taught but even to be disciplined, what had he done save to give free scope to my desires, and to offer me every opportunity, even if I had not sought it, to bend her to my will with threats and blows if I failed to do so with caresses? There were, however, two things which particularly served to allay any foul suspicion: his own love for his niece, and my former reputation for continence.

Why should I say more? We were united first in the dwelling that sheltered our love, and then in the hearts that burned with it. Under the pretext of study we spent our hours in the happiness of love, and learning held out to us the secret opportunities that our passion craved. Our speech was more of love than of the books which lay open before us; our kisses far outnumbered our reasoned words. Our hands sought less the book than each other's bosoms; love drew our eyes together far more than the lesson drew them to the pages of our text. In order that there might be no suspicion, there were, indeed, sometimes blows, but love gave them, not anger; they were the marks, not of wrath, but of a tenderness surpassing the most fragrant balm in sweetness. What followed? No degree in love's progress was left untried by our passion, and if love itself could imagine any wonder as yet unknown, we discovered it. And our inexperience of such delights made us all the more ardent in our pursuit of them, so that our thirst for one another was still unquenched.

In measure as this passionate rapture absorbed me more and more, I devoted ever less time to philosophy and to the work of the school. Indeed, it became loathsome to me to go to the school or to linger there; the labour, moreover was very burdensome, since my nights were vigils of love and my days of study. My lecturing became utterly careless and lukewarm; I did nothing because of inspiration, but everything merely as a matter of habit. I had become nothing more than a reciter of my former discoveries, and though I still wrote poems, they dealt with love, not with the secrets of philosophy. Of these songs you yourself well know how some have become widely known and have been sung in many lands, chiefly, methinks, by those who delighted in the things of this world. As for the sorrow, the groans, the lamentations of my students when they perceived the preoccupation, nay, rather the chaos, of my mind, it is hard even to imagine them.

A thing so manifest could deceive only a few, no one, methinks, save him whose shame it chiefly bespoke, the girl's uncle, Fulbert. The truth was often enough hinted to him, and by many persons, but he could not believe it, partly, as I have said, by reason of his boundless love for his niece, and partly because of the well-known continence of my previous life. Indeed we do not easily suspect shame in those whom we most cherish, nor can there be the blot of foul suspicion on devoted love. Of this St. Jerome in his epistle to Sabinianus (Epist. 48) says: "We are wont to be the last to know the evils of our own households, and to be ignorant of the sins of our children and our wives, though our neighbours sing them aloud." But no matter how slow a matter may be in disclosing itself, it is sure to come forth at last, nor is it easy to hide from one what is known to all. So, after the lapse of several months, did it happen with us. Oh, how great was the uncle's grief when he learned the truth, and how bitter was the sorrow of the lovers when we were forced to part! With what shame was I overwhelmed, with what contrition smitten because of the blow which had fallen on her I loved, and what a tempest of misery burst over her by reason of my disgrace! Each grieved most, not for himself, but for the other. Each sought to allay, not his own sufferings, but those of the one he loved. The very sundering of our bodies served but to link our souls closer together; the plenitude of the love which was denied to us inflamed us more than ever. Once the wildness of shame had passed, it left us more shameless than before, as shame died within us the cause of it seemed to us ever more desirable. And so it chanced with us, as in the stories that the poets tell, it once happened with Mars and Venus when they were caught together.

It was not long after this that Héloïse found that she was pregnant, and of this she wrote to me in the utmost exaltation, at the same time asking me to consider what had best be done. Accordingly, on a night when her uncle was absent, we carried out the plan we had determined on, and I stole her secretly away from her uncle's house, sending her without delay to my own country. She remained there with my sister until she gave birth to a son, whom she named Astrolabe. Meanwhile her uncle, after his return, was almost mad with grief; only one who had then seen him could rightly guess the burning agony of his sorrow and the bitterness of his shame. What steps to take against me, or what snares to set for me, he did not know. If he should kill me or do me some bodily hurt, he feared greatly lest his dear-loved niece should be made to suffer for it among my kinsfolk. He had no power to seize me and imprison me somewhere against my will, though I make no doubt he would have done so quickly enough had he been able or dared, for I had taken measures to guard against any such attempt.

At length, however, in pity for his boundless grief, and bitterly blaming myself for the suffering which my love had brought upon him through the baseness of the deception I had practiced, I went to him to entreat his forgiveness, promising to make any amends that he himself might decree. I pointed out that what had happened could not seem incredible to any one who had ever felt the power of love, or who remembered how, from the very beginning of the human race, women had cast down even the noblest men to utter ruin. And in order to make amends even beyond his extremest hope, I offered to marry her whom I had seduced, provided only the thing could be kept secret, so that I might suffer no loss of reputation thereby. To this he gladly assented, pledging his own faith and that of his kindred, and sealing with kisses the pact which I had sought of him—and all this that he might the more easily betray me.

CHAPTER VII. OF THE ARGUMENTS OF HÉLOÏSE AGAINST WEDLOCK—OF HOW NONE THE LESS HE MADE HER HIS WIFE

. . . After our little son was born, we left him in my sister's care, and secretly returned to Paris. A few days later, in the early morning, having kept our nocturnal vigil of prayer unknown to all in a certain church, we were united there in the benediction of wedlock, her uncle and a few friends of his and mine being present. We departed forthwith stealthily and by separate ways, nor thereafter did we see each other save rarely and in private, thus striving our utmost to conceal what we had done. But her uncle and those of his household, seeking solace for their disgrace, began to divulge the story of our marriage, and thereby to violate the pledge they had given me on this point. Héloïse, on the contrary, denounced her own kin and swore that they were speaking the most absolute lies. Her uncle, aroused to fury thereby, visited her repeatedly with punishments. No sooner had I learned this than I sent her to a convent of nuns at Argenteuil, not far from Paris, where she herself had been brought up and educated as a young girl. I had them make ready for her all the garments of a nun, suitable for the life of a convent, excepting only the veil, and these I bade her put on.

When her uncle and his kinsmen heard of this, they were convinced that now I had completely played them false and had rid myself forever of Héloïse by forcing her to become a nun. Violently incensed, they laid a plot against me, and one night, while I, all unsuspecting, was asleep in a secret room in my lodgings, they broke in with the help of one of my servants, whom they had bribed. There they had vengeance on me with a most cruel and most shameful punishment, such as astounded the whole world, for they cut off those parts of my body with which I had done that which was the cause of their sorrow. This done, straightway they fled, but two of them were captured, and suffered the loss of their eyes and their genital organs. One of these two was the aforesaid servant, who, even while he was still in my service, had been led by his avarice to betray me.

CHAPTER VIII. OF THE SUFFERING OF HIS BODY —OF HOW HE BECAME A MONK IN THE MONASTERY OF ST. DENIS AND HÉLOÏSE A NUN AT ARGENTEUIL

. . . The abbey, however, to which I had betaken myself was utterly worldly and in its life quite scandalous. The abbot himself was as far below his fellows in his way of living and in the foulness of his reputation as he was above them in priestly rank. This intolerable state of things I often and vehemently denounced, sometimes in private talk and sometimes publicly, but the only result was that I made myself detested of them all. They gladly laid hold of the daily eagerness of my students to hear me as an excuse whereby they might be rid of me; and finally, at the insistent urging of the students themselves, and with the hearty consent of the abbot and the rest of the brotherhood, I departed thence to a certain hut, there to teach in my wonted way. To this place such a throng of students flocked that the neighbourhood could not afford shelter for them nor the earth sufficient sustenance.

Here, as befitted my profession, I devoted myself chiefly to lectures on theology, but I did not wholly abandon the teaching of the secular arts, to which I was more accustomed, and which was particularly demanded of me. I used the latter, however, as a hook, luring my students by the bait of learning to the study of the true philosophy, even as the Ecclesiastical History tells of Origen, the greatest of all Christian philosophers. Since apparently the Lord had gifted me with no less persuasiveness in expounding the Scriptures than in lecturing on secular subjects, the number of my students in these two courses began to increase greatly, and the attendance at all the other schools was correspondingly diminished. Thus I aroused the envy and hatred of the other teachers. Those who sought to belittle me in every possible way took advantage of my absence to bring two principal charges against me: first, that it was contrary to the monastic profession to be concerned with the study of secular books; and, second, that I had presumed to teach theology without ever having been taught therein myself. This they did in order that my teaching of every kind might be prohibited, and to this end they continually stirred up bishops, archbishops, abbots, and whatever other dignitaries of the Church they could reach.

40 / THE BERNARDINE VISION

Abelard's most vehement critic was the great mystic St. Bernard (d. 1154), who was extremely hostile to the new dialectical movement as dangerous to the unity and stability of the faith. Bernard, however resembled the schoolmen in that he too had an additional foundation for faith besides revelation. Following suggestions of Augustine and Damiani, Bernard developed a full-fledged Christian mysticism in which the humblest member of the Church can have an immediate vision of God and experience His love. It might be questioned whether in the long run this mysticism, with its tendency to religious individualism, was not far more dangerous to sacerdotal authority than anything ever said by Abelard. Bernard's inclination toward a purified Church made him also the proponent of ideas which could easily lapse into Donatism.

Bernard is important in still another way: he was one of the creators of the cult of the Virgin Mary and the related supplanting of the wrathful, judging Old-Testament God by the loving self-sacrificing New-Testament Son and Savior, which sharply distinguishes the popular religious outlook of the twelfth and thirteenth centuries from early medieval religiosity. Bernard was both influenced by, and exerted an enormous influence upon, the new romanticism, emotionalism, and appreciation of feminine qualities, which were leading aspects of the cultural revolution of the twelfth century.

Although one of the great mystics of mankind, Bernard was not greatly loved by his contemporaries, who found him over-

bearing, authoritarian, and unreasonable. A French nobleman who joined the new stringent Cistercian order because of his puritanical attitude, he found the monastic life too placid and limited for his enormous energies and talents, and although he always claimed that he wanted only to be a Cistercian abbot, he spent the last twenty-five years of his life as a maker and adviser of popes, confidante of kings, preacher of crusades, and self-appointed moral arbiter of Europe.[20]

MARIOLOGY

. . . From all this it is clear, what is the stem proceeding from the root of Jesse, what is the Flower upon which rests the Holy Spirit. The Virgin, the *Genetrix Dei,* is the stem, her Son the Flower. Yes, the Son of the Virgin is that Flower "white and glowing red, chiefest among ten thousand"; the Flower upon which the Angels come to gaze, of which the perfume restores life to the dead; and as He Himself declares, a flower of the field, not of the garden. For the field blooms with flowers without human help; it is not sown nor tilled, nor enriched with nourishment. Thus it was with the womb of the Virgin: inviolate, untouched, it brought forth, as a prairie of living green, this Flower of immortal fairness, whose glory shall never fade. O Virgin, lofty stem, to what an exalted height dost thou attain! even to Him who sitteth upon the throne, unto the Lord of Glory. Nor is this strange, since thou sendest deeply into the ground the roots of humility.

O plant truly heavenly, more precious and pure than all others, truly the tree of life, which was found worthy to bear the fruit of salvation! Thy cunning, O malignant serpent, has overreached itself; thy falseness is made evident. Two charges thou hadst brought against the Creator; of untruth, and of envy: and in each thou hast been shown to have lied. He, to whom thou didst say, "Thou shalt by no means die," dies from the beginning; and the truth of the Lord endurest for ever. Tell me, if thou canst, what tree there is whose fruit can be an object of envy to him, to whom God has not denied this chosen stem and its lofty fruit? "He who spared not His own Son, how shall He not with Him also freely give us all things?"

You have now understood, I think, that the Virgin is that royal way, by which the Saviour came to us; proceeding from her womb, as a bridegroom from his chamber.

[20] J. Mabillon, ed., *Life and Works of St. Bernard,* transl. S. J. Eales (London: John Hodges, 1896), Vol. III, pp. 263–5, Vol. IV, pp. 316–17, 223–4, 361–2, 233–4, 235–6.

THE BEATIFIC VISION

I

. . . If, then, any of us finds it, with the Psalmist, good for him to draw near to God, and to speak more plainly, if any among us is so filled with an earnest longing [for those things that are above] that he desires to be dissolved and be with Christ; but desires it vehemently, thirsts for it ardently, and, without ceasing, dwells upon the hope of it: he shall, without doubt, receive the Word, and in no other form than that of the Bridegroom in the time of the visitation; that is to say, in the hour when he shall feel himself inwardly embraced, as it were, by the arms of wisdom, and shall receive a sweet inpouring of the Divine Love. For the desire of his heart shall be granted unto him, though he is still in the body as in a place of pilgrimage, and though only in part for a time, and that a short time. For when [the Lord] has been sought in watching and prayers, with strenuous effort, with showers of tears, He will at length present Himself to the soul; but suddenly, when it supposes that it has gained His Presence, He will glide away. Again He comes to the soul that follows after Him with tears; He allows Himself to be regained, but not to be retained, and anon He passes away out of its very hands. Yet if the devout soul shall persist in prayers and tears, He will at length return to it; He will not deprive it of the desire of its lips, but will speedily disappear again, and not return unless He be sought again with the whole desire of the heart. Thus, then, even in this body the joy of the Presence of the Bridegroom is frequently felt; but not the fulness of His Presence, because though His appearance renders the heart glad, the alternation of His absence affects it with sadness. And this the Beloved must of necessity endure, until, having laid down the burden of an earthly body, she shall be borne up upon the pinions, so to speak, of her earnest desires, and fly away, passing freely over the plains of contemplation as a bird through the air, and following in spirit her Beloved, whithersoever He goeth, without anything to hinder or retard. . . .

II

. . . May my soul die the death which, if I may so speak, belongs to angels; so that, departing from the remembrance of things present, and being divested not only of desire for, but also of the haunting ideas and images of, things corporeal and inferior, it may enter into pure relations with those in which is the image and likeness of purity. Of this nature, as I consider, is the ecstasy in which contemplation wholly or principally consists. For to be, while still living, delivered from the power of desires for things material is a degree of human virtue; but to be brought out of the sphere of material forms and ideas is a privilege of angelic purity. Yet each of these two is a Divine gift—each of them consists in coming out of yourself, in rising above yourself; but the one carries you only a little way, while the other carries you far indeed. Blessed is he who can say: "Lo, I have fled far away, and abode in solitude." He was not content to go forth unless he could go far away, so as to obtain repose. Have you over-passed the pleasures of the flesh, so that you no longer obey its lusts, nor are subject to its allurements? Then you have made progress; you have separated yourself [from the world]; but you have not the power to banish, by the mere purity of your spirit, and to rise entirely out of the reach of, the inrushing and thronging crowd of material images and ideas. Do not, at the point which you have thus far attained, promise yourself rest of soul. You mistake if you think that the place of repose, the secret of solitude, the habitation of peace, the stillness of serene light, is to be found on this side of your earthly existence. But show me the soul who has attained that point of freedom of which I speak, who can justly say: "Return unto thy rest, O my soul; for the Lord hath dealt bountifully with thee," and I will at once confess that he has found the rest desired. And this place is truly in a solitude, this dwelling is truly in the light, according to the prophet; a tabernacle for a shadow in the day-time from the heat, and for a place of refuge, and for a covert from storm and from rain; and of it holy David also says: "In the time of trouble He shall hide me in His pavilion: in the secret of His tabernacle shall He hide me. . . ."

THE CHURCH

. . . If the length of this discourse does not weary you, I will now try to assign these four temptations, in their order, to the Body of Christ, which is the Church. And I will endeavour to do this as briefly as possible. Consider the Primitive Church. Was it not at first pervaded in an extraordinary degree with the "terror that walketh by night?" For it was then, as it were, a night, when everyone who slew the saints thought that he was thus doing God service. But after that temptation was overcome, and that tempest stilled, she became glorious and illustrious, and, according to the promise made to her, was speedly placed in a position of worldly distinction. Then the enemy, vexed to have been frustrated, turned cunningly from the "nightly terror" to the "arrow that flieth by day," and with it wounded certain members of the Church. Vain and ambitious men rose up, greedy of reputation, and desired to make for themselves a name; and, going forth from the Church, their mother, they long afflicted her with various and perverse teachings. But this evil plague also was vanquished by the wisdom of the saints, as the former had been by the patience of the martyrs.

At the present time, by the mercy of God, the Church is free from each of these evils; but evidently it is still contaminated by "the pestilence that walketh in darkness." Woe to this generation [which is corrupted] by the leaven of the Pharisees, which is hypocrisy! If, indeed, that ought to be called hypocrisy which is so prevailing that it cannot be hidden, and so devoid of shame that it does not try to hide. At the present day a contagious corruption is creeping through the whole body of the Church, the more desperate of cure as it is universal, and the more dangerous because so deeply seated. If an heretic arose to wage against her an open war, she would exclude him from her bounds, and he would dry up and wither away; or if one attacked her with violence, she would peradventure hide herself from him. But at the present time whom shall she exclude, or from whom shall she hide herself? All are her friends, and all her enemies; all are her intimates, and all her adversaries; all are of her own household, and none at peace with her; all are very nearly related to her, and yet all are seeking their own interests. They are Ministers of Christ, and they are serving Antichrist. They are advanced to honour upon the goods of the Lord, and to the Lord they render no honour at all. From this proceeds that meretricious splendour, that habit fit for a comedian, that magnificence almost royal which you see every day. Because of this you see gold upon the bits of their horses, upon their saddles, and even upon their spurs; yes, their spurs shine more brightly than their altars. Because of this you see fine tables loaded with splendid services of plate, chased goblets, and, also, with viands correspondingly costly; then follow merry-makings and drunkenness, the guitar, the lyre, and the flute. Thence come groaning winepresses and storehouses full and overflowing with all manner of good things. Thence come vases of rich perfumes, and coffers filled with immense treasures. It is for the attainment of such objects that they desire to be, and are, Provosts of churches, Deans, Archdeacons, Bishops, Archbishops. For these dignities are not given for merit, but are disposed of in that infamous traffic which walketh in darkness.

It was once predicted [of the Church], and now the time of its fulfilment draws near: "Behold, in peace is my bitterness most bitter." It was bitter at first in the death of the martyrs; more bitter afterwards in the conflict with heretics; but most bitter of all now in the [evil] lives of her members. She cannot drive them away, and she cannot flee from them, so strongly established are they, and so multiplied are they above measure. The plague of the Church is inward; it is incurable. It is that which makes its bitterness most bitter, even in the midst of peace. But in what a peace! Peace it is, and yet it is not peace. There is peace from heathens, and from heretics; but not from her own sons. At this time is heard the voice of her complaining: "I have nourished and brought forth children, and they have rebelled against me." They have rebelled; they have dishonoured me by their evil lives, by their shameful gains, by their shameful trafficking, by, in short, their many works which walk in darkness. There remains only one thing—that the demon of noonday should appear, to seduce those who remain still in Christ, and in the simplicity which is in Him. He has, without question, swallowed up the rivers of the learned, and the torrents of those who are powerful, and (as says the Scripture) "he trusteth that he can draw up Jordan into his mouth"—that is to say, those simple and humble ones who are in the Church. For this is he who is Antichrist, who counterfeits not only the day, but also the noonday; who exalts himself above all that is called God or worshipped—whom the Lord Jesus shall consume with the Spirit of His Mouth, and destroy with the brightness of His Coming; for He is the true and eternal Noonday: the Bridegroom, and Defender of the Church, Who is above all, God blessed for ever. AMEN.

THE JEWS

. . . What is there in that [Jewish] people which is not crude and coarse, whether we consider their actions, their inclinations, their understanding, or even the rites with which they worship God? For their actions carried them [of old] into many wars, their inclinations are all devoted to the pursuit of gain, their intelligence stopped short in the thick husk of the letter of their Law, and their worship consists in shedding the blood of sheep and cattle. . . .

O how much worse were the last than the former ones! At first they were only useless, but the last came to be hurtful and poisonous. O nature not merely crude, but touched with viperous venom, to hate that Man, who not only cures the bodies of men, but saves their souls! O intelligence, coarse, dense, and, as it were, bovine, which did not recognise God even in His own works!

Perhaps the Jew will complain, as of a deep injury, that I call his intelligence bovine. But let him read what is said by the prophet Isaiah, and he will find that it is even less than bovine. For he says: "The ox knoweth his owner, and the ass his master's crib; but Israel doth not know, My people doth not consider." You see, O Jew, that I am milder than your own prophet. I have compared you to the brute beasts; but he sets you below even these. Or, rather, it is not the Prophet who says this in his own name; but he speaks in the Name of God, who declares Himself by the very works He does to be God. "Though ye believe not Me," He says, "believe the works"; and, "If I do not the works of My Father, believe Me not"; and not even that aroused them to understand. Not the flight of demons, not the obedience of the elements, nor life restored to the dead, was able to expel from their minds that stupidity bestial, and more than bestial, which caused them, by a blindness as marvellous as it was miserable, to rush headlong into that crime, so enormous and so horrible, of laying impious hands upon the Lord of Glory. . . .

LEARNING AND KNOWLEDGE

. . . I think we must in the first place inquire whether every kind of ignorance be a cause of condemnation? And it seems to me that this is not the case; that it is not every [kind or degree of] ignorance that is blamable, since there are many things—they are, indeed, innumerable —of which we are allowed to be ignorant without peril to our salvation. For example, if you are ignorant of some mechanical art, as that of the wheelwright, or of the mason, or some other of those industries which are carried on by men for the purposes of this present life, would that be an obstacle to your salvation? How many men are there who have been saved, being acceptable to God in character and actions, without having been acquainted even with the liberal arts (though these latter are more honourable and more useful both in learning and in practice)! How many persons does the Apostle enumerate in the Epistle to the Hebrews, who became dear to God, not by their acquaintance with polite literature, but by a pure conscience and by faith unfeigned! Others there were who pleased God in their life by the merits, not of their knowledge, but of their life. Peter and Andrew, and the sons of Zebedee, and all the rest of their fellow-disciples, were not drawn from the school of rhetoric or of philosophy, and yet the Saviour used them as instruments [by which to bring about] salvation throughout the earth. It was not because the wisdom in them was greater than that of all other men (as a certain holy man confesses of himself) but because of their faith and gentleness, that He saved them; yea, and made them Saints, and even teachers of others. They have made known to the world the ways of life, not by the sublimity of their preaching, or by the learning taught by human wisdom; but after that the world in its wisdom knew not God; it pleased Him to save by the foolishness of their preaching those who believed.

I may seem to you, perhaps, to speak too severely of knowledge; to blame, as it were, the learned, and to forbid the study of literature. But I would by no means do this. I am not ignorant how great are the services that have been rendered to the Church, and are rendered to her continually, by her learned sons, whether in repulsing the attacks of her enemies or in instructing the simple. . . .

There are those who wish to learn merely in order that they may know, and such curiosity is blamable. There are others who wish to learn for no other reason than that they may be looked upon as learned, which is a ridiculous vanity; and these will not escape the censure which a satiric poet levels against them when he says: "To know a thing is nothing in your eyes, unless some other person is aware of your knowledge." And others, again, desire to learn only that they may make merchandise of their knowledge, for example, in order to gain money or honours; and such trafficking is ignoble. But there are those who desire to learn that they may edify others; that is charity. And, lastly, there are some who wish to learn that they may be themselves edified; and that is prudence.

Of all these the two last are the only learners who do not fall into an abuse of knowledge; since they wish to know only that they may do good. . . .

41 / JUDAH HALEVI: THE FAITH AND HOPE OF MEDIEVAL ISRAEL

What was the response of intellectuals and scholars in the Jewish community of Western Europe to the abuse heaped upon the people of Israel by St. Bernard and other Christian leaders? What kind of faith and hope sustained medieval Jews through the long night of persecution that began in Christian Europe in the eleventh century and in the Islamic world in the twelfth century? The answers to these questions are evident from the following cry of the heart—at once anguished and serene, bitter and joyful—by Judah Halevi, the great Spanish Jewish scholar, poet, and spiritual leader, written in the 1130's.[21]

If the majority of us . . . would learn humility towards God and His law from our low station, Providence would not have forced us to bear

[21] Judah Halevi, *The Kuzari* (New York: Schocken Books, Inc., 1964), pp. 79, 107, 113, 226–7, 294–5. Reprinted by permission of Schocken Books.

it for such a long period. . . . Yet the majority may expect a reward, because they bear their degradation partly from necessity, partly of their own free will. For whoever wishes to do so can become the friend and equal of his oppressor by uttering one word, and without any difficulty. Such conduct does not escape the just Judge. If we bear our exile and degradation for God's sake, as is meet, we shall be the pride of the generation which will come with the Messiah, and accelerate the day of the deliverance we hope for. Now we do not allow any one who embraces our religion theoretically by means of a word alone to take equal rank with ourselves, but demand actual self-sacrifice, purity, knowledge, circumcision, and numerous religious ceremonies. The convert must adopt our mode of life entirely. We must bear in mind that the rite of circumcision is a divine symbol, ordained by God to indicate that our desires should be curbed, and discretion used, so that what we engender may be fitted to receive the divine Influence. God allows him who treads this path, as well as his progeny, to approach Him very closely. Those, however, who become Jews do not take equal rank with born Israelites, who are specially privileged to attain to prophecy, whilst the former can only achieve something by learning from them, and can only become pious and learned, but never prophets. . . .

The 'dead' nations which desire to be held equal to the 'living' people can obtain nothing more than an external resemblance. They built houses for God, but no trace of Him was visible therein. They turned hermits and ascetics in order to secure inspiration, but it came not. . . . We, however, since our heart, I mean the Holy House, was destroyed, were lost with it. If it be restored, we, too, will be restored, be we few or many, or in whichever way this may happen. For our master is the living God, our King, Who keeps us in this our present condition in dispersion and exile. . . .

The divine law imposes no asceticism on us. It rather desires that we should keep the equipoise, and grant every mental and physical faculty its due, as much as it can bear, without overburdening one faculty at the expense of another. If a person gives way to licentiousness he blunts his mental faculty; he who is inclined to violence injures some other faculty. Prolonged fasting is no act of piety for a weak person who, having succeeded in checking his desires, is not greedy. For him feasting is a burden and self-denial. Neither is diminution of wealth an act of piety, if it is gained in a lawful way, and if its acquisition does not interfere with study and good works, especially for him who has a household and children. He may spend part of it in almsgiving, which would not be displeasing to God; but to increase it is better for himself. Our law, as a whole, is divided between *fear, love,* and *joy,* by each of which one can approach God. Thy contrition on a fast day does nothing the nearer to God than thy joy on the Sabbath and holy days, if it is the outcome of a devout heart. Just as prayers demand devotion, so also is a pious mind necessary to find pleasure in God's command and law; that thou shouldst be pleased with the law itself from love of the Lawgiver. Thou seest how much He has distinguished thee, as if thou hadst been His guest invited to His festive board. Thou thankest Him in mind and word, and if thy joy lead thee so far as to sing and dance, it becomes worship and a bond of union between thee and the Divine Influence. Our law did not consider these matters optional, but laid down decisive injunctions concerning them. . . .

If I think of prominent men amongst us who could escape this degradation by a word spoken lightly, become free men, and turn against their oppressors, but do not do so out of devotion to their faith: is not this the way to obtain intercession and remission of many sins? . . . Besides this, God has a secret and wise design concerning us, which should be compared to the wisdom hidden in the seed which falls into the ground, where it undergoes an external transformation into earth, water and dirt, without leaving a trace for him who looks down upon it. It is, however, the seed itself which transforms earth and water into its own substance, carries it from one stage to another, until it refines the elements and transfers them into something like itself, casting off husks, leaves, etc., and allowing the pure core to appear, capable of bearing the Divine Influence. The original seed produced the tree bearing fruit resembling that from which it had been produced. In the same manner the law of Moses transforms each one who honestly follows it, though it may externally repel him. The nations merely serve to introduce and pave the way for the expected Messiah, who is the fruition, and they will all become His fruit. Then, if they acknowledge Him, they will become one tree. . . .

I only seek freedom from the service of those numerous people whose favour I do not care for, and shall never obtain, though I worked for it all my life. Even if I could obtain it, it would not profit me—I mean serving men and courting their favour. I would rather seek the service of the One whose favour is obtained with the smallest effort, yet it profits in this world and the next. This is the favour of God, His service spells freedom, and humility before Him is true honour. . . . Man is free in his endeavours and work. But he deserves blame who does not look for visible reward for visible work. For this reason it is written: 'Ye shall blow an alarm with the trumpets, and ye shall be remembered before the Lord your God (Num. x. 9) . . . They shall be to you for a memorial (ver. 10) . . . A memorial of blowing of trumpets' (Lev. xxiii. 24). God need not be reminded, but actions must be perfect to claim reward. Likewise must the ideas of the prayers be pronounced in the most perfect way to be considered as prayer and supplication. Now if thou bringest intention and action to perfection thou mayest

expect reward. This is popularly expressed by *reminding,* and 'the
Tōrāh speaks in the manner of human beings.' If the action is minus
the intention, or the intention minus the action, the expectation [for
reward] is lost, except in impossible things. It is, however, rather useful to show the good intention if the deed is impossible, as we express
this in our prayer: 'On account of our sins have we been driven out of
our land.' This sacred place serves to remind men and to stimulate
them to love God, being a reward and promise, as it is written: 'Thou
shalt arise and have mercy upon Zion, for the time to favour her, yea,
the set time is come. For thy servants take pleasure in her stones and
embrace the dust thereof' (Ps. cii. 14 sq.). This means that Jerusalem
can only be rebuilt when Israel yearns for it to such an extent that
they embrace her stones and dust.

42 / CHIVALRY,
THE NEW SENSIBILITY,
AND ROMANTIC LOVE

*The most original and creative aspect of twelfth-century
culture was the emergence of a new vernacular literature, first
in French and Spanish, then in German, and finally—in the thirteenth century—an Italian vernacular literature also appeared.
This literature, whose favorite forms were the feudal epic and the
adventure-romance, was the vehicle for the expression of a new
aristocratic style—chivalry and courtliness; a new sensibility—
marked by the frank revelation of deep emotions and an idealization of feminine qualities; and the ideal of romantic love—the
yearning for union between man and woman. This union in turn
was regarded as a mundane image of the soul's yearning for union
with God. The same blending of the sacred and secular worlds appears in the motif of the romantic hero's perilous quest for the
Holy Grail. The Grail was originally the chalice from which Jesus
drank at the Last Supper, but in the subtle imagination of the
romantic poets it came to symbolize the ineffable ideal, the perfected state of human happiness. In* The Song of Roland (A),[22] *the*

---

[22] *The Song of Roland,* transl. I. Butler (Boston: Houghton Mifflin Co., 1904),
pp. 129–30.

most famous of the feudal epics, the chivalric, courtly ideal, and even a trace of the new emotionalism are illustrated. The Story of the Grail *by Chrétien de Troyes, who wrote at the court of Champagne in the 1160's (B)* [23] *and* Parzival *by the great German poet Wolfram von Eschenbach, written c. 1200 (C),* [24] *exemplify the highest stage of development of the adventure-romance and exhibit the interrelated motifs and ideals that comprised the medieval romantic ethos. Behind the new sensibility and idealization of human love and femininity lies the motive of breakaway from the legalism, abstractness, hierarchy, and authoritarianism of the feudal-ecclesiastical complex and the desire for individual dignity and freedom. The literary products of this intellectual background represent the beginning of modern literature and are among the finest works of the European imagination. But as was to be the case with all succeeding romantic movements in Western Civilization, cynicism and disillusionment and the cold light of common day appeared almost immediately to undermine and sour the highflown idealism of the original romantic quest. This development is already evident in the work of another writer at the court of Champagne in the 1160's and 1170's, Andreas Capellanus (Andrew the Chaplain) (D).* [25]

A. THE SONG OF ROLAND: THE CHIVALRIC IDEAL

The day passes and night darkens, clear is the moon and bright the stars. The Emperor hath taken Saragossa. He commands a thousand Franks that they search the city, the synagogues and the mosques; with axes and mallets of iron they shatter the walls and the idols, till naught is left of their sorcery and their lies. The King believes in God and would do His service; and now the bishops bless the waters, and the paynims are brought to baptism. And if any among them gainsay Charles, he must hang or burn or perish by the sword. More than a hundred thousand are baptized and become true Christians, all save

[23] Chrétien de Troyes, *The Story of the Grail*, 2nd ed., transl. R. W. Linker (Chapel Hill, N. C.: The University of North Carolina Press, 1952), pp. 45–9. Reprinted by permission of The University of North Carolina Press.
[24] *The Parzival of Wolfram von Eschenbach*, transl. E. H. Zeydel and B. Q. Morgan (Chapel Hill, N. C.: University of North Carolina Press, 1951), pp. 294–5. Reprinted by permission of The University of North Carolina Press.
[25] Andreas Capellanus, *The Art of Courtly Love*, transl. J. J. Parry (New York: Columbia University Press, 1941), pp. 208–9. Reprinted by permission of Columbia University Press.

only the Queen; she will be brought a captive to fair France, and it is by love the King would have her converted.

The night passes and the clear day dawns. Charles has stuffed the tower of Saragossa with troops, leaving there a thousand stout knights, who keep the city in the name of the Emperor. The King gets to horse with all his men, and Bramimonde whom he takes with him as a captive; naught but good would he do her. And now in all joy and mirth they turn homewards; and in their strength and their might they passed Narbonne, and came to the proud city of Bordeaux; and there Charles left the horn of ivory filled with gold and mangons upon the altar of Saint Sevérin the baron, where it may still be seen of pilgrims. Thereafter Charles crossed the Gironde on great ships which he had there, and unto Blaye he bore his nephew, and Oliver, Roland's gentle comrade, and the Archbishop who was both wise and brave; he has the three lords laid in tombs of white marble, in Saint Romain, and there the barons lie even unto this day. The Franks commend them to God and his angels, and Charles rides on over hill and dale; he will make no stay until he comes to Aix, but hastens on till he reaches the entrance stair. And when he is come into his high palace, by messenger he summons his judges, Bavarians and Saxons, men of Lorraine and Friesland, Germans and Burgundians, Poitevins, Normans and Bretons, and the wisest of those of France. And then begins the trial of Ganelon.

The Emperor has returned from Spain, and come again to Aix, the fairest seat in France; he has gone up into his palace and has passed into the hall. To him comes Aude, that fair damsel, and saith to the King: "Where is Roland, the captain, who pledged him to take me as his wife?" Thereat Charles is filled with dolour and grief, he weeps and plucks his white beard, saying: "Sister, sweet friend, thou askest me of one who is dead. But I will make good thy loss to thee, and will give thee Louis—a better I cannot name—my son he is, and will hold my marches." "Lord, thy words are strange to me," Aude makes answer. "May it not please God or his saints or his angels that after Roland's death I should yet live." She loses her colour and falls at the feet of Charles, and lo, she is dead. God have mercy upon her soul. The barons of France weep and lament her.

B. CHRÉTIEN DE TROYES: ROMANTIC LOVE

At once she commands that one set the tables, and they are put in place and the people seated for supper.

They sat very little at their eating, but they took it with great liking. After eating they separated: those remained and slept who had kept watch the night before; those went out who were to keep vigil over the castle that night. There were fifty sergeants and squires who watched that night; the others made great efforts to make their guests comfortable. Those who take charge of putting him to bed place for him fine sheets and very dear coverings and a pillow for his head. The knight had that night all the ease and all the delight that one might know how to devise in a bed, except only the delight of maiden, if it might please him, or of lady, if it were allowed him. But he knew nothing of that, nor did he think of it either little or much, and he soon went to sleep, for he was not worried about anything. But his hostess, who was shut in her room, does not repose; he sleeps at his ease, and she thinks, who has in herself no defense against a battle which assails her. Much does she turn, and much jerk, much does she toss and move about. She has put on a short mantle of scarlet silk over her chemise, and set out on a venture, as a bold and courageous woman, but it is not aimlessly; rather she thinks that she will go to her guest and will tell him a part of her affair. Then she departed from her bed and went forth from her chamber in such fear that all her limbs tremble and her body sweats. Weeping she came from her room and comes to the bed where he is sleeping, and she weeps and sighs very strongly and bows and kneels and weeps so that she wets all his face with tears: she has not the boldness to do more.

So much has she wept that he awakens and is all dismayed and marvels at feeling his face wet, and he sees her on her knees before his bed, who was holding him tightly embraced around the neck, and he did her so much courtesy that he took her in his arms at once and drew her near him. So he said to her: "Fair one, what pleases you? Why have you come here?"

"Ha! gentle knight, mercy! For the sake of God and for His Son, I pray you that you do not hold me more vile because I have come here, although I am nearly naked. I never thought any folly nor malice nor villainy, for there is nothing alive in the world so grieving nor so caitiff that I am not more grieving. Nothing that I have pleases me, for never any day was I without ill, I am so ill-fortuned, nor shall I ever see another night except only this night, nor day except that of tomorrow; rather shall I slay myself by my hand. Of three hundred knights and ten with whom this castle was garnished there are not left herein but fifty; for two hundred and ten less than sixty has a very evil knight, Anguingueron, the seneschal of Clamadeu des Isles, led away and killed and imprisoned. For those who are put in prison I am as grieved as for the slain, for I know well that they will die there, for never again will they come forth. Because of me many worthy men are dead, and it is right that I be discomforted for that.

"Anguingueron has been at siege here before this castle a whole winter and a summer, without moving, and meantime his force grew, and ours has grown smaller and our foods exhausted so that there does not remain in here that on which a bee might feed. We are so entirely beaten that tomorrow, if God does not prevent it, this castle will be given up to him, for it cannot be defended, and I with it as a captive. But, certainly, rather than that he have me alive, I shall slay myself, so will he have me dead; then I do not care if he carries me away to Clamadeu, who thinks to have me: never will he have me, if he has me not empty of life and of soul, in any case, for I keep in a jewel chest of mine a knife of fine steel that I shall thrust in my body. Thus much I had to say to you. Now I shall go on my way again, and I shall let you rest."

Soon the knight will be able to boast if he dare, for never did she come weeping over his face for any other thing, whatever she make him understand, except because she would put in his heart to undertake the battle, if he dare, to defend her and her land. And he said to her:

"Dear friend, show a more cheerful face this night: comfort yourself; do not weep any more, and draw yourself toward me up here, and take the tears from your eyes. God, if it please Him, will do better for you tomorrow than you have said to me. Lie down beside me in this bed, for it is wide enough for our needs; today you will not leave me more."

And she said: "If it pleased you, so would I do."

And he kissed her, who held her grasped in his arms, so has he put her under the coverlet quite softly and wholly at ease and she suffers that he kiss her, nor do I believe that it annoys her. Thus they lay all night, the one beside the other, mouth to mouth, until morning when the day approaches. He solaced her so much that mouth to mouth, arm in arm, they slept until day broke. At daybreak the maiden returned to her chamber. Without serving girl and without chambermaid she dressed and attired herself so that she awoke no one by it. Those who had kept watch during the night, as soon as they could see the day, awakened those who were sleeping and made them rise from their beds, and they got up without delay, and the maiden within the hour repairs to her knight and says to him debonairly:

"Lord, God give you good day today! I believe indeed that you will not make long sojourn here. There will be nothing of staying: you will go away; it does not worry me, for I should not be courteous if it troubled me in any way, for we have given you herein no ease and no good. But I pray God that He may have a better hostel made ready for you where there is more bread and wine and salt and other good than in this one."

And he said: "Fair one, it will not be today that I go seek another hostel. Rather I shall have first put all your land in peace, if ever I can. If I find your enemy out there, it will trouble me if he sits there any longer, because you are grieved for nothing. But if I kill and conquer him I request your love as a reward, that it be mine; no other wages would I take."

She answers graciously: "Lord, you have now asked me for a very poor and despised thing, but if it were contradicted you, you would consider it pride; therefore I do not wish to deny it to you. Nevertheless do not say that I become your friend by such covenant nor by such law that you go to die for me; for it would be too great a pity, for neither your body nor your age is such, know this surely, that you could hold out or suffer strife or battle against so hard a knight nor so strong nor so large as is he who waits out there."

"That you will see," says he, "today, for I shall go fight against him; never will I give it up for any warning." She has built such plea with him that she blames him for it, and yet wishes it; but it often happens that one is wont to conceal one's wish when one sees a man well inclined to do his own liking, so that he may be more pleased to do it. And so she acts wisely, for she has put in his heart that for which she strongly blames him. He asks for his arms. They are brought to him and the gate was opened for him. They arm him and have him mount on a horse that they have made ready for him in the middle of the place. There is no one who does not show that he is worried, and who does not say: "Lord, God be your aid this day and give great ill to Anguingueron the seneschal, who has destroyed all this country."

All the men and women weep as they escort him to the gate, and when they see him outside the castle they all say in one voice: "Fair lord, that true Cross on which God suffered His Son to have pain guard you today from mortal peril, encumbrance and prison, and bring you back safely to a place where you may be at ease, which delights and pleases you!"

C. WOLFRAM VON ESCHENBACH: THE QUEST FOR THE GRAIL

Once again Sir Parzival
His fair wife could not but recall,
Her chasteness and her sweetness.
Could he with any meetness,
Another lady wooing,
Fall into faithless doing?
No, such love he'd ever shun.
Great constancy for him had won
A manly heart, a body strong,
Till to no other could belong
His love and his endeavor,
Save but his queen forever. . . .
He thought, . . .

"If toward the Grail I am to strive,
My heart must ever feel the drive
Toward the pure embrace and kiss
Which I gave up, too long to miss.
The while my eyes see happiness,
My heart knows nothing but distress—
Unlike are those positions.
Ah, under such conditions
I can't as happy know me.
May my good fortune show me
The way on which I best were led."
His armor lay before him spread.

   He pondered, "Since I have to miss
What they command who live in bliss, . . .
Since I of this am cheated,
I care not what becomes of me.
God does not wish my joy to see.
She who for love makes me to pine,
My wife, were our love, hers and mine,
So made as us to sever,
That we in love could waver,
Another love perhaps I'd gain.
But love for her from me has ta'en
All other love and joy I dreamed.
Of sadness I am unredeemed.
May fortune grant her pleasure
To those who seek full measure.
God, joy on all these throngs bestow!
From all these joys away I'll go."
He seized the harness, near him laid,
Which oft he'd donned without men's aid
And soon he had it on again.
He'll go in search of further pain.
When now the man who pleasure fled
Had armed himself from foot to head,
He saddled, all alone, his horse.
Shield and spear he took perforce.
They wept that he'd departed:
The sun rose when he'd started.

D. ANDREAS CAPELLANUS: AN ESSAY ON WOMAN

No woman knows how to keep a secret; the more she is told to keep it to herself, the harder she tries to tell it to everybody. No one to this day has been able to find a woman who could keep hidden anything confided to her, no matter how important it was or how much it seemed that to tell it would be the death of somebody. Whatever you intrust as a secret to the good faith of a woman seems to burn her very vitals until she gets the harmful secrets out of her. You cannot avoid this in a woman by ordering her to do the opposite . . . because every woman takes great pleasure in gossip; therefore be careful to keep your secret from every woman.

Every woman in the world is likewise wanton, because no woman, no matter how famous and honored she is, will refuse her embraces to any man, even the most vile and abject, if she knows that he is good at the work of Venus; yet there is no man so good at the work that he can satisfy the desires of any woman you please in any way at all.

Furthermore, no woman is attached to her lover or bound to her husband with such pure devotion that she will not accept another lover, especially if a rich one comes along, which shows the wantonness as well as the great avarice of a woman. There isn't a woman in this world so constant and so bound by pledges that, if a lover of pleasure comes along and with skill and persistence invites her to the joys of love, she will reject his entreaties—at any rate if he does a good deal of urging—or will defend herself against his importunity. No woman is an exception to this rule either. So you can see what we ought to think of a woman who is in fortunate circumstances and is blessed with an honorable lover or the finest of husbands, and yet lusts after some other man. But that is what a woman does who is too much troubled with wantonness.

Woman is also prone to every sort of evil. Whatever evil in this world is greatest, that any woman will commit without fear and for a trivial reason; by a little persuading anyone can easily incline her mind toward any evil. Besides there is not a woman living in this world, not even the Empress or the Queen, who does not waste her whole life on auguries and the various practitioners of divination, as the heathen do, and so long as she lives she persists in this credulousness and sins without measure again and again with the art of astrology. Indeed, no woman does anything without considering the proper day and hour for beginning it and without inaugurating it with incantation. They will not marry, or hold funeral rites for the dead, or start their sowing, or move into a new house, or begin anything else without consulting this feminine augury and having their actions approved by these witches. Therefore Solomon, that wisest of men, who knew all the evils and the misdeeds of womankind, made a general statement concerning their crimes and wickednesses when he said, "There is no good woman." Why therefore . . . , are you striving so eagerly to love that which is bad?

Indeed, a woman does not love a man with her whole heart, because there is no one of them who keeps faith with her husband or her lover; when another man comes along, you will find that her faithfulness wavers. For a woman cannot refuse gold or silver or any other gifts that are offered her, nor can she deny the solaces of her body when they are asked for. But since a woman knows that nothing so distresses her lover as to have her grant these to some other man, you can see how much affection she has for a man when, out of greed for gold or silver, she will give herself to a stranger or a foreigner and has no shame about upsetting her lover so completely and shattering the jewel of her own good faith. Moreover, no woman has such a strong bond of affection for a lover that if he ceases to woo her with presents she will not become luke-warm about her customary solaces and quickly become like a stranger to him. It doesn't seem proper, therefore, for any prudent man to fall in love with any woman, because she never keeps faith with any man; everybody knows that she ought to be spurned for the innumerable weighty reasons that have already been given.

43 / MEDIEVAL CITIES

The great religious and intellectual changes of the twelfth century were accompanied by the rise to prominence of a new class in European society: the bourgeoisie, or town dwellers, who were the product of the commercial expansion which had begun in the tenth century. Except for northern Italy and Flanders, it would be many centuries before the political power of the bourgeois would equal their economic importance, but in the cultural and religious life of the period the impact of urbanization was already evident. The interests and attitudes of the late twelfth-century bourgeois are made clear in a description of London in the year 1173 by an English churchman, William Fitz-Stephen (A).[26] *This piece of municipal patriotism may be compared with an account of the city of Milan in 1288 by an Italian churchman, Bonvesin della Riva (B).*[27] *In both descriptions there is the same*

[26] William Fitz-Stephen, *Description of the Most Noble City of London,* in E. K. Kendall, *Source Book of English History* (New York: The Macmillan Company, 1900), pp. 65–71.

[27] Bonvesin della Riva, "On the Marvels of the City of Milan," in *Medieval Trade in the Mediterranean World,* R. S. Lopez and I. W. Raymond, eds. (New York: Columbia University Press, 1955), pp. 61–6, 69. Reprinted by permission of Columbia University Press.

tendency to gross exaggeration and a strident, almost comic, effort to portray the writer's favorite city as a glorious and most blessed habitat. This chamber-of-commerce prose does not hide from the careful reader the authors' indications of the grave social, economic, and political problems of the medieval city, not the least of which were bad sanitation, wretched housing conditions for the majority of the townspeople, and overcrowding. Behind these municipal blurbs lies the isolation and fear of the bourgeois who had to look beyond the walls of his city at what was still an intensely rural and aristocratic society.

A. WILLIAM FITZ-STEPHEN: LONDON IN 1173

Of the Site Thereof

Among the noble cities of the world that Fame celebrates the City of London of the Kingdom of the English, is the one seat that pours out its fame more widely, sends to farther lands its wealth and trade, lifts its head higher than the rest. It is happy in the healthiness of its air, in the Christian religion, in the strength of its defences, the nature of its site, the honour of its citizens, the modesty of its matrons; pleasant in sports; fruitful of noble men. Let us look into these things separately. . . .

Of Religion

There is in the church there the Episcopal Seat of St. Paul; once it was Metropolitan, and it is thought will again become so if the citizens return into the island, unless perhaps the archiepiscopal title of Saint Thomas the Martyr, and his bodily presence, preserve to Canterbury where it is now, a perpetual dignity. But as Saint Thomas has made both cities illustrious, London by his rising, Canterbury by his setting, in regard of that saint, with admitted justice, each can claim advantage of the other. There are also, as regards the cultivation of the Christian faith, in London and the suburbs, thirteen larger conventual churches, besides lesser parish churches one hundred and twenty-six.

Of the Strength of the City

It has on the east the Palatine Castle, very great and strong, of which the ground plan and the walls rise from a very deep foundation, fixed with a mortar tempered by the blood of animals. On the west are two towers very strongly fortified, with the high and great wall of the city having seven double gates, and towered in like manner on the south, but the great fish-bearing Thames river which there glides, with ebb and flow from the sea, by course of time has washed against, loosened, and thrown down those walls. Also upwards to the west the royal palace is conspicuous above the same river, an incomparable building with ramparts and bulwarks, two miles from the city, joined to it by a populous suburb.

Of Gardens

Everywhere outside the houses of those living in the suburbs are joined to them, planted with trees, the spacious and beautiful gardens of the citizens.

Of Pasture and Tilth

Also there are, on the north side, pastures and a pleasant meadow land, through which flow river streams, where the turning wheels of mills are put in motion with a cheerful sound. Very near lies a great forest, with woodland pastures, coverts of wild animal, stags, fallow deer, boats and wild bulls. The tilled lands of the city are not of barren gravel but fat plains of Asia, that make crops luxuriant, and fill their tillers' barns with Ceres' sheaves.

Of Springs

There are also about London, on the north side, excellent suburban springs, with sweet, wholesome, and clear water that flows rippling over the bright stones; among which Holy Well, Clerken Well, and Saint Clements are frequented by greater numbers, and visited more by scholars and youth of the city when they go out for fresh air on summer evenings. It is a good city indeed when it has a good master.

Of Honour of the Citizens

That City is honoured by her men, adorned by her arms, populous with many inhabitants, so that in the time of slaughter of war under King Stephen, of those going out to muster twenty thousand horsemen and sixty thousand men on foot were estimated to be fit for war. Above all other citizens, everywhere, the citizens of London are regarded as conspicuous and noteworthy for handsomeness of manners and of dress, at table, and in way of speaking. . . .

Of Schools

In London three principal churches have by privilege and ancient dignity, famous schools; yet very often by support of some personage, or of some teachers who are considered notable and famous in philosophy, there are also other schools by favour and permission. On feast days the masters have festival meetings in the churches. Their scholars dispute, some by demonstration, others by dialectics; some recite enthymemes, others do better in using perfect syllogisms. Some are exercised in disputation for display, as wrestling with opponents; others for truth, which is the grace of perfectness. Sophists who feign are judged happy in their heap and flood of words. Others paralogize. Some orators, now and then, say in their rhetorical speeches something apt for persuasion, careful to observe rules of their art, and to omit none of the contingents. Boys of different schools strive against one another in verses, and contend about the principles of grammar and rules of the past and future tenses. . . .

Of the Ordering of the City

Those engaged in the several kinds of business, sellers of several things, contractors for several kinds of work, are distributed every morning into their several localities and shops. Besides, there is in London on the river bank, among the wines in ships and cellars sold by the vintners, a public cook shop; there eatables are to be found every day, according to the season, dishes of meat, roast, fried and boiled, great and small fish, coarser meats for the poor, more delicate for the rich, of game, fowls, and small birds. If there should come suddenly to any of the citizens friends, weary from a journey and too hungry to like waiting till fresh food is bought and cooked, with water to their hands comes bread, while one runs to the river bank, and there is all that can be wanted. However great the multitude of soldiers or travellers entering the city, or preparing to go out of it, at any hour of the day or night,—that these may not fast too long and those may not go supperless,—they turn hither, if they please, where every man can refresh himself in his own way. . . . Outside one of the gates there, immediately in the suburb, is a certain field, smooth (Smith) field in fact and name. Every Friday, unless it be a higher day of appointed solemnity, there is in it a famous show of noble horses for sale. Earls, barons, knights, and many citizens who are in town, come to see or buy. . . . In another part of the field stand by themselves the goods proper to rustics, implements of husbandry, swine with long flanks, cows with full udders, oxen of bulk immense, and wooly flocks. . . . To this city from every nation under heaven merchants delight to bring their trade by sea—. . . . This city . . . is divided into wards, has annual sheriffs for its consuls, has senatorial and lower magistrates, sewers and aqueducts in its streets, its proper places and separate courts for cases of each kind, deliberative, demonstrative, judicial; has assemblies on appointed days. I do not think there is a city with more commendable customs of church attendance, honour to God's ordinances, keeping sacred festivals, almsgiving, hospitality, confirming betrothals, contracting marriages, celebration of nuptials, preparing feasts, cheering the guests, and also in care for funerals and the interment of the dead. The only pests of London are the immoderate drinking of fools and the frequency of fires. To this may be added that nearly all the bishops, abbots, and magnates of England are, as it were, citizens and freemen of London; having there their own splendid houses, to which they resort, where they spend largely when summoned to great councils by the king or by their metropolitan, or drawn thither by their own private affairs.

Of Sports

Let us now come to the sports and pastimes, seeing it is fit that a city should not only be commodious and serious, but also merry and sportful; . . . But London . . . hath holy plays, representations of miracles which holy confessors have wrought, or representations of torments wherein the constancy of martyrs appeared. Every year also at Shrove Tuesday, that we may begin with children's sports, seeing we all have been children, the schoolboys do bring cocks of the game to their master, and all the forenoon they delight themselves in cock-fighting: after dinner, all the youths go into the fields to play at the ball.

The scholars of every school have their ball, or baton, in their hands; the ancient and wealthy men of the city come forth on horseback to see the sport of the young men, and to take part of the pleasure in beholding their agility. Every Friday in Lent a fresh company of young men comes into the field on horseback, and the best horseman conducteth the rest. Then march forth the citizens' sons, and other young men, with disarmed lances and shields, and there they practise feats of war. Many courtiers likewise, when the king lieth near, and attendants of noblemen, do repair to these exercises; and while the hope of victory doth inflame their minds, do show good proof how serviceable they would be in martial affairs.

In Easter holidays they fight battles on the water; a shield is hung upon a pole, fixed in the midst of the stream, a boat is prepared without oars, to be carried by violence of the water, and in the fore part thereof standeth a young man, ready to give charge upon the shield with his lance; if so be he breaketh his lance against the shield, and doth not fall, he is thought to have performed a worthy deed; if so be, without breaking his lance, he runneth strongly against the shield, down he falleth into the water, for the boat is violently forced with the tide; but on each side of the shield ride two boats, furnished with young men, which recover him that falleth as soon as they may. Upon the bridge, wharfs, and houses, by the river's side, stand great numbers to see and laugh thereat.

In the holidays all the summer the youths are exercised in leaping, dancing, shooting, wrestling, casting the stone, and practising their shields; the maidens trip in their timbrels, and dance as long as they can well see. In winter, every holiday before dinner, the boats prepared for brawn are set to fight, or else bulls and bears are baited.

When the great fen, or moor, which watereth the walls of the city on the north side, is frozen, many young men play upon the ice; some, striding as wide as they may, do slide swiftly; others make themselves seats of ice, as great as millstones; one sits down, many hand in hand to draw him, and one slipping on a sudden, all fall together; some tie bones to their feet and under their heels; and shoving themselves by a little picked staff, do slide as swiftly as a bird flieth in the air, or an arrow out of a cross-bow. Sometime two run together with poles, and hitting one the other, either one or both do fall, not without hurt; some break their arms, some their legs, but youth desirous of glory in this sort exerciseth itself against the time of war. Many of the citizens do delight themselves in hawks and hounds; for they have liberty of hunting in Middlesex, Hertfordshire, all Chiltern, and in Kent to the water of Cray. . . .

B. BONVESIN DELLA RIVA: MILAN IN 1288

In Praise of Milan's Housing

In regard to housing . . . the truth is there before the eyes of those who see. The streets in this city are quite wide, the palaces quite beautiful, the houses packed in, not scattered but continuous, stately, adorned in a stately manner.

1. Dwellings with doors giving access to the public streets have been found to number about 12,500, and in their number are very many in which many families live together with crowds of dependents. And this indicates the astonishing density of population of citizens.

2. The roofed commons [open to all] neighbors in those squares which are popularly called *coperti* [Arcades] almost reach the record number of sixty.

3. The court of the Commune, befitting such a great city, spreads over an area of ten *pertiche* or thereabouts. And in order to make this more easily understandable perchance to some people, [I shall specify that it] measures 130 cubits from east to west and 136 from north to south. In the midst of it stands a wonderful palace, and in the court itself there is a tower, in which are the four bells of the Commune. On the eastern side is a palace in which are the rooms of the podestà and

of the judges, and at its end on the northern side is the chapel of the podestà, built in honor of our patron, the Blessed Ambrose. And another palace prolongs the court on the north; so, similarly, on the west. To the south there is also the hall where the sentences of condemnation are publicly proclaimed.

4. The city itself is ringed as a circle, and its wonderful rounded shape is a mark of its perfection. . . .

5. . . . Outside the wall of the moat there are so many suburban houses that they alone would be enough to constitute a city. . . .

6. The main gates of the city are also very strong, and they reach the number of six. The secondary gates, named *pusterle*, are ten. . . .

7. The sanctuaries of the saints . . . are about two hundred in the city alone, having 480 altars. . . .

8. [In honor of the Virgin Mary] thirty-six churches have been built in the city, and undoubtedly there are more than 260 in the county (*comitatus*). . . .

9. The steeples, built in the manner of towers, are about 120 in the city. . . .

10. In the county there are pleasant and delightful localities, even stately towns, fifty in number; and among them is Monza, ten miles distant from the city, worthier to be named a city than a town. Indeed, 150 villages with castles are subject to the jurisdiction of our Commune, and among them there are a great many, each of which has more than five hundred inhabitants able to bear arms. And in these very towns as well as in the villages not only farmers and craftsmen live but also many magnates of high nobility. And there also are other isolated buildings, some of which are called mills and others, popularly, *cassine* [Farmhouses]—the infinite number of which I can hardly estimate. . . .

In Praise of Milan's Population

When considered in regard to population, it seems to me that it outshines all the other cities in the world.

1. In fact, its natives of both sexes have the peculiarity of being rather tall, jovial in appearance, and quite friendly, not deceitful, still less malicious in dealing with people from outside their town, and because of this they also are more highly considered abroad than are others. . . . They live decently, orderly, and magnificently; they use clothing that does them honor; wherever they may be, at home or elsewhere, they are quite free in spending, esteemed, honorable, goodhumored in customs and way of life. . . .

2. The population, as numerous in the city as in the county or in its district, increases every day, and the city spreads out with the [erec-

tion of new] buildings. How could the people not thrive where it is so glorious to live? For this reason, if citizens are counted together with strangers of all kinds they are found in all to be many more than 200,000 men [in the entire county]—each of them to be regarded as an able man at war. And we have not counted in their number men of different kinds exempted [from military service]—monks, canons, and other clerics and religious, both those professed and those living in their own homes with their servants. . . .

3. In the city, indeed, there are ten canonries, excluding from this number the house of canons [located] where the cathedral church is. But in the county there are seventy, not including seven canonries of the Order of the Humiliati, and the canons regular complete the number with twenty-one.

4. Then there are in the city ninety-four chapels. . . .

5. In the city there are six convents of monks, and the nunneries are eight. . . .

6. Again, in the city, including the suburbs, which are always to be regarded as included whenever the city is mentioned, there are ten hospitals for the sick, all properly endowed with sufficient temporal resources. The principal one of these is the Hospital of the Brolo, very rich in precious possessions; it was founded in 1145 by Goffredo de Bussero. In it, as its friars and deacons testify, at times and particularly in the days of dearth[?], when count is made, there are found more than five hundred poor bed patients and just as many more not lying down. All of these receive food at the expense of the hospital itself. Besides them, also, no less than 350 babies and more, placed with individual nurses after their birth, are under the hospital's care. Every sort of the poor people mentioned below, except the lepers, for whom another hospital is reserved, are received there; and they are kindly and bountifully restored to health, bed as well as food being provided. Also, all the poor needing surgical care are diligently cared for by three surgeons especially assigned to this task; the latter receive a salary from the Commune. In conclusion, the misery of no man who is in want meets refusal or rejection here. In the county, indeed, there are fifteen hospitals or thereabouts.

7. There are also houses of the Second Order of the Humiliati of each sex which in the city and the county reach the number of 220; inside them there is a copious number of persons leading the religious life while working with their own hands. . . .

8. The houses of the Order of St. Augustine of each sex undoubtedly are sixty. . . .

11. This, however, I affirm with certainty, that inside as well as outside the city, counting priests and other clerics of all orders . . . more than ten thousand religious are eating Ambrosian bread. . . .

12. What else can be said of the huge number of the multitude living in Milan and in the county? Silence; whoever can grasp it, let him grasp it. This, however, will be forgiven me: that I am by no means silent. For, as I roughly estimate—and many definitely assert the same —more than 700,000 mouths of the two sexes, including all infants as well as adults, obtain their sustenance from the surface of the Ambrosian earth. Every day—and it is wonderful in what manner—they receive, from the hand of God, Ambrosian food.

13. Why not, even if their number is so great, since in the city alone, with its dense population, there undoubtedly are 115 parishes, among which there certainly are some in each of which indeed more than five hundred families live, while in a few others about one thousand live?

14. Let therefore anyone who can count how many persons live in such a city. And if he is able to do it accurately, he will count up to the number of about 200,000, as I firmly believe. For it is certainly proved and supported by serious, careful investigation, that every day, taking into account the different seasons, 1,200 *modii* of grain and more are consumed in the city alone. That this is the truth of the matter, those who are wont to collect the tribute of the grain ground in the mills can certify.

15. Whoever wishes to know how many warriors there are in time of war should know that more than forty thousand—that is, counting each and all—live in this city who are able to fight the enemy with sword or lance or other weapon. . . .

16. In it and in its county more than ten thousand could easily maintain war horses [if] ordered by the Commune. . . .

17. There are in this city alone 120 doctors of both laws, and their college is believed to have no equal in the entire world, either in number or in learning. All these, ready to give [judicial] sentences, gladly take the money of the litigants.

18. The notaries are more than 1,500, among whom there are a great many who are excellent in drawing contracts.

19. The messengers of the Commune, popularly named *servitori*, undoubtedly are six hundred.

20. Six, indeed, are the principal trumpeters of the Commune, honorable and distinguished men. . . .

21. The experts in medicine, who are popularly named physicians, are twenty-eight.

22. The surgeons of different specialties, indeed, are more than 150, among whom are a great many who, obviously being excellent physicians, have derived from the ancestors of their family the ancient traditions of surgery. They are believed to have no equals in the other cities of Lombardy.

23. The professors of grammatical art are eight. They supervise

crowds of pupils, each professor with his rod, and teach grammar with great industry and diligence, surpassing the doctors of other cities, as I have clearly determined after careful examination.

24. There are fourteen doctors in the Ambrosian chant, of so excellent renown that because of them this city is noted for its crowds of clerics.

25. The teachers of the elements of reading and writing indeed number more than seventy.

26. The copyists, although there is no university (*Studium generale*) in the city, surpass the number of forty, and by writing books with their hands every day they earn their bread and other expenses.

27. Indeed, there are three hundred bakeries in the city (as one learns from the books of the Commune) which bake bread for the use of the citizens. There are also very many other bakeries exempt [from taxation] which serve monks or religious of each sex; of these I think there are more than a hundred.

28. The shopkeepers, who sell at retail an amazing amount of goods of all kinds, doubtlessly are more than a thousand.

29. The butchers number more than 440, and excellent meat of quadrupeds of all kinds, as suits our customs, is sold in great quantity in their shops.

30. There are more than eighteen fishermen [who catch] all kinds of fish—trout, carp, large eels, tench, grayling, eels, lampreys, crabs—and who every day bring a supply of large and small fish of every species from the lakes of our county. Those who bring fish from the rivers number more than sixty, and those who bring fish from the numberless mountain streams state that they are far more than four hundred.

31. The hostelries giving hospitality to strangers for profit number about 150.

32. The smiths who outfit quadrupeds with iron shoes number about eighty, and this indicates the multitude of horsemen and horses. How many are the saddlers, how many the smiths of bridles and spurs and stirrups, I pass over in silence.

33. The makers of the sweet-sounding brass bells which are attached to the breasts of horses—and which we do not know are made anywhere else—are more than thirty, and each of them has under him many assistants in his craft. . . .

In Praise of Milan's Fertility and Abundance of All Goods

When considered in regard to the fertility of territory and the abundance of all goods useful for human consumption, [its excellence] already is evident, but I shall explain it more plainly. . . .

17. Four general fairs are held in the city every year, that is, on the day of the ordination of the Blessed Ambrose, on the feast of the Blessed Lawrence, on the Ascension of the Blessed Mother of God, and on the feast of the Blessed Bartholomew. It is amazing to see almost innumerable merchants with their variety of wares and buyers flocking to all these fairs. Furthermore, ordinary markets are held in different parts of the city two days a week, that is, on Fridays and Saturdays. Indeed—and this is more [amazing]—practically anything that man may need is brought daily not only into special places but even into the [open] squares, and all that can be sold is loudly advertised for sale. Also, there are many fairs in the towns and villages of our county, being held every year on certain days. In many of them, indeed, there is a market every week, and merchants and buyers hasten to all of them in large numbers. It is evident, after [all] that has been said, that in our city it is a wonderful life for those who have money enough. Every convenience for human pleasure is known to be at hand here.

18. Also it is obvious that here any man, if he is healthy and not a good-for-nothing, may earn his living expenses and esteem according to his station. And it is worth noting that here the fecundity in offspring is just as prolific as the abundance of temporal goods. In fact, when on festive days one looks at the merry crowds of dignified men, both of the nobility and of the people, also at the bustling throngs of children incessantly scurrying here and there, and at the comely gatherings, comely groups of ladies and virgins going back and forth or standing on the doorsteps [of their homes], as dignified as if they were daughters of kings, who would say that he has ever met such a wonderful show of people this side or the other side of the sea? . . .

44 / THE RISE OF MONARCHY

Whatever strength monarchy in Western Europe had lost due to the forced abandonment of the ideology of theocratic kingship in the Gregorian-reform period, was rapidly recovered by the middle of the twelfth century. Taking advantage of cultural and economic changes, monarchy asserted its leadership in European society to a degree not seen in Western Europe since the fourth century by making use of the great improvements in law, administration, and finance. It needed only a strong per-

*sonality on the throne for a royal government to be able to assert
its authority over society, and to receive the loyalty of all classes
and groups, to an extent which prefigures the sovereignty of the
modern state. In Germany and England in the second half
of the twelfth century the royal power was in the hands of such
outstanding personalities, and the authority they were able to
wield and the awe and enthusiasm with which they were greeted
are illustrated in the following selections.*

*The forerunner, and in some ways, the model for the powerful
monarchs of the twelfth century, was the astute and ambitious
Norman duke who conquered England and ruled as William I
from 1066 to 1087. An Anglo-Saxon monk, one of the defeated
landed class of English society, has given us a balanced and
shrewd assessment of William the Conqueror's character and qualities as king, in which are intertwined the churchman's terror and
admiration at this new kind of medieval ruler (A).*[28]

*Frederick I Barbarossa (1152–1190), the second ruler of the
Hohenstaufen dynasty, was able to go a long way toward recon-
stituting the power of the emperor in Germany and northern
Italy. The enthusiasm with which this potential revival of royal
authority was hailed can be gauged from the* Deeds of Frederick, *the best royal biography of the twelfth century, which
was begun by Bishop Otto of Freising and concluded by Otto's
secretary Rahewin. Although Otto of Freising (d. 1158) was Frederick's uncle and therefore was naturally disposed in Frederick's
favor, his optimistic view of the emperor's charismatic qualities
is highly significant. A former Cistercian abbot and a great
scholar, whose* The Two Cities *(published in the 1140's) presented
a particularly pessimistic Augustinian view of secular authority,
Otto was fully able to arrive at an independent conclusion; his
eulogy of the emperor indicates a shift in popular attitudes toward greater acceptance of the leadership of the state in European society (B).*[29]

*Frederick's contemporary, Henry II of England (1154–1189),
was able to enjoy a much stronger tradition of royal power and
effective administration and law inherited from William the*

---

[28] *The Anglo-Saxon Chronicle*, transl. J. A. Giles (London, 1847), pp. 460–3.

[29] Otto of Freising, *The Deeds of Frederick Barbarossa*, transl. C. C. Mierow,
in *Records of Civilization*, Vol. 49 (New York: Columbia University Press, 1953),
pp. 24–5, 27, 115, 146–9, 180, 183–4, 185–6, 232, 234–5, 237–8. Reprinted by permission of Columbia University Press.

Conqueror and other Anglo-Norman rulers. The ease with which Henry vanquished Thomas Becket, the Archbishop of Canterbury, and asserted his full authority over the English church, with opposition from neither the English bishops nor, to any real extent, from the papacy itself, is again a portent of the emerging sovereign state (C).[30]

A. THE ANGLO-SAXON CHRONICLE: WILLIAM THE CONQUEROR

This king William, of whom we are speaking, was a very wise and a great man, and more honoured and more powerful than any of his predecessors. He was mild to those good men who loved God, but severe beyond measure towards those who withstood his will. He founded a noble monastery on the spot where God permitted him to conquer England, and he established monks in it, and he made it very rich. In his days the great monastery at Canterbury was built, and many others also throughout England; moreover this land was filled with monks who lived after the rule of St. Benedict; and such was the state of religion in his days that all that would, might observe that which was prescribed by their respective orders. King William was also held in much reverence: he wore his crown three times every year when he was in England: at Easter he wore it at Winchester, at Pentecost at Westminster, and at Christmas at Gloucester. And at these times, all the men of England were with him, archbishops, bishops, abbats, and earls, thanes, and knights. So also was he a very stern and a wrathful man, so that none durst do anything against his will, and he kept in prison those earls who acted against his pleasure. He removed bishops from their sees, and abbats from their offices, and he imprisoned thanes, and at length he spared not his own brother Odo. This Odo was a very powerful bishop in Normandy, his see was that of Bayeux, and he was foremost to serve the king. He had an earldom in England, and when William was in Normandy he was the first man in this country, and him did he cast into prison. Amongst other things the good order that William established is not to be forgotten; it was such that any man, who was himself aught, might travel over the kingdom with a bosom-full of gold unmolested; and no man durst kill another, however great the injury he might have received from him. He reigned over England and being sharp-sighted to his own interest, he surveyed the kingdom so thoroughly that there was not

---

[30] E. K. Kendall, *Source Book of English History* (New York: The Macmillan Company, 1900), pp. 57–8, 60–1.

G. C. Lee, *Source-Book of English History* (New York: Henry Holt and Co., 1900), pp. 130–1, 137.

a single hide of land throughout the whole, of which he knew not the possessor, and how much it was worth, and this he afterwards entered in his register. The land of the Britons was under his sway, and he built castles therein; moreover he had full dominion over the Isle of Man (Anglesey): Scotland also was subject to him from his great strength; the land of Normandy was his inheritance, and he possessed the earldom of Maine; and had he lived two years longer he would have subdued Ireland by his prowess, and that without a battle. Truly there was much trouble in these times, and very great distress; he caused castles to be built, and oppressed the poor. The king was also of great sternness, and he took from his subjects many marks of gold and many hundred pounds of silver, and this, either with or without right, and with little need. He was given to avarice, and greedily loved gain. He made large forests for the deer, and enacted laws therewith, so that whoever killed a hart or a hind should be blinded. As he forbade killing the deer, so also the boars; and he loved the tall stags as if he were their father. He also appointed concerning the hares, that they should go free. The rich complained and the poor murmured, but he was so sturdy that he recked nought of them; they must will all that the king willed, if they would live; or would keep their lands; or would hold their possessions; or would be maintained in their rights.

B. OTTO OF FREISING-RAHEWIN: FREDERICK BARBAROSSA

This, I think, has been the purpose of all who have written history before us: to extol the famous deeds of valiant men in order to incite the hearts of mankind to virtue, but to veil in silence the dark doings of the base or, if they are drawn into the light, by the telling to place them on record to terrify the minds of those same mortals.

Hence I judge those who write at this time to be in a certain measure happy. For, after the turbulence of the past, not only has an unprecedented brightness of peace dawned again, but the authority of the Roman empire prevails so greatly by reason of the virtues of our most victorious prince that the people living under his jurisdiction rest in humble quiet, and whatever barbarian or Greek dwells outside his bounds is overawed by the weight of his authority and trembles. . . . Things have changed for the better, and after the time of weeping the time of laughing has now come, and after the time of war, the time of peace. . . .

In the year 1800 since the founding of the City, but 1154 (1152) from the incarnation of the Lord, the most pious King Conrad departed this life in the springtime, on the fifteenth day before the Kalends of March [February 15]—that is, on the Friday following Ash Wednesday—in the city of Bamberg, as has been said. Wonderful to relate, it was possible to bring together the entire company of the princes, as into a single body, in the town of Frankfort, from the immense extent of the transalpine kingdom (as well as certain barons from Italy), by the third (fourth) day of the Nones of March (March 4)—that is, on Tuesday after *Oculi mei semper*. When the chief men took counsel together there concerning the choice of a prince—for this is the very apex of the law of the Roman empire, namely, that kings are chosen not by lineal descent but through election by the princes (this right it claims for itself as though by unique prerogative)—finally Frederick, duke of the Swabians, the son of Duke Frederick, was sought by all. By the favor of all he was raised to the rank of king. . . .

The king, inflamed with righteous anger by the tenor of a speech as insolent as it was unusual, interrupted the flow of words of those ambassadors concerning the jurisdiction of their republic and of the empire, as they were about to spin out their oration in the Italian fashion by lengthy and circuitous periods. Preserving his royal dignity with modest bearing and charm of expression he replied without preparation but not unprepared.

"We have heard much heretofore concerning the wisdom and the valor of the Romans, yet more concerning their wisdom. Wherefore we cannot wonder enough at finding your words insipid with swollen pride rather than seasoned with the salt of wisdom. You set forth the ancient renown of your city. You extoll to the very stars the ancient status of your sacred republic. Granted, granted! To use the words of your own writer, 'There was, there was once virtue in this republic.' 'Once,' I say. And O that we might truthfully and freely say 'now'! Your Rome—nay, ours also—has experienced the vicissitudes of time. She could not be the only one to escape a fate ordained by the Author of all things for all that dwell beneath the orb of the moon. What shall I say? It is clear how first the strength of your nobility was transferred from this city of ours to the royal city of the East, and how for the course of many years the thirsty Greekling sucked the breasts of your delight. Then came the Frank, truly noble, in deed as in name, and forcibly possessed himself of whatever freedom was still left to you. Do you wish to know the ancient glory of your Rome? The worth of the senatorial dignity? The impregnable disposition of the camp? The virtue and the discipline of the equestrian order, its unmarred and unconquerable boldness when advancing to a conflict? Behold our state. All these things are to be found with us. All these have descended to us, together with the empire. Not in utter nakedness did the empire come to us. It came clad in its virtue. It brought its adornments with it. With us are your consuls. With us is your senate. With us is your soldiery. These very leaders of the Franks must rule you by their counsel, these very knights of the Franks must avert harm from you with the sword. You boastfully declare that by you I have been summoned, that by you I have been made first a citizen and then the prince, that from you I have received what was yours. How lacking in reason, how void of truth this novel utterance is, may be left to your own judgment and to the decision of men of wisdom! Let us ponder over the exploits of modern emperors, to see whether it was not our divine princes Charles and Otto who, by their valor and not by anyone's bounty, wrested the City along with Italy from the Greeks and the Lombards and added it to the realms of the Franks. Desiderius and Berengar teach you this, your tyrants, of whom you boasted, on whom you relied as your princes. We have learned from reliable accounts that they were not only subjugated and taken captive by our Franks, but grew old and ended their lives in their servitude. Their ashes, buried among us, constitute the clearest evidence of this fact. But, you say: 'You came on my invitation,' I admit it; I was invited. Give me the reason why I was invited! You were being assailed by enemies and could not be freed by your own hand or by the effeminate Greeks. The power of the Franks was invoked by invitation. I would call it entreaty rather than invitation. In your misery you besought the happy, in your frailty the valiant, in your weakness the strong, in your anxiety the carefree. Invited after that fashion—if it may be called an invitation—I have come. I have made your prince my vassal and from that time until the present have transferred you to my jurisdiction. I am the lawful possessor. Let him who can, snatch the club from the hand of Hercules. Will the Sicilian, in whom you trust, perhaps do this? Let him take note of previous cases. Not yet has the hand of the Franks or the Germans been made weak. By God's help, if I live, that man will be able someday to test his own boldness. You demand the justice that I owe you. I say nothing of the fact that the prince should prescribe laws for the people, not the people for the prince. I pass over the fact that any possessor who is about to enter upon his possession should submit to no prejudicial conditions. Let us argue reasonably. You propose, as I understand it, to exact three oaths. I will discuss each separately. You say I must swear to observe the laws of my predecessors, the emperors, that are guaranteed you by their privileges, and likewise your good customs. You even add that I am to swear to defend the fatherland at the very risk of my life. To these two I make a single response. The things you demand are either just or unjust. If they are unjust, it will not be yours to demand nor mine to concede them. If they are just, I acknowledge that I am willing because of the obligation and that I am under obligation because of my willingness. Wherefore it will be unnecessary to affix an oath to an obligation to which I assent and an assent which is an obligation. For how could I infringe upon your just claims, since I desire to preserve for even the lowliest that which is theirs? How could I fail to defend the fatherland and especially the seat of my empire, even at

the risk of my life, when I have been giving thought to the restoration
of its frontiers so far as it is within my power, not without consideration of that same danger? Denmark, recently subjugated and restored
to the Roman world, has learned this, and perhaps more provinces
and more kingdoms would have perceived it if the present undertaking
had not intervened.

"I come to the third provision. You declare that I should personally
swear to pay you a certain sum of money. How disgraceful! You,
Rome, demand from your prince what some sutler should rather seek
from a peddler. With us, these demands are made of captives. Am I,
then, held in captivity? Am I weighed down by the enemies' bonds?
Do I not sit on my throne, renowned and attended by a great force of
valiant soldiers? Shall a Roman emperor be forced against his will
to be anyone's purveyor and not his benefactor? Hitherto I have been
accustomed to bestow my favors royally and munificently upon whom
I pleased, and as much as was seemly, and particularly to those who
have deserved well of me. For as due respect is properly demanded
from inferiors, so a fitting service is justly repaid by superiors. This
practice, received from my sainted parents, I have elsewhere observed.
Why should I deny it to my own citizens? Why should I not make the
City happy upon my entrance? All is justly denied to him who demands unjustly." . . .

In the middle of the month of October (1157) the emperor set out
for Burgundy to hold a diet at Besançon. . . . We must speak of the
ambassadors of the Roman pontiff, Hadrian. . . . The personnel of
the embassay consisted of Roland, cardinal priest of the title of St.
Mark and chancellor of the Holy Roman Church, and Bernard, cardinal priest of the title of St. Clement, both distinguished for their
wealth, their maturity of view, and their influence, and surpassing in
prestige almost all others in the Roman Church. . . . When this letter
had been read and carefully set forth by Chancellor Rainald in a faithful interpretation, the princes who were present were moved to great
indignation, because the entire content of the letter appeared to have
no little sharpness and to offer even at the very outset an occasion for
future trouble. But what had particularly aroused them all was the
fact that in the aforesaid letter it had been stated, among other things,
that the fullness of dignity and honor had been bestowed upon the
emperor by the Roman pontiff, that the emperor had received from
his hand the imperial crown, and that he would not have regretted
conferring even greater benefits (*beneficia*) upon him. . . . And the
hearers were led to accept the literal meaning of these words and to
put credence in the aforesaid explanation because they knew that the
assertion was rashly made by some Romans that hitherto our kings had
possessed the imperial power over the City, and the kingdom of Italy,
by gift of the popes, and that they made such representations and

handed them down to posterity not only orally but also in writing and in pictures. . . .

They returned without having accomplished their purpose, and what had been done by the emperor was published throughout the realm in the following letter (October, 1157):

"Whereas the Divine Sovereignty, from which is derived all power in heaven and on earth, has entrusted unto us, His anointed, the kingdom and the empire to rule over, and has ordained that the peace of the churches is to be maintained by the imperial arms, not without the greatest distress of heart are we compelled to complain to Your Benevolence that from the head of the Holy Church, on which Christ has set the imprint of his peace and love, there seem to be emanating causes of dissentions and evils, like a poison, by which, unless God avert it, we fear the body of the Church will be stained, its unity shattered, and a schism created between the temporal and spiritual realms. . . . And since, through election by the princes, the kingdom and the empire are ours from God alone, Who at the time of the passion of His Son Christ subjected the world to dominion by the two swords, and since the apostle Peter taught the world this doctrine: 'Fear God, honor the king,' whosoever says that we received the imperial crown as a benefice (*pro beneficio*) from the lord pope contradicts the divine ordinance and the doctrine of Peter and is guilty of a lie. . . ."

Now came the day (November 11, 1158) of the assembly, which brought the Roman emperor to the plains of Roncaglia. As all these, with a throng of lay princes (namely, dukes, margraves, counts, and consuls and judges from all the cities in Italy), surrounded Frederick, he enjoined upon the bishops only—together with a very few princes who were secretly cognizant of his plan—that they deliberate with him in the fear of God for a sound administration of affairs in Italy, that they might rejoice at the peace and tranquility of the Church of God, and that the royal power and glory of the empire might be advanced with due honor. This conference occupied three whole days. Finally, on the fourth day, the most serene emperor came into the assembly and, seated on a higher place, whence he might be seen and heard by all, with the venerable leaders whom we have named sitting in a circle around him, he spoke through an interpreter:

"Inasmuch as it has pleased the divine ordinance, whence comes all power in heaven and upon earth, that we should hold the helm of the Roman empire, we not unreasonably lay claim—in so far as we can of God's grace—to what is recognized as pertaining to the status of that office. And as we are not unaware that this is the duty of imperial majesty, that the wicked and disturbers of the peace be held in check by our zealous vigilance and the fear of punishment, the good raised up and sustained in the tranquility of peace, so we know what rights and what honors the sanction of divine as well as of human laws has assigned to the pinnacle of regal excellence. But we, though having the name of king, desire to hold our authority under the law and for preservation of each man's liberty and right rather than—in accordance with the saying, 'to do all things with impunity, this is to be a king'—to become arrogant through freedom from responsibility and to transform the task of ruling into pride and domination. By God's help, we shall not change our character with our fortune. We shall take care to maintain our authority by the very qualities through which it was first obtained. . . .

During the following days the emperor was occupied from morning until evening, in full and solemn court, dispensing judgments and justice. He listened attentively to complaints and appeals of rich and poor alike. He had four judges, namely Bulgar, Martin, James, and Hugo, eloquent and pious men, most learned in the law, doctors of law in the city of Bologna and teachers of many students. With these and other jurists present from various cities, he heard, deliberated, and decided matters. Remarking the great number of those who carried crosses—for this is the custom of the Italians, that those who have grievances carry a cross in their hands—he felt sorry for them and said that he marveled at the wisdom of the Latins, who gloried much in their knowledge of law, yet were so often found to be its transgressors. How niggardly they were of justice was clearly apparent from the number of those who were hungering and thirsting for righteousness. Therefore, by divine inspiration, he appointed particular judges for each diocese, not, however, from its own city, but either from the court or from another city. He did so for this reason: he feared that if a citizen were appointed to judge his own fellow citizens, he might readily be diverted from the truth by favor or hatred. And so it came about that of this great number of plaintiffs, there was scarcely any who did not rejoice at having secured either a complete victory in his suit, or his rights, or a satisfactory agreement with his adversary.

Then the emperor spoke earnestly about the justice of the realm and the regalia which, for a long time past, had been lost to the empire, either by reason of the impudence of usurpers or through royal neglect. As they could find no defense whereby to excuse themselves, both the bishops and the secular leaders and cities with one voice and one accord restored the regalia into the hand of the emperor.

C. HENRY II AND THOMAS BECKET

Peter of Blois: Henry II

You ask me to send you an accurate description of the appearance and character of the king of England. That surpasses my powers, for the genius of a Vergil would hardly be equal to it. That which I know however I will ungrudgingly share with you. Concerning David we read that it was said of him, as evidence for his beauty that he was ruddy. You may know then that our king is still ruddy, except as old age and whitening hair have changed his colour a little. He is of medium stature so that among small men he does not seem large, nor yet among large men does he seem small. His head is spherical, as if the abode of great wisdom and the special sanctuary of lofty intelligence. The size of his head is in proportion to the neck and the whole body. His eyes are full, guileless and dovelike when he is at peace, gleaming like fire when his temper is aroused, and in bursts of passion they flash like lightning. As to his hair he is in no danger of baldness, but his head has been closely shaved. He has a broad, square, lion-like face. His feet are arched and he has the legs of a horseman. His broad chest and muscular arms show him to be a strong, bold, active man. His hands show by their coarseness that he is careless and pays little attention to his person, for he never wears gloves except when he goes hawking. . . . Although his legs are bruised and livid from hard riding, he never sits down except when on horseback or at meals. On a single day, if necessary, he travels a journey of four or five days, and thus anticipating the plans of his enemies he baffles their devices by his sudden movements. . . . He is a passionate lover of the woods, and when not engaged in war he exercises with birds and dogs. . . . He does not loiter in his palace like other kings, but hurrying through the provinces he investigates what is being done everywhere, and is especially strict in his judgment of those whom he has appointed as judges of others. There is no one keener in counsel, of more fluent eloquence, no one who has less anxiety in danger or more in prosperity, or who is more courageous in adversity. If he has once loved any one, he rarely ceases to love him, while one for whom he has once taken a dislike he seldom admits to his favor. He always has his weapons in his hands when not engaged in consultation or at his books. When his cares and anxieties allow him to breathe he occupies himself with reading, or in a circle of clerks tries to solve some knotty problem. . . .

Herbert Bosham: The King Appoints Becket to the Primacy

The king was living at that time outside the kingdom beyond the seas and the chancellor was with him. On account of frequent hostilities on the part of the Welsh and other difficulties in the realm the king determined to send the chancellor to England. This mission he entrusted to the chancellor because the reasons for it were many and important and no one of his own men was so well fitted. Now the chancellor, after some days had been spent in making arrangements for the embassy, just before his departure went to the court at that time abiding in that stronghold of Normandy which is called Falaise, intending to simply take leave of the king and then set out upon his journey. But the king called him aside and said to him in secret, "You do not yet know in full the reason for your mission. It is my will that you should be archbishop of Canterbury." The chancellor, pointing to the gay fashion in which he was attired, said with a smile, "What a religious man, what a holy man you desire to place in the sacred seat and over that celebrated and sacred assembly of monks! Know surely that if by the will of God this should happen, you would speedily turn away your favour from me, and our friendship which is now so great would be changed into bitter hatred. For I am sure that you would assert many claims in ecclesiastical matters and you would demand some things which I could not quietly endure. Then jealous persons would seize the opportunity to interpose and not only would our friendship be destroyed but they would arouse perpetual hatred between us.". . .

But the king, not at all moved by these warnings of the chancellor which were prompted by his very affection, remained fixed in his purpose, and presently he gave careful and specific directions to the other envoys, men of importance, to make known his wish and desire in regard to the chancellor's promotion, to the sacred assembly of the metropolitan church and to the clergy of the kingdom. This he did in the chancellor's presence and addressing one of the envoys especially he said, "Richard" (it was Richard de Lucy), "if I were lying dead in my shroud, would you strive to have Henry, my first-born, exalted to the throne?" "Verily your majesty, I should do my utmost." And the king replied, "I wish you to use the same endeavour for the promotion of the chancellor to the seat of Canterbury."

Beginning of the Quarrel between Henry II and Becket

When the king was tarrying on his manor at Woodstock, with the archbishop and the great men of the land, among other matters a question was raised concerning a certain custom which obtained in England. Two shillings from each hide were given to the king's servants, who, in the post of sheriffs, guarded the shires. This sum the king wished to have enrolled in the treasury and added to his own revenue. The archbishop resisted him to the face, saying that it ought not to be exacted as revenue—"Nor will we," said he, "my lord king, give it as revenue, saving your pleasure; but if the sheriffs, and servants, and ministers of the shires shall serve us fitly, and maintain and defend our dependants, in no way will we be behindhand in contributing to their aid." But the king, taking ill this answer of the archbishop, said "By the eyes of God, it shall be given as revenue, and in the king's scroll shall it be writ; nor is it fit that thou shouldst gainsay, when no man would oppose your men against your will." The archbishop foreseeing and being aware lest by his sufferance a custom should be brought in whereby posterity should be harmed, answered, "By the reverence of the eyes by which you have sworn, my lord king, there shall be given from all my land or from the right of the Church not a penny." The king was silent, repulsed by the bold objection of the archbishop, but his indignation was not set at rest; for silently erewhile his fury from secular matters which seemed to be but little contrary to the archbishop, turned against the clergy, and his rage extended against the ministers of the church whose injuries specially redounded against the archbishop.

From the Constitutions of Clarendon (1164)

Of these acknowledged customs and dignities of the realm, a certain part is contained in the present writing. Of this part the heads are as follows:

1. If any controversy has arisen concerning the advowson and presentation of churches between laymen, or between laymen and ecclesiastics, or between ecclesiastics, it is to be considered or settled in the court of the lord king.

2. Churches of the fee of the lord king cannot be given perpetually without his assent and grant.

3. Clergymen charged and accused of anything, when they have been summoned by a justice of the king shall come into his court, to respond there to that which it shall seem good to the court of the king for them to respond to, and in the ecclesiastical court to what it shall seem good should be responded to there; so that the justice of the king shall send into the court of holy church to see how the matter shall be treated there. And if a clergyman shall have been convicted or has confessed, the church ought not to protect him otherwise.

4. It is not lawful for archbishops, bishops, and persons of the realm to go out of the realm without the permission of the lord king. And if they go out, if it please the lord king, they shall give security that neither in going nor in making a stay nor in returning will they seek evil or loss to the king or the kingdom.

5. Excommunicated persons ought not to give permanent security nor offer an oath, but only security and a pledge to stand to the judgment of the church, in order that they may be absolved.

6. Laymen ought not to be accused except by definite and legal accusers and witnesses, in the presence of the bishop, so that the archdeacon shall not lose his right, nor anything which he ought to

have from it. And if there are such persons as are blamed, but no one wishes or no one dares to accuse them, let the sheriff when required by the bishop cause twelve legal men of the neighbourhood or of the township to take an oath in the presence of the bishop that they will show the truth about it according to their conscience.

7. No one who holds from the king in chief, nor any one of the officers of his demesnes shall be excommunicated, nor the lands of any one of them placed under an interdict, unless the lord king, if he is in the land, first agrees, or his justice, if he is out of the realm, in order that he may do right concerning him; and so that what shall pertain to the king's court shall be settled there, and for that which has respect to the ecclesiastical court, that it may be sent to the same to be considered there.

8. Concerning appeals, if they should occur, they ought to proceed from the archdeacon to the bishop, from the bishop to the archbishop. And if the archbishop should fail to show justice, it must come to the lord king last, in order that by his command the controversy should be finally terminated in the court of the archbishop, so that it ought not to proceed further without the assent of the lord king.

9. If a contest has arisen between a clergyman and a layman or between a layman and a clergyman, concerning any tenement which the clergyman wishes to bring into charitable tenure, but the layman into a lay fief, it shall be settled by the deliberation of a principal justice of the king, on the recognition of twelve legal men, whether the tenement pertains to charity or to a lay fief, in the presence of that justice of the king. And if the recognition shall decide that it belongs to charity, the suit will be in the ecclesiastical court, but if to a lay fief, unless both are answerable to the same bishop or baron, the suit will be in the king's court. But if both shall be answerable concerning that fief before the same bishop or baron, the suit will be in his court, provided that the one who was formerly in possession shall not lose his possession on account of the recognition which has been made until it has been decided upon through the suit.

William Fitz-Stephen: Murder in the Cathedral

The Archbishop of York and the Bishops of London and Salisbury, with the Archdeacon of Poictiers (the Archdeacon of Canterbury was delayed on the sea by bad weather), having crossed the water, came to the King's court. He had already heard of the suspension and excommunication of the bishops. They repeat to him the whole story. They lay all the blame upon the Archbishop; they declare him to be guilty of treason in what he has done. Falsehood doubles his offence. It had been told the King that the Archbishop was making the circuit of the kingdom at the head of a large body of men. The King asks the Archbishop of York and the Bishops of London and Salisbury to advise him what to do. "It is not our part," they say, "to tell you what must be done." At length one says, "My lord, while Thomas lives, you will not have peace or quiet or see another good day." On hearing this, such fury, bitterness, and passion took possession of the King, as his disordered look and gesture expressed, that it was immediately understood what he wanted.

When they saw his emotion, four knights, barons of the king's household, seeking to please him, named Reginald Fitz Urse, William de Traci, Hugh de Morville, Richard Brito having sworn the death of the Archbishop, departed sailing from different ports. By the guidance of the devil, the old enemy of all good, they met at the same hour on the morrow at the castle of the family of Broc, at Saltwood.

Whilst we were lately assembled in council before our lord and king, and supposed we were going to discuss important matters connected with the Church, . . . we were told by some who are just come over from England, that certain enemies of the archbishop, provoked to madness, it is said, by frequent causes of exasperation, have suddenly set upon him, and—I can hardly write for my tears—have attacked his person and put him to a cruel death. At the first words of the messenger the king burst into loud lamentations, and exchanged his royal robes for sackcloth and ashes, acting more like a friend than the sovereign of the deceased. At times he ceased his cries and became stupid; after which he burst again into cries and lamentations louder than before. Three whole days he spent in his chamber, and would receive neither food nor consolation, but by the excess of his grief it seemed as if he had thoroughly made up his mind to die.

45 / VARIETIES OF RELIGIOUS EXPERIENCE

One of the most important phenomena of the twelfth century was the spread of lay piety, the serious acceptance of Christianity by all ranks of society. This involved, however, not only the intensification of the religious life of Europe in such forms as the Virgin cult (A),[31] but also the growth of religious individ-

[31] D. C. Munro, *Translations and Reprints* (Philadelphia: University of Pennsylvania Press), Vol. II, No. 4, pp. 1–2.

*ualism with its concomitant form of popular heresy. By the latter
part of the twelfth century Donatism was widespread in northern Italy, and was adhered to by the Waldensians and similar
sects (B),*[32] *while the rich civilization of the cities of southern
France was beginning to be dominated by supporters of the
Albigensian heresy, a revival of the ancient Manichean doctrine
of the struggle between the god of light and the god of darkness
(C).*[33] *The Catholic Church, led at Rome by canon lawyers who
were able administrators but mediocre in pastoral work, encum-
bered by a monastic order which was rapidly losing both its zeal
and social utility (D),*[34] *and blemished by frequent scandals in
clerical life (E),*[35] *was very tardy in adjusting to meet the needs
of lay society and to counter the rising tide of antisacerdotalism.
By the early thirteenth century, attacks on the papacy and the
priesthood were coming not only from the heretics but from many
conscientious and devout laymen, such as the great German poet
Walther von der Vogelweide (F).*[36]

A. A THIRTEENTH-CENTURY VIRGIN TALE BY JACQUES DE VITRY

A certain very religious man told me that this happened in a place
where he had been staying. A virtuous and pious matron came frequently to the church and served God most devoutly, day and night.
Also a certain monk, the guardian and treasurer of the monastery, had
a great reputation for piety, and truly he was devout. When, however,
the two frequently conversed together in the church concerning religious matters, the devil, envying their virtue and reputation, tempted
them very sorely, so that the spiritual love was changed to carnal.
Accordingly they made an agreement and fixed upon a night in which
the monk was to leave his monastery, taking the treasures of the
church, and the matron was to leave her home, with a sum of money
which she should secretly steal from her husband.

After they had fled, the monks on rising in the morning, saw that the

[32] J. H. Robinson, *Readings in European History* (Boston: Ginn & Co., 1904),
Vol. I, pp. 380–1.

[33] J. H. Robinson, *Readings in European History* (Boston: Ginn & Co., 1904),
Vol. I, pp. 381–3.

[34] *The Chronicle of Jocelin of Brakelond*, King's Classics, transl. E. Clarke
(London, 1903), pp. 60–2.

[35] J. H. Robinson, *Readings in European History* (Boston: Ginn & Co., 1904),
Vol. I, 378–9.

[36] J. H. Robinson, *Readings in European History* (Boston: Ginn & Co., 1904),
Vol. I, p. 375.

receptacles were broken and the treasures of the church stolen; and not finding the monk, they quickly pursued him. Likewise the husband of the said woman, seeing his chest open and the money gone, pursued his wife. Overtaking the monk and the woman with the treasure and money, they brought them back and threw them into prison. Moreover so great was the scandal throughout the whole country and so much were all religious persons reviled that the damage from the infamy and scandal was far greater than from the sin itself.

Then the monk restored to his senses, began with many tears to pray to the blessed Virgin, whom from infancy he had always served, and never before had any such misfortune happened to him. Likewise the said matron began urgently to implore the aid of the blessed Virgin whom, constantly, day and night, she was accustomed to salute and to kneel in prayer before her image. At length, the blessed Virgin very irate, appeared and after she had upbraided them severely, she said, "I am able to obtain the remission of your sins from my son, but what can I do about such an awful scandal? For you have so befouled the name of religious persons before all the people, that in the future no one will trust them. This is an almost irremediable damage."

Nevertheless the pious Virgin, overcome by their prayers, summoned the demons, who had caused the deed, and enjoined upon them that, as they had caused the scandal to religion, they must bring the infamy to an end. Since, indeed, they were not able to resist her commands, after much anxiety and various conferences they found a way to remove the infamy. In the night they placed the monk in his church and repairing the broken receptacle as it was before, they placed the treasure in it. Also they closed and locked the chest which the matron had opened and replaced the money in it. And they set the woman in her room and in the place where she was accustomed to pray by night.

When, moreover, the monks found the treasure of their house and the monk, who was praying to God just as he had been accustomed to do; and the husband saw his wife and the treasure; and they found the money just as it had been before, they became stupefied and wondered. Rushing to the prison they saw the monk and the woman in fetters just as they had left them. For one of the demons was seen by them transformed into the likeness of a monk and another into the likeness of a woman. When all in the whole city had come together to see the miracle, the demons said in the hearing of all, "Let us go, for sufficiently have we deluded these people and caused them to think evil of religious persons." And, saying this, they suddenly disappeared. Moreover all threw themselves at the feet of the monk and of the woman and demanded pardon.

Behold how great infamy and scandal and how inestimable damage the devil would have wrought against religious persons, if the blessed Virgin had not aided them.

B. PETER WALDO, AS DESCRIBED IN AN
EARLY–THIRTEENTH-CENTURY CHRONICLE

And during the same year, that is the 1173rd since the Lord's Incarnation, there was at Lyons in France a certain citizen, Waldo by
name, who had made himself much money by wicked usury. One
Sunday, when he had joined a crowd which he saw gathered around a
troubadour, he was smitten by his words and, taking him to his house,
he took care to hear him at length. The passage he was reciting was
how the holy Alexis died a blessed death in his father's house. When
morning had come the prudent citizen hurried to the schools of
theology to seek counsel for his soul, and when he was taught many
ways of going to God, he asked the master what way was more certain
and more perfect than all others. The master answered him with this
text: "If thou wilt be perfect, go and sell all that thou hast," etc.

Then Waldo went to his wife and gave her the choice of keeping
his personal property or his real estate, namely, what he had in ponds,
groves and fields, houses, rents, vineyards, mills, and fishing rights.
She was much displeased at having to make this choice, but she kept
the real estate. From his personal property he made restitution to those
whom he had treated unjustly; a great part of it he gave to his two
little daughters, who, without their mother's knowledge, he placed
in the convent of Font Evrard; but the greatest part of his money he
spent for the poor. A very great famine was then oppressing France
and Germany. The prudent citizen, Waldo, gave bread, with vegetables and meat, to every one who came to him for three days in every
week from Pentecost to the feast of St. Peter's bonds.

At the Assumption of the blessed Virgin, casting some money among
the village poor, he cried, "No man can serve two masters, God and
mammon." Then his fellow-citizens ran up, thinking he had lost his
mind. But going on to a higher place, he said: "My fellow-citizens
and friends, I am not insane, as you think, but I am avenging myself
on my enemies, who made me a slave, so that I was always more careful of money than of God, and served the creature rather than the
Creator. I know that many will blame me that I act thus openly. But
I do it both on my own account and on yours; on my own, so that
those who see me henceforth possessing any money may say that I
am mad, and on yours, that you may learn to place hope in God and
not in riches."

On the next day, coming from the church, he asked a certain citizen,
once his comrade, to give him something to eat, for God's sake. His
friend, leading him to his house, said, "I will give you whatever you
need as long as I live." When this came to the ears of his wife, she was
not a little troubled, and as though she had lost her mind, she ran to

the archbishop of the city and implored him not to let her husband beg bread from any one but her. This moved all present to tears.

[Waldo was accordingly conducted into the presence of the bishop.] and the woman, seizing her husband by the coat, said, "Is it not better, husband, that I should redeem my sins by giving you alms than that strangers should do so?" And from that time he was not allowed to take food from any one in that city except from his wife.

C. THE ALBIGENSIANS, AS DESCRIBED BY AN EARLY–FOURTEENTH-CENTURY INQUISITOR

It would take too long to describe in detail the manner in which these same Manichaean heretics preach and teach their followers, but it must be briefly considered here.

In the first place, they usually say of themselves that they are good Christians, who do not swear, or lie, or speak evil of others; that they do not kill any man or animal, nor anything having the breath of life, and that they hold the faith of the Lord Jesus Christ and his gospel as Christ and his apostles taught. They assert that they occupy the place of the apostles, and that, on account of the above-mentioned things, they of the Roman Church, namely the prelates, clerks, and monks, and especially the inquisitors of heresy, persecute them and call them heretics, although they are good men and good Christians, and that they are persecuted just as Christ and his apostles were by the Pharisees.

Moreover they talk to the laity of the evil lives of the clerks and prelates of the Roman Church, pointing out and setting forth their pride, cupidity, avarice, and uncleanness of life, and such other evils as they know. They invoke, with their own interpretation and according to their abilities, the authority of the Gospels and the Epistles against the condition of the prelates, churchmen, and monks, whom they call Pharisees and false prophets, who say, but do not.

Then they attack and vituperate, in turn, all the sacraments of the Church, especially the sacrament of the eucharist, saying that it cannot contain the body of Christ, for had this been as great as the largest mountain Christians would have entirely consumed it before this. They assert that the host comes from straw, that it passes through the tails of horses, to wit, when the flour is cleaned by a sieve (of horse hair); that, moreover, it passes through the body and comes to a vile end, which, they say, could not happen if God were in it.

Of baptism, they assert that water is material and corruptible, and is therefore the creation of the evil power and cannot sanctify the soul, but that the churchmen sell this water out of avarice, just as they sell earth for the burial of the dead, and oil to the sick when they anoint them, and as they sell the confession of sins as made to the priests.

Hence they claim that confession made to the priests of the Roman Church is useless, and that, since the priests may be sinners, they cannot loose nor bind, and, being unclean themselves, cannot make others clean. They assert, moreover, that the cross of Christ should not be adored or venerated, because, as they urge, no one would venerate or adore the gallows upon which a father, relative, or friend had been hung. They urge, further, that they who adore the cross ought, for similar reasons, to worship all thorns and lances, because as Christ's body was on the cross during the passion, so was the crown of thorns on his head and the soldier's lance in his side. They proclaim many other scandalous things in regard to the sacraments.

Moreover they read from the Gospels and the Epistles in the vulgar tongue, applying and expounding them in their favor and against the condition of the Roman Church in a manner which it would take too long to describe in detail; but all that relates to this subject may be read more fully in the books they have written and infected, and may be learned from the confessions of such of their followers as have been converted.

D. THE CHRONICLE OF JOCELIN OF BRAKELOND: A TWELFTH-CENTURY ABBOT

The abbot Samson [37] was of middle stature, nearly bald, having face neither round nor yet long, a prominent nose, thick lips, clear and very piercing eyes, ears of the nicest sense of hearing, arched eyebrows, often shaved; and he soon became hoarse from a short exposure to cold. On the day of his election he was forty and seven years old, and had been a monk seventeen years. He had then a few grey hairs in a reddish beard, and a very few in a black and somewhat curly head of hair. But within fourteen years after his election it became as white as snow.

He was a man remarkably temperate, never slothful, of strong constitution, and willing to ride or walk till old age gained upon him and moderated such inclination. On hearing the news of the Cross being taken, and the loss of Jerusalem, he began to use under garments of horsehair and a horsehair shirt, and to abstain from flesh and flesh meats. Nevertheless, he desired that meats should be placed before him at table for the increase of the alms dish. Sweet milk, honey and such like sweet things he ate with greater appetite than other food.

He abhorred liars, drunkards and talkative folk; for virtue ever is consistent with itself and rejects contraries. He also much condemned persons given to murmur at their meat or drink, and particularly monks

---

[37] Abbot of Bury Saint Edmunds in England.

who were dissatisfied therewith, himself adhering to the uniform course he had practised when a monk. He had likewise this virtue in himself, that he never changed the mess set before him.

Once when I, then a novice, happened to be serving in the refectory, I wished to prove if this were true, and I thought I would place before him a mess which would have displeased any other than him, in a very black and broken dish. But when he looked at it, he was as one that saw it not. Some delay took place, and I felt sorry that I had so done; and snatching away the dish, I changed the mess and the dish for a better, and brought it to him; but this substitution he took in ill part, and was angry with me for it.

An eloquent man was he, both in French and Latin, but intent more on the substance and method of what was to be said than on the style of words. He could read English books most admirably, and was wont to preach to the people in English, but in the dialect of Norfolk, where he was born and bred; and so he caused a pulpit to be set up in the church for the ease of the hearers, and for the ornament of the church. The abbot also seemed to prefer an active life to one of contemplation, and rather commended good officials than good monks. He very seldom approved of any one on account of his literary acquirements, unless he also possessed sufficient knowledge of secular matters; and whenever he chanced to hear that any prelate had resigned his pastoral care and become an anchorite, he did not praise him for it. He never applauded men of too compliant a disposition, saying, "He who endeavours to please all, ought to please none."

E. ARCHBISHOP EUDES RIGAUD: RECORDS OF DIOCESAN VISITATIONS IN NORMANDY

On the fourteenth day before the Kalends of April [March 19, 1248] we visited the chapter of Rouen. We found that they talked in the choir, in violation of their rule. Clerks wandered about the church and chatted with women while the service was going on. They did not observe the rule in regard to entering the choir, and chanted the psalms too fast without making the pauses. . . . In short, they failed to observe many other of the rules, and their temporalities were badly managed.

As for the canons themselves, we found that Master Michael of Berciac was accused of incontinence, likewise Lord Benedict. Likewise Master William of Salmonville of incontinence, theft, and homicide. Likewise Master John of St. Laud of incontinence. Likewise Master Alain of frequenting taverns, drunkenness, and gaming. Likewise Peter of Euleige of carrying on business.

On the *nones* of May [May 7, 1256] we visited the chapter of St.

Firmat. There are fifteen secular canons and a prior there; six canons in residence. Firmin, the vicar of the prior, farms the prebends of the said canons. Morell, the choir clerk, is a rough fellow (*percussor*). Regnaud of Stampis is accused of incontinence, and has a boy with him whom he supports. Bartholomew, the vicar of the cantor, sometimes get drunk and then does not get up to matins. Roger, one of the canons, occasionally frequents taverns. John, the vicar of the dean, is a tipsy fellow. We accordingly admonished Bartholomew, the cantor's vicar, for his drinking, and likewise John, the dean's vicar, and Roger, the canon, for going to the tavern, and Regnaud of Stampis for his licentiousness, and bade the said Bartholomew, John, Roger, and Regnaud to avoid these offenses. Likewise we ordered that Morell, the choir clerk, who was given to striking and evil speaking, should be corrected as he deserved, and also Firmin, the vicar, for farming the prebends, else we should come down upon them with a heavy hand.

On the Kalends of May [May 1, 1258] we visited the nunnery of St. Savior. There were sixty-three nuns. They did not have books enough: we ordered that these should be procured. The rule of silence was not properly observed: we commanded that it should be. We admonished them to go to confession every month. We enjoined that they should not keep dogs, birds, or squirrels, and should send away those that they had. Each nun has a chest of her own. We ordered the abbess to see what these contained, and that she should have them opened, and that the iron fastenings should be removed. When they receive new gowns they do not return the old ones. We ordered that no nun should dare to give away her old gown without the permission of the abbess.

F. WALTHER VON DER VOGELWEIDE: THE PAPACY AS WOLF

St. Peter's chair is filled to-day as well
   As when 'twas fouled by Gerbert's [37a] sorcery;

For he consigned himself alone to hell,
   While this pope thither drags all Christentie.
Why are the chastisements of Heaven delayed?
   How long wilt thou in slumber lie, O Lord?

Thy work is hindered and thy word gainsaid,
   Thy treasurer steals the wealth that thou hast stored.
Thy ministers rob here and murder there,
   And o'er thy sheep a wolf has shepherd's care.

[37a] Gerbert of Aurillac, who ruled as Pope Sylvester II at the end of the tenth century, had a posthumous reputation as a sorcerer.

46 / INNOCENT III: REASSERTION OF PAPAL LEADERSHIP

The greatest pope of the twelfth and thirteenth centuries, Innocent III (1198–1216), made extensive and, in some respects, successful efforts to meet the challenge of religious, economic, and political change. He reformed and tightened ecclesiastical administration and discipline and countered the threat of heresy by founding a special ecclesiastical court that developed into the papal inquisition, by encouraging new religious orders suited to meet the new social and intellectual world of the thirteenth century, and by preaching the Albigensian crusade against the heretics in southern France. He also succeeded in asserting papal authority against the powerful English and German monarchies, although in the former case he was assisted by the unpopularity and rashness of King John (1199–1216) and in the latter instance by a dispute over the imperial throne following the premature death of Barbarossa's son Henry VI (1190–1197), who had greatly frightened the papacy by uniting the German and Sicilian crowns.

Innocent's conception of papal authority in Europe may be gauged from the following selections from letters which he wrote on the imperial-succession crisis. It will be noted that while he was in many respects more moderate than Gregory VII (No. 34A), he nevertheless had a high sense of the ultimate plenitude of papal power. The strong legalistic tone of his statement of papal authority reflects the domination of the see of Peter in the twelfth and thirteenth centuries by canon lawyers, of whom Innocent was himself one of the most illustrious.[38]

I

How great the harmony between the kingdom and the priesthood ought to be is shown by Christ Himself, Who is King of kings and Lord of lords, a priest through all eternity, according to the order of

[38] *Regestum Innocentii III papae super negotio Romani imperii*, F. Kempf, ed., *Miscellanea Historiae Pontificiae* (Rome: Pontificia Università Gregoriana, 1947), pp. 6–7, 46–8, 91–2, 98–9, 167–9. By permission of F. Kempf, S.J.

Melchizedek. For he descended according to the nature of flesh assumed equally from sacerdotal and royal lineage, to underscore this that the blessed Peter said to those who had converted to the faith of Christ: "You are a chosen race, a royal priesthood." And Christ is thus addressed in the Apocalypse: "You have made us a kingdom and a priesthood to our God." For these are two cherubs who, with their wings joined, are described as guarding the mercy seat, facing each other from either end. These are two marvelous and beautiful columns placed beside the door in the vestibule of the temple; a line of twelve cubits measures their circumference. These are the two great lights which God placed in the firmament of heaven: a greater light to rule the day and a lesser light to rule the night. These are the two swords about which the apostles said: "Behold, there are two swords here."

II

In Genesis we read that Melchizedek was king and priest, but king of Salem and priest of the Most High, that is, king of the polity and priest of the Deity. Clearly, if there is a difference between the polity and the Deity, there is likewise a difference between the kingdom and the priesthood. For Melchizedek prefigured Christ—Who, on his robe and on his thigh, had the name inscribed: King of kings and Lord of lords, priest through all eternity, according to the order of Melchizedek—in order to signify the harmony which ought to exist between the kingdom and the priesthood. For this reason too, Christ descended according to the nature of flesh assumed equally from royal priestly ancestry—to signify, nevertheless, the preeminence of the priesthood to the kingdom. . . . For he who receives tithes is greater than he who pays tithes, and he who is blessed inferior to him who blesses. The Apostle confirms this when he speaks of the matter, saying: "It is beyond dispute that the inferior is blessed by the superior. . . ." For although the kings as well as the priests are anointed according to divine law, nevertheless, the kings are anointed by the priests, and not the priests by the kings. He who is anointed is inferior to him who anoints, and the anointer is superior to the anointed. . . . Hence it is that God called the priests gods, but termed the kings princes: "You shall not revile your gods," He said, "nor curse the prince of your people. . . ." It is also said, not by anyone, but by God, and not to anyone, but to the prophet, not to one of royal race, but to one of the priests who were in Anathoth: "I have set you over nations and kingdoms, to root out and to destroy, to build and to plant." Similarly it is said to Peter, but more excellently: "You are Peter," it is said, "and on this rock I will build My church, and whatever you shall bind on earth, shall be bound in heaven; and whatever you shall loose on earth, shall be loosed in heaven. . . ." To princes power is given on earth, but to priests power is given also in heaven. The former have power over bodies only, the latter have power also over souls. Wherefore, to that degree by which the soul is more worthy than the body, by so much is the priesthood more worthy than the kingdom. . . . Single rulers have single provinces, and single kings have single kingdoms; but Peter rules them all, with as much latitude [of power] as plenitude, because he is the vicar of Him, Whose is the earth, and the fulness thereof, the world, and all those who dwell therein.

III

The provision of the Roman Empire pertains to us principally and finally: principally, because it was transferred from Greece through the Roman Church, especially for the defense of the Church; finally, because, although he may receive the crown of the kingdom elsewhere, nevertheless the emperor receives the final benediction and the crown of the Empire from the Apostolic See. When we heard, therefore, that the votes of the princes in the election were divided, we were all the more concerned about the division, because the welfare of the Empire, for the abovementioned reasons, especially pertains to us. For now not only does the Church desire to have a devoted defender because of the many and great necessities of the Christian people, but the entire Empire is known to need a suitable provider. . . .

IV

. . . [The Lord] set two great lamps in the firmament of heaven, one to illuminate the day, the other to shine in the darkness. In same fashion, He ordained two great dignities in temporal affairs, in the firmament of the Church, which is called by the name of heaven: the first to illuminate the day, that is, to guide spiritual men in spiritual matters and loose souls deceived by diabolical fraud from the bondage of sin, for, because of the power given to it, those whom it binds and looses on earth, God shall consider bound and loosed in heaven; the other to shine in the darkness, to punish heretics stricken by darkness of mind, the enemies of the Christian faith, whom the rising sun has not regarded from on high, to punish injuries done to Christ and Christians, and to use the power of the earthly sword to avenge wrongdoers and praise good men. And just as in an eclipse of the moon, the darkness becomes darker still, and the dimness of the fog becomes stronger, in the same way, after the defection of the emperor, the insanity of heretics and the violence of pagans against faithful Catholics grows more perfidious and cruel in its manifold iniquity. . . .

V

. . . But just as we, who, because of our duty of apostolic servitude, owe justice to all, do not wish our jurisdiction to be usurped by others, in the same way we do not wish to arrogate the rights of the princes to ourselves. We recognize, therefore, as indeed we ought to do, that the right and power of electing a king, who will afterwards be promoted into the Empire, belongs to those princes to whom it is known to pertain by law and by ancient usage. This is especially true because this right and power came to them through the Apostolic See, which transferred the Roman Empire from the Greeks to the Germans in the person of the magnificent Charles. But the princes, too, ought to recognize, and do recognize (for they had done so in our presence) that the right and authority of examining the person whom they have elected as king, and of promoting him to the imperial power belongs to us who anoint, consecrate, and crown him. For it is regularly and generally observed that the right of examining a man belongs to him who has the right to give him the benediction. If the princes, not only in disharmony, but even in harmony, should elect a sacrilegious man or an excommunicate as king, a tyrant or a fool, a heretic or a pagan, ought we to anoint, consecrate, and crown this sort of man? May God forbid it in every way! . . .

47 / ST. FRANCIS OF ASSISI: THE WAY OF THE SPIRIT

The ability of the thirteenth-century Church to control the consequences of lay piety and education and social and economic change depended to a very large extent on the effectiveness of the two new religious orders of friars, the Franciscans and Dominicans. The Franciscan approach to the reassertion of Church leadership was by way of a direct emotional, spiritual appeal, emulating the pure devotion and imitation of Christ of St. Francis of Assisi (d. 1226). St. Francis was an Italian nobleman who received a religious call to live as the Savior had lived, "taking nothing for the way," but existing as a mendicant, to go out on the highways and into the cities and to summon men to

*God by a direct emotional appeal and the purity of his own life.
With St. Francis, the personal, mystical strain in medieval religiosity reaches its fulfillment. His message and his disciples
had an enormous popularity in thirteenth-century society, especially in urban areas. In the following selections we have one of
the vast number of legends and stories told about him by his disciples (A); nearly all of his own writings that have survived, or
perhaps that he ever found it necessary or worthwhile to put
down (B); and finally a modern assessment of his religious approach, which to the present day exercises a powerful attraction
for many sensitive minds (C).*[39]

A. FROM THE LITTLE FLOWERS OF ST. FRANCIS

It happened one time that the Brothers were serving the lepers
and the sick in a hospital, near to the place where St. Francis was.
Among them was a leper who was so impatient, so cross-grained, so
unendurable, that everyone believed him to be possessed of the devil,
and rightly enough, for he heaped insults and blows upon those who
waited upon him, and what was worse, he continually insulted and
blasphemed the blessed Christ and his most holy Mother the Virgin
Mary, so that there was no longer anyone who could or would wait
upon him. The Brothers would willingly have endured the insults and
abuse which he lavished upon them, in order to augment the merit
of their patience, but their souls could not consent to hear those which
he uttered against Christ and his Mother. They therefore resolved to
abandon this leper, but not without having told the whole story exactly
to St. Francis, who at that time was dwelling not far away.

When they told him, St. Francis betook himself to the wicked leper;
"May God give thee peace, my most dear brother," he said to him as
he drew near.

"And what peace," asked the leper, "can I receive from God, who
has taken away my peace and every good thing, and has made my
body a mass of stinking and corruption?"

St. Francis said to him: "My brother, be patient, for God gives us
diseases in this world for the salvation of our souls, and when we
endure them patiently they are the fountain of great merit to us."

"How can I endure patiently continual pains which torture me day
and night? And it is not only my disease that I suffer from, but the
friars that you gave me to wait upon me are unendurable, and do not
take care of me as they ought."

[39] P. Sabatier, *Life of St. Francis of Assisi,* transl. L. S. Houghton (New York:
Charles Scribner's Sons, 1905), pp. 142–3, 255–7, 305–6, 337–9, xx–xxii, xxiii.

Then St. Francis perceived that this leper was possessed by the spirit of evil, and he betook himself to his knees in order to pray for him. Then returning he said to him: "My son, since you are not satisfied with the others, I will wait upon you."

"That is all very well, but what can you do for me more than they?"

"I will do whatever you wish."

"Very well; I wish you to wash me from head to foot, for I smell so badly that I disgust myself."

Then St. Francis made haste to heat some water with many sweet-smelling herbs; next he took off the leper's clothes and began to bathe him, while a Brother poured out the water. And behold, by a divine miracle, wherever St. Francis touched him with his holy hands the leprosy disappeared and the flesh became perfectly sound. And in proportion as the flesh was healed the soul of the wretched man was also healed, and he began to feel a lively sorrow for his sins, and to weep bitterly. . . . And being completely healed both in body and soul, he cried with all his might: "Woe unto me, for I have deserved hell for the abuses and outrages which I have said and done to the Brothers, for my impatience and my blasphemies."

B. THE WRITINGS OF ST. FRANCIS

The Rule of 1221

By the holy love which is in God, I pray all the friars, ministers as well as others, to put aside every obstacle, every care, every anxiety, that they may be able to consecrate themselves entirely to serve, love, and honor the Lord God, with a pure heart and a sincere purpose, which is what he asks above all things. Let us have always in ourselves a tabernacle and a home for him who is the Lord God most mighty, Father, Son, and Holy Spirit, who says: "Watch and pray always, that you may be found worthy to escape all the things which will come to pass, and to appear upright before the Son of man."

Let us then keep in the true way, the life, the truth, and the holy Gospel of Him who has deigned for our sake to leave his Father that he may manifest his name to us, saying, "Father, I have manifested thy name to those whom thou hast given me, and the words which thou hast given me I have given also unto them. They have received them, and they have known that I am come from thee, and they believe that thou hast sent me. I pray for them; I pray not for the world, that they may have joy in themselves. I have given them thy words, and the world hath hated them, because they are not of the world. I pray not that thou shouldst take them out of the world, but that thou wilt keep them from the evil. Sanctify them through the truth; thy word is truth. As thou hast sent me into the world I have also sent them into the world, and for their sake I sanctify myself that they may themselves be sanctified in the truth; and neither pray I for these alone, but for all those who shall believe on me through their words, that we all may be one, and that the world may know that thou hast sent me, and that thou lovest them as thou hast loved me. I have made known unto them thy name, that the love wherewith thou hast loved me may be in them and I in them."

PRAYER

Almighty, most high and sovereign God, holy Father, righteous Lord, King of heaven and earth, we give thee thanks for thine own sake, in that by thy holy will, and by thine only Son and thy Holy Spirit thou has created all things spiritual and corporeal, and that after having made us in thine imagine and after thy likeness, thou didst place us in that paradise which we lost by our sin. And we give thee thanks because after having created us by thy Son, by that love which is thine, and which thou hadst had for us, thou hast made him to be born very God and very man of the glorious and blessed Mary, ever Virgin, and because by his cross, his blood, and his death thou hast willed to ransom us poor captives. And we give thee thanks that thy Son is to return in his glorious majesty to send to eternal fire the accursed ones, those who have not repented and have not known thee; and to say to those who have known and adored thee and served thee by repentance, "Come, ye blessed of my Father, inherit the kingdom prepared for you from before the foundation of the world." And since we, wretched and sinful, are not worthy to name thee, we humbly ask our Lord Jesus Christ, thy well-beloved Son, in whom thou art well pleased, that he may give thee thanks for everything; and also the Holy Spirit, the Paraclete, as it may please thee and them; for this we supplicate him who has all power with thee, and by whom thou hast done such great things for us. Alleluia.

And we pray the glorious Mother, the blessed Mary, ever Virgin, St. Michael, Gabriel, Raphael, and all the choir of blessed Spirits, Seraphim, Cherubim, Thrones, Dominions, Principalities and Powers, Virtues and Angels, Archangels, John the Baptist, John the Evangelist, Peter, Paul, and the holy Patriarchs, the Prophets, the Holy Innocents, Apostles, Evangelists, Disciples, Martyrs, Confessors, Virgins, the blessed ones, Elijah and Enoch, and all the saints who have been, shall be, and are, we humbly pray them by thy love to give thee thanks for these things, as it pleases thee, sovereign, true, eternal and living God, and also to thy Son, our most holy Lord Jesus Christ, and to the Holy Spirit, the Comforter, forever and ever. Amen. Alleluia.

And we supplicate all those who desire to serve the Lord God, in the bosom of the Catholic and Apostolic Church, all priests, deacons, sub-deacons, acolytes and exorcists, readers, porters, all clerks, all monks and nuns, all children and little ones, paupers and exiles, kings, and princes, workmen and laborers, servants and masters, the virgins, the continent and the married, laics, men and women, all children, youths, young men and old men, the sick and the well, the small and the great, the peoples of every tribe and tongue and nation, all men in every part of the world whatsoever, who are or who shall be, we pray and beseech them, all we Brothers Minor, unprofitable servants, that all together, with one accord we persevere in the true faith and in penitence, for outside of these no person can be saved.

Let us all, with all our heart and all our thought, and all our strength, and all our mind, with all our vigor, with all our effort, with all our affection, with all our inward powers, our desires, and our wills, love the Lord God, who has given to us all his body, all his soul, all his life, and still gives them every day to each one of us. He created us, he saved us by his grace alone; he has been, he still is, full of goodness to us, us wicked and worthless, corrupt and offensive, ungrateful, ignorant, bad. We desire nothing else, we wish for nothing else; may nothing else please us, or have any attraction for us, except the Creator, the Redeemer, the Saviour, sole and true God, who is full of goodness, who is all goodness, who is the true and supreme good, who alone is kind, pious, and merciful, gracious, sweet, and gentle, who alone is holy, righteous, true, upright, who alone has benignity, innocence, and purity; of whom, by whom, and in whom is all the pardon, all the grace, all the glory of all penitents, of all the righteous and all the saints who are rejoicing in heaven.

Then let nothing again hinder, let nothing again separate, nothing again retard us, and may we all, so long as we live, in every place, at every hour, at every time, every day and unceasingly, truly and humbly believe. Let us have in our hearts, let us love, adore, serve, praise, bless, glorify, exalt, magnify, thank the most high, sovereign, eternal God, Trinity and Unity, Father, Son, and Holy Spirit, Creator of all men, both of those who believe and hope in him and of those who love him. He is without beginning and without end, immutable and invisible, ineffable, incomprehensible, indiscernible, blessed, lauded, glorious, exalted, sublime, most high, sweet, lovely, delectable, and always worthy of being desired above all things, in all the ages of ages. Amen.

The Canticle of the Sun

O most high, almighty, good Lord God, to thee belong praise, glory, honor, and all blessing!

Praised be my Lord God with all his creatures, and specially our brother the sun, who brings us the day and who brings us the light;

fair is he and shines with a very great splendor: O Lord, he signifies to us thee!

Praised be my Lord for our sister the moon, and for the stars, the which he has set clear and lovely in heaven.

Praised be my Lord for our brother the wind, and for air and cloud, calms and all weather by the which thou upholdest life in all creatures.

Praised be my Lord for our sister water, who is very serviceable unto us and humble and precious and clean.

Praised be my Lord for our mother earth, the which doth sustain us and keep us, and bringeth forth divers fruits and flowers of many colors, and grass.

Praised be my Lord for all those who pardon one another for his love's sake, and who endure weakness and tribulation; blessed are they who peaceably shall endure, for thou, O most Highest, shall give them a crown.

Praised be my Lord for our sister, the death of the body, from which no man escapeth. Woe to him who dieth in mortal sin! Blessed are they who are found walking by thy most holy will, for the second death shall have no power to do them harm.

Praise ye and bless the Lord, and give thanks unto him and serve him with great humility.

St. Francis' Will

See in what manner God gave it to me, to me, Brother Francis, to begin to do penitence; when I lived in sin, it was very painful to me to see lepers, but God himself led me into their midst, and I remained there a little while. When I left them, that which had seemed to me bitter had become sweet and easy.

A little while after I quitted the world, and God gave me such faith in his churches that I would kneel down with simplicity and I would say: "We adore thee, Lord Jesus Christ, here and in all thy churches which are in the world, and we bless thee that by thy holy cross thou hast ransomed the world."

Besides, the Lord gave me and still gives me so great a faith in priests who live according to the form of the holy Roman Church, because of their sacerdotal character, that even if they persecuted me I would have recourse to them. And even though I had all the wisdom of Solomon, if I should find poor secular priests, I would not preach in their parishes without their consent. I desire to respect them like all the others, to love them and honor them as my lords. I will not consider their sins, for in them I see the Son of God and they are my lords. I do this because here below I see nothing. I perceive nothing corporally of the most high Son of God, if not his most holy Body and

Blood, which they receive and they alone distribute to others. I desire above all things to honor and venerate all these most holy mysteries and to keep them precious. Whenever I find the sacred names of Jesus or his words in indecent places, I desire to take them away, and I pray that others take them away and put them in some decent place. We ought to honor and revere all the theologians and those who preach the most holy word of God, as dispensing to us spirit and life.

When the Lord gave me some brothers no one showed me what I ought to do, but the Most High himself revealed to me that I ought to live according to the model of the holy gospel. I caused a short and simple formula to be written, and the lord pope confirmed it for me.

Those who presented themselves to observe this kind of life distributed all that they might have to the poor. They contented themselves with a tunic, patched within and without, with the cord and breeches, and we desired to have nothing more.

The clerks said the office like other clerks, and the laymen *Pater noster*.

We loved to live in poor and abandoned churches, and we were ignorant and submissive to all. I worked with my hands and would continue to do so, and I will also that all other friars work at some honorable trade. Let those who have none learn one, not for the purpose of receiving the price of their toil, but for their good example and to flee idleness. And when they do not give us the price of their toil, let us resort to the table of the Lord, begging our bread from door to door. The Lord revealed to me the salutation which we ought to give: "God give you Peace!"

Let the Brothers take great care not to receive churches, habitations, and all that men build for them, except as all is in accordance with the holy poverty which we have vowed in the Rule, and let them not receive hospitality in them except as strangers and pilgrims.

I absolutely interdict all the brothers, in whatever place they may be found, from asking any bull from the court of Rome, whether directly or indirectly, under pretext of church or convent or under pretext of preachings, nor even for their personal protection. If they are not received anywhere let them go elsewhere, thus doing penance with the benediction of God.

I desire to obey the minister-general of this fraternity, and the guardian whom he may please to give me. I desire to put myself entirely into his hands, to go nowhere and do nothing against his will, for he is my lord.

Though I be simple and ill, I would, however, have always a clerk who will perform the office, as it is said in the Rule; let all the other brothers also be careful to obey their guardians and to do the office according to the Rule. If it come to pass that there are any who do not the office according to the Rule, and who desire to make any other change, or if they are not Catholics, let all the Brothers, wherever they may be, be bound by obedience to present them to the nearest custode. Let the custodes be bound by obedience to keep him well guarded like a man who is in bonds night and day, so that he may not escape from their hands until they personally place him in the minister's hands. And let the minister be bound by obedience to send him by brothers who will guard him as a prisoner day and night until they shall have placed him in the hands of the Lord Bishop of Ostia, who is the lord, the protector, and the correcter of all the Fraternity.

And let the Brothers not say: "This is a new Rule"; for this is a reminder, a warning, an exhortation; it is my Will, that I, little Brother Francis, make for you, my blessed Brothers, in order that we may observe in a more catholic way the Rule which we promised the Lord to keep.

Let the ministers-general, all the other ministers and the custodes be held by obedience to add nothing to and take nothing from these words. Let them always keep this writing near them, beside the Rule; and in all the chapters which shall be held, when the Rule is read let these words be read also.

I interdict absolutely, by obedience, all the Brothers, clerics and laymen, to introduce glosses in the Rule, or in this Will, under pretext of explaining it. But since the Lord has given me to speak and to write the Rule and these words in a clear and simple manner, without commentary, understand them in the same way, and put them into practice until the end.

And may whoever shall have observed these things be crowned in heaven with the blessings of the heavenly Father, and on earth with those of his well-beloved Son and of the Holy Spirit, the consoler, with the assistance of all the heavenly virtues and all the saints.

And I, little Brother Francis, your servitor, confirm to you so far as I am able this most holy benediction. Amen.

C. PAUL SABATIER: THE CHRISTIAN LIFE ACCORDING TO ST. FRANCIS

. . . Jesus went indeed into the desert, but only that he might find in prayer and communion with the heavenly Father the inspiration and strength necessary for keeping up the struggle against evil. Far from avoiding the multitude, he sought them out to enlighten, console, and convert them.

This is what St. Francis desired to imitate. More than once he felt the seduction of the purely contemplative life, but each time his own spirit warned him that this was only a disguised selfishness; that one saves oneself only in saving others.

When he saw suffering, wretchedness, corruption, instead of fleeing he stopped to bind up, to heal, feeling in his heart the surging waves of compassion. He not only preached love to others, he himself was ravished with it; he sang it, and what was of greater value, he lived it.

There had indeed been preachers of love before his day, but most generally they had appealed to the lowest selfishness. They had thought to triumph by proving that in fact to give to others is to put one's money out at a usurious interest. "Give to the poor," said St. Peter Chrysologus, "that you may give to yourself; give him a crumb in order to receive a loaf; give him a shelter to receive heaven."

There was nothing like this in Francis; his charity is not selfishness, it is love. He went, not to the whole, who need no physician, but to the sick, the forgotten, the disdained. He dispensed the treasures of his heart according to the need and reserved the best of himself for the poorest and the most lost, for lepers and thieves.

The gaps in his education were of marvellous service to him. More learned, the formal logic of the schools would have robbed him of that flower of simplicity which is the great charm of his life; he would have seen the whole extent of the sore of the Church, and would no doubt have despaired of healing it. If he had known the ecclesiastical discipline he would have felt obliged to observe it; but thanks to his ignorance he could often violate it without knowing it, and be a heretic quite unawares.

We can now determine to what religious family St. Francis belongs.

Looking at the question from a somewhat high standpoint we see that in the last analysis minds, like religious systems, are to be found in two great families, standing, so to say, at the two poles of thought. These two poles are only mathematical points, they do not exist in concrete reality; but for all that we can set them down on the chart of philosophic and moral ideas.

There are religions which look toward divinity and religions which look toward man. Here again the line of demarcation between the two families is purely ideal and artificial; they often so mingle and blend with one another that we have much difficulty in distinguishing them, especially in the intermediate zone in which our civilization finds its place; but if we go toward the poles we shall find their characteristics growing gradually distinct.

In the religions which look toward divinity all effort is concentrated on worship, and especially on sacrifice. The end aimed at is a change in the disposition of the gods. They are mighty kings whose support or favor one must purchase by gifts.

Most pagan religions belong to this category and pharisaic Judaism as well. This is also the tendency of certain Catholics of the old school for whom the great thing is to appease God or to buy the protection of the Virgin and the saints by means of prayers, candles, and masses.

The other religions look toward man; their effort is directed to the heart and conscience with the purpose of transforming them. Sacrifice disappears, or rather it changes from the exterior to the interior. God is conceived of as a father, always ready to welcome him who comes to him. Conversion, perfection, sanctification become the pre-eminent religious acts. Worship and prayer cease to be incantations and become reflection, meditation, virile effort; while in religions of the first class the clergy have an essential part, as intermediaries between heaven and earth, in those of the second they have none, each conscience entering into direct relations with God. . . .

For him, as for St. Paul and St. Augustine, conversion was a radical and complete change, the act of will by which man wrests himself from the slavery of sin and places himself under the yoke of divine authority. Thenceforth prayer, becomes a necessary act of life, ceases to be a magic formula; it is an impulse of the heart, it is reflection and meditation rising above the commonplaces of this mortal life, to enter into the mystery of the divine will and conform itself to it; it is the act of the atom which understands its littleness, but which desires, though only by a single note, to be in harmony with the divine sympathy.

48 / ST. THOMAS AQUINAS: THE WAY OF THE INTELLECT

The Dominican solution to the problems of the thirteenth-century Church was to emphasize the primacy of intellect, and to insist that intellectual quests would support the teachings of faith. The Dominican friars dominated the papal inquisition; they were "the order of preachers," the defenders of the faith. As such, the Dominicans were particularly concerned with demonstrating that the corpus of Aristotelian science—having been made available in the twelfth and early thirteenth centuries as a result of the heroic efforts of translators working in Spain and Sicily with the assistance of Moslem scholars—was in large part compatible with Christian revelation.

The Dominicans were very strong in the philosophy and theology faculties of the University of Paris, where their greatest thinker, St. Thomas Aquinas (d. 1274), worked out a vast, balanced, harmonious intellectual system showing how most of the teachings of the faith could be substantiated by reason and sci-

ence (I) and the emerging sovereign state made compatible with Christian mortality (II). Thomas' efforts were considered excessively rash by many conservative churchmen, and his philosophy erroneous by Oxford Franciscan scholars, but in the middle decades of the thirteenth century, it did appear to many that the Dominican intellectual re-enforcement of the old faith had met with a high degree of success. Thomas' effort to produce a comprehensive summa of theology in conformity with all known science and philosophy reflected the encyclopedic, summarizing inclination of thirteenth-century thought, and partly accounts for the measure of acceptance which his work received. Since the sixteenth century Thomism has been the official philosophy of the Catholic Church.[40]

I. WHETHER GOD EXISTS?

We proceed thus to the Third Article:—

Objection 1. It seems that God does not exist; because if one of two contraries be infinite, the other would be altogether destroyed. But the name *God* means that He is infinite goodness. If, therefore, God existed, there would be no evil discoverable; but there is evil in the world. Therefore God does not exist.

Obj. 2. Further, it is superfluous to suppose that what can be accounted for by a few principles has been produced by many. But it seems that everything we see in the world can be accounted for by other principles, supposing God did not exist. For all natural things can be reduced to one principle, which is nature; and all voluntary things can be reduced to one principle, which is human reason, or will. Therefore there is no need to suppose God's existence.

On the contrary, It is said in the person of God: *I am Who I am* (*Exod. iii.* 14).

I answer that, The existence of God can be proved in five ways.

The first and more manifest way is the argument from motion. It is certain, and evident to our senses, that in the world some things are in motion. Now whatever is moved is moved by another, for nothing can be moved except it is in potentiality to that towards which it is moved; whereas a thing moves inasmuch as it is in act. For motion is nothing else than the reduction of something from potentiality to actuality. But nothing can be reduced from potentiality to actuality, except by something in a state of actuality. Thus that which is actually

---

[40] *Summa Theologica,* A. C. Pegis, ed., *Basic Writings of St. Thomas Aquinas* (New York: Random House, 1945), Vol. I, pp. 21–3, Vol. II, p. 744. Reprinted by permission of Random House.

hot, as fire, makes wood, which is potentially hot, to be actually hot, and thereby moves and changes it. Now it is not possible that the same thing should be at once in actuality and potentiality in the same respect, but only in different respects. For what is actually hot cannot simultaneously be potentially hot; but it is simultaneously potentially cold. It is therefore impossible that in the same respect and in the same way a thing should be both mover and moved; *i.e.*, that it should move itself. Therefore, whatever is moved must be moved by another. If that by which it is moved be itself moved, then this also must needs be moved by another, and that by another again. But this cannot go on to infinity, because then there would be no first mover, and, consequently, no other mover, seeing that subsequent movers move only inasmuch as they are moved by the first mover; as the staff moves only because it is moved by the hand. Therefore it is necessary to arrive at a first mover, moved by no other; and this everyone understands to be God.

The second way is from the nature of efficient cause. In the world of sensible things we find there is an order of efficient causes. There is no case known (neither is it, indeed, possible) in which a thing is found to be the efficient cause of itself; for so it would be prior to itself, which is impossible. Now in efficient causes it is not possible to go on to infinity, because in all efficient causes following in order, the first is the cause of the intermediate cause, and the intermediate is the cause of the ultimate cause, whether the intermediate cause be several, or one only. Now to take away the cause is to take away the effect. Therefore, if there be no first cause among efficient causes, there will be no ultimate, nor any intermediate, cause. But if in efficient causes it is possible to go on to infinity, there will be no first efficient cause, neither will there be an ultimate effect, nor any intermediate efficient causes; all of which is plainly false. Therefore it is necessary to admit a first efficient cause, to which everyone gives the name of God.

The third way is taken from possibility and necessity, and runs thus. We find in nature things that are possible to be and not to be, since they are found to be generated, and to be corrupted, and consequently, it is possible for them to be and not to be. But it is impossible for these always to exist, for that which can not-be at some time is not. Therefore, if everything can not-be, then at one time there was nothing in existence. Now if this were true, even now there would be nothing in existence, because that which does not exist begins to exist only through something already existing. Therefore, if at one time nothing was in existence, it would have been impossible for anything to have begun to exist; and thus even now nothing would be in existence—which is absurd. Therefore, not all beings are merely possible, but there must exist something the existence of which is necessary.

But every necessary thing either has its necessity caused by another, or not. Now it is impossible to go on to infinity in necessary things which have their necessity caused by another, as has been already proved in regard to efficient causes. Therefore we cannot but admit the existence of some being having of itself its own necessity, and not receiving it from another, but rather causing in others their necessity. This all men speak of as God.

The fourth way is taken from the gradation to be found in things. Among beings there are some more and some less good, true, noble, and the like. But *more* and *less* are predicated of different things according as they resemble in their different ways something which is the maximum, as a thing is said to be hotter according as it more nearly resembles that which is hottest; so that there is something which is truest, something best, something noblest, and, consequently, something which is most being, for those things that are greatest in truth are greatest in being, as it is written in *Metaph*. ii. Now the maximum in any genus is the cause of all in that genus, as fire, which is the maximum of heat, is the cause of all hot things, as is said in the same book. Therefore there must also be something which is to all beings the cause of their being, goodness, and every other perfection; and this we call God.

The fifth way is taken from the governance of the world. We see that things which lack knowledge, such as natural bodies, act for an end, and this is evident from their acting always, or nearly always, in the same way, so as to obtain the best result. Hence it is plain that they achieve their end, not fortuitously, but designedly. Now whatever lacks knowledge cannot move towards an end, unless it be directed by some being endowed with knowledge and intelligence; as the arrow is directed by the archer. Therefore some intelligent being exists by whom all natural things are directed to their end; and this being we call God.

II. WHETHER LAW IS ALWAYS DIRECTED TO THE COMMON GOOD?

We proceed thus to the Second Article:—

Objection 1. It would seem that law is not always directed to the common good as to its end. For it belongs to law to command and to forbid. But commands are directed to certain individual goods. Therefore the end of law is not always the common good.

Obj. 2. Further, law directs man in his actions. But human actions are concerned with particular matters. Therefore law is directed to some particular good.

Obj. 3. Further, Isidore says: *If law is based on reason, whatever is based on reason will be a law.* But reason is the foundation not only of what is ordained to the common good, but also of that which is directed to private good. Therefore law is not directed only to the good of all, but also to the private good of an individual.

On the contrary, Isidore says that *laws are enacted for no private profit, but for the common benefit of the citizens.*

I answer that, As we have stated above, law belongs to that which is a principle of human acts, because it is their rule and measure. Now as reason is a principle of human acts, so in reason itself there is something which is the principle in respect of all the rest. Hence to this principle chiefly and mainly law must needs be referred. Now the first principle in practical matters, which are the object of the practical reason, is the last end: and the last end of human life is happiness or beatitude, as we have stated above. Consequently, law must needs concern itself mainly with the order that is in beatitude. Moreover, since every part is ordained to the whole as the imperfect to the perfect, and since one man is a part of the perfect community, law must needs concern itself properly with the order directed to universal happiness. Therefore the Philosopher, in the above definition of legal matters, mentions both happiness and the body politic, since he says that we call those legal matters *just which are adapted to produce and preserve happiness and its parts for the body politic.* For the state is a perfect community, as he says in *Politics* i.

49 / THE MEDIEVAL UNIVERSITY

By the time of Aquinas the university had fully become the center of European intellectual life. These selections reveal the problems of medieval university life: the struggle to obtain institutional independence, the authorities' occasional fear of heretical tendencies on the part of the professors, and the febrile condition of the students. Universities have not changed much since the thirteenth century.[41]

PRIVILEGE OF PHILIP AUGUSTUS TO THE STUDENTS AT PARIS IN 1200

In the Name of the sacred and indivisible Trinity, amen. Philip, by the grace of God, King of the French.

[41] D. C. Munro, *Translations and Reprints* (Philadelphia: University of Pennsylvania Press), Vol. II, No. 3, pp. 4–14, 17–18, 19–20.

Let all men know, now and in the future, that for the terrible crime owing to which five of the clergy and laity at Paris were killed by certain malefactors, we shall do justice as follows: that Thomas, then provost, concerning whom more than all others the students have complained, because he denies the deed, we shall consign to perpetual imprisonment, in close confinement, with meagre fare, as long as he shall live; unless, perchance, he shall choose to undergo publicly at Paris the ordeal by water. If he attempts that and fails, he shall be condemned. If he succeeds, never henceforth at Paris nor anywhere else in our own land shall he be our provost or bailiff; nor elsewhere, if we are able to prevent it; nor shall he in the future enter Paris.

And if through the full and legal examination, which we have entrusted to two of our faithful servants, Walter, the chamberlain, and Philip de Levis [to be conducted] without making any exception of persons, by the invocation of the Christian faith and by the fidelity which they owe to us, their liege lord, and through the oath which they have sworn to us concerning our honor and advice, we are able to learn what further we can and ought to do in the matter, we will do it without any hesitation, for God's honor and our own. Moreover, concerning the others who are in prison for the same crime, we will act thus: we will detain them in perpetual imprisonment, in our custody, unless they perfer to undergo the ordeal by water and to prove their innocence by God's witness. If they fail in that, we shall consider them condemned; unless, perchance, some of them having been fully tried shall be found innocent, or being found less guilty, shall be freed from captivity by us, on the intercession of the scholars. Those, moreover, who have fled we consider *ipso facto* condemned, and we shall cause all the counts in our land to swear that they will diligently seek them out and if they are able to seize any one of them, they will seize him and send him to us at Paris.

Also, concerning the safety of the students at Paris in the future, by the advice of our subjects we have ordained as follows: we will cause all the citizens of Paris to swear that if any one sees an injury done to any student by any layman, he will testify truthfully to this, nor will any one withdraw in order not to see [the act]. And if it shall happen that any one strikes a student, except in self-defense, especially if he strikes the student with a weapon, a club or a stone, all laymen who see [the act] shall in good faith seize the malefactor or malefactors and deliver them to our judge; nor shall they withdraw in order not to see the act, or seize the malefactor, or testify to the truth. Also, whether the malefactor is seized in open crime or not, we will make a legal and full examination through clerks or laymen or certain lawful persons; and our count and our judges shall do the same. And if by a full examination we or our judges are able to learn that he who is accused, is guilty of the crime, then we or our judges shall immediately inflict a penalty, according to the quality and nature of the crime; notwithstanding the fact that the criminal may deny the deed and say that he is ready to defend himself in single combat, or to purge himself by the ordeal by water. . . .

Also our judges shall not lay hands on the chief of the students at Paris for any crime whatever. But if that official ought to be arrested, he shall be arrested and guarded after arrest by the ecclesiastical judge, in order that whatever is judged legal by the church, may be done with the chief. But if students are arrested by our count at such an hour that the ecclesiastical judge can not be found and be present at once, our count shall cause the culprits to be guarded in some student's house without any ill-treatment, as is said above, until they are delivered to the ecclesiastical judge.

Concerning the lay servants of the students, who do not owe to us *burgensiam* or *residentiam*, and do not live by traffic, and through whom the scholars do not do any injury to anyone, it shall be as follows: neither we nor our judge will lay hands on them unless they commit an open crime, for which we or our judge ought to arrest them. In accordance, truly, with the tenor of the privilege which we have granted to the students at Paris, we are not willing that the canons of Paris and their servants should be included in this privilege. But we wish the servants of the canons at Paris and the canons of the same city to have the same liberty which our predecessors ought to have granted to them and which we ought to. Also, on account of the above-mentioned conventions or on account of this charter, we shall not be liable to lawsuit except in our own courts.

In order, moreover, that these [decrees] may be kept more carefully and may be established forever by a fixed law, we have decided that our present count and the people of Paris shall affirm by an oath, in the presence of the scholars, that they will carry out in good faith all the above-mentioned. And always in the future, whoever receives from us the office of count in Paris, among the other initiatory acts of his office, namely, on the first or second Sunday, in one of the churches of Paris,—after he has been summoned for the purpose,—shall affirm by an oath, publicly in the presence of the scholars, that he will keep in good faith all the above-mentioned. And that these decrees may be valid forever, we have ordered this document to be confirmed by the authority of our seal and by the characters of the royal name, signed below. . . .

STATUTES OF GREGORY IX FOR THE UNIVERSITY OF PARIS IN 1231

Gregory, the bishop, servant of the servants of God, to his beloved sons, all the masters and students of Paris—greeting and apostolic benediction.

Paris, the mother of sciences, like another Cariath Sepher, a city of letters, stands forth illustrious, great indeed, but concerning herself she causes greater things to be desired, full of favor for the teachers and students. There, as in a special factory of wisdom, she has silver as the beginnings of her veins, and of gold is the spot in which according to law they flow together; from which the prudent mystics of eloquence fabricate golden necklaces inlaid with silver, and making collars ornamented with precious stones of inestimable value, adorn and decorate the spouse of Christ. There the iron is raised from the earth, because, when the earthly fragility is solidified by strength, the breastplate of faith, the sword of the spirit, and the other weapons of the Christian soldier, powerful against the brazen powers, are formed from it. And the stone melted by heat, is turned into brass, because the hearts of stone, enkindled by the fervor of the Holy Ghost, at times glow, burn and become sonorous, and by preaching herald the praises of Christ.

Accordingly, it is undoubtedly very displeasing to God and men that any one in the aforesaid city should strive in any way to disturb so illustrious grace, or should not oppose himself openly and with all his strength to any who do so. Wherefore, since we have diligently investigated the questions referred to us concerning a dissension which, through the instigation of the devil, has arisen there and greatly disturbed the university, we have decided, by the advice of our brethren, that these should be set at rest rather by precautionary measures, than by a judicial sentence.

Therefore, concerning the condition of the students and schools, we have decided that the following should be observed: each chancellor, appointed hereafter at Paris, at the time of his installation, in the presence of the bishop, or at the command of the latter in the chapter at Paris—two masters of the students having been summoned for this purpose and present in behalf of the university—shall swear that, in good faith, according to his conscience, he will not receive as professors of theology and canon law any but suitable men, at a suitable place and time, according to the condition of the city and the honor and glory of those branches of learning; and he will reject all who are unworthy without respect to persons or nations. Before licensing anyone, during three months, dating from the time when the license is requested, the chancellor shall make diligent inquiries of all the masters of theology present in the city, and of all other honest and learned men through whom the truth can be ascertained, concerning the life, knowledge, capacity, purpose, prospects and other qualities needful in such persons; and after the inquiries, in good faith and according to his conscience, he shall grant or deny the license to the candidate, as shall seem fitting and expedient. The masters of theology and canon law, when they begin to lecture, shall take a public oath that they will give true testimony on the above points. The chancellor shall also swear, that, he will in no way reveal the advice of the masters, to their injury; the liberty and privileges being maintained in their full vigor for the canons at Paris, as they were in the beginning. Moreover, the chancellor shall promise to examine in good faith the masters in medicine and arts and in the other branches, to admit only the worthy and to reject the unworthy.

In other matters, because confusion easily creeps in where there is no order, we grant to you the right of making constitutions and ordinances regulating the manner and time of lectures and disputations, the costume to be worn, the burial of the dead; and also concerning the bachelors, who are to lecture and at what hours, and on what they are to lecture; and concerning the prices of the lodgings or the interdiction of the same; and concerning a fit punishment for those who violate your constitutions or ordinances, by exclusion from your society. And if, perchance, the assessment of the lodgings is taken from you, or anything else is lacking, or an injury or outrageous damage, such as death or the mutilation of a limb, is inflicted on one of you; unless through a suitable admonition satisfaction is rendered within fifteen days, you may suspend your lectures until you have received full satisfaction. And if it happens that any one of you is unlawfully imprisoned, unless the injury ceases on a remonstrance from you, you may, if you judge it expedient, suspend your lectures immediately.

We command, moreover, that the bishop of Paris shall so chastise the excesses of the guilty, that the honor of the students shall be preserved and evil deeds shall not remain unpunished. But in no way shall the innocent be seized on account of the guilty; nay rather, if a probable suspicion arises against anyone, he shall be detained honorably and on giving suitable bail he shall be freed, without any exactions from the jailors. But if, perchance, such a crime has been committed that imprisonment is necessary, the bishop shall detain the criminal in his prison. The chancellor is forbidden to keep him in his prison. We also forbid holding a student for a debt contracted by another, since this is interdicted by canonical and legitimate sanctions. Neither the bishop, nor his official, nor the chancellor shall exact a pecuniary penalty for removing an excommunication or any other censure of any kind. Nor shall the chancellor demand from the masters who are licensed an oath, or obedience, or any pledge; nor shall he receive any emolument or promise for granting a license, but be content with the above-mentioned oath.

Also, the vacation in summer is not to exceed one month, and the bachelors, if they wish, can continue their lectures in vacation time. Moreover, we prohibit more expressly the students from carrying weapons in the city, and the university from protecting those who disturb the peace and study. And those who call themselves students but do not frequent the schools, or acknowledge any master, are in no way to enjoy the liberties of the students.

Moreover, we order that the masters in arts shall always read one lecture on Priscian, and one book after the other in the regular courses. Those books on natural philosophy which for a certain reason were prohibited in a provincial council, are not to be used at Paris until they have been examined and purged of all suspicion of error. The masters and students in theology shall strive to exercise themselves laudably in the branch which they profess; they shall not show themselves philosophers, but they shall strive to become God's learned. And they shall not speak in the language of the people, confounding the sacred language with the profane. In the schools they shall dispute only on such questions as can be determined by theological books and the writings of the holy fathers.

Also, about the property of the scholars who die intestate or do not commit the arrangement of their affairs to others, we have determined to arrange thus: namely, that the bishop and one of the masters, whom the university shall appoint for this purpose, shall receive all the property of the defunct, and placing it in a suitable and safe spot, shall fix a certain date, before which his death can be announced in his native country, and those who ought to succeed to his property can come to Paris or send a suitable messenger. And if they come or send, the goods shall be restored to them, with the security which shall have been given. If no one appears, then the bishop and masters shall expend the property for the soul of the departed, as seems expedient; unless, perchance, the heirs shall have been prevented from coming by some good reason. In that case, the distribution shall be deferred to a fitting time.

Truly, because the masters and students, who harassed by damages and injuries, have taken a mutual oath to depart from Paris and have broken up the school, have seemed to be waging a contest not so much for their own benefit as for the common good; we consulting the needs and advantage of the whole church, wish and command that after the privileges have been granted to the masters and students by our most dearly beloved son in Christ, the illustrious King of the French, and amends have been paid by the malefactors, they shall study at Paris and shall not be marked by any infamy or irregularity on account of their staying away or return.

It is not lawful for any man whatever to infringe this deed of our provision, constitution, concession, prohibition and inhibition or to act contrary to it, from rash presumption. If anyone, however, should dare to attempt this, let him know that he incurs the wrath of almighty God and of the blessed Peter and Paul, his apostles.

Given at the Lateran, on the Ides of April [April 13], in the fifth year of our pontificate.

STATUTES OF ROBERT DE COURCON FOR PARIS IN 1215

R., servant of the cross of Christ, by the divine mercy cardinal priest of the title of St. Stephen in Monte Celio and legate of the apostolic seat, to all the masters and scholars at Paris—eternal safety in the Lord.

Let all know, that having been especially commanded by the lord pope to devote our energy effectively to the betterment of the condition of the students at Paris, and wishing by the advice of good men to provide for the tranquillity of the students in the future, we have ordered and prescribed the following rules:

No one is to lecture at Paris in arts before he is twenty-one years old. He is to listen in arts at least six years, before he begins to lecture. He is to promise that he will lecture for at least two years, unless he is prevented by some good reason, which he ought to prove either in public or before the examiners. He must not be smirched by any infamy. When he is ready to lecture, each one is to be examined according to the form contained in the letter of lord P. bishop of Paris (in which is contained the peace established between the chancellor and the students by the judges appointed by the lord pope, approved and confirmed namely by the bishop and deacon of Troyes and by P., the bishop, and J., the chancellor of Paris).

The treatises of Aristotle on logic, both the old and the new, are to be read in the schools in the regular and not in the extraordinary courses. The two Priscians, or at least the second, are also to be read in the schools in the regular courses. On the feast-days nothing is to be read except philosophy, rhetoric, *quadrivialia*, the Barbarism, the Ethics, if they like, and the fourth book of the Topics. The books of Aristotle on Metaphysics or Natural Philosophy, or the abridgements of these works, are not to be read, nor the writings of Master David of Dinant, the heretic Amauri, or the Spaniard Mauricius.

In the promotions and meetings of the masters and in the confutations or arguments of the boys or youths there are to be no festivities.

But they may call in some friends or associates, but only a few. We also advise that donations of garments and other things be made, as is customary or even to a greater extent, and especially to the poor. No master lecturing in arts is to wear anything except a cope, round and black and reaching to the heels—at least, when it is new. But he may well wear a pallium. He is not to wear under the round cope embroidered shoes and never any with long bands.

If anyone of the students in arts or theology dies, half of the masters of arts are to go to the funeral one time, and the other half to the next funeral. They are not to withdraw until the burial is completed, unless they have some good reason. If any master of arts or theology dies, all the masters are to be present at the vigils, each one is to read the psalter or have it read. Each one is to remain in the church, where the vigils are celebrated, until midnight or later, unless prevented by some good reason. On the day when the master is buried, no one is to lecture or dispute.

We fully confirm to them the meadow of St. Germain in the condition in which it was adjudged to them.

Each master is to have jurisdiction over his scholars. No one is to receive either schools or a house without the consent of the occupant, if he is able to obtain it. No one is to receive a license from the chancellor or any one else through a gift of money, or furnishing a pledge or making an agreement. Also, the masters and students can make among themselves or with others agreements and regulations, confirmed by a pledge, penalty or oath, about the following matters: namely, if a student is killed, mutilated or receives some outrageous injury—if justice is not done; for fixing the prices of lodgings; concerning the dress, burial, lectures and disputations; in such a manner, however, that the university is not scattered or destroyed on this account.

We decide concerning the theologians, that no one shall lecture at Paris before he is thirty-five years old, and not unless he has studied at least eight years, and has heard the books faithfully and in the schools. He is to listen in theology for five years, before he reads his own lectures in public. No one of them is to lecture before the third hour on the days when the masters lecture. No one is to be received at Paris for the important lectures or sermons unless he is of approved character and learning. There is to be no student at Paris who does not have a regular master.

CONDEMNATION OF ERRORS AT PARIS IN 1241

These are the articles rejected as contrary to true theology and condemned by Odo, the chancellor of Paris, and the masters ruling in theology at Paris, in the year of our Lord 1240, on the second Sunday after the octaves of Christmas.

The first [error] is, that the Divine essence in itself will not be seen by any man or angel.

We condemn this error, and by the authority of William, the bishop, we excommunicate those who assert and defend it. Moreover, we firmly believe and assert that God in His essence or substance, will be seen by the angels and all saints, and is seen by glorified spirits.

The second, that although the Divine essence is one in Father, Son and Holy Ghost, nevertheless that as far as regards form it is one in Father and Son, but not one in these with the Holy Ghost; and yet this form is the same as the Divine essence.

We condemn this error, for we firmly believe that the essence or substance is one in the Father and Son and Holy Ghost, and the essence is the same in regard to form.

The third, that the Holy Ghost, as it is a bond of affection or love, does not proceed from the Son, but only from the Father.

We condemn this error, for we firmly believe, that as it is a bond of affection or love, it proceeds from both.

The fourth, that glorified spirits are not in the empyreal heaven with the angels, nor will the glorified bodies be there, but in the aqueous or crystalline heaven, which is above the firmament; which they also presume to think concerning the blessed Virgin.

We condemn this error, for we firmly believe, that angels and sanctified souls and corporeal bodies will occupy the same corporeal place, namely, the empyreal heaven.

The fifth, that the bad angel was bad from his very creation, and never was anything but bad.

We condemn this error, for we firmly believe that he was created good, and afterward through sinning he became bad.

The sixth, that an angel can at the same moment be in different places, and can be omnipresent if he chooses.

We condemn this error, for we firmly believe, that an angel is in one definite place; so that, if he is here, he is not elsewhere at the same moment; for it is impossible that he should be omnipresent, for this is peculiar to God alone.

The seventh, that many truths, which are not God, have existed eternally.

We condemn this error, for we firmly believe, that one truth alone, which is God, has existed eternally.

The eighth, that the beginning, the present time, the creation and the passion may not have been created.

We condemn this error, for we firmly believe, that each is both created and creature.

The ninth, that he who has greater talents, will of necessity have greater grace and glory.

We condemn this error, for we firmly believe, that God will give grace and glory to each one according to what he has decided and foreordained.

The tenth, that the bad angel never had ground, whereon he was able to stand, nor even Adam in his state of innocence.

We condemn this error, for we firmly believe, that each one had ground, whereon he was able to stand, but not anything by which he was able to profit.

JACQUES DE VITRY: STUDENT LIFE AT PARIS

Almost all the students at Paris, foreigners and natives, did absolutely nothing except learn or hear something new. Some studied merely to acquire knowledge, which is curiosity; others to acquire fame, which is vanity; others still for the sake of gain, which is cupidity and the vice of simony. Very few studied for their own edification, or that of others. They wrangled and disputed not merely about the various sects or about some discussions; but the differences between the countries also caused dissensions, hatreds and virulent animosities among them, and they impudently uttered all kinds of affronts and insults against one another.

They affirmed that the English were drunkards and had tails; the sons of France proud, effeminate and carefully adorned like women. They said that the Germans were furious and obscene at their feasts; the Normans, vain and boastful; the Poitevins, traitors and always adventurers. The Burgundians they considered vulgar and stupid. The Bretons were reputed to be fickle and changeable and were often reproached for the death of Arthur. The Lombards were called avaricious, vicious and cowardly; the Romans, seditious, turbulent and slanderous; the Sicilians, tyrannical and cruel; the inhabitants of Brabant, men of blood, incendiaries, brigands and ravishers; those of Flanders, fickle, prodigal, gluttonous, yielding as butter, and slothful. After such insults, from words they often came to blows.

I will not speak of those logicians, before whose eyes flitted constantly "the lice of Egypt," that is to say, all the sophistical subtleties, so that no one could comprehend their eloquent discourses in which, as says Isaiah, "there is no wisdom." As to the doctors of theology, "seated in Moses' seat," they were swollen with learning, but their charity was not edifying. Teaching and not practicing, they have "become as sounding brass or a tinkling cymbal," or like a canal of stone, always dry, which ought to carry water to "the bed of spices." They not only hated one another, but by their flatteries they enticed away the students of others; each one seeking his own glory, but caring not a whit about the welfare of souls.

Having listened intently to these words of the Apostle, "If a man desire the office of a bishop, he desireth a good work," they kept multiplying the prebends, and seeking after the offices; and yet they sought the work decidedly less than the preëminence, and they desired above all to have "the uppermost rooms at feasts and the chief seats in the synagogue, and greetings in the market." Although the Apostle James said, "My brethren, be not many masters," they on the contrary were in such haste to become masters, that most of them were not able to have any students, except by entreaties and payments. Now it is safer to listen than to teach, and a humble listener is better than an ignorant and presumptuous doctor. In short, the Lord had reserved for Himself among them all, only a few honorable and timorous men, who had not stood "in the way of sinners," nor sat down with the others in the envenomed seat.

50 / SIR WALTER OF HENLEY: A THIRTEENTH-CENTURY TREATISE ON HUSBANDRY

The thirteenth century marks the high tide of medieval prosperity; at the end of the century the long medieval depression set in, lasting, at least north of the Alps, until the mid-fifteenth century. The great majority of the European nobility were far removed from the great issues of the time; except for the top stratum of great aristocrats, they were retiring to their estates and settling down to the peaceful lives of petty landlords and country gentlemen. In this selection, a mid-thirteenth-century English gentleman imparts his experienced knowledge of good husbandry.[42]

This is the treatise on husbandry that a good man once made, whose name was Sir Walter of Henley; and this he made to teach those who have lands and tenements and may not know how to keep all the points of husbandry, as the tillage of land and the keeping of cattle,

---

[42] *Walter of Henley's Husbandry*, transl. E. Lamond (London: Longmans, Green and Co., 1890), pp. 3, 5, 13–35, *passim*.

from which great wealth may come to those who will hear this teaching and then do as is found written herein.

The father having fallen into old age said to his son, Dear Son, live prudently towards God and the world. With regard to God, think often of the passion and death that Jesus Christ suffered for us, and love Him above all things and fear Him and lay hold of and keep His commandments; with regard to the world, think of the wheel of fortune, how man mounts little by little to wealth, and when he is at the top of the wheel, then by mishap he falls little by little into poverty, and then into wretchedness. Wherefore, I pray you, order your life according as your lands are valued yearly by the extent, and nothing beyond that. If you can improve your lands by tillage or cattle or other means beyond the extent, put the surplus in reserve, for if corn fail, or cattle die, or fire befall you, or other mishap, then what you have saved will help you. If you spend in a year the value of your lands and the profit, and one of these chances befall you, you have no recovery except by borrowing, and he who borrows from another robs himself; or by making bargains, as some who make themselves merchants, buying at twenty shillings and selling at ten. It is said in the proverb, "Who provides for the future enjoys himself in the present." You see some who have lands and tenements and know not how to live. Why? I will tell you. Because they live without rule and forethought and spend and waste more than their lands are worth yearly, and when they have wasted their goods can only live from hand to mouth and are in want, and can make no bargain that shall be for their good. The English proverb says, "He that stretches farther than his whittle will reach, in the straw his feet he must stretch." Dear son, be prudent in your doings and be on your guard against the world, which is so wicked and deceitful. . . .

TO SOW YOUR LANDS

Sow your lands in time, so that the ground may be settled and the corn rooted before great cold. If by chance it happens that a heavy rain comes or falls on the earth within eight days of the sowing, and then a sharp frost should come and last two or three days, if the earth is full of holes and the frost will penetrate through the earth as deep as the water entered, and so the corn, which has sprouted and is very tender, will perish. There are two kinds of land for spring seed which you must sow early, clay land and stony land. Why? I will tell you. If the weather in March should be dry, then the ground will harden too much and the stony ground become more dry and open, so it is necessary that such ground be sown early, that the corn may be nourished by the winter moisture.

TO FREE LANDS FROM TOO MUCH WATER

Chalky ground and sandy ground need not be sown so early, for these are two evils escaped to be overturned in great moisture, but at sowing let the ground be a little sprinkled. And when your lands are sown let the marshy ground and damp ground be well ridged, and the water made to run, so that the ground may be freed from water. Let your land be cleaned and weeded after St. John's Day; before that is not a good time. If you cut thistles fifteen days or eight before St. John's Day, for each one will come two or three. Let your corn be carefully cut and led into the grange.

TO MAKE THE ISSUE OF THE GRANGE

When the stock of the grange is taken, place there a true man in whom you trust, who can direct the provost rightly, for one often sees that the grange-keeper and barn-keeper join together to do mischief. Make your provost and barn-keepers fill the measures, so that for every eight bushels a cantle shall be left for the waste which takes place at the putting in and taking from the barn, for in the comble is fraud. How? I will tell you. When the provost has rendered account for the return of the grange, then cause the bushel which he filled with grain to be proved. If the bushel be large then four heaped up will make five, more or less; if it be smaller five will make six; if smaller six will make seven; if still smaller eight will make nine, and so on for each, more or less. Now some of these provosts will only render account for eight in the seam, whether the bushel be large or small, and if the bushel be large there is great deceit. If the return of your grange only yields three times the seed sown you will gain nothing unless corn sells well.

FOR HOW MUCH YOU SHALL SOW AN ACRE

You know surely that an acre sown with wheat takes three ploughings, except lands which are sown yearly; and that, one with the other, each ploughing is worth sixpence, and harrowing a penny, and on the acre it is necessary to sow at least two bushels. Now two bushels at Michaelmas are worth at least twelvepence, and weeding a halfpenny, and reaping fivepence, and carrying in August a penny; the straw will pay for the threshing. At three times your sowing you ought to have six bushels, worth three shillings, and the cost amounts to three shillings and three halfpence, and the ground is yours and not reckoned.

HOW YOU OUGHT TO CHANGE YOUR SEED

Change your seed every year at Michaelmas, for seed grown on other ground will bring more profit than that which is grown on your own. Will you see this? Plough two selions at the same time, and sow the one with seed which is bought and the other with corn which you have grown: in August you will see that I speak truly.

HOW YOU OUGHT TO KEEP AND PREPARE MANURE

Do not sell your stubble or take it from the ground if you do not want it for thatching; if you take away the least you will lose much. Good son, cause manure to be gathered in heaps and mixed with earth, and cause your sheepfold to be marled every fortnight with clay land or with good earth, as the cleansing out of ditches, and then strew it over. And if fodder be left beyond that estimated to keep your cattle cause it to be strewed within the court and without in wet places. And your sheep-house and folds also cause to be strewed. And before the drought of March comes let your manure, which has been scattered within the court and without, be gathered together. And when you must cart marl or manure have a man in whom you trust to be over the carters the first day, that he may see that they do their work well without cheating, and at the end of the day's work see how much they have done, and for so much must they answer daily unless they are able to show a definite hindrance. Put your manure which has been mixed with earth on sandy ground if you have it. Why? I will tell you. The weather in summer is hot, and the sand hot and the manure hot; and when these three heats are united after St. John's Day the barley that grows in the sand is withered, as you can see in several places as you go through the country. In the evening the earth mixed with manure cools the sand and keeps the dew, and thereby is the corn much spared. Manure your lands, and do not plough them too deeply, because manure wastes in descending. Now I will tell you what advantage you will have from manure mixed with earth. If the manure was quite by itself it would last two or three years, according as the ground is cold or hot; manure mixed with earth will last twice as long, but it will not be so sharp. Know for certain that marl lasts longer than manure. Why? Because manure wastes in descending and marl in ascending. And why will manure mixed last longer than pure manure? I will tell you. Of manure and the earth which are harrowed together the earth shall keep the manure, so that it cannot waste by descending as much as it would naturally. I tell you why, that you may gather manure according to your power. And when your manure has been spread and watered a little, then it is time that it should be turned over; then the earth and the manure will profit much together. And if you spread your manure at fallowing it shall be all the more turned over at a second ploughing, and at sowing shall come up again and be mixed with earth. And if it is spread at second ploughing at sowing it is all the more under the earth and little mixed with it, and that is not profitable. And the nearer the fold is to the sowing the more shall it be worth. At the first feast of our Lady enlarge your fold according as you have sheep, either more or less, for in that time there is much manure.

HOW YOU OUGHT TO INSPECT YOUR CATTLE

Sort out your cattle once a year between Easter and Whitsuntide—that is to say, oxen, cows, and herds—and let those that are not to be kept put to fatten; if you lay out money to fatten them with grass you will gain. And know for truth that bad beasts cost more than good. Why? I will tell you. If it be a draught beast he must be more thought of than the other and more spared, and because he is spared the others are burdened for his lack. And if you must buy cattle buy them between Easter and Whitsuntide, for then beasts are spare and cheap. And change your horses before they are too old and worn out or maimed, for with little money you can rear good and young ones, if you sell and buy in season. It is well to know how one ought to keep cattle, to teach your people, for when they see that you understand it they will take the more pains to do well.

HOW YOU OUGHT TO KEEP BEASTS FOR THE PLOUGH

You must keep your plough beasts so that they have enough food to do their work, and that they be not too much overwrought when they come from the plough, for you shall be put to too great an expense to replace them; besides, your tillage shall be behindhand. Do not put them in houses in wet weather, for inflammation arises between the skin and the hair and between the skin and the wool, which will turn to the harm of the beasts. And if your cattle are accustomed to have food, let it be given at midday by one of the messers or the provost, and mixed with little barley, because it is too bearded and hurts the horses' mouths. And why shall you give it them before some one and with chaff? I will tell you. Because it often happens that the oxherds steal the provender, and horses will eat more chaff for food and grow fat and drink more. And do not let the fodder for oxen be given them in a great quantity at a time, but little and often, and then they will eat and waste little. And when there is a great quantity before them they eat their fill and then lie down and ruminate, and by the blowing of their breath they begin to dislike the fodder and it is wasted. And let the cattle be bathed, and when they are dry curry them, for that will do them much good. And let your cows have enough food, that the milk may not be lessened. And when the male calf is calved let it have all the milk for a month; at the end of the month take away a teat, and from week to week a teat, and then it will have sucked eight weeks, and put food before it, that it may learn to eat. And the female calf shall have all the milk for three weeks, and take from it the teats as with the male. And let them have water in dry weather within the houses and without, for many die on the ground of a disease of the lungs for lack of water. Further, if there be any beast which begins to fall ill, lay out money to better it, for it is said in the proverb, "Blessed is the penny that saves two.". . .

TO SELL IN SEASON

Buy and sell in season through the inspection of a true man or two who can witness the business, for often it happens that those who render account increase the purchases and diminish the sales. If you must sell by weight, be careful there, for there is great deceit for those who do not know to be on their guard.

VIEW OF ACCOUNT

Have an inspection of account, or cause it to be made by some one in whom you trust, once a year, and final account at the end of the year. View of account is made to know the state of things as well as the issues, receipts, sales, purchases, and other expenses, and for raising money. If there is any let it be raised and taken from the hands of the servants. For often it happens that servants and provosts by themselves or by others make merchandise with their lord's money to their own profit and not to the profit of their lord, and that is not lawful. And if arrears appear in the final account let them be speedily raised, and if they name certain persons who owe arrears, take the names, for often it happens that servants and provosts are debtors themselves, and make others debtors whom they can and ought not, and this they do to conceal their disloyalty.

HOW SERVANTS AND PROVOSTS OUGHT TO BEHAVE

Those who have the goods of others in their keeping ought to keep well four things: To love their lord and respect him, and as to making profit, they ought to look on the business as their own, and as to outlays, they ought to think that the business is another's, but there are few servants and provosts who keep these four things altogether, as I think, but there are many who have omitted the three and kept the fourth, and have interpreted that contrary to the right way, knowing well that the business is another's and not theirs, and take right and left where they judge best that their disloyalty will not be perceived. Look into your affairs often, and cause them to be reviewed, for those who serve you will thereby avoid the more to do wrong, and will take pains to do better.

51 / THE ADVANCE OF ROYAL LEADERSHIP

In the midst of thirteenth-century peace and prosperity, it appeared that the church was succeeding in reasserting its leadership in medieval society. But in the middle years of the century there was new evidence of a shift of popular attitudes toward acceptance of royal leadership. The Hohenstaufen emperor Frederick II (1220–1250) was acclaimed as a sort of demigod in southern Italy, as in the following eulogy by the ecclesiastical writer Nicholas of Bari (A).[43] *The terrified papacy preached a crusade against the Hohenstaufen dynasty, extirpated the family, and brought in the brother of the French king Louis IX (1226–1270) to rule southern Italy.*

By the first decade of the fourteenth century it was evident that this was a great tactical error. The French Capetian kings had always been on good terms with the papacy, partly because they were too weak to act in any other way, until the end of the twelfth century. The thirteenth century's most important political developments were the extension of the sovereignty of the French crown and administration over the whole country, and the rise of a skilled and aggressive bureaucracy loyal to the monarchy and not to much else. This great turning point in French political history was partly disguised by the saintly qualities of Louis IX, who was canonized soon after his death. This only gave the Capetian monarchy added prestige. As is evident in the second selection (B) [44]—*which comes from Joinville's Life of St. Louis, the first medieval royal biography written by a layman* —*Louis aroused veneration and enthusiasm not far removed from that accorded Frederick II. In the first decade of the fourteenth century Louis IX's grandson, Philip IV the Fair, found it easy to*

[43] *Deutsches Archiv*, Vol. XI (1954), pp. 169–74, transl. John F. Benton. By permission of Monumenta Germaniae Historica.

[44] J. H. Robinson, *Readings in European History* (Boston: Ginn & Co., 1904), Vol. I, pp. 213–8.

humiliate and subjugate the Vicar of Christ and to destroy the medieval papacy.

A. NICHOLAS OF BARI: EULOGY OF FREDERICK II

"Great is our Lord, and great is his power: and of his wisdom there is no number." This short statement is a precept overflowing with abundance and adorned with all manner of precious stones. . . . King David, that wonderful harpist and remarkable prophet, prophesied in the aforesaid precept about two emperors, namely the celestial emperor, who rules winds and sea, who spoke and they were made, who commanded and the universe was created, and the terrestrial lord, the magnificent Emperor Frederick, anointed with the oil of gladness before the kings of the universe. First he prophesied about the Son, and secondly about His successor in lordship.

This accords in all ways with the greatness of Christ, since He is the great king over all gods, and his power was great when he triumphed over the devil, and in the assembly of the Church Militant he brought forth and taught great wisdom, so that the gospel says, "Never did man speak like this" from the beginning.

And how it suits the earthly emperor is now to be shown. . . . The emperor is our great lord in his noble breeding, since he derives his lineage from the emperors and kings of the world. He that cometh from heaven is above all, i.e., he who descends from the imperial seed is more noble than all. That saying of Solomon can be said of him: "Her husband is honorable in the gates, when he sitteth among the senators of the world" and "Blessed is the land whose king is noble." His nobility is most pure gold, from which the most precious vessels of the temple are cast. . . .

He is great, greater, and greatest: great since he is king of Sicily, greater since he is king of Jerusalem, greatest since he is Roman emperor. He it is whom the Lord crowned with glory and honor, and set over the work of his hands. O lord wonderful, humble, and sublime! O lord expressible and ineffable! O happiness of princes, o joy of the populace, no one is to be found more sublime than him, nor more humble. . . .

All the days from the Nativity of the Lord up to Epiphany are said to be especially the days of the Lord, and in those days, i.e., within those days, that is, on the Feast of St. Stephen which is immediately after the Nativity, justice was born. Justice refers to the lord Emperor Frederick, who is so greatly our justice in this world, who renders unto everyone his due: to God three things, fear, honor, and love; to kings, concord; to his subjects, grace and mercy. The Lord caused this thing to come to pass and it is wonderful in our eyes that the emperor should have been born on the day of St. Stephen. For Stephen means he who is crowned, and on his day the lord crowned with a many-layered diadem proceeded to his birth, so that the interpretation of the name alluded to his dignity and earthly matters accorded with the heavenly. . . .

Ho, then, dear ones, let us praise him along with the angel Gabriel. Hear us say: Ave, lord emperor, full of the grace of God, the lord is with thee. . . . Blessed art thou amongst kings, that is, over all kings, and blessed is the fruit of thy womb, that is, that most beautiful fruit King Conrad, your beloved son, in whom you are well pleased. . . .

B. JOINVILLE: ST. LOUIS

I

As I have heard say, our sainted king Louis was born on the feast of St. Mark the evangelist, after Easter [1214]. . . . God, in whom he put his trust, watched over him always, from his infancy to the end, but especially in his childhood, when he had greatest need of his care, as you shall hear later. God saved his soul through the pious care of his mother, who taught him to believe in God and to love him, and kept him surrounded by devout and religious people. Even as a child she made him attend the daily services and listen to the sermons on feast days. He remembered hearing his mother often say that she would rather that he were dead than that he should commit a mortal sin.

In his youth he had sore need of God's aid, for his mother, who came from Spain, had neither relatives nor friends in the whole kingdom of France. And when the barons of France saw that their king was a child and the queen mother a foreign woman, they made the count of Boulogne their head and treated him in all things as their lord. After the king had been crowned there were certain barons who demanded that the queen should give them extensive lands, and when she would not they assembled at Corbeil. And the sainted king has told me how he and his mother, who were at Montlhéry, dared not return to Paris until their supporters there came for them in arms. He told me, too, that all the way from Montlhéry to Paris the roads were full of men, armed and unarmed, and that they all called on our Lord to grant the king a long and happy life and defend him from his enemies. And God did even so, as you shall hear.

II

[Joinville, a prominent lord in Champagne, joins Louis' crusade against Egypt.]

While I was on foot with my knights, and wounded, as I have just been relating, the king came along with his own body of troops, amidst a great shouting and noise of trumpets and kettledrums, and halted on the highroad. Never have I seen knight so noble, for he stood head and shoulders above all his attendants, a golden helmet on his head, and in his hand a German sword.

As soon as he came to a halt the good knights in his following, whom I have already named to you, rushed pell mell upon the Turks. And then followed a splendid feat of arms; none drew bow or crossbow, but it was a combat at close quarters, with sword and battle-ax, between the Turks and our people, all mixed up together. One of my squires, who had escaped [from a previous encounter] with my banner and returned to me, loaned me one of my Flemish stallions, which I mounted and rode off side by side with the king.

[In the midst of a council of war as to the course to be pursued] the constable, Monseigneur Imbert de Beaujeu came to the king to tell him that his brother, the count of Artois, was defending himself in a house at Mansourah and needed aid. The king said, "Constable, go you ahead and I will follow you." And I said to the constable that I would go with him and be his knight, for which he thanked me heartily. So we set out for Mansourah. . . .

As we came down along the river bank, between the brook and the river, we saw the king near the river, and that the Turks were pushing back our troops toward the river, driving them on with furious strokes of battle-ax and sword. So great was the havoc that some of our people thought to escape by swimming across the river to the duke of Bourgoyne's side, which, however, they were unable to do, for the horses were weary and the day grown very hot; so that, as we came down, we saw the river full of lances and shields, and of drowning men and horses who perished there.

We came presently to a little bridge or culvert over the brook, and I said to the constable that we would better stay and guard it, "for, if we leave it, they will rush across it to attack the king, and if our men are assailed from both sides at once they are likely to succumb." So we did this. And men said that we should all have been lost that day if it had not been for the king's being there in person. For the sire of Courtenay and Monseigneur Jean de Saillenay told me how six Turks seized the king's horse by the bridle and were going to take him prisoner, and how he, with great slashing sword cuts, delivered himself from them unaided. And when his men saw how the king defended himself they took heart, and some of them gave up trying to get across the river and came to his support. . . .

[The constable went to seek aid, leaving Joinville and two other knights to hold the bridge, which they did, in spite of many wounds.] At sunset the constable brought a company of crossbowmen, who ranged themselves in front of us; and when the Saracens saw them preparing to discharge their crossbows they took to flight and left us. Then the constable said to me, "Seneschal, this is well done; now you must go to the king, and do not leave him until he dismounts at his own tent." Just as I reached the king, Monseigneur Jean de Valery came and said, "Sire, Monseigneur de Châtillon requests that you assign to him the rear guard." This the king did gladly, and then we set out. As we went long I got him to take off his helmet, and I lent him my iron one so that he might get some air. . . .

After we had passed the river there came to him Henry de Ronnay, marshal of the hospital, and kissed his hand, all in armor as it was. The king asked if he could give him any tidings of his brother, the count of Artois, and he said he could indeed, for he was sure the count of Artois was in paradise. "But O sire," said the marshal, "be of good comfort; for never did a king of France win greater honor than has fallen to you. You have swum a river in order to fight your enemies; you have routed them and driven them from the battlefield, have captured their tents and engines of warfare, and to-night you shall sleep in their camp." And the king replied that God be praised for all that he had done for him; but great tears fell from his eyes.

III

One day in Pentecost the saintly king was at Corbeil, where there were eighty chevaliers. After dinner the king came down into the courtyard beneath the chapel and was talking in the gateway with the count of Brittany, the father of the present duke, God keep him! Master Robert de Sorbonne came seeking me and, taking me by the hem of my cloak, led me to the king; and all the other gentlemen followed us. So I said to Master Robert, "Master Robert, what do you want with me?" and he said to me, "If the king should seat himself here in the courtyard and you should go and sit above him on the same bench, would you think yourself blameworthy?" And I replied that I should. And he said, "Then you are also blameworthy when you wear finer clothes than the king, for you array yourself in ermine and cloth of green, which the king never does."

"But," I said, "Master Robert, saving your grace, I am not to blame in wearing ermine and cloth of green, for it is the habit of dress that has come down to me from my father and my mother. But you, on the contrary, are much to be blamed, for your father was a villein and your mother was a villein, and you have forsaken the dress of your father and your mother, and wear finer camelot than the king." And I took the skirt of his outer coat and that of the king's and said to him, "Look now, if I do not speak the truth." Then the king set himself to speak in defense of Master Robert with all his might.

Afterward my lord the king called my lord Philip, his son, the father of the present king, and King Thibaut, and, seating himself at the entrance to his oratory, he put his hand on the ground and said to them, "Sit here close by me so that no one can hear us." "O sire," they said, "we dare not seat ourselves so close to you." Then he said to me, "Seneschal, sit here," which I did, and so close to him that my garments touched his. Then he made them sit down after me and said to them, "You did very wrong, you who are my sons, not to do at once what I commanded; see that it does not happen again." And they said that it should not.

Then he said to me that he had summoned us in order to confess to me that he had been wrong in defending Master Robert against me. "But," he said, "I saw that he was so thunderstruck that he was in sore need of my aid. However, do not mind anything I may have said in defense of Master Robert; for, as the seneschal told him, you should always dress neatly and well, for your ladies will love you the better for it, and your servants value you the more. As the philosopher says, one should array oneself, both as to clothing and arms, in such a manner that the men of sense of his generation cannot cry that he dresses too well, nor the young people that he dresses too poorly."

IV

When it was summer King Louis went and sat him down in the forest of Vincennes after mass, taking his place under an oak tree, and making us sit down by him. Then those who had anything to say to him might come without the interposition of any usher or other attendant. Then he would ask of them, "Is there any one here who has any case to be decided?" and those who had a case would rise; then he would say, "All must keep silence, for we must take up one matter after another." And then he called M. de Fontaines and M. Geoffrey de Villette, and said to one of them, "Hand the brief to me"; and when he saw anything to better in the words of those who spoke for another, he corrected them with his own mouth.

Sometimes in summer I have seen him in order to dispose of his people's affairs, come into the garden in Paris dressed in a coat of camelot, with a sleeveless garment of linsey-woolsey, a cloak of black taffeta about his shoulders, his hair carefully dressed, but with no headdress save a hat of white peacock feathers. He would have carpets spread down so that we might sit about him, and all the people who had business to bring before him stood round about. And then he would attend to them in the manner I have described above in the forest of Vincennes.

52 / THE BEGINNINGS OF ENGLISH CONSTITUTIONALISM

The use of representative institutions to obtain consent or impart information was widespread in the thirteenth century. But only in England was representative government to endure into the modern world. This was at least in part due to the failure of Roman law to be absorbed in England and, instead, the development of the distinctive English common-law system, using the jury, which retained the Germanic idea that law resided in the community. In the following selections are given first an example of the use of the jury in the twelfth century (A); [45] *an account by the contemporary monastic chronicler Roger of Wendover of the dispute between King John and the English barons in 1215, arising out of the barons' feeling that the royal government had violated the law of the land (B);* [46] *selections from the Magna Carta of 1215, emphasizing the principle that the king cannot violate the due process of the law in his own interests, and that the barons, as the leaders of the community of the realm, can coerce him to maintain the law (C);* [47] *and finally an example of a summons of representatives of shires and towns to join the lords and king's council in parliament at the end of the thirteenth century (D).* [48]

A. IMPANELLING OF A JURY BY A WRIT OF NOVEL DISSEISIN

The king to the sheriff, etc. A hath complained unto us that B unjustly and without judgment hath disseised him of his freehold in C within 30 years last past, and therefore we command you that if the

[45] G. Booth, *The Nature and Practice of Real Actions* (New York, 1808), p. 91.
[46] Roger of Wendover, *Chronica Majora,* transl. J. A. Giles (London, 1849), Vol. II, pp. 320–4.
[47] G. C. Lee, *Source Book of English History* (New York: Henry Holt & Co., 1900), pp. 175, 178–9.
[48] G. C. Lee, *Source Book of English History* (New York: Henry Holt & Co., 1900), p. 183.

aforesaid A shall make you secure to prosecute his claim, then cause that tenement to be reseised, and the chattels which were then in it, and the same tenement with the chattels shall be in peace until the first assize when our justices shall come into those parts, and in the meantime cause twelve free and lawful men of that visne [neighborhood] to view that tenement, and their names to be put into the writ, and summon them by good summoners, that they be before the justices aforesaid, at the assize aforesaid, ready to make recognizance thereupon, and put by gages and safe pledges the aforesaid B, or, if he shall not be found, his bailiff, that he may be then there to hear that recognizance, etc. And have there the summoners, the names of the pledges, and this writ, etc.

B. ROGER OF WENDOVER: KING JOHN AND THE BARONS

A.D. 1215; which was the seventeenth year of the reign of king John; he held his court at Winchester at Christmas for one day, after which he hurried to London, and took up his abode at the New Temple; and at that place the above-mentioned nobles came to him in gay military array, and demanded the confirmation of the liberties and laws of king Edward, with other liberties granted to them and to the kingdom and church of England, as were contained in the charter, and above-mentioned laws of Henry the First; they also asserted that, at the time of his absolution at Winchester, he had promised to restore those laws and ancient liberties, and was bound by his own oath to observe them. The king, hearing the bold tone of the barons in making this demand, much feared an attack from them, as he saw that they were prepared for battle; he however made answer that their demands were a matter of importance and difficulty, and he therefore asked a truce till the end of Easter, that he might, after due deliberation, be able to satisfy them as well as the dignity of his crown. After much discussion on both sides, the king at length, although unwillingly, procured the archbishop of Canterbury, the bishop of Ely, and William Marshal, as his sureties, that on the day pre-agreed on he would, in all reason, satisfy them all, on which the nobles returned to their homes. The king however, wishing to take precautions against the future, caused all the nobles throughout England to swear fealty to him alone against all men, and to renew their homage to him; and, the better to take care of himself, he, on the day of St. Mary's purification, assumed the cross of our Lord, being induced to this more by fear than devotion . . .

In Easter week of this same year, the above-mentioned nobles assembled at Stamford, with horses and arms; for they had now induced almost all the nobility of the whole kingdom to join them, and constituted a very large army; for in their army there were computed to be two thousand knights, besides horse soldiers, attendants, and foot soldiers, who were variously equipped . . . all of these being united by oath, were supported by the concurrence of Stephen archbishop of Canterbury, who was at their head. The king at this time was awaiting the arrival of his nobles at Oxford. On the Monday next after the octaves of Easter, the said barons assembled in the town of Brackley; and when the king learned this, he sent the archbishop of Canterbury, and William Marshal earl of Pembroke, with some other prudent men, to them to inquire what the laws and liberties were which they demanded. The barons then delivered to the messengers a paper, containing in great measure the laws and ancient customs of the kingdom, and declared that, unless the king immediately granted them and confirmed them under his own seal, they would, by taking possession of his fortresses, force him to give them sufficient satisfaction as to their before-named demands. The archbishop with his fellow messengers then carried the paper to the king, and read to him the heads of the paper one by one throughout. The king when he heard the purport of these heads, derisively said, with the greatest indignation, "Why, amongst these unjust demands, did not the barons ask for my kingdom also? Their demands are vain and visionary, and are unsupported by any plea of reason whatever." And at length he angrily declared with an oath, that he would never grant them such liberties as would render him their slave. . . .

As the archbishop and William Marshal could not by any persuasions induce the king to agree to their demands, they returned by the king's order to the barons, and duly reported all they had heard from the king to them; and when the nobles heard what John said, they appointed Robert Fitz-Walter commander of their soldiers, giving him title of "Marshal of the army of God and the holy church," and then, one and all flying to arms, they directed their forces toward Northampton. . . .

King John, when he saw that he was deserted by almost all, so that out of his regal superabundance of followers he scarcely retained seven knights, was much alarmed lest the barons would attack his castles and reduce them without difficulty, as they would find no obstacle to their so doing; and he deceitfully pretended to make peace for a time with the aforesaid barons, and sent William Marshal earl of Pembroke, with other trustworthy messengers, to them, and told them that, for the sake of peace, and for the exaltation and honour of the kingdom, he would willingly grant them the laws and liberties they required; he also sent word to the barons by these same messengers, to appoint a fitting day and place to meet and carry all these matters into effect. The king's messengers then came in all haste to London, and without deceit reported to the barons all that had been deceitfully imposed on them; they in their great joy appointed the fifteenth of June for the king to meet them, at a field lying between Staines and Windsor. Accordingly, at the time and place pre-agreed on, the king and nobles came to the appointed conference, and when each party had stationed themselves apart from the other, they began a long discussion about terms of peace and the aforesaid liberties. . . . At length, after various points on both sides had been discussed, king John, seeing that he was inferior in strength to the barons, without raising any difficulty, granted the underwritten laws and liberties, and confirmed them by his charter.

C. MAGNA CARTA, 1215

No free man shall be taken or imprisoned or dispossessed, or outlawed, or banished, or in any way destroyed, nor will we go upon him, nor send upon him, except by the legal judgment of his peers or by the law of the land.

To no one will we sell, to no one will we deny, or delay right or justice.

Since, moreover, for the sake of God, and for the improvement of our kingdom, and for the better quieting of the hostility sprung up lately between us and our barons, we have made all these concessions; wishing them to enjoy these in a complete and firm stability forever, we make and concede to them the security described below; that is to say, that they shall elect twenty-five barons of the kingdom, whom they will, who ought with all their power to observe, hold, and cause to be observed, the peace and liberties which we have conceded to them, and by this our present charter confirmed to them; in this manner, that if we or our justiciar, or our bailiffs, or any one of our servants shall have done wrong in any way toward any one, or shall have transgressed any of the articles of peace or security; and the wrong shall have been shown to four barons of the aforesaid twenty-five barons, let those four barons come to us or to our justiciar, if we are out of the kingdom, laying before us the transgression, and let them ask that we cause that transgression to be corrected without delay. And if we shall not have corrected the transgression, or if we shall be out of the kingdom, if our justiciar shall not have corrected it within a period of forty days, counting from the time in which it has been shown to us or to our justiciar, if we are out of the kingdom; the aforesaid four barons shall refer the matter to the remainder of the twenty-five barons, and let these twenty-five barons with the whole community of the country distress and injure us in every way they can; that is to say by the seizure of our castles, lands, possessions, and in such other ways as they can until it shall have been corrected according to their judgment, saving our person and that of our queen, and those of our children; and when the correction has been made, let them devote themselves to us as they did before.

D. SUMMONS OF REPRESENTATIVES OF SHIRES AND TOWNS TO PARLIAMENT (1295)

The king to the sheriff of Northamptonshire. Since we intend to have a consultation and meeting with the earls, barons and other principal men of our kingdom with regard to providing remedies against the dangers which are in these days threatening the same kingdom; and on that account have commanded them to be with us on the Lord's day next after the feast of St. Martin in the approaching winter, at Westminster, to consider, ordain, and do as may be necessary for the avoidance of these dangers; we strictly require you to cause two knights from the aforesaid county, two citizens from each city in the same county, and two burgesses from each borough, of those who are especially discreet and capable of labouring, to be elected without delay, and to cause them to come to us at the aforesaid time and place.

Moreover, the said knights are to have full and sufficient power for themselves and for the community of the aforesaid county, and the said citizens and burgesses for themselves and the communities of the aforesaid cities and boroughs separately, then and there for doing what shall then be ordained according to the common counsel in the premises; so that the aforesaid business shall not remain unfinished in any way for defect of this power. And you shall have there the names of the knights, citizens and burgesses and this writ.

Witness the king at Canterbury on the third day of October.

[Identical summonses were sent to the sheriffs of each county.]

53 / JEAN DE MEUN: CORRUPTION AND DEGENERACY

In the late 1270's a university-educated bourgeois, Jean de Meun, wrote a long continuation to a traditional work of courtly love, The Romance of the Rose. *Not only is de Meun's poem the greatest achievement of thirteenth-century French literature; it is a social document of the greatest importance. He re-*

veals the dispassionately realistic and, in fact, cynical attitude of the bourgeois intellectual toward aristocratic courtliness; even more, he lays bare the growing corruption, degeneracy, and rottenness of medieval culture, the increasing disillusionment with the old ideals, and the loss of faith in traditional leadership. Greed, selfishness, and irresponsibility appear in this poem to be characteristic of all the middle and higher ranks of society. The faith and idealism that distinguished twelfth-century culture has turned cold and sour.[49]

Many a servant has a happy heart
Bearing his charcoal through the Place de Grève
Untroubled by the burden, since he works
In patience. He will hop and skip and jump
Toward Saint Marcel for his poor meal of tripe,
Nor ever hoard his pennyworth of wealth,
But in the tavern all his savings spend;
Then back to bear his burdens, not in pain
But in pure joy, for he has earned his bread
And ne'er is tempted to defraud or steal.
Returning to the tavern, he will drink
And live as live he should. Rich are all such,
Abundantly, in thinking they've enough;
God knows they're honester than usurers.
No usurer can actually be rich,
For covetousness makes him suffer want.
    Whoever it displeases to hear the truth,
I say no merchant ever lives at ease;
He has for life enlisted in the war
Of gain, and never will acquire enough.
Though what he has he fears to lose, he runs
After the remnant which he'll ne'er possess.
His only thought's to get his neighbor's goods.

As well he might tremendous effort make
To drink up at a draft the river Seine,
Which more supplies no matter how he drinks.
This is the anguish, this is the distress,
This is the greedy fire that ever burns,
This is the dolor, this the constant fight

[49] From the book *The Romance of the Rose* by Guillaume de Lorris and Jean de Meun. Translated into English verse by Harold W. Robbins. Edited by Charles W. Dunn. Copyright, ©, 1962 by Florence L. Robbins. Reprinted by permission of E. P. Dutton & Co., Inc. Pp. 109–111, 114–115, 162, 169, 170–171.

That wounds his heart with fear of future want.
The more he gets, the more he seems to lack.
  "Doctor and lawyer both such fetters wear,
And, if they sell their skill for cash, they'll hang
By such a rope. The one would gladly see,
So sweet and pleasant does he find his gain,
Threescore in place of every invalid;
The other fain would have, for every suit,
Thirty at least or ten or twenty score,
So strongly he's by selfishness impelled.
As bad divines are who overrun the earth,
Preaching to gain favor, honor, wealth;
Their hearts feel like distress; they live in sin.
But worst are those who purchase their soul's death
By following Vainglory's treacherous path.
Deceived are such deceivers, for such priests
Are never profitable to themselves
Whatever good they may for others do;
For evil purpose, when it fails its end,
May yet produce a sermon that does good.
The hearers may a good example take
The while Vainglory damns the sermoner.
  "Leaving the Preachers, we'll of misers speak.
No love nor fear of God have they who hoard
More than they need of treasure in their chests
When out-of-doors they see the shivering poor
And starving hungry. God will make them pay.
Who lead such lives a triple vengeance feel:
The toil by which they wealth acquire; the fear
In which they ceaselessly their treasures guard;
The pain with which they leave them at the end.
In such a torment misers live and die.
All is from lack of love, so scarce on earth.
If such men loved, they would be loved again,
And perfect love would reign throughout the world.
No evil would be done; the more one had,
The more to those who were in want he'd give
Or lend for charity, nor usury,
Provided their intentions were the best
And they were not with idleness attaint.
No poverty or wealth would then be seen
But where it was deserved, throughout the earth.
But so degenerate is all the world
That it has put up love for sale; no man
Loves but for his own profit, or for gift

Or service he may gain. E'en women sell
Themselves; may all such bargains have bad end!
    Thus by Deceit are all on earth disgraced,
And goods once common portioned out to few,
Who, bound in chains by Avarice, submit
Their native freedom to vile servitude—
Slaves to the gold that in their coffers lies.
Themselves and not their goods are prisoners.
Such wretched, earthy toads are riches' slaves.
They cannot understand that wealth's no good
Except to spend; they think it's but to keep,
Which is not true. They never deign to use
But always hoard their cash. They may go hang,
For spite of all their pains it will be spent
When in the end they die and spendthrift heirs
Shall dissipate it all most joyfully;
Then little good of it the misers have.
Nor are they sure to keep it until then;
Tomorrow's rising sun may see it snatched away."

. . . .

    All day you've urged, and haven't finished yet,
That I renounce my lord for some rude love—
I know not what. To Carthage one might go
And search from west to east, from north to south,
And live until one's teeth fell out for age,
Scouring the earth with utmost diligence
Until all had been seen, and yet not find
The sort of love that you've described to me.
When gods of old before the giants fled,
And Chastity, Good Faith, and Law withdrew,
That love, I ween, was swept clean from the earth,
Or so dismayed it lost itself in flight.
Even ponderous Justice fled at last.
All left the world—they couldn't stand the wars—
To make their habitations in the skies,
Descending thenceforth but in miracles.
The gods were driven out by force of Fraud,
Who now with outrage holds their heritage.
    "Not even Tully, who took careful pains
To search all secret writings, could find out,
For all his ingenuity, that e'er
In all the ages since the world began
Have there been couples more than three or four
Who knew this perfect love; and I believe,

For never have I read of such a thing,
That fewer yet who lived in Tully's time
Proved by their words that they were such-like friends.
Am I more wise than Tully? I should be
A sottish fool were I to search for love
That is not to be found upon the earth.
Where should I look for what does not exist?
Can I fly with the cranes beyond the clouds
As did in truth the swan of Socrates?
I'll silent be; I've no such foolish hope.
The gods would think I threatened Paradise,
As did the giants once, and hurl their bolts
At me.

. . . .

In quite a different style lives Poverty;
Depressed by shame and misery, she feels
Her heart too much afflicted by disgrace,
So much she has to beg and be refused.
However she may try, she'll not escape
The universal blame for all her works.
She is unloved, and vilified by all.
One never thinks of her except to plan
His action so that he may her avoid.
Naught can so grieve a man as falling in
With Poverty; this debtors know full well
Who've spent their all and fear a gallows end.
Full well one knows this who is forced to beg
And suffer much ere folk will give him aid;
And one who's felt the joy of love should know
This just as well; for Ovid truly says,
'Poor men have not wherewith to pasture love.'
    "Poverty makes a man despair and hate
And live a martyr till he lose his mind.
For Heaven's sake, from such fate guard yourself!

. . . .

"Writings that emphasize degeneracy
Prove that in our first parents' early days
Loyal and true was love—not mercenary.
Most precious was that glorious Golden Age!
Men were not greedy for fine clothes or food.
They gathered acorns in the woods for bread. . . .

    "Upon such beds as I've described to you,
Free from all thought of harlotry or rape,

Those who were pleased to play the game of love
With kisses and embraces would unite.
In groves the verdant trees stretched out their limbs,
Protecting thus the lovers from the sun
With curtains and pavilions made of leaves.
There carried on their play and caroling

And lazy pleasantries this folk secure,
Void of all care except to lead their lives
In frank and joyous amiability.
Not yet had king or prince brought despotism
To pinch and rob the folk. All equals were.
Not yet for private property they strove.
Well did they know this saying is no lie
Or foolishness: 'There's no companionship
'Twixt Love and Seignory.' Whom Love unites
Either's supremacy will quickly separate."

54 / THE DISSOLUTION OF THE MEDIEVAL WORLD ORDER

By 1300 it was finally clear that the brave efforts made by Innocent III, St. Francis, and St. Thomas Aquinas, in their different ways, to preserve the leadership of the Church in the face of political, intellectual, and economic change had ultimately failed. Leadership had passed to the secular state, and in the writings of the two greatest thinkers at the beginning of the fourteenth century we can see the breakdown of the medieval world order. The Italian poet and philosopher Dante Alighieri (1265– 1321), on the one hand, summed up much of medieval religiosity in his Divine Comedy. *But his treatise* On Monarchy *justifies the leadership of the king in society, invoking, among other arguments, a novel pragmatic justification. Although Dante was particularly concerned with supporting the claims of the German emperor, his work may be taken as a general study of government, and it indicates the shift in the European ethos in the direction of the modern state (A).*[50]

[50] *De Monarchia*, transl. F. J. Church (London: The Macmillan Co., 1879), pp. 179, 184–5, 202–3, 216, 220, 221, 223–4, 229–30, 239–40, 251–2, 257, 260–2, 269–70, 271–2, 274–5, 277–8, 282–3, 292–3, 294–5, 302, 303, 304.

Dante's contemporary, the English Franciscan philosopher William of Ockham (1299–1350), was even more radical; his work made a shambles of the world order of the thirteenth century (B).[51] *By insisting on a strong nominalist philosophical position, he destroyed the Thomist harmony of science and revelation, leaving only simple faith and mystical experience as the shaky foundations of Church doctrine. Ockham was, however, only bringing to a conclusion the philosophical trend prevalent among the great Franciscan scholars who dominated Oxford from the late decades of the thirteenth century. Similarly, his attack on papal authority reflected the attitudes of the radical wing of the Franciscan order, which had been growing more and more critical of Rome since the mid-thirteenth century.*

A. DANTE: THE PRINCIPLES OF POLITICAL LIFE

. . . Temporal Monarchy, then, or, as men call it, the Empire, is the government of one prince above all men in time, or in those things which are measured by time. Three great questions are asked concerning it. First, there is the doubt and the question, is it necessary for the welfare of the world? Secondly, did the Roman people take to itself by right the office of Monarchy? And thirdly, does the authority of the Monarchy come from God directly, or only from some other minister or vicar of God? . . .

The proper work of the human race, taken as a whole, is to set in action the whole capacity of that understanding which is capable of development: first in the way of speculation, and then, by its extension, in the way of action. And seeing that what is true of a part is true also of the whole, and that it is by rest and quiet that the individual man becomes perfect in wisdom and prudence; so the human race, by living in the calm and tranquility of peace, applies itself most freely and easily to its proper work; a work which, according to the saying: "Thou hast made him a little lower than the angels," is almost divine. Whence it is manifest that of all things that are ordered to secure blessings to men, peace is the best. And hence the word which sounded to the shepherds from above was not riches, nor pleasure, nor honour, nor length of life, nor health, nor strength, nor beauty; but

---

[51] *The De Saramento Altaris of William of Ockham*, T. B. Birch, ed. and transl. (Burlington, Iowa: Lutheran Literary Board, 1930), pp. 115, 123, 125, 433, 435. Reprinted by permission of Board of Publication of the United Lutheran Church in America.

Guillelmi de Ockham Opera Politica, Vol. I, J. G. Sikes, ed. (Manchester: Manchester University Press, 1940), pp. 43–4, 57, 59, 65. Translated by permission of Manchester University Press.

peace. For the heavenly host said: "Glory to God in the highest, and on earth, peace to men of goodwill." Therefore also, "Peace be with you," was the salutation of the Saviour of mankind. For it behoved Him, who was the greatest of saviours, to utter in His greeting the greatest of saving blessings. And this custom His disciples too chose to preserve; and Paul also did the same in his greetings, as may appear manifest to all.

Now that we have declared these matters, it is plain what is the better, nay the best, way in which mankind may attain to do its proper work. And consequently we have seen the readiest means by which to arrive at the point, for which all our works are ordered, as their ultimate end; namely, the universal peace, which is to be assumed as the first principle for our deductions. As we said, this assumption was necessary, for it is as a sign-post to us, that into it we may resolve all that has to be proved, as into a most manifest truth. . . .

The Monarch is the only one who can be fitted in the best possible way to govern. Which is thus proved: Each thing is the more easily and perfectly qualified for any habit, or actual work, the less there is in it of what is contrary to such a disposition. Therefore, they who have never even heard of philosophy, arrive at a habit of truth in philosophy more easily and completely than' those who have listened to it at odd times, and are filled with false opinions. For which reason Galen well says: "Such as these require double time to acquire knowledge." A Monarch then has nothing to tempt appetite, or, at least, less than any other man, as we have shown before; whereas other princes have much; and appetite is the only corrupter of righteousness, and the only impediment to justice. A Monarch therefore is wholly, or at least more than any other prince, disposed to govern well: for in him there may be judgment and justice more strongly than in any other. But these two things are the pre-eminent attributes of a maker of law, and of an executor of law, as that most holy king David testified when he asked of God the things which were befitting the king, and the king's son, saying: "Give the king thy judgment, O God, and thy righteousness unto the king's son."

We were right then when we assumed that only the Monarch can in the best way fit other men. Therefore it follows that Monarchy is necessary for the best ordering of the world. . . .

It was by right, and not by usurpation, that the Roman people assumed to itself the office of Monarchy, or, as men call it, the Empire, over all mankind. For in the first place it is fitting that the noblest people should be preferred to all others; the Roman people was the noblest; therefore it is fitting that it should be preferred to all others. By this reasoning I make my proof; for since honour is the reward of goodness, and since to be preferred is always honour, therefore to be preferred is always the reward of goodness. It is plain that men are ennobled for their virtues; that is, for their own virtues or for those of their ancestors; for nobleness is virtue and ancestral wealth, according to Aristotle in his Politics; and according to Juvenal, "There is no nobleness of soul but virtue," which two statements refer to two sorts of nobleness, our own and that of our ancestors. . . .

That which is helped to its perfection by miracles is willed by God, and therefore it is of right. . . . The Roman Empire has been helped to its perfection by miracles; therefore it was willed by God, and consequently was and is by right. . . .

Whoever works for the good of the state, works with Right as his end. This may be shown as follows. Right is that proportion of man to man as to things, and as to persons, which, when it is preserved, preserves society, and when it is destroyed, destroys society. The description of Right in the Digest does not give the essence of right, but only describes it for practical purposes. If therefore our definition comprehends well the essence and reason of Right, and if the end of any society is the common good of its members, it is necessary that the end of all Right is the common good. Therefore Cicero says well in the first book of his *Rhetoric:* "Laws must always be interpreted for the good of the state." If laws do not aim at the good of those who live under them, they are laws only in name; in reality they cannot be laws. For it behoves them to bind men together for the common good; and Seneca therefore says well in his book "on the four virtues": "Law is the bond of human society." It is therefore plain that whoever aims at the good of the state, aims at the end of Right; and therefore, if the Romans aimed at the good of the state, we shall say truly that they aimed at the end of Right. . . .

Two things therefore have been made clear: first, that whoever aims at the good of the state aims at right; and secondly, that the Roman people in bringing the world into subjection, aimed at the public weal. Therefore let us argue thus: Whoever aims at right, walks according to right; the Roman people in bringing the world into subjection aimed at right, as we have made manifest in the preceding chapter. Therefore in bringing the world into subjection the Roman people acted according to right, consequently it was by right that they assumed the dignity of Empire. . . .

That people then, which conquered when all were striving hard for the Empire of the world, conquered by the will of God. For God cares more to settle a universal strife than a particular one; and even in particular contests the athletes sometimes throw themselves on the judgment of God, according to the common proverb: "To whom God makes the grant, him let Peter also bless." It cannot, then, be doubted that the victory in the strife for the Empire of the world followed the judgment of God. The Roman people, when all were striving for the Empire of the world, conquered; it will be plain that so it was, if we consider the prize or goal, and those who strove for it. The prize or goal was the supremacy over all men; for it is this that we call the Empire. None reached this but the Roman people. Not only were they the first, they were the only ones to reach the goal. . . .

Christ, as Luke, who writes His story, says, willed to be born of the Virgin Mary under an edict of Roman authority, so that in that unexampled census of mankind, the Son of God, made man, might be counted as man: and this was to carry out that edict. Perhaps it is even more religious to suppose that it was of God that the decree issued through Caesar, so that He who had been such long years expected among men should Himself enroll himself with mortal man.

Therefore Christ, by His action, enforced the justice of the edict of Augustus, who then wielded the Roman power. And since to issue a just edict implies jurisdiction, it necessarily follows that He who showed that He thought an edict just, must also have showed that He thought the jurisdiction under which it was issued just. . . .

The present question, then, concerning which we have to inquire, is between the two great luminaries, the Roman Pontiff and the Roman Prince: and the question is, does the authority of the Roman Monarch, who, as we have proved in the second book, is the monarch of the world, depend immediately on God, or on some minister or vicar of God; by whom I understand the successor of Peter, who truly has the keys of the kingdom of heaven? . . .

Now three classes of men chiefly strive against the truth which we are trying to prove.

First, the Chief Pontiff, Vicar of our Lord Jesus Christ and the successor of Peter, to whom we owe, not indeed all that we owe to Christ, but all that we owe to Peter, contradicts this truth, urged it may be by zeal for the keys; and also other pastors of the Christian sheepfolds, and others whom I believe to be only led by zeal for our mother, the Church. These all, perchance from zeal and not from pride, withstand the truth which I am about to prove.

But there are certain others in whom obstinate greed has extinguished the light of reason, who are of their father, the devil, and yet pretend to be sons of the Church. They not only stir up quarrels in this question, but they hate the name of the most sacred office of Prince, and would shamelessly deny the principles which we have laid down for this and the previous questions.

There is also a third class called Decretalists, utterly without knowledge or skill in philosophy or theology, who, relying entirely on their Decretals (which doubtless, I think, should be venerated), and hoping, I believe, that these Decretals will prevail, disparage the power of the Empire. And no wonder, for I have heard one of them, speaking of these Decretals, assert shamelessly that the traditions of the Church are the foundations of the faith. May this wickedness be taken away from the thoughts of men by those who, antecedently to the traditions of the Church, have believed in Christ the Son of God, whether to come, or present, or as having already suffered; and who from their faith have hoped, and from their hope have kindled into love, will, the world doubts not, be made co-heirs with Him.

And that such arguers may be excluded once for all from the present debate, it must be noted that part of Scripture was *before* the Church, that part of it came *with* the Church, and part *after* the Church. . . .

Although the moon has not light of its own abundantly, unless it receives it from the sun, yet it does not therefore follow that the moon is from the sun. Therefore be it known that the being, and the power, and the working of the moon are all different things. For its being, the moon in no ways depends on the sun, nor for its power, nor for its working, considered in itself. Its motion comes from its proper mover, its influence is from its own rays. For it has a certain light of its own, which is manifest at the time of an eclipse; though for its better and more powerful working it receives from the sun an abundant light, which enables it to work more powerfully.

Therefore I say that the temporal power does not receive its being from the spiritual power, nor its power which is its authority, nor its working considered in itself. Yet it is good that the temporal power should receive from the spiritual the means of working more effectively by the light of the grace which the benediction of the Supreme Pontiff bestows on it both in heaven and on earth. Therefore we may see that the argument of these men erred in its form, because the predicate of the conclusion is not the predicate of the major premiss. The argument runs thus: The moon receives her light from the sun, which is the spiritual power. The temporal power is the moon. Therefore the temporal power receives authority from the spiritual power. "Light" is the predicate of the major premiss, "authority" the predicate of the conclusion; which two things we have seen to be very different in their subject and in their idea. . . .

Again, from the first book of Kings they take the election and the deposition of Saul; and they say that Saul, an enthroned king was deposed by Samuel, who, by God's command, acted in the stead of God, as appears from the text of Scripture. From this they argue that, as that Vicar of God had authority to give temporal power, and to take it away and bestow it on another, so now the Vicar of God, the bishop of the universal Church has authority to give the sceptre of temporal power, and to take it away, and even to give it to another. And if this were so, it would follow without doubt that the authority of the Empire is dependent on the Church, as they say.

But we may answer and destroy this argument, by which they say that Samuel was the Vicar of God: for it was not as Vicar of God that he acted, but as a special delegate for this purpose, or as a messenger bearing the express command of his Lord. For it is clear that what God commanded him, that only he did, and that only he said. . . .

No vicar, whether human or divine, can be equal in power to the master whose vicar he is, which is at once obvious. We know that the successor Peter had not equal authority with God, at least in the works of nature; he could not make a clod of earth fall upwards, nor fire to burn in a downward direction, by virtue of the office committed to him. Nor could all things be committed to him by God; for God could not commit to any the power of creation, and of baptism, as is clearly proved. . . .

Although the successor of Peter has power to bind and to loose, as belongs to him to whom the office of Peter was committed, yet it does not therefore follow that he has power to bind and to loose the decrees of the Empire, as our opponents say, unless they further prove that to do so belongs to the office of the keys, which we shall shortly show is not the case. . . .

They say that the two swords of which Peter spake mean the two kinds of rule which we have spoken of; but this we wholly deny, for then Peter's answer would not be according to the meaning of the words of Christ; and also we say that Peter made, as was his wont, a hasty answer, touching only the outside of things. . . .

Certain persons say further that the Emperor Constantine, having been cleansed from leprosy by the intercession of Sylvester, then the Supreme Pontiff, gave unto the Church the seat of Empire which was Rome, together with many other dignities belonging to the Empire. . . . The dignity of the Empire was what Constantine could not alienate, nor the Church receive. . . . The Empire had its power while the Church was either not existing at all, or else had no power of acting. Therefore the Church is not the cause of the power of the Empire, and therefore not of its authority either, for power and authority mean the same thing. . . .

Again, if the Church had power to bestow authority on the Roman Prince, she would have it either from God, or from herself, or from some Emperor, or from the universal consent of mankind, or at least the majority of mankind. There is no other crevice by which this power could flow down to the Church. But she has it not from any of these sources; therefore she has it not at all. . . .

Man had need of two guides for his life, as he had a twofold end in life; whereof one is the Supreme Pontiff, to lead mankind to eternal life, according to the things revealed to us; and the other is the Emperor, to guide mankind to happiness in this world, in accordance with the teaching of philosophy. . . . God alone elects, God alone confirms: for there is none higher than God. . . .

I have unravelled the truth of the questions which I asked: whether the office of Monarchy was necessary to the welfare of the world;

whether it was by right that the Roman people assumed to themselves the office of Monarchy; and, further, that last question, whether the authority of the Monarch springs immediately from God, or from some other. Yet the truth of this latter question must not be received so narrowly as to deny that in certain matters the Roman Prince is subject to the Roman Pontiff. For that happiness, which is subject to mortality, in a sense is ordered with a view to the happiness which shall not taste of death. Let, therefore, Caesar be reverent to Peter, as the first-born son should be reverent to his father, that he may be illuminated with the light of his father's grace, and so may be stronger to lighten the world over which he has been placed by Him alone, who is the ruler of all things spiritual as well as temporal.

B. THE OCCAMIST REVOLT

Nominalism

. . . Quantity is not a thing really distinct from substance and quality, but any quantity is really the same as substance, and any quantity is really the same as quality; . . .

Only a diversity of modes of signification suffices to distinguish one concept from another; not that no thing may be signified absolutely through one, but that it may be signified by another. So also it is obvious from these two "homo" and "homines"; for it is impossible to grant any thing signified through one that may not be signified through the rest; yet it is false to say, "man is species." So the identity of significators through some species or genera obtains with the distinction of species and of genera; and, as was frequently proved, genera or species are not, unless concepts or names. . . . And indeed there are no categories except certain predicables and signs of things and simple terms; from which are made combinations true and false; but simple terms of this kind can be distinct to such a degree that the predication of one on another is impossible; although no thing through one is signified, but that the same thing may be signified by the rest; as no substantial or accidental thing is signified through this name "angelus" but that it may be signified through this name "angeli," and conversely; and indeed it is not inconsistent to posit that distinct predicables imply the same thing; notwithstanding, therefore, that substance, quality, and quantity may be distinct categories; yet every quantity could be a thing not really distinct from substance and quality. But it must be observed that such categories are not only signs fixed arbitrarily, of whatever kind the words are; but are also concepts or intentions of the mind which are signs naturally signifying things; and indeed as words can be distinguished, notwithstanding the identity of the things signified, so concepts or intentions of the mind can be distinguished, although they do not signify distinct things.

And thus these names "substance," "quality," and "quantity" may be distinct, although the things signified may not be distinct.

The Limits of Papal Authority

What was the true power of the material sword and the true dominion of temporal sovereignty, both before the coming of Christ and among the infidels, is shown in the following manner. The true dominion is that dominion of sovereignity which God gives to certain men, which it is also illegal for others to take from them: a dominion not merely allowed to them but granted by Him Who has the power to grant the true and legitimate dominion. And God, as we read in Deuteronomy II, gave to the sons of Esau, Moab, and Ammon, who were infidels, certain lands and territories which He did not allow the faithful to take from them. They, therefore, although they were infidels, had the true and legitimate dominion of temporal sovereignty, no matter how much they may have abused it. Further, he who is anointed king by a special divine command, is not merely allowed to have the power of the material sword, but is granted this power by God, because royal unction is not legitimate without legitimate power. Moreover, God ordered the prophet Elijah, as we read in III Kings XIX, to anoint Azael as king over Syria although he was an infidel. Therefore did Azael have the legitimate power of the sword. On this subject, it is added in the same place: "Whosoever shall escape from the sword of Azael shall Jehu slay." Again, he has the true dominion of temporal sovereignty—and not merely a dominion God allows him to keep—if the faithful are obliged to render unto him those things which he says are his; for no man is obliged to give to a tyrant or usurper those things which they appropriate by plunder or pillage. But Christ desired and instructed that the faithful should render unto Caesar those things which he claimed were his, saying: Render unto Caesar the things that are Caesar's"; therefore that Caesar, namely Tiberius, who was an infidel, had the true and legitimate dominion of temporal sovereignty. . . .

We reply to [Pope] Innocent IV that although the emperor is crowned by the pope, and receives a sword in a sheath from him, he does not, therefore, pull out the sword and brandish it to show that he is inferior to the pope in temporal affairs. For he need not, unless he is willing to do so, receive a sword in a sheath from him, and likewise, he need not, unless he so wishes, be crowned by him. For there were many true emperors who were not crowned by the supreme pontiff because they did not feel that the supreme pontiff was worthy of any honor. Therefore, when it pleases the emperor to be crowned by the pope, it also pleases him to receive a sword in a sheath from him, to pull out this sword and to brandish it, in order to show that he has been equipped with the mediating material sword, to use it, whenever necessary, to do full justice to all and especially to defend Christians who are suffering from injustice. . . .

Moreover, since it is said in the aforementioned allegation that even temporal laws do not scorn to imitate the sacred canons, we reply that this is not necessarily true. For when laws are established concerning those matters which pertain to the pontifical powers, nothing which is ordained by the emperor or by any one else is valid, even though it agrees with or favors the cause of the pope or other clerics, unless it has been approved by the supreme pontiff. Other laws, however, are absolutely valid without the canons; they do not have to imitate the sacred canons as long as they are reasonable and just. Nevertheless, if they should be injust, they can be abrogated by just canons. Therefore, although the pope may occasionally be able to judge laws, nevertheless, he does not have the power to abrogate laws regularly. And therefore, the supreme lay power neither does nor ought to devolve upon the pope, although it can devolve upon him if he does not use the divine law to establish anything unjust. . . .

Moreover, in a question of faith, any Catholic is allowed to appeal the decision of an heretical pope, because the matter concerns him. For a question of faith touches all and pertains to all Christians in every way . . . , although in this case it is not absolutely necessary to appeal the decision of an heretical pope, even if he has pronounced an opinion which is clearly in opposition to Catholic truth. For every such opinion, which is contrary to divine law, is *ipso facto* null and void, even if it has not been challenged by an appeal. In this case, therefore, it would be sufficient to indict the heretical pope. Indeed, if no judge were found who was willing for the pope to be accused, or who dared to hear the accusation, it would have sufficed if a few men had proclaimed publicly, either in words or in writing, that the pope was an heretic, by stating the reason or reasons why he was heretical. In a case of such proportions, the proclamation should have been carried out in accordance with divine and natural law, which all Catholics are obliged to obey, even as in any case in which a man appeals the decision of some other judge. For all Catholics should have had so much respect for a proclamation of this sort, in favor of the Christian faith, that they would have duly defended the proclaimer, unless he had been convicted of false proclamation, and all his confederates, against any one who spoke for the pope, either truly or falsely: each man doing his duty because of his need for salvation, and in a manner suitable to his status in society. . . .